# Digital Filmmaking

## The Changing Art and Craft of Making Motion Pictures

### Second Edition

## Thomas A. Ohanian
## Michael E. Phillips

**Focal
Press**

Boston    Oxford    Auckland    Johannesburg    Melbourne    New Delhi

## Avid Press™ Books

*The Avid Handbook, Third Edition*
Steve Bayes

*The Digital Producer*
Curtis Poole and Ellen Feldman

*Digital Filmmaking, Second Edition*
Thomas A. Ohanian and Michael E. Phillips

Focal Press is an imprint of Butterworth–Heinemann.

Copyright © 2000 by Butterworth–Heinemann

 A member of the Reed Elsevier group

 Recognizing the importance of preserving what has been written, Butterworth—Heinemann prints its books on acid-free paper whenever possible.

 Butterworth-Heinemann supports the efforts of American Forests and the Global ReLeaf program in its campaign for the betterment of trees, forests, and our environment.

ISBN 0-240-80427-9

The publisher offers special discounts on bulk orders of this book.
For information, please contact:
Manager of Special Sales
Butterworth-Heinemann
225 Wildwood Avenue
Woburn, MA 01801-2041
Tel: 781-904-2500
Fax: 781-904-2620

For information on all Focal Press publications available, contact our World Wide Web home page at: http://www.focalpress.com

10 9 8 7 6 5 4 3 2 1

Printed in the United States of America

*For Michele, Eric, Ian, Evan, Howard,
Helene, Ming, and Dad.*

*For Lisa Marie.*

# Contents

## production  87

### 5  The Technology of Film: Timecode on Film, Computerized Cameras, Motion-control, and Pre-editorial During Production  89

# postproduction   109

## 7  The Film Laboratory  125

# Foreword

A revolution is taking place in the art and science of image-making for visual entertainment. It's causing changes so profound in the ways we create motion pictures and other visual media that it can only be described as the advent of the digital renaissance.

Our society is in an era of change so rapid that it may be remembered for centuries for that reason. Digital image processing and computer animation were once exotic fields. They are now a part of our daily lives. Communicating with others is becoming all about ones and zeros. Cellular technology, broadcast satellites, multimedia platforms, and interactive software are now fully a part of our cultural landscape. Kids today understand technology and interactivity at an instinctive level. It's practically in their DNA. This first generation raised on video games and personal computers…they get it. They get it the way a fish gets water. Decades of commercials, combined with MTV and the graphic, hyperkinetic style that it pioneered, have reconditioned the human visual cortex to a much higher rate of image replacement. We process information not over a period of minutes but in seconds. We have been re-wired. And we like it.

And the trend is accelerating toward an even greater diversity of media, with more cable channels, more networks, more information access, and more sources of entertainment images at our fingertips. These new markets and formats, from the interactive to the Internet, are supplemented by electronic delivery systems of increasing speed and quality, from DTV to DVD.

What meaning this current environment of technical evolution and revolution has to the filmmaker is twofold. Obviously, the demand for visual production of every kind is increasing, with new opportunities and platforms for creativity, but more importantly, the emergence of new tools and open mind sets is giving storytellers the means to realize their wildest visions.

With advances in software, and the recent reductions in cost, and multiple increases in processing speed of the hardware, the long-awaited digital age of filmmaking is finally at hand. The parallel democratization of computing, from the new accessibility of powerful high-end mainframes to the burgeoning sophistication of personal computers like the Mac and PC, is leading to the greater empowerment of the filmmaker. With the advent of real-time digital image manipulation, performance capture, telemetry suits, and nonlinear editing systems, the process begins to resemble conventional filmmaking … except that the result is computer-generated imagery, with all the incredible possibilities which that offers. It's all about making people more intuitive, more free, and more human in the act of creation, while using the most advanced technology available. The growing accessibility of these new digital tools is revolutionizing the entertainment business by demonstrating to technology-adverse directors and producers that they can realize fantastic imagery, and still retain the creative control and sense of personal accomplishment they experience with conventional photography.

And bear in mind that none of this requires the director or producer to take a graduate course in computer science. Most directors cannot load a camera, or read a light meter, or trim a carbon arc. Most are not proficient at many of the technical crafts which make basic filmmaking possible. And they don't have to be. Directors are generalists who work with teams of specialists to achieve results. It is required of them only that they be able to visualize what is needed, and then articulate those needs to the cinematographer or the production designer or the dolly grip or the composer, or whoever is actually doing the work at hand.

My interest in the digital revolution originated with my desire to make better movies. Starting with *The Abyss*, and continuing on *Terminator 2* and *True Lies*, I found myself, inadvertently really, at the cutting edge of animation software development. I'm not saying I sat down and wrote code at an SGI workstation, but I was in a position to stimulate development. This was an unpremeditated process. I just wanted some neat imagery, and that was the way to get it.

Since then I have come to appreciate that high-resolution digital image manipulation has sweeping ramifications, throughout the production process, throughout the delivery of those images to the consumer, and throughout the ancillary product markets. On the one hand, I was seeing the creative renaissance in film images made possible by the computer; on the other hand, downstream I was seeing all of these emerging markets, for digital assets like characters and environments, that would run on computers. I wanted to be where the action was, because by getting heavily involved in digital image processing and computer animation software, I believed I could be in a position to creatively capitalize on these new markets as they would define themselves in the next few years. I therefore made a conscious decision to put myself on the front lines, to learn how to use these powerful new tools, and to help create new ones, if necessary, in order to make my work better.

What you are about to read encompasses a depth and range of areas in digital filmmaking. The thoughts are drawn from some of the best craftsmen in the entertainment industry, people actively working in the digital realm to break down the barriers between the technical and the artistic.

We're all still trying to figure out what it all means and how to utilize it, taking bold steps and bold falls, watching one another as we colonize this brave new world. But a few things are clear to me, and they give me strength:

1. No matter what the platform, no matter what the delivery system, a good show is still a good show.
2. No computer or piece of software ever had an original idea; entertainment is made by people for people.
3. Creative people will use these new tools, and their creativity will be empowered by them.

The whole digital arena is a learning center for filmmakers and storytellers, who will come away with the realization that the only limit on what they can achieve is their own imaginations.

James Cameron
February 1995

# Preface
## to the Second Edition

In the first edition of this book, we felt quite strongly that the use of digital cameras, digital editing, and digital projection would enable a whole new breed of filmmakers. There will still be those with classical training in the filmmaking process, but, at the same time, there will be a new, and perhaps more intriguing, group of filmmakers who have no training in how images are put together but who want to tell a story—to tell *their* story.

In the end, whether a filmmaker is commanding a group of thousands, such as James Cameron did with a crew that at times reached as high as five thousand persons, or whether a filmmaker is commanding a team of three or four persons, the goal is the same. For each and every one of us, storytelling is at the heart of every moment when we pick up a camera, make an edit, or write a word of dialogue.

Whether it is the home enthusiast who owns a digital camera, who creates a program and streams it to friends and relatives over the Internet, or the big-budget filmmaker who is desperately striving to make a film-opening deadline, digital technologies offer tremendous benefits.

And yet, digital technologies are only tools. They must be used skillfully, and with temperance, all the while taking into account the end goals: to tell a story and to communicate.

It is for our love of filmmaking (one an editor, the other a director), inventing, and storytelling that we have written this book.

Thomas A. Ohanian
Michael E. Phillips
December, 1999

# Acknowledgments

There are a number of individuals who have contributed their time and counsel to this effort. This book would not be complete without both acknowledging and gratefully thanking them.

Aaton: Jean-Pierre Beauviala, Alain Bellet; AbelCineTech: Peter Abel; Alcatel Network Systems: Michael Newsom; American Zoetrope: Francis Coppola, Kim Aubry; Arriflex Corporation: Russell Guenther, Marc Shipman-Mueller; Balsmeyer & Everett/Syzygy Digital Cinema: Randy Balsmeyer, Michael Arias; Banned From The Ranch Entertainment: Van Ling; Cinema Products: Ed Digiulio; Rick Baker & Associates/Cinovation Studios, Inc.: Rick Baker; Debbie Perillard; Dolby Laboratories: Eileen Tuuri, Bill Mead, Christopher Irwin; Dream Quest Images: Hoyt Yeatman, Mark Galvin; Evertz Microsystems, Ltd.: Carter Lancaster; Alan Lambshead; Filmlook: Bob Faber; Kleiser/Walczak Construction Company: Jeff Kleiser; Lucasfilm: Gary Rydstrom, Lynne Hale; ModaCAD, Inc.: Maurizio Vecchione; Panavision: John Farrand; The Post Group/Digital Film Group: Joe Leggett, Jr.; PowerProduction Software: Paul Clatworthy, Sally Ann Walsh, Ray Walsh; Skyview Film and Video: Jack Tohtz; Sony Digital Picture Editorial: Steven B. Cohen; Steven Katz, Scott Billups, Howard Smith, Fraser Heston, Martha Coolidge, Richard Marks, Anne Goursaud, Steven Poster, Tony Westman, Basil Pappas, Kyle Shannon, Joel Cox, Neil Travis, Steven J. Cohen, Mia Goldman, Joe Hutshing, David Brenner, Michael Tronick, Ed Salier, Fred Gallo, Glen Scantlebury, Diane Shapiro, Peter Fasciano, Nathan Mackinnon, Stefan Boroda, Nora Barry, Richard Edlund, Bob Mazza, Ed Jones, Marty Shindler, Brad Kuehn, Tracy Dennison, Tom Scott, James Cameron, George Lucas, Jeffrey Krebs.

Aatonbase, Keylinker, and OriginC+ are trademarks of the Aaton Corporation; Aaton and AatonCode are registered by the Aaton Corporation; Academy Award is registered by the Academy of Motion Picture Arts and Sciences; Acmade is a trademark; Photoshop, After Effects are trademarks of the Adobe Corporation; QuickTake, QuickTime are trademarks of the Apple Computer Corporation; Macintosh, Powerbook, Quadra, and Power Macintosh are registered by the Apple Computer Corporation; Arriflex is registered by the Arriflex Corporation; AVI is a trademark; Film Composer, Media Composer, MediaMatch, Media Recorder Telecine, and OMF are trademarks of Avid Technology, Inc.; BVE Logger is registered by the BVE Corporation; Cinefusion is a trademark; Cyberware is a trademark; Flame is a trademark of Discrete; Dolby, Dolby Stereo, and the double-D symbol are trademarks of Dolby Laboratories Licensing Corporation; DTS is a registered symbol; ElectricImage is a trademark of the ElectricImage; Cineon, KeyKode, Kodak Photo-CD, Kodak Picture Exchange, and Kodak PROfiLE CD are trademarks of the Eastman Kodak Corporation; Keylog is a trademark of Evertz Microsystems, Inc.; Excalibur is trademarked by Filmlab Systems; Filmlook is registered by Filmlook, Inc.; flexFile is a trademark; MetaFlow is a trademark of the Flo-Freeform Plasticity

Company; Hazeltine is registered by the Hazeltine Corporation; KAI's Power Tools is a trademark of HSC Software; Synthespian is registered by the Kleiser/Walczak Construction Company; Kodika is a trademark; Lightworks is registered by Lightworks; Excel, Microsoft Word, and Windows are trademarks of the Microsoft Corporation; Final Draft is a trademark; ModaDRAPE, ModaFINITY, and ModaSKETCH are trademarks of ModaCAD, Inc.; Montage Picture Processor is a trademark of the Montage Corporation; Nagra is a trademark; Emmy is registered by the National Academy of Television Arts and Sciences; Panavision is registered by the Panavision Corporation; Pantone is registered by the Pantone Corporation; Polaroid is a trademark of the Polaroid Corporation; Domino, Harry, and Paintbox are trademarks of the Quantel Corporation; Smartslate is a trademark; Costume Pro and StoryBoard Quick are trademarks of PowerProduction Software; Movie Magic, Scriptor, Vocabulate are trademarks of Screenplay Systems; SDDS is a registered symbol by Sony Dynamic Digital Sound, Inc.; Steenbeck is registered by the Steenbeck Corporation; Touchbase is trademarked; Ultimatte is registered by the Ultimatte Corporation; Virtus Walkthrough Pro is a trademark of the Virtus Corporation.

# Introduction

When we wrote the first edition of *Digital Filmmaking* in 1995, the use of digital technologies by filmmakers was largely evident in digital special effects. Awash in the imagery of special effects–laden films such as *Terminator 2, Judgment Day*, and *The Abyss*, when most of us thought of the term "digital filmmaking," we most often concentrated on the special visual effects category. Recall, however, that these were the days before films such as *Titanic, The Matrix*, and *Star Wars Episode One: The Phantom Menace*, which, together, combined to push the world of special visual effects to an even higher plane.

Although filmmakers were using video to acquire their images and eventually transfer them to film for theatrical projection, both the cost of this process and the quality of these images left something to be desired, especially when compared to the quality of the projected film image.

Recall also that the notion of the "Cinema of the Future," as well as the delivery and exhibition processes for films, which would be affected by digital technology had not yet been introduced in practice to the public.

In the short time that has passed since the first edition of this book, enormous changes have taken place and are rapidly evolving in the area of digital filmmaking. In 1999, digital projections of images stored on computer hard disks were made for a variety of films, ranging from *The Phantom Menace* to *Tarzan*. Although they were not quite up to the overall contrast ratio of the projected film image, the message was clear: Technology will evolve and the use of digital projectors that will replace the projection of film is no longer a theory—it will occur.

Digital Filmmaking

# Preproduction and Previsualization

# 1 From Filmmaking to Digital Filmmaking

For years the process of making films has essentially remained unchanged. Up until the late 1980s, the manner by which a filmmaker went about creating a film was little different than the process used by another filmmaker halfway around the world. Filmmaking had developed a methodology that did not require any substantial changes. Of course, processes and components improved—sound appeared, film frame rates were standardized at 24 frames per second, film stocks improved, and camera lenses became faster. However, the essential steps that one took to complete a film remained largely unchanged.

There have been technical leaps that brought forth new artistic looks that would define styles for years and scores of films to follow. The deep focus black-and-white photography of James Wong Howe and Gregg Toland, and the stylized sound techniques borrowed from the radio industry have influenced many filmmakers.

When we think of "filmmaking" it is important to be aware of filmmaking as a term that is applied to many different types of presentations. While we may first think of the feature film "experience", where we sit in a theater and watch the efforts of the filmmaker, there are also documentaries, short animated films, and so forth.

Perhaps one of the most astonishing changes that came about in terms of the intrusion into traditional filmmaking was George Lucas's *Star Wars* (1977). With innovative technology that allowed the filmmakers the ability to exactly repeat camera movements, multiple passes for backgrounds, foregrounds, and lighting effects yielded some of the most astounding special visual effects sequences ever seen. There were, of course, unsuccessful attempts to use this new technology in other films—a result of the filmmakers forgetting that it is the story and not the special effects that carry a film. And yet, it is now apparent that this technical leap certainly shows the impact that digital technology will have on the entire filmmaking process. Heralded by the ingeniousness of Lucas's work, the huge technological leaps that have occurred since now comprise not only a new set of tools for the filmmaker, but enable the filmmaker to create new worlds and images.

Such a clear and decisive change in the way that special visual effects were accomplished raised the expectations not only of filmmakers, but also of audiences. Such viewer sophistication has occurred, through the mid-1990s, that it has been left to filmmakers to push technology as quickly as possible in order to achieve what previously had been either impossible or economically restrictive.

This book outlines the changing methodology of filmmaking. Whether a documentary or a feature film, the technology and the artistry of making films are being impacted greatly as a confluence of film, television, and computer capabilities combine to form a new and exciting way of providing a new set of rules to understand, to use, and to break, in the quest of telling a story.

The term *digital filmmaking* refers to a methodology that combines certain traditional filmmaking techniques with new capabilities that have come about through the integration of computers, digital image manipulation, disk recording, and networking. Digital technologies entering the art and craft of filmmaking is akin to the incorporation of sound in motion pictures. When sound was introduced in filmmaking, it had a dramatic impact on how films were made. Directors, actors, and screenwriters were all affected. Some succeeded, and some did not. However, while the introduction of digital technology is analogous to the introduction of sound, there are important differences.

Sound was an immediate introduction. One moment the capability did not exist, and the next moment sound was everywhere. Further, once sound was introduced, its basic capabilities did not rapidly change.

Conversely, digital technologies have been introduced more gradually. Machine-readable film edge numbers are years old, but only recently has the importance of this technology been understood in digital filmmaking. As with any new methodology, once there are enough pieces in place, the user gets to stand back and see the whole picture, or the redefinition of the parts into digital filmmaking.

Incorporating digital technologies into the world of filmmaking will revolutionize and redefine filmmaking. Computers, and the software that is written to run on them, will be used in all facets of making a film. There are currently computers that are used to control the cameras that expose the film; there are computers that are used to create backgrounds where actors cannot possibly be, say, in space suits on the planet Mars; and there are even computers in the armrests of theater seats which allow the filmgoer to determine how a movie should end: should the villain live or die?—the audience gets to decide!

Computers, which reduce information to the digital bit, allow creative individuals the power to combine these bits into new forms. Digital technologies can process the information more efficiently than any manual process. Filmmakers, eager to make as many films as possible, always struggle with the film's schedule. Will the filmmaker complete the film in the allotted amount of time, or will the filmmaker find that the film is being released before it is really ready? Using digital technologies will better ensure that the filmmaker will be able to accomplish the job.

It is important to understand how films have traditionally been made—the procedures followed, and the personnel required. This chapter describes the traditional art and craft of making motion pictures and describes the various personnel. The tools and techniques used, and the decisions that are made in bringing a film to the screen, are all affected by emerging digital filmmaking technologies.

## INDUSTRY VIEWPOINTS

### George Lucas—Filmmaker/ Lucasfilm

George Lucas is one of the defining forces in digital filmmaking technology and methodology. Providing new, easier methods to make films has been a career-long ambition. When one considers a brief history of

**Figure 1-1** Photo of George Lucas, courtesy of Lucasfilm, Ltd. All rights reserved. Photograph by Minsei Tominaga.

the actions that Lucas has taken to redefine the filmmaking process, it quickly becomes apparent that he has a vision of filmmaking's future.

In 1979 Lucas created the Computer Division of Lucasfilm to explore new uses of computers in film editing, sound, and visual effects. Three products resulted: EditDroid™, SoundDroid™, and the Pixar Image™ Computer. In 1984 he pioneered film-oriented, computerized nonlinear editing through the premiere of EditDroid and SoundDroid. Through the years 1988 to 1994, Lucas's Industrial Light & Magic (ILM) made further breakthroughs on films such as *The Abyss, Terminator 2: Judgment Day, Death Becomes Her, Jurassic Park, The Mask,* and *Forrest Gump.* Says Lucas,

My primary interest in developing digital technology was to speed up the filmmaking process so that I could get my ideas accomplished in a more efficient way. I was trying to improve my ability to make movies since much of the filmmaking process is still 19th century. Digital technology saves vast amounts of time and energy. It allows the filmmaker to be more creative—be it special effects or post-production—and makes the job of filmmaking easier.

Being in San Francisco and remote from Hollywood has made it easier to facilitate new technology.

We've developed a method of operating that's more facile. I can't be several places at one time, yet I constantly have to be involved in the postproduction process on our projects. We use telecommunications at Skywalker Ranch and ILM to send shots back and forth. We are currently working on technologies which will allow the filmmaker to work on the elements and transmit them to multiple locations. It leads to what's been dubbed "nonlinear filmmaking"—filmmaking that isn't assembly line fashion, but a much more integrated approach.

I like to put the sound department on a project at the same time that the picture department is working on the film. It helps people be creatively involved when we they can see what a scene looks like. It's a much more integrated process when picture, sound, and visual effects are all going on at the same time and we're able to focus on all aspects of the process. We are able to create a visual storyboard—a "videomatic" which ILM can use for reference to render a shot. The process used to be very clumsy—it was old-fashioned animation which would take two weeks. We can now complete the same work in one day. Our methods make the whole process much easier and faster. You can see a rough cut that has music and effects much more quickly.

Historically, the biggest change in filmmaking was the introduction of sound. The special requirements of sound altered the filmmaking process. Digital filmmaking is the equivalent to the introduction of sound. I think we are going to have the freedom of opening up sound, visual effects, and picture editing so that changes to a film can be made anywhere and at any time. . . .

I've had a long interest in digital technology from EditDroid to SoundDroid to Pixar to laser printing—all these tools recycle themselves. All of the things that we are doing will be rewritten once again. I do feel that I pushed digital technology and helped it come into being—now everyone is trying to push the frontier in technology. It will eventually create a more democratic filmmaking environment. Anyone will be able to create movies. Pretty soon you'll be doing it on your PC.

## THE PROCESS AND THE PEOPLE WHO MAKE FILMS

### Collaboration Defines Filmmaking

Filmmaking is a collaborative art. The art form itself is communication, using pictures, motion, colors, sound, music, and the spoken word to convey a message. This chapter covers some of the key people involved and how each must communicate with others to complete the film. Each person has a view of how the film will look when it is finished. For the process to run smoothly, communication must be established among the different disciplines.

The filmmaking process consists of three major categories: Preproduction, Production, and Postproduction. Within each category, there are many people creating, reshaping, and producing elements that will form the final film.

Shown in Figure 1-2 is the traditional, linear

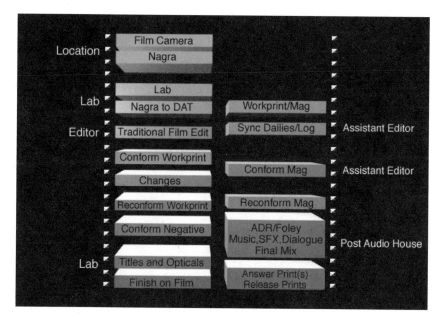

**Figure 1-2** A flowchart outlining the traditional linear process of how a film is made. Illustration by Jeffrey Krebs.

process of how a film is made. Many of the elements that make up this process are entirely redefined by the incorporation of digital filmmaking methods. Because feature films have the most people involved, there is a complex division of labor and much paperwork.

## PREPRODUCTION

### The Screenwriter

The screenwriter of a film has a word processor that allows him to change his mind at any time. Several versions can be saved and reviewed and these versions can be easily broken up into high and low budget versions as well as first or final draft versions.

For the filmmaking process, the main output is the printed page that will be photocopied and distributed to various departments. The first stage is script breakdown and budgeting. The word processor represents the beginning of the digital process of computers touching the traditional film world. In ensuing chapters of this book, the reader will find examples of how information is created, shared, and distributed.

### Script Breakdown

Normally, each page of a script is broken down into eighths of a page. Filmmaking days can be described in the number of pages shot per day. For example, on shooting day 14, a total of $5\frac{3}{8}$ pages were completed.

For each script scene, the breakdown person creates a list of actors, extras, props, and locations. Also indicated is whether the scene is an interior or exterior and whether it is a day or night shoot. This information helps determine the film's budget and scheduling. Scheduling is handled by the first assistant director. Information from the script breakdown is used by other departments to determine the requirements of costumes, hair and makeup, props, and locations, as all elements are listed on a scene-by-scene basis.

### Budgeting

Budgeting covers the cost of the entire film. Both above-the-line and below-the-line costs are included. Above-the-line costs are usually for the producer, director, some A-list actors, some directors of photography, and some editors. From the breakdown of the script, each scene can be viewed, needed elements are

noted, the type of shooting crew necessary is determined, and so on.

Package costs are calculated, such as camera and lighting packages, based on a weekly rental or on a per-job basis. Crew members are based on an hourly rate with overtime rates applied. The budget is broken down into workflow such as preproduction, production, and postproduction.

### Scheduling

The next step is for the first assistant director to take the script breakdown sheets and to schedule the film. Scheduling could be based around the main actor's availability. If a film has several high-priced actors, shooting these actors as close together as possible to avoid any contractual overages is important.

Location choices may depend on whether the scenes are interior/exterior and day/night shoots. A first assistant director will factor into the schedule alternative plans in case of weather changes or if talent becomes unavailable due to illness. No matter the difficulties encountered, the schedule must allow shooting to continue. Any delays or down days can cost a production hundreds of thousands of dollars.

### Casting

The director will give an indication of the type, look, and age range for the roles to be cast. The casting director will then consult a database of talent and make a casting call for actors and actresses, typically requiring a short biography and an 8 × 10 black-and-white glossy photograph (head shots). These head shots are sorted, and actors that fit the general description are called in for a screen test. Screen tests are usually conducted with the casting director and director. These tests are usually videotaped, and, once final candidates are chosen, some actual tests on film can be made. Through a process of reviews and callbacks, the principal actors are selected for a film. The casting director usually has complete control over the casting of extras and bit parts. The casting director will negotiate the contracts and make the deals for the final cast.

### Production Designer

The production designer is responsible for the overall look of the film and works very closely with the director to achieve the mood and feel of the story. Based on the director's overall vision for the film, the production designer sets the style, colors, and textures for the film. Perhaps the genre is *film noire,* where the color scheme is to be in the range of red, to provide a feeling of fear, danger, or sexual overtones. For example, in *Color of Night* (1994), a lead character is unable to see the color red. This factor is used by the director and production designer, and in situations where the character is in danger, the color red is distinct. A car that swerves into frame is red while the rest of the items in the frame are largely monochromatic.

Whether it is the opening title sequence of *North By Northwest* (1959), with its intersecting lines signifying the circuitous pathway that both the story and the characters will take, or the black-garbed Mrs. Robinson waiting at the end of a totally white corridor in *The Graduate* (1967), signifying the ubiquitous black widow awaiting her prey, conscious decisions of production design, art direction, and costume design are discussed and implemented.

The production designer also supervises the search for locations and works with the location scout to find the right settings for the feel of the film.

## Location Scout

The location scout goes on location and brings back pictures based on the description set forth by the director and production designer. Location scouts also work closely with film bureaus in each state, which provide a library of photographs, descriptions, and maps. If a producer is based in New York, and is making a film that takes place in both Montana and New Mexico, she can call the film bureaus in these states and provide them with a verbal description of the locations. The bureaus then search through their databases and provide the producer with 8 × 10 photos of possible locations. These databases may be very low-tech—often a filing system of index cards. There may be several attempts before the exact location can be found.

## Set Designer

The set designer is responsible for overseeing and executing the plans for the set and is responsible for drafting detailed blueprints from drawings and verbal descriptions provided by the production designer. The set designer is also responsible for the type of construction elements used to create and build the set. Set designers work closely with the cinematographer to ascertain which parts of the set will be used, based on

the blocking plans the director has created for each actor, and which sections will be lit and photographed. These detailed drawings are then used by the prop construction crew to build the needed elements. Once the set has been constructed, the set designer works closely with the set decorator.

## Set Decorator

The set decorator is responsible for the visual look of the film through the use of furniture, carpeting, drapery, and the different artifacts that a character would be most likely to have. All these elements help to shape the character's personality, creating a background that would probably take too much time to tell in words or in situations. For example, a camera panning across a series of trophies, high school football pictures and uniforms instantly conveys to the audience that this character is an athlete who is accustomed to being a winner.

One important distinction is that set elements are considered different from props because they belong to the set and not to the actor. If an actor uses one of the set elements, then it technically becomes a prop. If in the previous example an actor picks up one of the trophies and throws it against the wall, the trophy ceases being a set element and is now a prop.

## Property Master

The property master is responsible for any props that are used by the actors. He or she will break down the script, select the props required for each scene, budget for the required props, and finally acquire them. The property master must maintain these props for the duration of the production and is responsible for their placement with the actors.

## Costume Designer

The costume designer is responsible for researching and designing the costumes and related accessories such as hats, gloves, and jewelry. Working closely with the production designer to determine appropriate periods and styles, there is much research that must be done to ensure that time periods are correctly represented. There is nothing more disconcerting to the moviegoer than to see a fashion or accessory that did not yet exist in the film's period. While the moviegoer may not be aware of exactly what is wrong, subconsciously the visual message will be scrambled and will ultimately cause the viewer to question the validity of what is being seen. Costume designers utilize catalogs, old movies, and newsreels to determine the look and feel of costumes and accessories. They oversee all costume making, fitting, and renting for the entire production.

A knowledgeable costume designer understands the importance of working closely with the director of photography to determine the requirements for color and texture, and with the set designer to ensure that the costumes will not clash with the set decor. Certain colors may be attributed to a character to accentuate a certain personality trait. In addition, costumes and set decoration can be used in conjunction to blend or extrude a character from the environment. There are also scientific studies of human visual perception which have shown that certain color combinations are likely to cause specific reactions. For example, let's say that the filmmaker has filmed a background shot which has red filtration so that the entire shot is bathed in a hazy, red glow. Now, the director has a female character running from one side of the frame to the other. She is wearing a bright green sweater. Combinations such as red and green are often used to signify frenetic energy, panic, and anxiety.

## Makeup Artist

The makeup artist is responsible for researching and designing the makeup for principal actors and extras, and he or she works with the production designer to coordinate makeup with costume. Depending upon the type of makeup required for a character, there is research involved to create the look of a certain time period. The actor thus uses props, costumes, and makeup to realize a role. Any departure from what the audience expects as visual details that define a character will be perceived as something which is not quite correct. The makeup artist will also work closely with the director of photography to determine the photographic requirements for makeup.

The makeup artist prepares the makeup schedule and helps coordinate other makeup artists in the group. The hair stylist must also research the appropriate style of hair to fit the story line and time period, and may also care for wigs and maintain the hairstyles of actors between takes.

## Production Illustrator

The production illustrator provides sketches and storyboards for different departments. These illustra-

tions can be simple sketches that show the layout of a futuristic city. Or they can be a series of drawings, or storyboard, that actually depicts the visual breakdown of an entire scene as the director has planned for it to be shot.

Many directors utilize complex storyboarding to visually plan how a scene is to be covered. Intricate and meticulous detail covering camera placement, lenses, and movement can be of great assistance to the production and postproduction teams as the film is shot and edited. There are many examples where highly detailed storyboards were used to create celebrated film sequences. Director Alfred Hitchcock was perhaps the most famous user of storyboards, and there are many books which show the elaborate storyboards he commissioned. Sequences such as "The Crop Duster Sequence" in *North By Northwest* (1959), "The Shower Sequence" in *Psycho* (1960), and "The Attic Attack Sequence" in *The Birds* (1963) are all indicative of excellent storyboarding. Students of cinema will also find the CAV laserdisc version of Martin Scorsese's *Raging Bull* (1980) helpful in that it contains intricate storyboards of various boxing sequences.

The images in figure 1-3 show the relation of drawn storyboards and the finished visuals from the 1991 film, *Terminator 2: Judgment Day.*

In order to create storyboards, the production illustrator must be familiar with shot description, continuity, and camera angles. The illustrator works closely with the director to work out an idea, a camera move, or the different camera angles that will be used for a sequence before the scene is shot. Depending upon the detail, the storyboard can also provide clues as to the pace of the scene and an indication of the editing style desired.

Sometimes sketches may be used to create interest in the concept of the film prior to the film being sold and put into production. These storyboards can be used to sell the script to potential investors and to provide a pictorial idea of the script beyond the written word. These boards also are used by the production manager to break down a schedule, and then by the director of photography to further break down shots, and prepare lighting and camera angles.

Storyboards are critical when sequences involve special and visual effects departments. Precise planning as to how opticals and elements are to be used in final composited shots begins with detailed storyboards. Without knowing exactly how the live action components of a composite shot should be accomplished, and how this element relates to the final vis-

**Figure 1-3** Three frames which show the relation of drawn storyboards and the finished visuals. This sequence, which outlines the transformation of a computer-generated T1000 figure to live actor Robert Patrick, is even more noteworthy as it was executed while the camera was tracking swiftly backward with the actor in motion. Clearly, filmmakers are now, more than ever, free to create action unencumbered by the locked-down camera angle which had been so often required for shooting effects elements. From *Terminator 2: Judgment Day* (1991). Courtesy of Carolco Pictures and Twentieth-Century Fox, Ltd. All rights reserved.

ual effects shot, much time and money can be wasted later in fixing something that could have easily been accomplished during the shooting stage.

There are many individuals and disciplines involved under the banner of special and visual effects departments. The production illustrator and the visual coordinator will meet and perhaps the matte painter will then be required to plan the background elements that must be painted in order to create sets that do not exist. Creating a sixteenth-century castle so that actors in period costume can walk across a drawbridge will usually require some form or combi-

nation of matte painting and miniatures. Further, a location that exists only in the imagination, such as that in a science fiction story, will demand the artificial creation of the landscape and backgrounds. The matte painter will also communicate with the director of photography for the film, and there may be a separate director of photography assigned to photograph only the mattes.

## PRODUCTION

### Director of Photography

The director of photography (DP) interprets the written page and the director's vision into moving images. The techniques of lighting and camera are combined to tell a story pictorially. The choice of film negative type, lighting equipment, and camera lenses all fall to the domain of the DP. Lighting can set the mood, develop character, and hide and reveal specific details in order to draw an audience into the story. The DP also approves the set dressing, costumes, hair, and makeup and works closely with the Key Grip, the Gaffer, and the Camera Operator.

### Camera Operator

The Camera Operator is responsible to the Director and the DP in terms of composition, focus, and camera movement. Any item relating to what the camera actually sees and what is captured on the film frame is the responsibility of the Camera Operator. He or she is one of the few people on the set who can reject a take as being faulty or can call for a cut.

### Key Grip

The key grip is responsible to the DP and will communicate with the DP at all times to perform the camera moves that the director and DP have designed. One of the most important jobs that the key grip has is to either facilitate or actually create the movement of a camera via dolly, boom, jib, or crane. Certainly, the type and quantity of equipment that the key grip is responsible for is quite relevant.

### Gaffer

The Gaffer is responsible to the DP in all areas of lighting, including maintenance and selection of electrical equipment. Under consultation with the DP, the gaffer will place and set levels for each light. The gaffer is also responsible for listing all the needed lighting equipment—which can be a formidable array.

## Production Sound Mixer

The production sound mixer (figure 1-4) is responsible for recording all production sound, either synchronous (sync) or wild. The term *wild sound* refers to sound that does not have a synchronous picture, or it could be the recording of sound effects which are available on the location and may be either hard to obtain or to create at a later time. Note that often a shot is referred to as being MOS, which is film shot without sound being recorded. The Nagra™ audio tape recorder is one of the most popular devices for the recording of sound for film.

The production sound mixer is responsible for both the direct and mixed quality of the sound and for hiring the boom operator and the boom assistant. When several microphones are used, all lines are run through a separate mixer to create the desired level for each mic. Some of these mics may be hidden on an actor's body while another mic, a shotgun mic, is mounted on a boom and held just outside of the visible frame area. The sound editor will often be given choices—some of the sound sources will be separate, while others will be mixed together. He or she will then choose based on sound quality or proximity, as the scene's requirements dictate. The production sound mixer is also responsible for all sound reports and delivery of all sound elements to the film transfer facility. The production mixer, like the camera operator, is also one of the few people that can refuse a take based on quality.

## Script Supervisor/Continuity

A script supervisor will assist the director or assistant director during shooting by ensuring that dialogue is adhered to, or, if changed, is noted accordingly (figure 1-5). The script supervisor will also keep the script notes and create a lined script (figure 1-6) that shows the editor how a scene was covered.

It is important to be able to know exactly how a character reacted in a specific scene, what the character was wearing, and what the camera was photographing. The continuity person will keep track of all these details. If a character wore a brown dress in one scene and enters a store, interior store scenes with the actress must have her wearing the same dress. Similarly, if a character is smoking a cigarette, continuity must be preserved from shot to shot; otherwise, a cigarette which has just been lit may be incorrectly cut against another take of the character where the cigarette is almost out.

**Figure 1-4** A production sound mixer at work on location in this vintage photograph. Courtesy of The Academy of Motion Picture Arts and Sciences.

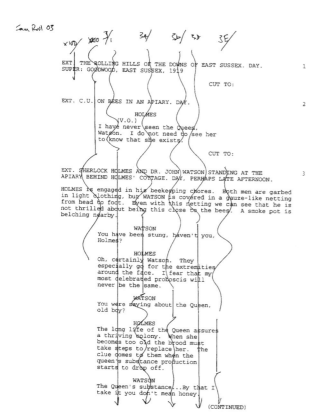

**Figure 1-6** A sample of a lined script which shows coverage for each scene. Courtesy of Gary Locke.

## Developing and Printing the Film

Shown in figure 1-7 is an example of a camera and sound report. All film and sound elements are sent to the film lab for developing and printing. Using the camera and sound reports, prints are created based on the selections that the director made during shooting. These are known as *circled takes,* and represent the takes that the director feels can be utilized during the editing stage. Usually, several takes will be circled as certain parts of each take are used to create one complete scene during editing.

Once the film has been developed and printed, the resulting workprint and the mag stock are synced together into select rolls. These rolls are created with all the takes for a scene so that the producer, director, DP, and editor can screen the film. Others can attend this screening of the dailies with the director's permission. Notes will be taken concerning performances, quality of both picture and sound, and which takes are preferred for editing.

## POSTPRODUCTION

Shown in figure 1-8 is a Magnasync Moviola film editing machine, circa 1960. By working closely with the director, the editor begins to create and craft a story cut by cut. Editing is a process of selecting takes

**deluxe laboratories**
137 North Serrano Ave., Hollywood, CA 90027 (213) 462-6171

**CAMERA REPORT**
**SOUND REPORT**                     No. 451079

DATE 3.28.95     CUSTOMER ORDER NUMBER EZ #69321
COMPANY         UNIVERSAL TELEVISION
DIRECTOR Hanson    CAMERAMAN/RECORDIST STEPHEN LIGHTHILL
PRODUCTION NUMBER OR TITLE    EARTH 2
MAGAZINE NUMBER 75   ROLL NUMBER A-6
TYPE OF FILM / EMULSION 5287·109·1702

PRINT CIRCLED TAKES ONLY: ☐ ONE LITE   ☐ TIMED

| SCENE NO. | TAKE | DIAL | PRINT | REMARKS |
|-----------|------|------|-------|---------|
| 33 | 3 | 260 | 260 | |
| 33A | 9 | 480 | 220 | |
| | 2 | 540 | 60 | |
| | 8 | 730 | 240 | |
| | 7 | 950 | 200 | 2nd Stx |
| | | | | |
| | | | | |
| | | | | |
| | | | | |
| | | | | |
| | | 6 | 670 | |
| | | N6 | 280 | |
| | | W | 50 | |
| | | T | 1000 | |
| | | | | |
| | | | | |
| | | | | |
| **TOTAL** | | | | |

All contracts with this company are accepted with the understanding that all film delivered to it is covered by the owner against loss. This company takes every necessary precaution for the safekeeping of the film, but assumes no responsibility for its loss.
DEL-62 (10/90)

**Figure 1-7** An example of a camera and sound report. Courtesy of Deluxe Laboratories.

interaction and communication between postproduction and production. The editor may find that some shots are needed to make a scene play better, and upon hearing this, the director may elect to get those shots before leaving the location. The editor may work with one or more assistant editors to locate material needed, or to send material to the lab for previewing a dissolve or a special effect. There is also a great deal of work in logging shots, as frames are added and removed to create the first cut. Each of the head or tail frames must be labeled and arranged so that the editor can have quick access to these elements if the need arises. Screenings of the edited scene or reel are then held and the director will then ask the editor to make any changes that are required. This cyclical process continues until the reels are finely tuned and the final cut is accomplished.

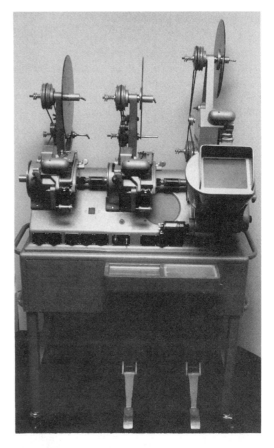

**Figure 1-8** Magnasync Moviola film editing machine, circa 1960. Courtesy of Skyview Film and Video.

and shots, and knowing how much to show of one image before changing to another image. The pace, rhythm, and flow are dictated by the cut of one picture against another. Although there are many talented people who have yet to contribute, when the editor begins cutting, this is the first time that the disparate elements come together and feel like a film.

During the editing process, there is simultaneous

## Negative Cutter

Once the final cut has been created, the edited reels are sent to a negative cutter. It is necessary to recreate the cuts that the editor made on the workprint, but this must be done on the original camera negative, yielding an exact duplicate of the workprint. This very tedious job is also a very serious affair as the negative cutter is handling the original camera negative. If a mistake is made during this stage, there is no backup film which can be used. Cutting the negative is the ultimate final cut. Negative cutters take the original camera rolls that have been logged by roll number. As each cut is added to the final reel, they are searched by both roll and film edge number, cut to exactly match the workprint, and segmented into the final reels. These reels are then sent off to the lab to create the answer print.

## Visual Effects Producer

The visual effects producer supervises the plan for realizing the film's visual effects. Each scene that has a special visual effect is noted and described as fully as possible. The visual effects producer works with the director, the visual effects art director, and the visual effects DP. Visual effects run the gamut from the arcane to the fantastic, from effects that have been seen in many films to effects that are entirely new.

Effects can be as basic as a person who is clinging to a cliff and is about to fall. This effect can be achieved by first shooting the two different elements. First, the actor is shot against a blue screen while providing the needed actions that the director desires. Next, a second element is shot: the cliff without the actor. These two film elements are then combined to create the final composite. The blue areas around the actor are removed, or keyed out, allowing the cliff picture to become the new background for the actor. When both elements have been carefully planned and executed, the audience will believe they are seeing their favorite actor hanging from the edge of a cliff.

## Re-recording Mixer

The re-recording mixer's responsibilities include the mixing of dialogue, music, sound effects, and the creation of atmosphere, such as adding echo or reverb to provide a new feeling for a scene. There are a wide variety of tools that the re-recording mixer uses, such as digital signal sound processors, compressors, limit-

ers, and equalizers. Generally, the process of taking sounds and changing them in some way is known as *sweetening*. This term is used because heretofore all sound elements have been recorded dry or clean, meaning that the sound elements have not yet been influenced by the environment of the scene in which the sound element must exist. An actor speaking in a crowded room will sound much different than one speaking in a large empty warehouse, and while the actor's dialogue may often sound the same when dry, the re-recording mixer will add the proper ambience to the voice. Clearly, there is nothing more disconcerting for a filmgoer than to see a visual of a person talking on the phone to someone and hearing both voices clearly. Instead, it is more convincing if one of the voices sounds as if it is traveling through a phone line. It must sound a bit more tinny and more distant, because this is what the viewer's mind expects to hear. The re-recording mixer works closely with both director and editor, and they must all be able to translate a visual description into an aural perception. The director may comment, "Make it sound big or empty."

The re-recording mixer is also responsible for the recording of any additional dialogue. This is often required when an actor's line was badly recorded because of extraneous location noise. Lines may even be rewritten in order to change the direction of the story or to help fix a scene which requires further explanation. This may only become apparent during the editing stage.

This process is known as ADR, or additional dialogue replacement. The ADR process is accomplished by playing back the scene in question in a loop while the actor matches the timing and delivery of the lines, in sync with the on-screen visual. In addition, by now seeing the scene as it has been edited, the actor can add further to the emotional content of the scene. Each take is recorded and either portions or the entire take is used in the final mix.

The re-recording mixer also works with a foley artist and a supervising sound editor. The sound editor coordinates the efforts of the music editor and re-recording mixer. He or she is responsible for the quality of all sound elements, with the exception of music, and works with the ADR and foley elements. A foley artist watches a scene and recreates many of the sound effects that the scene requires such as a series of footsteps walking to a door, the jangling of keys, and the opening of a door. A foley artist must have a sense of timing that matches the action on the screen. These newly created sound effects are carefully recorded and then accurately placed in synchronization with the picture during the final mix.

Foley work is done on a foley stage, which has many different types of floor and ground samples such as concrete, gravel, and sand, all of which are used to recreate specific environments. Some of the objects that a foley artist uses to create sounds are shown in figure 1-9. There are also sounds that the foley artist is not capable of creating, and these will be created by a sound designer. A sound designer uses recording techniques and multiple layers of sound to create specific effects. For example, the tools offered by sophisticated, digital audio workstations were used to create many of the underwater submarine sounds found in *The Hunt For Red October* (1990). When the filmgoer sees a close-up of a torpedo speeding through the water, the sounds heard are products of a sound designer's talent.

Another technique of sound design is using a different sound in concert with an original recording. For example, the sound designer may augment a person's scream by adding an underlying and layered sound of a lion's roar. Further, there are clearly needs for sound design when one thinks of new environments where the audience does not have a preconceived notion as to how things should sound. How, for example, does a door slam sound in outer space? It is left to the director and sound designer to answer such a question.

All of these sound elements are then combined by the re-recording mixer and mixed into the final picture soundtrack. A typical film can have hundreds of tracks of sound, along with hundreds of alternate tracks. The tracks are mixed down to either a stereo master or into a six-track master used in surround-sound theaters.

## Scoring Mixer

The scoring mixer is responsible for recording all the music in the film. This may consist of a full orchestra or electronic instrumentation. The scoring mixer works closely with the music composer in creating and capturing music. The music editor then takes the recorded music and is responsible for all technical aspects of the music track. He or she will ensure that the music is in proper sync with the cues set forth by the composer and director, and will place the music elements in relation to the dialogue and effects tracks so that the re-recording mixer can create the final soundtrack.

## Titles and Effects Supervisor

The titles and effects supervisor is responsible for producing the main titles and end credits for a film, and he or she works closely with the director and the visual effects supervisor. This includes supervision of title design and creation of titles and optical effects. Titles can be as simple as still image black-and-white cards to very sophisticated computer-generated

**Figure 1-9** Foley work and the various objects that a foley artist uses to recreate sounds. Courtesy of The Academy of Motion Picture Arts and Sciences.

animation. The optical effects can be as simple as a dissolve where an outgoing picture blends into an incoming picture, to something as complicated as restructuring a shot that must be repositioned, enlarged, reversed, and then chroma keyed onto another picture in order to create the composite effect. Some of these effects will be created in several passes and may cause a generational loss in quality and an accumulation of film grain. It is the responsibility of the effects supervisor to create the highest quality optical effect. This sometimes requires the use of larger format film types that greatly reduce generational loss.

## The Color Timer

The color timer sets the density, contrast, and color from scene to scene. By working with three colors (red, green, blue) other colors can be created. By increasing or decreasing all colors equally, a scene can be brightened or darkened. The color timer works closely with the DP and the director to achieve the mood of the film. Terms such as colder and warmer are used to describe a scene and a mood. An answer print is then created and screened for the director and DP. The "Color by—" credit at the end of a film identifies the laboratory responsible for the color timing.

During the screening, notes are taken, and the footage is marked for additional color correction. For example, let's say that 353 feet into the film there is an interior shot which the director wants warmed up. The footage is marked and later loaded on a Hazeltine. The Hazeltine is a machine that analyzes the film negative and sets the initial timing lights. By aligning the positive print alongside and in sync with the negative, the notes based on the positive are matched to the negative during the Hazeltine process. Usually, three to four passes at the answer print are required to create the release print. The release print is the final selection of the answer print where the entire print meets the look that the director and DP are trying to achieve.

## The Collaborative Process of Filmmaking

Each of the people involved in making a film must relate an idea to their coworkers and assistants; there may be hundreds of people involved. Film is a collaborative art, and efforts must be coordinated to create a single film. Hundreds of questions may be asked

and answered daily, and some answers will not be apparent until the film has been shot. Any hesitation or mistake due to a failure of communication can increase the budget of the film. Filmmaking is the art of communication, visualization, and organization.

## INDUSTRY VIEWPOINTS

### Howard Smith—Film Editor

*Strange Days* (1995), *Two Bits* (1995), *The Saint of Fort Washington* (1993), *Glengarry Glen Ross* (1992), *Point Break* (1991), *After Dark My Sweet* (1990), *The Abyss* (1989), *River's Edge* (1987), *Near Dark* (1987), *Tex* (1982).

For editor Howard Smith, the use of digital, nonlinear editing systems has been a rewarding experience not only due to the effect it has had on his ability to try new ideas, but also in its position in the digital filmmaking environment. For Smith, a veteran of some of the most memorable films that have showcased story lines and the skills of many talented actors, filmmaking is less about technology as it is about telling a story. Says Smith,

> I teach a course called "Film Editing for Screenwriters" where the focus is on the script. Film was first a

**Figure 1-10** Photo of Howard Smith. Courtesy of Howard Smith.

visual medium in which sound came later and became very powerful. If a screenwriter understands camera and the mechanics of the cinematic language and editing and the selection of images, that person will be able to previsualize the fiction feature film. For example, there is nothing as rewarding as a very good chase sequence, but people think that the answer is to escalate the action—to have 400 car crashes instead of six. What really makes a sequence work is when the audience involvement escalates, and a writer can conceive of a good sequence if he or she understands editing and camera. I, as an editor, cannot make something wonderful if I don't have the elements. In the editing room, you finally see things come to life. That's why I believe the script is so important.

Some of these new technologies let you learn this language as you are sitting at the computer. You can read all the books on filmmaking, but you have to edit to learn editing. Editors will often let their assistants cut a scene or two to gain experience, but with digital systems, assistants can conceivably cut the entire film themselves on their own time—that is an extraordinary opportunity to learn.

Smith sees a whole new approach to filmmaking as more individuals utilize computers and networking capabilities. He continues,

What I see as being exciting is when the ones and zeroes can speak to each other—it will give us a greater sense of cross-communication. When there is a free flow of language among director, editor, photographer, and so on, it is a true collaboration. How great films get made is that you have a lot of people who are communicating with each other. The important point of not losing any details is one of the great benefits of being digital. The key to this will be networking systems together. If I can be working on my cut visually and the script supervisor is giving me input directly, it's a very fluid atmosphere and it keeps stimulating you to try new ideas. Or, if I'm finishing a cut of a scene and the material is immediately picked up by our sound man in Colorado, we can be very far apart geographically and connected digitally. A casting director has something that he or she wants to get across, and they can create a sketch on the computer that is so rich and detailed that the director or the editor can see what they want to accomplish in a fraction of the time that it may normally take.

If directors sit down and discover what can be done by editing digitally, they'll also lose their fear of visual effects and prove that this technology is accessible. What they'll find is that digital technology is allowing us in visual conception to create worlds that we only imagine. It's possible to make an alien world

out of lights and sets and backgrounds, and even filmmakers who are doing realistic drama can benefit from this—it's not just the science fiction films.

When I learned to edit, I learned the Moviola and the flatbed at the same time. I used to do all my first assemblies on the Moviola, then I would switch to the KEM. Over the past few years I had looked at the videotape- and laserdisc-based editing systems, and I always felt that they were no better than the Moviola. Francis Coppola made the new technology safe to think about when he coined the term "Electronic Cinema."

Now, digital editing has far exceeded my expectations. It has allowed me to do something that would have taken so much time. You can smooth out your sound almost effortlessly—and the sequence plays 100% better. The fact that I can actually add sound effects, background effects and can make crossfades between the audio tracks is amazing. You are showing a cut to a director with multitracks of sound and the director says, "My God, this film really works!" For performances, if I have four ten-minute takes and I am looking for another reading, on film I have to wind down the film, physically get to it, thread it up, watch it, and so forth. With digital, you just point to the footage you want and it's there.

As a result, you are less likely to be lazy and more likely to do your homework. I am attracted to pieces that have strong performances—a specific example is, let's say, the actor has done a line and it is slightly different in each take and very subtly different. You really quickly edit together just those lines, and you play them one after another—just that becomes an extraordinary evaluative tool. I think digital editing maximizes squeezing the absolute best of what the whole movie has to offer. The shaping of material is really intensified and allowed to have stronger reign—you are less worried about wondering whether you have the best material.

Smith points out how communication is essential to the filmmaking process. He says,

James Cameron is a director whose genius is that he can conceive of a sequence that is very filmic and that relies on all of the state-of-the-art tools. We'll have a shot with a matte painting, then blue screen, then miniatures with live action composited. Now, not any of these shots creates the illusion, but he knows how to put together a series of images that comes together and is extraordinary where the accumulation of cutting gives you the sense that you've seen something that you really haven't. An example is the diving sequence in *The Abyss*—it is made up of many little pieces of extraordinary special visual effects, but taken together it really gives you the impression that he has filmed this huge wreck, and you really feel that you have arrived at this special place. The ability to communicate and talk and to figure out how we were going to realize this sequence was evident in making that film. . . .

When I was cutting *Two Bits* I tried things that I may not have tried otherwise. There are three major sequences in this film where if we didn't have digital nonlinear we would not have gone down a particular road. After you get some experience in editing, you know that there aren't a thousand ways to cut a scene; basically you've got only a handful. We tried something where the feeling was, "This can't possibly work"—actually the feeling we had was that there was only a 2% chance that it would work. We said, "Let's just do it"—it took maybe ten minutes to recut this one sequence—a running chase sequence—suddenly, what would not have worked in our brains was working on the screen and it was jaw-dropping

and we saw it and realized it and we said, "My God, this works, and it works brilliantly," and everything you would have discussed would have pointed to the answer, "Don't bother."

You can start and then store every possibility that you come up with and you don't lose it. Film directors and film editors don't ever again have to face losing a particular cut because the options are preserved. It so closely relates to how you respond to what's good and bad—you can see the work you are doing in a better way because you can look back at the work that you did on the sequence some time ago. Making something the very finest it can be starts out with using the tools correctly and digital filmmaking helps you in your conceptualization, where the different tools—right now, for me, the editing tool— is actually becoming part of the conceptualization. And that is radically new and revolutionary.

# 2

# Introduction to Digital Filmmaking

In this chapter, we describe the developing digital filmmaking methods and how technological innovations are redefining how films are made. The previous chapter contained an outline of the multitude of individuals involved and the accepted and traditional filmmaking process, honed by years of experience, trial, and error. For almost 100 years filmmaking has seemed not to change very much. Film is put in a camera, exposed, edited, sound is added, and viewers are, usually, either enthralled or disappointed. However, filmmaking has, indeed, experienced a change. The gradualness of the various changes, however, has been so slow, and based on refinements to analog technology, to cause the casual observer to be unaware that change was taking place.

In the 1990s the various disciplines of filmmaking, such as photography, editing, sound, and special visual effects all underwent significant changes. As each of those disciplines have sought out digital tools and solutions, a great synergy appeared. When we examine each of these labors—those of editing, sound design, computer-generated special visual effects, etc.—we see overwhelming evidence of the redefinition of the entire process of filmmaking.

Digital tools present the opportunity to change the filmmaking process because the process is no longer tied to or defined by the limitations of analog technology. We may casually dismiss the notion that how films are made will change and that the people who make films will simply become more efficient and creative as a result of using digital tools. However, a significant aspect of digital filmmaking is that the process will no longer remain serial in nature. Rather, the different artisans on a film will work in parallel, and it is this work method which will be quite different and new.

Within this change and redefinition, job categories will also undergo a redefinition. Whereas an assistant film editor has had a very traditional job

definition with specific job tasks, the digital film assistant will be required to do new tasks and will be required to be more computer savvy than ever.

So many new aspects of making a film are appearing that it is difficult for the traditionally trained film director, producer, writer, et al., to keep up with the new methods of accomplishing his or her vision. It is most important that the filmmaker have an overall vision not only of the project being created, but of the methods which will be used to accomplish the project.

While one need not become an expert at, say, the specifics of how a strip of film can be input into a computer, changed in some way, and output back to a strip of film, simply knowing that this technology is available is a crucial piece of information to the filmmaker who is wondering, "This story needs this, but I don't know how to accomplish it. If I can't accomplish it, why go down this story route?"

Often, a filmmaker is left free to dream about creating an environment or characters but may not be allowed the freedom without understanding how the story could be accomplished within the real limitation of budget considerations. In the new world of filmmaking, being a visionary, being an artist, also requires an understanding of what digital filmmaking techniques can offer.

Digital filmmaking can be thought of as a combination of filmmaking methods that are dominated by digital solutions and tools that have created new means of accomplishing old tasks. Second, some of these new digital tools have combined to create new capabilities, heretofore unavailable to the filmmaker. The traditional triad of preproduction, production, and postproduction (and the forgotten, but critical phase of distribution) that any film undergoes is affected by these new sets of tools and capabilities.

There is a vast difference in the look that films have taken during the last twenty years. While the early silent movie made use of title cards to convey dialogue in the absence of synchronized sound, the simple look of these films is a far cry from the fantastic images of modern films. Shown in figure 2-1 (see page 81 [color insert]) is an example of just how far the filmmaking industry has come in delivering to an audience an enormously successful action film that makes use of ground-breaking special effects.

It would be very wrong to think of digital filmmaking as being a series of methods used only to create films which are dominated by special effects. Rather, digital filmmaking methods are for all aspects of filmmaking—the action adventure film, the murder mystery, the drama, the comedy.

While one particular technique in the digital filmmaking tool set may be used to create some fantastic three-dimensional character, that same technique may be used to fix some error that was not seen in the frame. Or a particular digital filmmaking method may be used to ascertain if something is or is not feasible before more costly tests are done. In all cases, it is the task to be accomplished that dictates the tool to be used; it should never be the other way around.

Of course, there are certainly instances where specific sequences could not have been accomplished without knowing that technology would be there to save the day. The fantastic dinosaurs found in the film *Jurassic Park* or the wire-removal techniques used on *Cliffhanger* are examples of very difficult scenes that are dependent upon either existing technologies, or technologies created specifically for the purpose of accomplishing specific scenes.

And, with each groundbreaking film, new digital filmmaking methods are being added to the range of tools available to the filmmaker. As film, video, and computers are used, the range of tools that the filmmaker has will become quite astounding.

Two very different editing systems for filmmakers, a film flatbed editor and its digital counterpart, the digital, nonlinear edit system, are shown in figures 2-2 and 2-3.

## FILM CATEGORIES

Although most people generally tend to think of films as having scripts and actors, this is certainly not always true. Watching a documentary film can often be one of the most fascinating and exciting moviegoing experiences. If a story is interesting and captured well, a rendering which is not dramatized is very rewarding. Documentary films, by and large, are not at all script driven. Nor will they tend to have professional actors. The filmmaker, armed with an outline, places a camera in a situation and documents the surroundings and its inhabitants. During the postproduction stage, the all-important editorial sessions will bring shape to the film that has been shot.

There are feature films, documentary films, live action short films, feature length animated films, special venue films, and many others. To lose track of

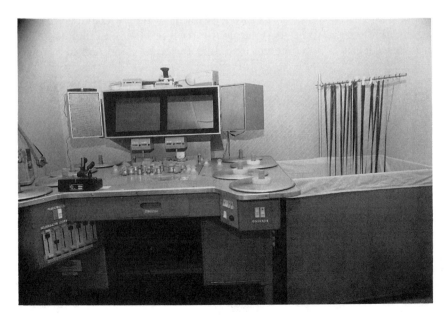

**Figure 2-2** The flatbed film editor, with strips of film hanging in the film bin. Photo by Michael E. Phillips.

**Figure 2-3** The flatbed's digital counterpart, the digital, nonlinear edit system. Courtesy of Avid Technology, Inc.

these various film types is to lose sight of the massive film audiences there are in the world and, most importantly, the widely divergent distribution forms that a film may take.

## Film—A World Perspective

While most individuals, when first asked to name the center of international filmmaking, will most likely respond, "Hollywood, California in the United States of America," it is worth pausing to evaluate this statement. Certainly, Hollywood, given its history as the site of the industry whose sole purpose is to create filmmaking and the place that markets its films very successfully throughout the world has achieved legendary status as the film capitol of the world.

In the category of feature films, the United States of America creates approximately 400 feature films each year. Manila, the Philippines, with far fewer resources, creates approximately 200 feature films. Bombay, India creates at least five times the number of films created in America. For sheer numbers of films created, many parts of the world rival Hollywood.

In terms of execution, artistic and technical innovation, it is widely held that Hollywood attracts wonderfully talented craftspeople. But this is quite arguable. For years and years, film experts felt that there were two centers of film production—Hollywood and London. London, in recent times, has fallen from the list in terms of the actual number of films produced, while, at the same time, maintaining quite a large pool of very talented filmmakers and craftspeople.

While Hollywood may have the latest in technological apparatus, a Third World country, and the filmmaker in that country, may only have a camera and an old, but trusty, editing system. The only things that the two locations, and the personalities in the two locations, may have in common are A) film is exposed, and B) both are trying to make the best film possible within their operating scales.

For our purposes, we must not forget that what is old news to one segment of the filmmaking community may turn out to be a revelation to filmmakers in a different land. It is, therefore, important to communicate all of the developments that filmmaking is undergoing as we incorporate digital filmmaking techniques.

## The Digital Filmmaking Experience

There are many trends in the world of filmmaking. With the appetite for increased programming fueled by diverse markets such as cable television, home videocassettes, and interactive applications, many efforts have been put in place to try and obtain the best possible results with the most economical budgets.

Creating lavish films and films of good value without spending more money than necessary is, or should be, the economic responsibility of all filmmakers. Today, with such a large demand for films that will find their way first into theaters, but more likely in the lucrative ancillary markets, filmmakers must find ways to make films more economically, while not sacrificing the film's quality. With excellent planning, these objectives are possible.

What follows is a description of the digital filmmaking experience. In chapters to follow, each of the major facets of digital filmmaking will be expanded upon. Most of the technology, operability, and acceptance by the filmmaker are in place today. Only a few items are not presently available, but they will be in a matter of only a few years.

## INDUSTRY VIEWPOINTS

### Fraser Heston—Director/Writer

*Needful Things* (1994)

For film director Fraser Heston, the use of digital, nonlinear editing for feature film post-production has been a very rewarding experience. Heston, who along with editor Rob Kobrin, decided to use a digital editing system for the Castle Rock production of *Needful Things,* comments on the differences between traditional film editing and digital, nonlinear editing. Says Heston,

**Figure 2-4** Photo of Fraser Heston. Courtesy of Fraser Heston.

First, let me say that for me digital editing is the most impressive advancement since color film and sound. It has changed the way that a director can think about making films, and it really frees your mind to experimentation. However, the small screen on the digital system is forgiving, and while you can make mistakes on any screen, you really need to see your work on the big screen to know how a scene is going to play.

Of additional importance to Heston is the advanced sound capabilities of the digital editing system. He continues,

Sound is so important—it's intangible really—but it's definitely crucial. Even if we were filling in blank spaces with wind sound effects, you can just drop in the compact disc and cut the sounds into place so easily. There's nothing worse than watching your cut and you have a car driving by with absolutely no sound. But if you use the digital editing system correctly, you can drop in the sound of the car going past, and you remain in that visual experience, you are not taken out of it—so why not give yourself every opportunity to have the best possible presentation and experience?

I would count flexibility, speed, non-destructiveness, and nonlinear as the combination that presents the filmmaker with an incredible tool. But you have to be disciplined with the tool—you can become wrapped up in it. You must be well organized and understand file management. Most importantly, you are a director—you must make your choices and stick with them. Ultimately, this technology is a lot more fun to work with and it's great to see an idea unfold before your eyes—you get to see the changes immediately and you can see optical effects almost instantly. . . .

What I think is going to be very interesting is seeing companies that begin to develop interactive movies and games that require live action and computer animation. The line has already been blurred, because there are already huge amounts of computer generated imagery in feature films. But, even so, there will always be an overriding need for a creative hand in directing these projects. Whatever technology we filmmakers use, we must not only understand the technology, we must understand when and when not to use it.

## Preserving and Sharing Information

One of the most important aspects of the digital filmmaking methodology is to preserve as much information as possible. This means that once information is originated, it is not lost. Instead, it is cataloged and made accessible to all members who need access. Most importantly, this availability must be present throughout all stages, even through the distribution stage.

One of the greatest contributions of the studio system was standardizing a record keeping and paperwork system for film production. Detailed record keeping, cross-referencing, and file retrieval are all tasks that computers can do, and they allow for much easier sharing of this information.

As an example of this contribution, suppose a specific sound effect has been created in a very quick fashion very early on in the production. As the various phases of the film are encountered, without rigorous labelling and cataloging, this particular sound effect might be lost—not an unlikely occurrence since it was only created to give an idea of what was necessary. After all, who would have thought that it would be used in the final version? In fact, who could have predicted that the very sound effect that was quickly created would have been so difficult to recreate? Lastly, who paused to give thought that the sound effect would have been a perfect signature signal for the home video game version of the movie?

It is the nature of segment-based work, where work done may end up being duplicated, often quite needlessly, and with little emphasis given to the preservation of information that contributes to quite a great deal of inefficiency.

Just as importantly, it is necessary to be completely clear as to what the responsibilities are for each of the various departments in any film. By being able to share and access common information, this becomes possible.

## Preproduction, Production, Postproduction, and Distribution

While this book has been divided into three major sections, preproduction, production, and postproduction (and we have added distribution as an important, but rarely mentioned stage), it is critical to remember that when digital filmmaking completely comes into fruition, it will be as a process that does not make clear, distinguished lines between these different phases. Rather, digital filmmaking, as a methodology, will blur all lines which currently characterize the various stages of filmmaking.

How will films be made using digital filmmaking

methods? The truth is that many films are being made now using various components of digital filmmaking. Eventually, there will be so many of the individual components in place that entire processes will become dependent upon the digital tools and methods. This will be true digital filmmaking. What follows is a view of where we are going and the various digital filmmaking components along the way.

## WHY FILMMAKING IS CHANGING

Consider the 35mm motion picture. Until only recently, most feature films were shot using 35mm film. The 35mm film negative was loaded into the camera, exposed, and processed. Then a print was made from the processed negative, and this print was the film that the editor cut together to form the movie. There just weren't that many additional visual elements used in the presentation. Films, for decades and decades, were made in this fashion: Shoot the live action, edit the film, finish the sound for the film, put the titles and credits on the film, and show the film.

In the late 1980s, the integration of many types of media into the feature film began. Today, depending on the look that the director wants, a film may include material shot on 35mm film, 16mm, Super 8, professional videotape formats (such as D2 and 1″), and consumer videotape formats (such as Hi 8 and VHS). These formats can be enhanced or degraded through electronic means. Since these different formats will record images in different ways, integrating many formats into one feature film can provide exciting visual results; it all depends upon what the filmmaker is trying to express visually.

Technological manipulation of film has increased dramatically. For example, if a period piece is being filmed and it simply wouldn't be correct to see telephone poles in the frame, technology is used to fix the shot after it has been filmed. Using electronic painting systems to erase the telephone poles and replace these sections with a sky background is the only viable alternative. It would be unlikely that the poles could be physically removed! Also, the viewing audience has grown in sophistication and expectation, with an increased pressure on filmmakers to deliver new images. Now, more than ever, there is a reliance on new technologies to facilitate these images.

Any adoption of a new methodology or a new technology must take into account two issues: 1) does the new way decrease the cost of getting the film into distribution, or 2) is there a different benefit, such as increased creativity? Change for the sake of change in the film world is not common practice! There must be reasons for setting the known methods on end and a justification for bringing in new technology.

Through it all, it will be the filmmaker who knows how to harness these digital filmmaking methods with taste and creativity, to always present the story first, and not shrouded by the technological means by which the story was achieved.

## The Digital Filmmaking Flowchart

One way to minimize the amount of difficulty that may be encountered is to take the time to carefully think about the path of all the elements. A film flowchart is extremely helpful to show exactly where the film is at any specific moment. Figure 2-5 is an example of a film flowchart created by Kim Aubry for the Francis Ford Coppola film *Bram Stoker's Dracula*. Note how every process is outlined and shows interdependencies.

Unfortunately, often new methods are attempted without adequate preparation. As the film industry adapts to a digital filmmaking methodology, there will be experiments to affirm that something works as advertised. Without this confidence, the film industry will continue to operate under an à la carte basis, where only a few sections are accomplished digitally. A flowchart serves as a blueprint for the production, and at any point, anyone involved in the production can glance at the flowchart and know what has transpired. Figure 2-6 shows a flowchart that will serve as a digital filmmaking guideline. Each major concept that forms the fabric of the flowchart will be transformed and improved.

What follows is a description of digital filmmaking and the various procedures that form its methodology.

## PREPRODUCTION

For our purposes, let us take a feature film through the four stages of filmmaking by applying digital filmmaking techniques.

## The Script

The script is created with a word processor, and the digital files can be copied, changed, and distributed. There are software packages which include standard scriptwriting template forms and tools to determine how many times a character says a particular word, or how many times a character makes an appearance. Once a script is created, it may be changed over time. However, once a script and monies are approved, what begins is an inexorable march to the motion picture theater.

A script is next broken down into each scene, and scenes are grouped according to what can be shot in a specific location or time. Maximizing the use of each location, type of equipment, props, and a dizzying set of other variables must all be balanced.

Information flows between the scripting stage and the script breakdown stage. If a script calls for tens of thousand of extras for a scene, the filmmakers must take into account the location, the physical constraints, the cost of mounting such a scene, and many other logistics. Questions arise, such as: "Can we afford to do this? How will we get the people in and out? What type of security forces will we need? Are we obligated to provide meals?" If no answers are forthcoming to these practical questions, does the script get changed, or, if writer and director are adamant that the scene must stay, new questions arise, such as: "Can we mount the scene by shooting the backgrounds with just a few hundred people? Can we then take these pieces of film and digitally replicate the people to create a more expansive scene that will look as if there are thousands of people present?" If so, then the intent of the script carries forth. The production is not unduly burdened with the cost of mounting the scene, and digital filmmaking has provided a solution to the problem.

Digital filmmakers rely heavily on software programs that take scripts, facilitate their breakdown, and serve as preparation for other departments. Most importantly, all the generated information will not be lost. If a special effects house is bidding on a series of visual effects shots, and they are receiving a very rough draft of the script, imagine receiving the script with actual voice notes from the director, that explain the effect's intent. As the project is tracked through different departments, it will be useful to have this oral subtext. As early on as the screenwriting stage, collaboration and the cataloging of that collaboration can be very valuable to all involved.

Asking questions such as "Can it be done? How could we go about showing that? Is it even achievable?" may lead to proof of concept tests. This category of preproduction is known as the previsualization stage.

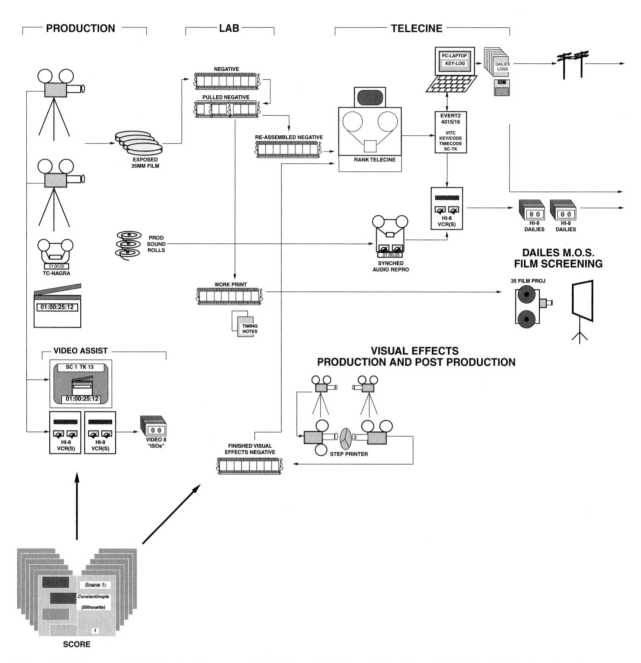

**Figure 2-5** An example of a film flowchart created for the Francis Ford Coppola film, *Bram Stoker's Dracula*. Flowchart by and courtesy of Kim Aubry.

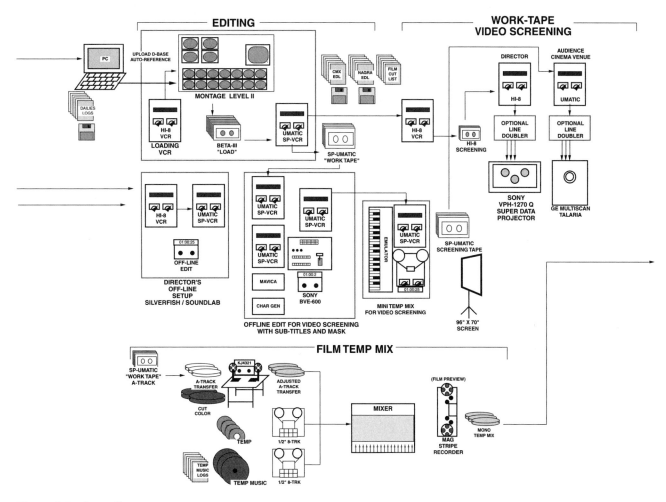

**Figure 2-5** *(page 2)*

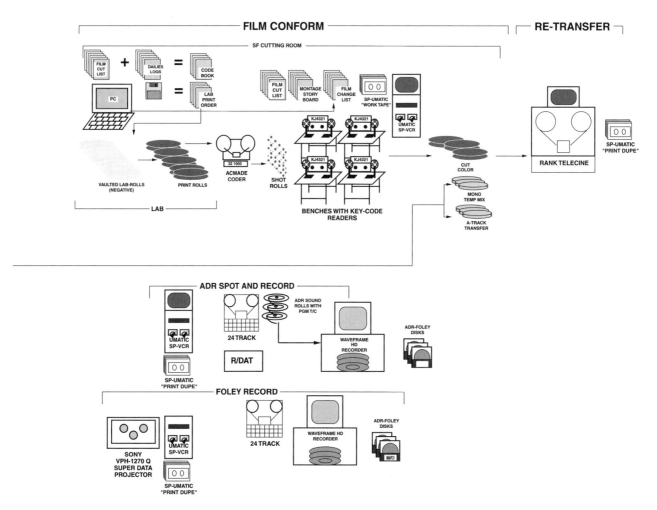

**Figure 2-5** *(page 3)*

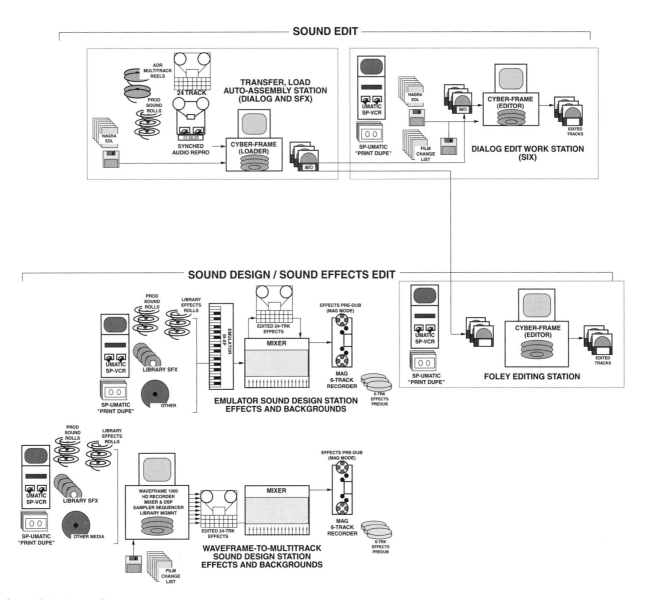

**Figure 2-5**  (page 4)

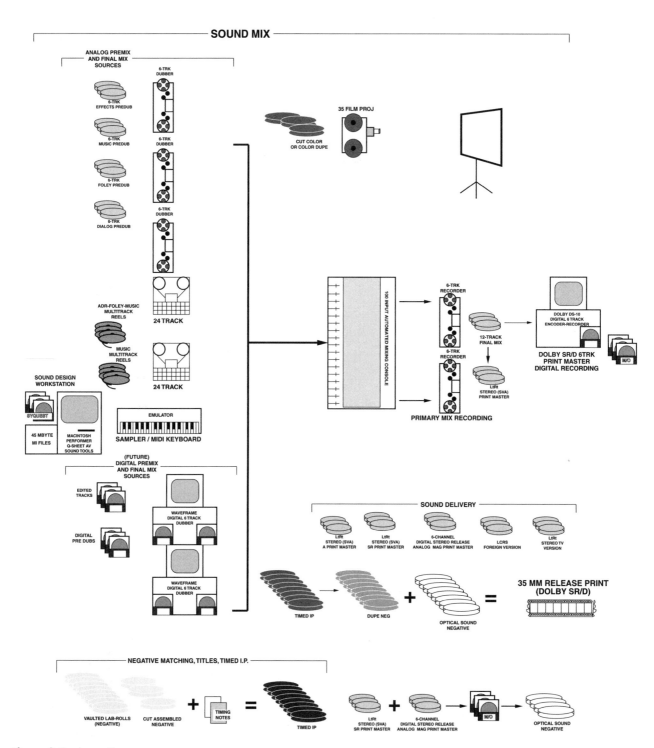

**Figure 2-5** *(page 5)*

## ── MUSICAL SCORE ──

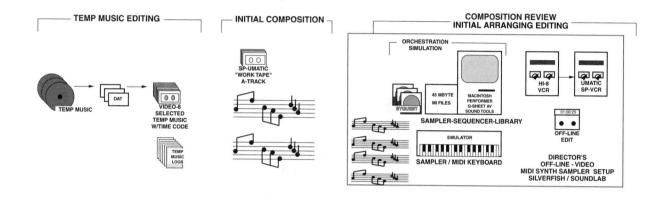

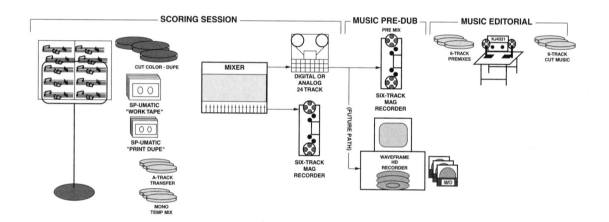

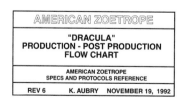

| AMERICAN ZOETROPE |
|---|
| **"DRACULA"**<br>**PRODUCTION - POST PRODUCTION**<br>**FLOW CHART** |
| AMERICAN ZOETROPE<br>SPECS AND PROTOCOLS REFERENCE |
| REV 6      K. AUBRY      NOVEMBER 19, 1992 |

**Figure 2-5**  (page 6)

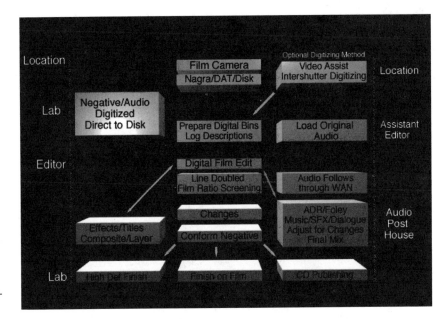

**Figure 2-6** A flowchart which represents the digital filmmaking process. Illustration by Jeffrey Krebs.

## INDUSTRY VIEWPOINTS

### Tim McGovern—SVP of Creative and Technical Affairs, Sony Pictures Imageworks

For Tim McGovern, filmmakers are increasingly turning to Sony Pictures Imageworks (SPI) for a whole spectrum of work. McGovern clearly is excited by the manner and rapidity with which digital technology is affecting the filmmaking process.

McGovern oversees four departments that service different aspects of feature film production and three that support other media. For feature films, the Previsualization department creates 3-D animated storyboards on their PC-based production systems at the planning preproduction phase; during production the Camera Department is responsible for plate, blue screen, and miniature photography; R&D creates hardware and software solutions to visual EFX problems that do not have off-the-shelf solutions, and Digital Productions is responsible for the computer animation and digital compositing work performed on a huge array of Silicon Graphics Workstations.

Three other SPI Departments are responsible for production as it relates specifically to commercial music video, special venue ride films, and video games. Says McGovern, "Because entertainment is so diversified, the idea that a digital character we create

**Figure 2-7** Photo of Tim McGovern, Courtesy of Sony Pictures Imageworks.

will be used in a film for Sony Pictures, then reused in the ride film, the interactive film, and the video game is a reality and a justification for SPI to be active on all these fronts." Says McGovern,

We are involved at all stages of production but we encourage filmmakers to come talk to us before the scripts are written, because we feel that we can really help in the conceptual stage. Sometimes we need to point out things that are more difficult than necessary, and show the writer or director ways that make it more do-able. Other times it actually feels like we are freeing the writer or director when we show them how much we can actually achieve using digital techniques. Obviously, we prefer the latter situation to the former, but it's our job to give them the realistic appraisal, and it's up to them how they proceed. The amazing thing is that more films use this technology than ever in subtle ways, and more films than ever are being made that rely heavily on it and couldn't have been made without it. . . .

We scan 4 perf (standard 35mm) film at 3K × 4K, and 8 perf (VistaVision) at 4K × 6K with ten bits per pixel. At this resolution and color depth we preserve one billion colors and all the detail we believe necessary to reproduce the original negative. Once it becomes digital, there is a wide variety of things we can do to it. We can combine any number of other digital elements either real or computer generated in a digital composite, running on Silicon Graphics workstations. SPI employs a variety of the software packages such as Alias, Cinefusion, SoftImage, Wavefront/TDI, and Parallax; as well as a substantial amount of proprietary software developed by its own Software R&D department, to create the computer generated elements and complete digital composites.

McGovern cites the 1993 film, *In The Line of Fire,* as requiring deft digital handiwork. Says McGovern,

This is an excellent example where using digital technology allowed the filmmakers to make believable scenes without incurring huge expenses. For one of the crowd scenes, we shot 1500 people in five different groupings. We then took the five shots with hundreds of extras and weaved them into one shot with thousands of extras. As a result, when you look at the shots, it looks as if there are ten thousand people. In other shots, we took footage from the Bush/Clinton campaign, removed the real candidate, and replaced him with the actor candidate in the film. Political campaigns are supposed to look big; without these techniques it really would have been too costly. It would have dramatically affected the scope and authenticity of the film. . . .

If you figure that you want 10,000 extras and you have to pay each extra $50 a day, that's $500,000 for one day of shooting. Plus, there is a whole set of logistics that you don't have to worry about anymore; for example, how do you feed 10,000 people or where do you put 10,000 people?

McGovern also sees great benefit in being able to take advantage of wide networks in order to send material from one location to another. He says,

We are watching all these technologies closely, and we are participating in an ATM network experiment with Pac-Tel that connects a Southern California Net to a Northern California Net. Unfortunately these systems are still point-to-point, but the speeds are about 15 mb/sec which is great if you're on the net and academic if you're not. . . .

We will often do work and send the work to location where the director is shooting. The director can see what we're doing and comment. Because post-production time is shrinking simultaneously as the complexity and shot counts are increasing, we've got to have better communication with the director during all phases of production. Often the director is remote for large portions of this schedule. When money is no object, satellite services are available, as witnessed with Steven Spielberg reviewing post-production EFX on *Jurassic Park* during principal photography in Poland on *Schindler's List*. That's not for everyone, a lower cost digital alternative to 1/2″ VHS tapes through Federal Express is clearly needed, and I believe we are closer to that now than ever with the advent of high speed networks. Soon D1 video will be able to be played in real time over a network, and delivered anywhere phone lines can go.

## Previsualization

Previsualization allows us to see and judge concepts in an unfinished form. Previsualization can occur prior to principal photography or during production. Usually, the results are not seen by the initial audiences for the film though there can be ancillary uses for previsualization material. Perhaps that material will be used to create a director's special edition laserdisc version of the film to illustrate the film's previsualization methods. There are several major categories where these techniques are used.

These categories consist of:

1. Set construction and lighting considerations.
2. Art, costume, and makeup uses.
3. Casting roles.
4. Location scouting and property searches.
5. Storyboarding and script visualization with images and audio.
6. Feasibility studies to determine the possibility of achieving a specific effect.

Below is a brief explanation of the capabilities of one category, set and lighting. An in-depth description of each category is made in chapter four.

## Set Construction and Lighting Considerations

Digital technology can be used to create software environments of a set or location that already exists, or has not yet been constructed. These software versions allow the filmmaker to see what the room looks like from the perspective of the camera, using specific camera lenses, and operating in three-dimensional space.

For example, if a scene is to be shot in a large room, computer software can be used to recreate a realistic, three-dimensional view. Critical information, such as where space is limited, where set objects should be placed, and where, given the physical limitations, a fixed camera can and cannot go, can provide a great advantage for the filmmaker. Where lights can be placed, and how shadows will be cast, can all be previsualized. With accurate previsualization, knowing what equipment to bring, and knowing, a priori, where problems may occur can be invaluable pieces of information.

Once the set is visualized, it may be determined that, given a specific camera angle, the set must be lengthened, therefore requiring more construction time and materials. Alternatively, it may be discovered that the set can be reduced, and that an extra four meters of set are no longer necessary. All of these decisions can be made before the expensive stages are encountered.

## Script and Previsualization: An Interconnected Process

Films usually do not take a long time from inception to completion. The average time from initial photography to the film's opening is approximately nine months. However, the script and previsualization stage can last for quite some time during which a great deal of information can be created. Notes about how a character should sound for the sound design department, notes about the color scheme a character will wear, examples of computer generated foregrounds that serve as guides for the times when backgrounds are shot with live actors—all of these invaluable notes must be accessible to the filmmakers.

## The Script Supervisor and Logging

As the production begins, there are three major forms of information acquisition: the camera(s) recording the event, the sound recorder, and the script supervisor. The script supervisor's job is to make in-depth notations to the film.

As shown in the flowchart, an electronic version of the script is available and we will find the supervisor making notes directly onto a logging template marking the relation of film to sound and when a scene and take began. The diagram shows the links among film camera, sound recording, and logging application. Envision the supervisor using a handheld computer whose input comes via a pen.

Supervisors, who work all day and night with pencil and notebook in hand, won't have to change their style of information gathering. What will change, however, is that the endless transcribing, duplication of work, and the frustrating loss of information will become quite infrequent.

## The Camera, Sound, and On-Location Digital Recording Processes

Film camera and sound recorder work in parallel. The output of the film camera is converted to a video signal (video tap) that allows the image to be recorded to videotape. Viewing this video tap recording allows the director to make judgments.

In the flowchart, the output of the video tap and the sound recorder is captured by an on-location digital recorder that will replace the videotape recorder. By recording picture and sound to digital disks, each take can be viewed quickly. Heretofore, the digital technologies that are in use during the scripting and previsualization stages have been somewhat invisible to the cast and crew members. Here, however, a new concept is being introduced—digital recording, review, and manipulation.

## On-Set/On-Location Previsualization, Editorial, and Compositing

During the shooting stage, we may utilize components of the previsualization stage. Let's say we have a scene in which an actor is being photographed in front of a blue screen that will later be optically removed to composite the actor with a computer generated background. By digitizing the shot of the actor, it can be composited through the use of an on-location compositing system. This system takes the shot of the actor, filmed just moments ago, and combines it with the computer background. The director can view the composite and judge whether the take is sufficient or must be redone.

This on-set and on-location manipulation extends to editing as well. After digitizing the output of the film camera and sound recorder, this new material can be edited. Take, for example, a difficult scene that a director must complete. Time may be running short, and there is pressure to wrap the scene. If a director is concerned whether a scene can be successfully put together during editing, that is, whether there is enough essential coverage to make the scene work, using on-location editing may help remove this anxiety.

## THE LABORATORY

The film negative arrives into the laboratory and is developed. Usually a positive, or workprint, is created from the film negative, and it is this workprint that the film editor cuts. However, with digital filmmaking methods, the laboratory and what happens to the film at this stage involve different sections of the flowchart.

## The Telecine

A telecine is a device that is used to transfer film images from a film roll to either videotape or to digital disk. The film is transferred to videotape and is then digitized into the digital, nonlinear editing system. Or, the videotape stage is circumvented, and the film is transferred directly from the telecine to computer disks used for editing. Directions regarding what sections of film to transfer, or what sections of the film to print, can be obtained by a merging of data. Since the script supervisor's notes are accessible to the on-location digital recorder, or directly merged into the logging application in the transfer facility, directions and notes for each film take can be brought forth through this digital filmmaking phase. Telecine sessions will proceed in a semi-automated (eventually completely automated) state as the required sections of film are transferred directly to disk.

## Electronic Dailies

Whether in videotape or digital form, the film has been transferred and exists in a form known as electronic dailies. What has happened to the all-important sound? There are two possibilities—either the sound was synchronized to the picture during the telecine stage, or the sound was transferred directly from the original recordings to computer disk.

## Dailies Projection

One of the traditional parts of feature filmmaking is the projection of dailies for cast and crew who gather to view footage usually shot the previous day. When using workprint, the normal methodology is to synchronize magnetic track to picture and to run picture and sound. There is certainly a great feeling of anticipation surrounding this event. For the feature filmmaker, projecting dailies is a traditional part of being a filmmaker—that moment when you experience either joy or sorrow over some of the footage you labored so hard to capture!

However, digital filmmaking does impact on the method by which dailies are screened. There are clearly those film projects that will continue to print film and project dailies. However, there are also many films where workprint will not exist. Instead, dailies will be watched either on videotape or off digital disk.

For dailies projected using digital filmmaking methods, immediate changes are most apparent in the area of sound. Referring to the flowchart, note that sound can flow from the digital editing system directly to a device which we will label the digital audio follower. If workprint is being projected, it need not be synced to magnetic track. Instead, the digital audio follower will play the appropriate sound files in sync with the picture. The files exist either on the digital audio follower, or on the digital edit system connected via a computer network to the audio follower. The benefits of this method include a complete removal of magnetic track from the film cutting room and removing the necessity of manually synchronizing sound to picture.

How is this miraculous synchronization achieved between picture and sound? Returning to the flowchart, our electronic dailies have been loaded into the digital, nonlinear editing system. At the same time, the precious log of information from telecine or from the script supervisor is imported into the edit system. It is this log, cataloging the relationships between film and sound, that directs the digital audio follower to play its digital audio files with either the projected film or videotape transfer.

## THE EDITORIAL STAGE

Digital filmmaking requires digital, nonlinear editing. Referring to the flowchart, note that the digital dailies, log, and sound files travel to the digital edit system where tools reside that range from common film optical effects, such as fades and dissolves, to more advanced features, such as blue screen compositing and multiple audio tracks. By utilizing these multiple audio tracks, the editor can create temporary (temp) dubs which can be played during screenings. By putting together such soundtracks, and mixing them within the editing system, the editor is better able to give the director a view of not only what the finished movie will look like, but also what the finished movie will sound like. It is one thing to see a huge explosion with no sound effects, and quite another to see it with seven layered sound effects built upon one another, along with some music that was quickly sampled from a compact disc!

### Editorial Interaction with Parallel Operations

Referring to the flowchart, notice that the editing system works in concert with, for example, the special visual effects department. It may be necessary to incorporate intricate computer generated material into a sequence being edited. Working in parallel is crucial when deadlines are very tight, especially given the nature of special visual effects. Being efficient with directions and objectives is very important. In the past, filmmakers would describe how a particular effect should look when completed, but there could be a great deal of difference with what was described and what the effects house delivered. Each iteration is time, and the extra time may jeopardize placing a film in a theater on a specific date.

As editorial proceeds, it will be necessary to share files among various workstations used in digital filmmaking. Rather than describe the effect to the visual effects house, the editor may decide to composite a rough example of the effect at low picture resolution. However, by giving the effects house a visual blueprint, there is greater synergy between editorial and visual effects.

## INDUSTRY VIEWPOINTS

### Frank Kerr—Film Director

*Patriots* (1994)

For film director Frank Kerr, the use of a digital, nonlinear editing system on his 1994 film *Patriots* was his first foray into the world of digital filmmaking. Director Kerr comments on the benefits of using a DNLE system and its impact on his filmmaking:

> By eliminating or shortening much of the mechanical process of film editing, using a digital, nonlinear system left me to concentrate on creative decision making. Selected takes were reviewed on-screen and then cut into the body of the picture with the touch of a button. The advantages of this process over the traditional, cumbersome method of cut and splice editing were evident in both time savings and creative flexibility.

For his film, *Patriots,* Kerr utilized not only digital editing for picture, but also a digital audio workstation for the sound design and track-lay stages. It is illustrative to document Kerr's outlook on the digital filmmaking post-production process, especially as it relates to *Patriots.* Says Kerr,

> I had mixed feelings while participating in this new wave of digital, nonlinear film editing. It was sober-

**Figure 2-8** Photo of Frank Kerr. Courtesy of Frank Kerr.

ing to realize that many of the traditional methods of film postproduction will soon become past history. But while this is sad news for those who love the touch of film and tape, the greater artistic freedom resulting from this new technology should be welcomed by anyone involved in the creative process.

The positive aspects of digital editing are found in the shortening of the postproduction process which, in turn, allows more time to make creative choices. Also, by going directly from film to videotape and to digital, there was no need for screening dailies and the picture quality was outstanding. The entire workprint aspect of filmmaking has essentially been eliminated by this process which is good news for budget-conscious producers. Finally, the integrity of sound quality was maintained from the field right through the mix, as there was no generational loss as we followed a digital audio route.

On the downside, digital editing is in its infancy, and a producer must expect some stumbles along the way, as with any new product. Traditional film-related services are only now learning to work with the digital, nonlinear technology. In my experience, sound houses, negative cutters, and laboratories are, for the most part, still trying to get up to speed with this new way of doing business. Sufficient contingency time should be allotted by the producer to absorb delays until the process is better understood and mastered by these related services.

Kerr also feels that future developments in digital filmmaking will not essentially change the role of the film director, but will provide additional options. He concludes,

> I don't see the new technology changing the filmmaking style of directors but it will make the job easier. With new technologies such as capturing images directly from the film camera and into the digital editing system, the director is able to quickly see performance and camera results and can make adjustments accordingly. In fact, entire scenes can be cut by the editor before sets are abandoned. This technology will be especially useful when budget is a concern for the filmmaker.

## Networking

Note also how this parallel work stage involves connecting different systems over local, wide, cross-country, and even cross-continent networks. It will become commonplace for files to be sent to different participants. A film may be shooting in Milan, Italy, but by editing on location, and transferring picture and sound files over high-speed networks, the effects

house, located on another continent, can see what is being done in Italy without waiting for an air courier service. The filmmaker can make comments and offer feedback. Sound applications abound and many films have benefitted from using high-speed networks that allow filmmakers in one country to accomplish audio dubbing while the actors are in a different country. Working in parallel has never been optimized in traditional filmmaking. This parallelism, file sharing, and networking form the glue that holds together the digital filmmaking methodology.

## Screening

Screening a film, for the financiers or for audience previews, usually takes place on film. Often, the sound mix is inferior, sound effects are missing, and the overall result is that the film appears undone, which, of course, it is. Optical effects, such as dissolves, superimpositions, and computer-intensive special effects are also usually missing.

Digital filmmaking methods can greatly improve this experience. This is especially true as more video is used to screen films. The advantage is that the optical effects created during editing will be preserved. The disadvantage is that the viewer is looking at video rather than film but there are technological advancements occurring to make video adequate for the screening stage by using large-screen projection systems and doubling the number of video lines.

## Changes

During the course of screening or previewing the film, changes may be required. These changes are made in the digital editing system, and if a workprint is being projected, a list is generated and the workprint will be updated. Also, the sound for these screenings can be output directly from the editing system, eliminating the need for costly audio work. The savings from doing this can be considerable. On a two-hour film that is previewed four times the amount saved would be about $20,000.

## Sound Sweetening and Mixing

Film directors, in general, have always been plagued with the sound elements for films. In traditional filmmaking, the pictures have been cut and completed and then the sound phase begins. Since the average time spent in soundtrack laying, dubbing, and mixing is approximately six to eight weeks, the director must finalize the picture that much sooner. This can put enormous pressure on the director who is faced with requiring changes to the picture up until the last possible moment.

Digital filmmaking that utilizes digital audio workstations begins the process of sound work earlier by sharing cut sequences from the editing system. The editor can send a newly cut sequence along the network to the sound design department. This sequence may change, but the majority of work for initial sound design and track lay can proceed. There is a huge advantage in allowing the director to take time away from the back end of the schedule—that normally allowed for the entire sound work process—and applying it to the production and editorial stages.

## Libraries for Picture and Sound

Libraries are useful throughout the digital filmmaking process. During preproduction, the filmmaker who wants to include certain period piece photographs of a street scene in Rome, Italy, has the ability to tap into and browse through a visual library. During editing, if the editor finds that a scene needs to have a refined sound effects track, the editor can poll the network, access the sound library, perform a search for a specific effect, and download it. Within a very short amount of time, a time-consuming task can be accomplished quite easily. It is also clear that on-demand libraries, and subscriptions to such libraries, will become commonplace.

## FINISHING THE FILM

### The Film Negative

When the postproduction process is complete, a negative cut list, which describes exactly what pieces of original film negative will be used in the final film, is generated along with an optical list, with special directives to the laboratory. Information in the database can be sent to the laboratory via modem. The laboratory will receive these directives digitally, in a format that relates to their specific and time-honored handwritten sheets.

### Timing Lite Information

Timing lites, which determine the amount of light and color that a film will be exposed to in creating the release print, use a red, green, blue, and color/gray scale. The editor may have utilized tools from the digital, nonlinear edit system to affect changes in how a shot looks, for example, from color to black-and-white during mid-shot. If so, the film negative for this shot will be changed during timing. Translating information from the edit system so that the laboratory can understand what the editor and director have tried to do, represents pieces of information that should not be lost. Even if this information only serves to point the laboratory in a beginning direction, it is quite better than duplicating 100% of the work.

## Computerized Workprint and Negative Location Tables

A crucial step in completing any film is conforming the original negative. Digital technologies are being introduced to this process as well. A negative cut list can be transmitted from the network, or simply carried on a floppy disk, and an edge code reader then facilitates the automatic rolling down of that reel to the exact frame line that must be cut (it must be stressed that this is not an automatic frame cutter, but, rather, an automatic frame finder). The human negative cutter then cuts the negative and begins to assemble the show. Early studies have shown that this process may save as much as 30% of the time that it takes to cut the negative for an average feature film.

## FILM EXHIBITION AND DISTRIBUTION

### Theater and Film or Television and Video?

Each year the feature film theater is visited by fewer people. The major reason cited is that viewers are waiting to see films on videocassette. Films such as documentaries may not even make it to the theater. Instead, the film may have been made specifically for television or for distribution on videotape.

### Ancillary and New Markets

A developing trend is that filmmakers are finding that there are several markets for their productions. Take the documentary filmmaker who is making a film that is primarily intended for television. As new outlets for programming arise, such as High Definition Television (HDTV) and Compact Disc Interactive (CD-I), the documentary filmmaker may find that there is a great afterlife for the film. These various afterlives, better known as ancillary and new markets, have previously been unforeseeable and a documentary that does not do well at the box office can now become quite profitable as a home video, CD-I, or CD-ROM release. The possibilities of ensuring that the investment turns a profit increase dramatically as ancillary and new markets for the film are defined and researched before the film's cameras begin rolling. Also it is wise to note what occurs on the sets of major motion pictures whose producers have contracted for game versions of the film. After photography has been completed on a major set, before the set is struck, a different crew, this one responsible for the interactive game version, arrives and shoots any material required for the game.

## Electronic Distribution

There is a great deal of research and testing being done to determine if programming can be delivered electronically. Often, this type of distribution has been referred to as arena programming. The name recalls instances, typically sporting events such as boxing matches, that are beamed into a civic auditorium. In parts of the world where cable television has made sufficient progress, pay-per-view and special request services have rendered arena-type programming extinct. However, there are many parts of the world where satellite programming on a one-night basis still occurs.

Today, the majority of testing is concentrated on the electronic delivery of films to the theater via high-capacity, high-speed telephone lines, and the displaying of the images on large screens. From a central location, thousands of miles away, several films could be sent at specific timed intervals into a cinema complex. There would be no film projectors or film cannisters; indeed, no actual film would be involved in the presentation of the film! There are expenditures to put such a system in place, as well as the cost of maintaining the distribution lines. Anti-piracy safeguards would be necessary to ensure that the film was not duplicated or transmitted to unauthorized viewers. Quality control would be improved—no focus problems, film print scratches, film jitter, etc. Time, experimentation, and advances in technology will provide the answer to this most important issue.

In the chapters to follow, issues relating to specific areas of digital filmmaking are discussed in-depth. The world of filmmaking, whether the feature film, the documentary, or the short live action film, is changing. The filmmaker must understand how technological developments have ushered in such a change and must think about how the digital filmmaking process can be used to better accomplish storytelling.

## INDUSTRY VIEWPOINTS

### Kim Aubry—Vice-President, Engineering and Technology, American Zoetrope

As vice-president for engineering and technology at American Zoetrope, Kim Aubry's chief responsibilities include bridging new technology and technological processes to the largely non-technical process of filmmaking. A former technical director, reporter, and producer for public radio, Aubry's early career included mixing film soundtracks and documentary work in the early 1980s. Aubry's love of film is apparent when one notes that his career has included early work as a film projectionist. Aubry came to Zoetrope

**Figure 2-9**  Photo of Kim Aubry. Courtesy of Kim Aubry.

after the company had experimented with early forms of Electronic Cinema, in the period following Francis Coppola's *One From The Heart*. Says Aubry,

At that time, Zoetrope was developing methods to create films using electronic production and postproduction methods. Zoetrope is a company that provides Francis Coppola with the capability he requires to make the films that he may write, produce, or direct. We also provide postproduction and creative services for other filmmakers.

In the early 1970s, Francis Coppola was one of the first American directors to use flatbeds as opposed to the venerable upright Moviola for feature film editing. . . . ironic because in a way flatbeds are more linear in the way film materials are handled and organized. But Francis loves new technology, loves trying new things, and loves applying them to filmmaking.

Over the years, Aubry has been exposed to and helped develop many of the working methods that characterize Zoetrope today. In the following paragraphs, Aubry reflects on the past, present, and future Zoetrope.

## A History of Technical Innovation

Zoetrope's innovative desire to further Electronic Cinema methodology led the company to create a hybrid system to offer high-speed sound dubbing. A large number of flatbed transports were linked together and a mixing facility was built. Aubry says,

In these early days of "Electronic Cinema," the late 1970s and early 1980s, New York and Hollywood dubbing stages were very low-tech and inflexible. From a facilities standpoint, sound postproduction was a very noncompetitive, stagnant business. With the advent of Dolby optical stereo and improved 70mm six channel "split-surround" magnetic sound, *Apocalypse* was an artistic and technological watershed. But Zoetrope was really just borrowing from current music recording studio technology; we were one of the first to use an automated mixing console for feature film dubbing. We developed a computer hard disk system to store automation information and pioneered the use of SMPTE timecode to synchronize 35mm magnetic dubbers with nonperforated, multitrack studio tape machines, and industrial VCRs because locking film sound to video picture was even more significant in some respects than locking up multitrack transports. Many of the techniques that eventually became standard procedure we had to develop because they didn't exist. . . .

At the time, Zoetrope consisted of film traditionalists and others who were video users excited about computers. This contributed to the merging of different technologies. Coppola felt that his concept of electronic cinema should include and take advantage of all the work that was going on in television and that these tools should apply to filmmaking.

Zoetrope's innovation is also evident in the continued search for technology which must bridge the world of film with that of video dailies and electronic editing. Says Aubry,

In 1989, Zoetrope built a custom "telecine assist rack pod" in road cases to augment local telecine facilities with the necessary peripherals for making video dailies. All the correct editorial data was burned into video character generated windows, encoded into VITC, and even stored in personal computer database files. In 1991, Zoetrope and Evertz Microsystems Ltd. of Ontario co-developed "Key-Log," a computer logging and management program for real-time data capture during video dailies telecine transfer and for uploading into nonlinear editing systems.

## On Previsualization

On-set previsualization techniques during the filming of *Apocalypse Now* and *One From the Heart* included the use of camera video taps, Ultimatte video compositing and electronic off-line editing. Director Coppola viewed rushes of *Apocalypse Now* footage on Betamax 1 videotapes in the Philippine jungles. Zoetrope acquired the first prototype Videola for in-house film-to-tape dailies transfers. Eventually, this was replaced with a Rank telecine. During *One From the Heart* production, dailies tapes were delivered to the "Silverfish," an airstream motor-home that serves as the director's private on-set trailer and provides video-assist recording, playback audio supervision, and off-line editing. Coppola is able to intercut telecined materials from previous shooting days with just photographed scenes recorded on the camera's video tap. Viewing materials juxtaposed in this way helps the director provide coverage and even economize on photography. Aubry says,

Francis fell in love with the Hi-8 videotape format when he first saw it at a private demo in early 1989 and felt it had applications beyond the manufacturer's stated intention—an image acquisition camcorder. Zoetrope took delivery of some of the earliest production industrial decks and has used Hi-8 as an in-house standard for video dailies, telecine masters, and for other purposes. Because Hi-8 equipment did not initially support many of the standard editing machine interface standards and protocols, we had to concoct some fairly unorthodox "black boxes" to make the equipment work in a larger system. Some of those boxes are now commercially manufactured and many of the features lacking in early Hi-8 have now been included in newer models, thanks in large part to direct personal communication between the manufacturer's CEO and Francis Coppola's Zoetrope.

Integral to the success of Electronic Cinema is minute attention to detail during a film's pre-visualization stage. Aubry says that, in the early 1980s,

> . . . before the appearance of powerful and affordable Macintosh computers, Zoetrope began to develop a software program called Ulysses, running on an Apollo workstation for creating storyboards and merging script text with pre-recorded soundtracks and musical scores. Armed with a computerized storyboard and database of location notes, one could generate budgets and schedules, and change them as the storyboard changes. Other workstations would run editorial software; film editing would be accomplished digitally.

Previsualization, and the preservation of data during the logging and creation of materials in these early stages of production is of prime importance in being able to know what elements were created and the location of those elements. Continues Aubry,

> Good organization is needed because filmmaking has become so specialized; it's separate units, fiefs actually, all doing their piece. But frequently, the director innovates or creates something valuable early in pre-production but no one logged the tapes in such a way that the material can be found later in postproduction. This has been continuing source of frustration to Francis and to other directors.

## Creating the Workflow

Equally important is a highly detailed work flow diagram of how the production will proceed from the moment the film cameras begin to roll up, until the final delivery of the film. Aubry says,

> I've set up all electronic postproduction paths for over a dozen projects, from low-budget films up to major features including *The Godfather, Part III*, and *Bram Stoker's Dracula*. On *Godfather III*, the idea of editing a $40 million film electronically was not understood by people outside of Zoetrope. . . . I had to spend a lot of time explaining what we were trying to accomplish; why film had to be transferred to tape in

a certain way, and so forth. But now, in 1994, I go back to the same labs and facilities—even the studios!—and people are really knowledgeable about this technology. A lot has happened in a very short time.

## On Future Working Methods

As the pictures that we do at Zoetrope incorporate computer generated animation, digital compositing, and more visual effects, moving and manipulating all digital frames of 4K × 6K pixels becomes necessary. The technology that allows us this phenomenal control of each picture element for each frame of the motion picture is relatively new, tremendously expensive, and painfully slow. What is more, it is in a state of constant flux. Avoiding these techno-bottlenecks becomes an essential part of the supervision of postproduction. The cost and schedule implications of every decision become enormous. This is why you must have a detailed plan of how you are going to approach the film in advance of starting.

For digital, nonlinear editing on location, Aubry notes that American Zoetrope is interested in investigating editing directly from the video assist. He comments that if the production crew is shooting a background for a composite shot for which a computer-generated foreground element will be utilized, actually compositing the shot on set to see if the just filmed take will work would provide invaluable and instantaneous feedback to the filmmakers. With the advent of new digital filmmaking tools and methods and the rapid improvement and innovation characterizing this growth, Aubry points out certain items he feels are important for making the technology even more accessible to the filmmaker:

> At this point we have digital, nonlinear editing systems that display 24 fps source material at 24 fps, which is a vast improvement over a 30 fps 2:3 pulldown display of 24 fps original material. However, seeing complete video frames would be an improvement over the current technology which halves vertical resolution by discarding one field. A screen refresh rate of 72 Hz at 24 fps would make the display unambiguous.

One aspect of digital filmmaking is the development of parallel work activities both in local and remote locations. Notes Aubry,

> Telecommutation is very important to filmmaking. Globalizing the work is very significant and will change many of the ways that we make films.

## INDUSTRY VIEWPOINTS

### Rob Kobrin—Editor

*Needful Things* (1993), *Columbus: A Journey to Discovery* (Interactive)

For Rob Kobrin, an editor who has done pioneering work on a variety of nonlinear editing systems, technical advancements in the digital filmmaking process have been exciting to track, develop, and utilize. Says Kobrin,

I have experienced three major areas of technical development that have contributed to my work in digital filmmaking: first was the development of sophisticated digital signal processing. For audio, it has given us sound design capabilities that now allow us to modify production sound to meet our editorial needs, and to create sounds that are new and intriguing. For picture, the advent of JPEG compression meant that it was finally possible to digitize massive sequences of images at resolutions that were workable. Now digital film workstations are opening up a new era of editorial solutions to production challenges, allowing us to create whole new visual realms with which to amaze and entertain our audiences.

Second, the advancement of hard drive storage has made it viable both technically and economically to use these digital systems to create feature films. In just a few short years we have gone from struggling to store and manage what were overwhelming amounts of data, to today where it is possible to contain all the footage for a feature film on a single array. I am stunned by the rapidity with which hard drive technologies have developed and dropped in cost.

The third major development which is now affecting my working process is networking and interactivity. The ability to share media and compositions between digital workstations of different but complementary functionality opens the door to active collaboration—and film is the most collaborative art I've ever experienced. I think it will not only affect the process and economics of filmmaking, but lead to films of unprecedented imagination.

Kobrin feels that there are overwhelming reasons to utilize digital filmmaking methods. Continues Kobrin,

Film editing is slow and destructive in that when you make a change, the previous version is necessarily destroyed. This creates inhibition to making changes, which creates a lot of anxiety and has even been known to lead to fist fights in the cutting room! Traditional film opticals are slow, expensive, and limited in their ability to fulfill the filmmaker's vision. On my last show, we replaced the skies in two shots with stock footage of approaching storms, so as to create a mood of impending danger. A subtle, but effective trick that we simply would not have played without the effectiveness and efficiency of digital compositing. . . .

I foresee that postproduction in the future will occur entirely with malleable, interchangeable digital media moving about in a networked environment. Design functions will occur at low resolution, and final presentation reproduced at high resolution, analogous to the workprint/negative relationship. As technical processes become more complex and abstract, none of us will be able to control all of the filmmaking processes. We will all have to rely on the expertise of our specialized colleagues, but those human interactions should become freer, more creative, and more satisfying.

**Figure 2-10** Photo of Rob Kobrin. Courtesy of Rob Kobrin.

## INDUSTRY VIEWPOINTS

### Basil Pappas—Film and Digital, Nonlinear Editor

Editor: "CityKids" (ABC/Jim Henson Productions), "GhostWriter" (PBS); Episodic Television: "Parent-

**Figure 2-11** Photo of Basil Pappas. Courtesy of Basil Pappas.

Digital image creation, compositing, and computer graphics will give filmmakers new abilities to realize stories and ideas while HDTV image compositing and digital film to disk scanning techniques will make high quality compositing available to lower budget productions. Eastman Kodak's Cineon will almost certainly usher in the era of total computer domination of film effects. High speed fiber optical data transfer will make delivery of daily work elements, as well as works in progress, an instantaneous process. Everyone will be capable of increased productivity, and more participation in the collaborative process will be possible by more people without regard to physical distance. Digital networks will be the key to future collaborative working environments.

Motion Picture film stocks will continue to evolve technically, becoming a dry, non-silver process, and will always be the medium of choice for acquisition. High speed digital scanning of these to-be-invented stocks will result in no delay waiting for digital dailies.

One of the more exciting developments recently has been the introduction of digital disk recorders that are compatible with the telecine environment. Designed to automate the collection of critical data relating to location audio timecode, film keykode or ink numbers, and video timecode, these devices are compatible with nonlinear editing systems and will also record to disk the same images and sound that are simultaneously being recorded to tape. The result is a more productive editing environment, eliminating the time-consuming process of logging and digitizing, and ensuring total accuracy in the numbered data. Of course, the digital images and sound themselves are as pristine as possible, not having to go through a tape generation. Subsequent audio postproduction using these very same audiofiles will eventually ensure first generation audio quality to the end product, whether that be on the air broadcast or theatrical film release.

hood," "Cheetah"; Dialog/Foley Editor: *Homeless: Feature Film*; Editor: "HDTV: RWANDA."

Nonlinear feature/television film post production supervision: *Vanya on 42nd Street* (Sony Classics), *Mississippi* (New Line), "The Stand" (ABC/Laurel), "Guy Hanks" (NBC).

Editor Basil Pappas has been in the forefront of the development of nonlinear editing systems for film. Pappas, who has been involved with the design and testing phases of many such systems, is most intrigued by the potential of digital, nonlinear editing systems. He says,

> The introduction of the computer into the production and postproduction process is the single most significant advance in the film world during my career. Nonlinear editing systems and remote logging software, as well as the introduction of data files to bring the numbered information from picture negative and location audio into the editing process, has been equally significant in providing me with the ability to manage the entire post process.

Pappas, who has built a reputation as a creative film editor who has mastered and utilized many of the concepts that define digital filmmaking, observes the various technologies that are growing in use in the field of filmmaking. He continues,

For Pappas, who pays strict attention to the sound elements for the programs that he edits, audio and the advancements that are being made in digital audio are particularly important. Says Pappas,

> Digital audio recording and editing will become the standard way of handling all soundtrack elements, from location, to editing, to dialog editing, ADR, Foley, music composition, recording, sound effects, re-recording and mastering. Why? Less weight and physical size, faster handling and delivery, more creative options, vastly improved reproduction quality, ease of replacement work, and confirmations as changes happen, less physical labor, and more productivity per human hour.

All these technologies will also translate into compatibility with digital broadcast methods either via air, fiber telephone technology, computer network, or any other distribution process grouped into the information superhighway concept. Totally compatible digital delivery resulting in a no-loss delivery and distribution network of the future.

Pappas, who considers it his responsibility to explain the new methods of filmmaking to his clientele, also feels that there are some unclear aspects that arise when technical concerns meet creative wishes. Says Pappas,

Today's filmmaker is increasingly reliant on very sophisticated technical machines to support the creative endeavors. The most misunderstood aspect for filmmakers today is that the filmmaker may feel it necessary to rely on the technology in order to envision an idea, and many filmmakers seem to have lost much of their ability to previsualize. But truly creative thinking will always be ahead of the technology, as well it should. The end product starts and ends with good creative imagination. Digital techniques don't make an end product better, they make it possible.

# 3 Scripting, Breakdown, Scheduling, and Budgeting

Screenwriting was one of the first areas of filmmaking to benefit from computers. It is easy to understand why. Move this sentence to the end? No problem! Just "copy and paste" it into its new position.

## SCRIPTING

There are several computer programs available that are actually scriptwriting applications. These provide the functions of both word processor and script layout. Programs such as Scriptor by Screenplay Systems support text imported from other word processing programs. Final Draft is a professional scriptwriting software package from Mac Toolkit.

Normally, a screenwriter writes the screenplay using a word processor. The writer can use style sheets and there are global styles for scene headings, action, character, dialogue, parenthetical, and transition. These styles can be saved as settings and used any time a new screenplay is to be written. The settings can be accessed directly through a key function, or recorded as part of the style sheet script. For example, the style sheet for "Character" may call for:

Normal + Caps, Indent: 2 inches. Keep with next: Dialog.

This means that each time that character is chosen from the style sheet, the program will use what has been chosen as the normal font, usually twelve-point Courier, will capitalize the entire entry, although it may not have been typed that way, and space it two inches from the margin. Whenever the return key is entered, it then automatically sets up the style sheet for dialog with the settings created for dia-

log. For example, a character named John may be written as:

John

But when the style is applied to that line, it will appear as:

JOHN

Macros are used by computer applications and will record a certain repeated function and allow that function to be assigned to the keyboard. For example, all the characters in a script can each have their own function key. Instead of repeatedly typing in a character's name, a function key can be hit once and it will type the name, apply the style sheet for the character, and leave the user ready to write that character's dialog.

Once the screenplay is written, it will be one continuous file with page breaks. Part of the style sheet may have a "keep with next" function. This means that a script line(s) cannot be separated from the next set of lines. If a page break occurs, the character and his or her dialog are not separated.

An application like Scriptor formats the imported screenplay based on certain user criteria. There are different templates for screenplays, TV movies, and stage. Templates refer to common layouts accepted for script presentation. For a feature film, the user selects "screenplay." The script can be immediately formatted based on the application's defaults. Scriptor has several options available when implementing page numbering. The pages will be numbered consecutively from page 1–end depending upon the total number of pages. The user can select "create A & B pages" and the program will retain all original page numbers and create the A & B pages to accommodate newly written scenes or additional material. Some of the same options are available for scene numbering as are available for page numbering, such as "number scenes from beginning to end, create A & B scenes, and remove all scene numbers." Both page numbers and scene numbers can have a custom user start other than 1. For example, the user may want to start page numbering at 10 and scene numbering at 20. This is easily accomplished and saves a great deal of time.

The program Scriptor uses information to determine if there is a new scene, such as if the line begins with INTERIOR or EXTERIOR, or their abbreviations: INT. and EXT. When Scriptor encounters these phrases it numbers the scene "+1" from the previous scene. Sometimes the writer will want a scene counted, even though it may not necessarily be a new scene. Perhaps the scene is a flashback within a scene that references another scene in the script. This needs to be counted in terms of the total scenes, but does not need to separated.

The following shows the resulting screenplay format after using SCRIPTOR.

*THE AGENT exits as HOLMES sits and continues his scan of the newspaper. There is a MUFFLED BELLOWING from some other room, then we hear the SNUFFLING and SHUFFLING of THE AGENT as he returns.*

AGENT
There will be someone along for you in a minute, sir.

HOLMES
Is there a problem?

AGENT
With what, sir?

HOLMES
I thought I heard a shout.

AGENT
That was Mr. Pinkerton, sir.

HOLMES
And . . .

AGENT
And what, sir?

HOLMES
And is there a problem?

AGENT
You keep asking that, sir.

HOLMES
Why was Mr. Pinkerton shouting?

AGENT
Oh. It annoys Mr. Pinkerton to hear me swallowing my phlegm, sir.

*Mercifully, A MAN ENTERS the office. He is ROGER KEATS; a handsome, rugged man in his late thirties.*

KEATS
You are Sherlock Holmes?

Scriptor will process the script and create page breaks. Often, the page break is needed to occur during a character's dialog. The program will split the dialog at a sentence break, place an indication (more) at the bottom of the page, put (continued) at the top of the next page with the character's name and (cont'd) after it. There is also an "X-Change" option that will indicate where script changes have been made. If the program encounters an asterisk (*) at the beginning of a line, it will note it as a change. Multiple lines will also be noted as changed if the lines are embodied within brackets: [ ].

A cast list can be generated. This list contains all characters in alphabetical order. It also lists the amount of sides per character. Sides is the number of dialog parts for each actor. It lists the page and the scene number reference for each actor's side, such as the one on the next two pages.

## SCHEDULING

Scheduling is usually done by the Unit Production Manager (UPM) or the First Assistant Director (1st AD). Any mistakes made during this stage can cost thousands of dollars to the budget. This can be caused by omission of important elements, such as actors not being where they must be, missing props, unnecessary extra days added to the shooting schedule, and the lack of a secondary shooting schedule for weather delays or illness. Otherwise, the filmmaker may be faced with having hundreds of crew members and actors waiting to work but with nothing to do.

Report For The Consulting Detective

| Page | Scene | Scene identification | Scene length |
|------|-------|----------------------|--------------|
| 1 | 1 | EXT. THE ROLLING HILLS OF THE DOWNS OF EAST SUSSEX | 2/8 |
| 1 | 2 | EXT. C.U. ON BEES IN AN APIARY. DAY. | 2/8 |
| 1 | 3 | EXT. SHERLOCK HOLMES AND DR. JOHN WATSON STANDING | 3 — |
| 4 | 4 | INT. HOLMES' STUDY. EARLY EVENING. | 2 — |
| 6 | 5 | EXT. LONDON, SPECIFICALLY WHITEHALL. | 2/8 |
| 6 | 6 | INT. THE DIOGENES CLUB. LATE AFTERNOON. | 7/8 |
| 7 | 7 | INT. VISITOR'S ROOM. LATE AFTERNOON. | 3 — |
| 11 | 8 | EXT. THE PORT OF BOSTON. DAY. | 2/8 |
| 11 | 9 | EXT. THE DOCKS. DAY. | 1 3/8 |
| 12 | 10 | EXT. COURT STREET. DAY. | 3/8 |
| 13 | 11 | INT. THE PINKERTON DETECTIVE AGENCY. DAY. | 2 — |
| 15 | 12 | INT. PINKERTON AGENCY CORRIDOR. | 6 4/8 |
| 22 | 13 | EXT. THE DOCKS. DAY. | 4/8 |
| 22 | 14 | EXT. RAILROAD STATION. NIGHT. | 6/8 |
| 23 | 15 | EXT. WASHBURN'S P.O.V. | 3/8 |
| 23 | 16 | INT. RAILROAD COMPARTMENT. NIGHT. | 1 7/8 |
| 25 | 17 | INT. RAILROAD COMPARTMENT. LATER THAT NIGHT. | 1 6/8 |
| 27 | 18 | INT. SLEEPING CAR. MUCH LATER. NIGHT. | 5/8 |
| 28 | 19 | INT. SLEEPING CAR, AS BEFORE. | 2/8 |
| 28 | 20 | INT. KEATS'S BUNK. | 1/8 |
| 28 | 21 | INT. SLEEPING CAR, AS BEFORE. | 3 2/8 |
| 31 | 22 | EXT. AN OPEN HORSE DRAWN CAB. DAY | 1 2/8 |
| 33 | 23 | INT. COWPER'S OFFICE. DAY. | 2 5/8 |
| 36 | 24 | EXT. THE SAME OPEN, HORSE DRAWN CAB. DAY. | 7/8 |
| 37 | 25 | EXT. THE CAB. AS BEFORE. | 2/8 |
| 37 | 26 | EXT. TRAIN IN MOTION. NIGHT. | 1/8 |
| 37 | 27 | INT. PASSENGER CAR ON TRAIN. NIGHT. | 1 3/8 |
| 38 | 28 | EXT. THE TRAIN CONTINUING ON THROUGH THE NIGHT. | 2/8 |
| 39 | 29 | EXT. MANOIR SOIE. DAY. L.S. | 1 4/8 |
| 40 | 30 | INT. MANOIR SOIE. DAY. | 3 5/8 |
| 44 | 31 | INT. THE DINING ROOM. DAY. | 2 — |
| 46 | 32 | EXT. THE PARK. NIGHT. | 6/8 |
| 47 | 33 | EXT. ANOTHER PART OF THE PARK, NEAR THE MUSICIAN | 2/8 |
| 47 | 34 | EXT. THE BLANKET. NIGHT, AS BEFORE. | 3/8 |
| 47 | 35 | EXT. NEW ORLEANS STREET. NIGHT. | 2 — |
| 49 | 36 | INT. MANOIR SOIE. NIGHT. | 1 3/8 |
| 51 | 37 | INT. TOP OF THE STAIRS. NIGHT. | 3/8 |
| 51 | 38 | INT. WASHBURN'S ROOM. NIGHT. | 3/8 |
| 52 | 39 | INT. HOLMES' P.O.V. | 4 6/8 |
| 57 | 40 | EXT. NEW ORLEANS STREET. DAY. | 2 — |
| 59 | 41 | EXT. QUARTER OF THE DAMNED. DAY | 4 — |
| 63 | 42 | INT. MANOIR SOIE. THE SITTING ROOM. DAY. | 5 4/8 |
| 69 | 43 | INT. LONDSDALE'S. DAY. | 6/8 |
| 70 | 44 | EXT. NEW ORLEANS STREET. DAY. | 6/8 |
| 71 | 45 | EXT. HOLMES AND WASHBURN, AS BEFORE. | 2/8 |
| 71 | 46 | INT. ESPIRITU'S PARLOR. DAY. | 3 4/8 |
| 75 | 47 | EXT. NEW ORLEANS STREET, OUTSIDE ESPIRITU'S PARLOR | 1 3/8 |
| 76 | 48 | EXT. A QUIET, SUBURBAN STREET. NIGHT. | 4/8 |
| 77 | 49 | EXT. ANOTHER SUBURBAN STREET. NIGHT. HOLMES. | 5/8 |
| 77 | 50 | INT. THE GILLES MANSION, AND THE MASKED BALL. | 3 6/8 |
| 81 | 51 | INT. GILLES' BALLROOM. | 2 6/8 |
| 84 | 52 | INT. GILLES' MAIN ROOM. NIGHT. | 3/8 |
| 86 | 53 | EXT. GILLES' PORTICO. NIGHT. | 1 4/8 |

| | | | |
|---|---|---|---|
| 87 | 54 | INT. GILLES' MANSION. THE BALLROOM. | 1 2/8 |
| 89 | 55 | INT. GILLES' MANSION. THE BALLROOM. | 3 6/8 |
| 93 | 56 | INT. MANOIR SOIE. THE FOYER. NIGHT. | 3/8 |
| 93 | 57 | INT. THE SITTING ROOM. NIGHT. | 5 2/8 |
| 99 | 58 | INT. MANOIR SOIE. TOP OF THE STAIRS. NIGHT. | 2/8 |
| 99 | 59 | INT. WASHBURN'S ROOM. NIGHT. | 4 — |
| 103 | 60 | INT. DEE-DEE'S ROOM. NIGHT. | 1 4/8 |
| 105 | 61 | INT. POLICE STATION CORRIDOR. DAY. | 2/8 |
| 105 | 62 | INT. VACHON'S OFFICE. DAY | 4 6/8 |
| 110 | 63 | EXT. A TAXI CARRIAGE ON A NEW ORLEANS STREET. | 3/8 |
| 110 | 64 | EXT. GILLES' MANSION. DAY. | 6 1/8 |
| 117 | 65 | INT. MANOIR SOIE. THE SITTING ROOM. DAY. | 1 1/8 |
| 118 | 66 | INT. MANOIR SOIE. THE DINING ROOM. DAY. | 3/8 |
| 118 | 67 | INT. MANOIR SOIE. THE KITCHEN. DAY. | 2 3/8 |
| 121 | 68 | INT. MANOIR SOIE. THE CELLAR. | 1 — |
| 122 | 69 | INT. MANOIR SOIE. THE CELLAR. LATER. | 2 6/8 |
| 125 | 70 | INT. ACADIAN HALL. NIGHT. | 6/8 |
| 126 | 71 | EXT. QUARTER OF THE DAMNED. NIGHT. | 1/8 |
| 126 | 72 | INT. ACADIAN HALL. NIGHT. | 4/8 |
| 126 | 73 | EXT. QUARTER OF THE DAMNED. NIGHT. | 2/8 |
| 127 | 74 | INT. ACADIAN HALL. NIGHT. | 5/8 |
| 127 | 75 | EXT. QUARTER OF THE DAMNED. NIGHT. | 2/8 |
| 128 | 76 | INT. ACADIAN HALL. NIGHT. AS BEFORE. | 1/8 |
| 128 | 77 | EXT. QUARTER OF THE DAMNED. NIGHT. | 1/8 |
| 128 | 78 | INT. ACADIAN HALL. NIGHT, AS BEFORE. | 1/8 |
| 128 | 79 | EXT. QUARTER OF THE DAMNED. NIGHT. | 1/8 |
| 128 | 80 | INT. ACADIAN HALL. NIGHT, AS BEFORE. | 1/8 |
| 128 | 81 | EXT. QUARTER OF THE DAMNED. NIGHT. | 1/8 |
| 128 | 82 | INT. ACADIAN HALL. NIGHT, AS BEFORE. | 2/8 |
| 129 | 83 | EXT. QUARTER OF THE DAMNED. NIGHT. | 2/8 |
| 129 | 84 | INT. ACADIAN HALL. NIGHT, AS BEFORE. | 6/8 |
| 130 | 85 | EXT. QUARTER OF THE DAMNED. NIGHT. | 2/8 |
| 130 | 86 | INT. MANOIR SOIE. THE SITTING ROOM. | 7 1/8 |
| 137 | 87 | INT. RAILROAD COMPARTMENT. NIGHT. | 5/8 |
| 138 | 88 | INT. HOLMES' STUDY. GOODWOOD COTTAGE. LATE NIGHT. | 2 7/8 |

First page: 1    Last page: 141    Total pages: 141
First scene: 1    Last scene: 88    Total scenes: 88

When one considers that it may cost as much, if not more than $100,000 a day to keep a location shoot going, even one day lost to weather represents considerable funds.

Even though a computer can assist the scheduling and breakdown process, it does not preclude the need for the scheduling person to know every detail of the story and to be intimate with the script. Traditionally, the UPM or 1st AD takes the script and the script breakdown sheets. These sheets are color coded based on:

| | |
|---|---|
| Exterior Day: | Yellow |
| Interior Day: | White |
| Exterior Night: | Green |
| Interior Night: | Blue |

The UPM then starts breaking out the actual elements. This is done by underlining or using highlighting pens of certain colors for the different elements. These elements are determined in the following way:

| | |
|---|---|
| Red: | Cast and speaking parts |
| Yellow: | Extras and silent bits |
| Green: | Extras and atmosphere |

| | |
|---|---|
| Orange: | Stunts |
| Blue: | Special Effects |
| Violet: | Props |
| Pink: | Vehicles and animals |
| Brown: | Sound Effects |

When using the scheduling program, the file that was imported from Scriptor already contained much of this information. Once imported into the program, a strip board would have already been created in scene order. The appropriate colors were attached to each scene depending on EXT, INT, DAY, or NIGHT. Scene headings and characters for each scene were already written into the breakdown sheets. Parameters can be changed as the UPM continues the breakdown process.

Clicking on Scene One brings that scene to the forefront for extra data entry. This information is the header information used on the strips. The scheduling board is a six- or eight-panel board that holds about twenty-five strips of different colors, coded to the type of scene. Production boards can be constructed from a variety of material, but due to cost, cardboard is inexpensive and popular. The breakdown sheet is the heart of scheduling programs to provide the infor-

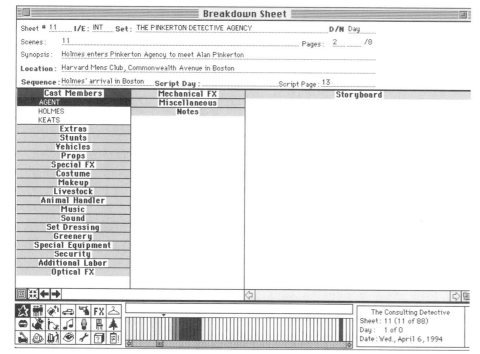

**Figure 3-1** The breakdown sheet is the heart of a scheduling program. Scheduling software by Screenplay Systems.

mation required for reports, schedules, and budget preparation (figure 3-1).

Information that needs to be added to the breakdown schedule is a synopsis of the scene, the location where the scene will be shot, and the sequence, meaning whether the scene is part of a montage of other scenes in a flashback, and the script day. The script day is the flow of time as determined by the story and not by the shooting schedule. An entire film may take place over a lifetime or in "real time." The information gives a clue to the director and actors as to where they are in the story as films are typically shot out of story order. All information here is printed as "header" information on each of the strips (figure 3-2).

Below the header information are the elements of each broken down. Under cast members is a list of all known characters. Clicking on the character pops up another data entry box for additional information. Here the actor is given his or her ID #, real name, address, phone number, and other pertinent information such as agent's name and number, and the actor's salary rate. This information can be exported to the budgeting program to determine how many days a specific actor will work.

Categories in the elements view are: cast members, extras, stunts, vehicles, props, special EFX, costumes, makeup, livestock, animal handler, music, sound, set dressing, greenery, special equipment, security, additional labor, optical FX, mechanical EFX,

miscellaneous, and notes. Sheets can be duplicated for alternate scenes, and data can simply be changed or removed to create an updated report. Once the breakdown of the script has been completed, the UPM is ready for scheduling.

Scheduling a film is based on a variety of parameters. Based on the order and outcome of these parameters, a schedule can be shortened, lengthened, or optimized. There is a certain order of priority used when scheduling a film. These priorities are:

*Location:* once a film has completed its scenes at one location, it is very costly to move to another location and have to return to the first location for additional filming.

*Cast:* depending on an actor's availability, cast can greatly influence a schedule. A good UPM understands the trade-offs of budget versus cast availability. For example, the UPM may have to decide between an extra day of shooting versus using extra cameras to cover the scene in less time.

*Day or night shoots:* if a film is being made using cast and crew who are members of unions, there are rules governing turnaround time, meaning the amount of time talent and crew can be made to work. There is a minimum time granted between these types of shoots and the UPM is aware of these shooting conditions.

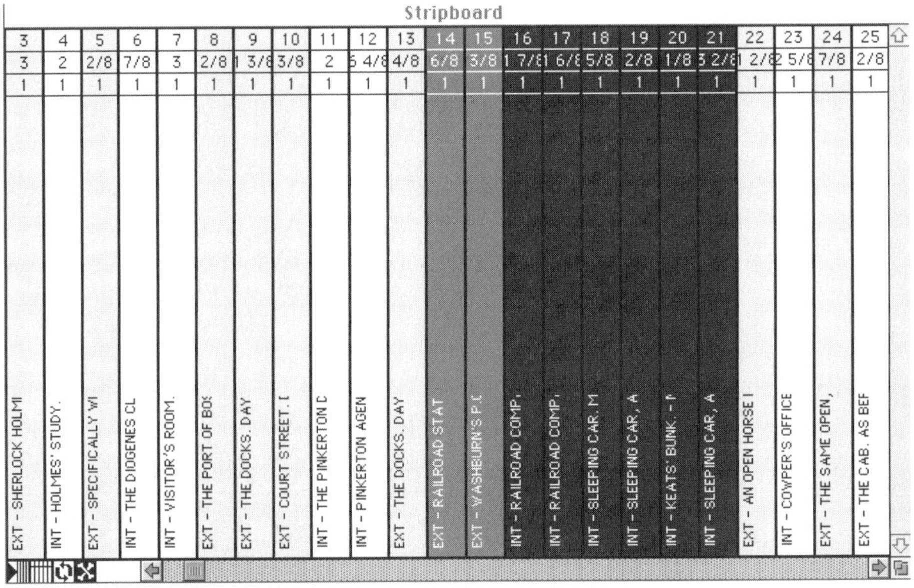

**Figure 3-2** An example of header information seen in strip view. Scheduling software by Screenplay Systems.

*Exterior or interior shoots:* it is customary to shoot exterior shots before interior shots, and important to have a back-up schedule available due to weather conditions.

*Shooting in or out of continuity:* for emotional continuity, it is easier for director and actors to shoot all scenes at a single location in the order that the scenes unfold in the story. Other criteria such as seasonal changes, weather, special effects, and geography impact the schedule. The UPM must know the schedule intimately and must know how one small change may impact the overall schedule.

The sort/select portion of the scheduling program is very powerful, and the criteria it offers for sorting are quite extensive and changes in the schedule can be quickly viewed. Fine tuning can then be achieved by moving the strips as though they were actually on a scheduling board. Information such as production start and finish, travel days, holidays, and whether the production is on a five or six day work week is tracked. The scheduling portion of the program will enter the "down days" as it encounters them in the schedule. Part of the UPM's fine tuning is based on the number of pages a director can actually accomplish per day. A director may be able to shoot, say, only seven pages in a day. Based on the length of each scene, days can also be broken out based on this criteria.

The schedule can be printed on both paper and cardboard strips so that the entire scheduling board and panels can be carried into the field. There is also a barcode printed on each strip so that changes in the field, such as a last moment dropout of an actor, can be quickly updated in the computer program upon the UPM's return. The order of the strips is read by a light pen and the order of the strips in the program is reset to match that in the scheduling book. Information in the scheduling program that relates to budget is exported in a file that can be read by the budgeting program. This includes talent, crew, and equipment.

## BUDGETING

Budgeting is the overall defining factor that determines whether a film will be made. Investors want to see a budget breakdown before giving a project the go ahead. Studios want to see the budget before green lighting the deal. Several companies have created budgeting programs that are designed specifically for film production. Some of the more widely used programs are those by Screenplay Systems and by Mac-TOOLKIT.

What typically separates these programs from other accounting programs is the terminology, interface, and accounting tools used for film production. Both programs use a three-level form of interface. Each level shows more detail in terms of how monies are being referenced, updated, and calculated. MOVIE MAGIC is divided into three major sections: the topsheet, the account level, and the detail level. To access the different categories, the user can go to the topsheet to see the major categories of the budget, the page on which the detailed portion of that budget appears, and the total from that category. The user navigates to different parts of the budget by clicking on each category. New categories can be entered or existing categories can be deleted.

By going one level down for the topsheet/category level, the user can access the account level. There is no limit to the number of accounts each category can have. It is very easy to access other accounts, or drop down an additional level into the details of each account. It is at this level that actual dollar amounts are entered for each item in the account. Each line has a description, an amount, a unit, and a rate associated with it. Contractual charges can be applied to each budget. These contractual charges include a percentage to be applied to the four default categories of contingency, completion bond, insurance, and overhead.

One of the several unique features of MOVIE MAGIC is the ability to apply fringes to any account, or a specific detail within that account. Fringes are percentages added to a budget that encompass such things as sales tax, unemployment taxes, and so forth. A percentage for each of these fringes can be entered along with a detailed description. A limit can also be applied to each of these entries for fringes that do use them. Perhaps a category has a greater budget than the percentage called for by that fringe, and in that case the total in the category would never be higher than the cutoff set, regardless of the budget and its percentage.

Subgroups is another valuable feature and it allows the user to create subgroups of certain parts of the budget. For example, several lighting packages (such as basic, medium, and full blown) can be stored, and any one can be included or excluded from the budget. A production company can compare packages and use the one that best meets the film's needs. Subcategories can be applied to other accounts such as actors, locations, film stock, cameras, and laboratory costs.

The library function is the ability to save portions of a budget, to be used in other budgets. You could think of the library as being a rate book for different services. Libraries can be created for each lab in the city, and then used as subgroups based on the budget requirements of the project. Any budget can be globally changed to another currency where the whole budget will be converted, or just one category or account can be changed. For example, perhaps the director wishes to hire a French director of photography and the rate is in French francs. The currency exchange can be applied to that category only and then converted to US dollars for the total budget.

Once the budget estimate has been completed, all data can be exported into other accounting programs and spreadsheets. Budgets can also be formatted into industry format or studio specific budgets, as many of the templates are supplied with the program. Templates for studios such as Universal, Disney, Warner Brothers, Home Box Office, and so forth are available.

The use of computers and digital technology has already touched the initial stages of a film's creation. From writing the screenplay to preparing for the shoot, computers have assisted from idea to preproduction. The data has been shared by several different programs and can continue to be shared throughout the production process.

## INDUSTRY VIEWPOINTS

### Elizabeth Rodeno—Production Manager, Film and Commercial Productions

For Elizabeth Rodeno, the use of computerized scheduling and budgeting software has had a tremendous effect on her job, as well as on those of the production coordinator and assistant director. Rodeno, a veteran of film and commercial productions, utilizes a Macintosh computer with an internal fax modem which brings her in instant contact with any production throughout the world. Software packages that Rodeno regularly uses include: Movie Magic Budgeting & Scheduling, Excel, Microsoft Word, and Touchbase. Says Rodeno,

**Figure 3-3**  Photo of Elizabeth Rodeno. Courtesy of Elizabeth Rodeno.

Within two days, I can effectively read, breakdown the script, and schedule the film in a variety of ways, for example, five versus six day weeks or thirty versus thirty-six day schedules. I will then have a good idea of what it will take to create a budget for the film. After consulting with the producers, I can effortlessly make changes and redo both the schedule and budget within hours.

Rodeno credits the use of computer technology with being able to greatly enhance her productivity. She continues,

Before using this new technology, it would take many days with a pencil and eraser in breaking down each scene, completing strips for the board and rearranging them. Some say the old way of scheduling helped you learn the script and the board. But, actually, instead of going over your work to check it once or twice you are often duplicating tasks—often really mundane tasks such as whether the scene is Day or Night—and you could be doing this 600 to a thousand times! The use of a database has made the production manager's job more creative and less manual. I still learn the script and the board, but with a much clearer mind.

The use of software has also enhanced Rodeno's ability to create the budget for a film. Says Rodeno,

Budgeting a film is so much easier and more accurate than using a pencil and eraser. I cannot think of any reason to go back to the old methods of making changes while you may be wondering if you forgot a line in your addition. When you need to change sales tax figures for a different state or increase the worker's compensation fee that a payroll company misquoted to you, you just enter the change and the computer does it for you. And it doesn't miss a line number at 2 A.M.!

Another important aspect in the developing digital filmmaking environment is the promise that sharing information and networking capabilities will result in greater communication for the various filmmaking departments. Continues Rodeno,

The development of improved databases is helping us communicate while low cost servers and compatible computers that break the barriers between Macintosh and DOS computers will help change the office. I look forward to the day when all departments will talk to each other via the computer. I would love the art department to deliver via disk or via server their budget per location or set so that I can incorporate the information into my budget. I would like the production coordinator to be able to generate vendor lists tied directly to my budget and budget line numbers. I would like to see the accountant deliver the rough cost report to me via our office server. All this will lead to less paper in the office. The Production department of a film generates more paper than any other aspect of filmmaking and much of it is obsolete the day it is distributed.

Rodeno is also an advocate of using remote communications to provide as much off-site support as is necessary for a film production. She says,

The modem has been tremendously valuable to me. My AD, who is finishing up another job in Minnesota, can send me his latest version of the schedule without spending a fortune on fax paper, and it allows me to make changes prior to printing between 40 and 80 pages. I used the modem on the last show to send notes to the editor and additional lines of dialogue to the producer for approval. It saved a lot of time, and I didn't have to pull the script supervisor or the director off the set for a 20 minute phone call.

Rodeno can easily imagine the working methods of a digital filmmaking production office. She continues,

For the production minded, a digital filmmaking center would include a server and workstations for the art and costume departments and would include drawing, CAD, and budgeting, and scheduling capabilities. There would be workstations for the coordinator and accountant who would be linked together to deal with vendor status and purchase orders. As an example, the storyboard artist could send the director's ideas to the art department, the art department could send the revamped ideas to the costume designer for color and theme ideas concerning a particular location or set. A variation on this is that the location manager could scan in photos of chosen locations, and the director could look at them at home or in the office. The production manager could look at them, and the art department could refer to them from wherever their workstation is located.

Really, the digital filmmaking center wouldn't be a center at all, it would be a digital filmmaking network, and it would save considerably on fuel and drive time. The production team would still meet for location scouts, wardrobe fittings, walkthroughs of sets, and the like, but we just wouldn't have to drive every day to the same location and set up. Instead, our true office could be at home.

# 4 Previsualization

## ENVISIONING THE FINISHED FILM

Previsualization is largely underutilized by today's filmmaking community. However, its capabilities are so vast and powerful, that more efficient filmmaking can proceed. We can define previsualization as methods that allow the filmmaker to envision how elements of the film will look prior to principal photography. It is important to note that previsualization is not a new term and has been part of filmmaking from the moment that a director made sketches on a restaurant napkin outlining how a shot should look through the camera, or from the moment that an art director moved little cardboard cutouts to signify where various set pieces should be placed.

Any tool that provides a filmmaker with the ability to plan ahead and to work out problems and issues before the expensive and time limited production phase of filmmaking begins are forms of previsualization. Some forms are highly visual, such as visualizing what a set will look like before it is constructed, but others, such as budgeting and scheduling, are also forms of previsualization.

Previsualization has become so sophisticated today that it is easy to shoot a test with a computer controlled camera, using a stand-in actor against blue screen. The data points that represent where the camera was in space and time are stored, and that pathway is imported into a three-dimensional computer rendering of a set. Suddenly, the actor is moving in 3-D space with the artificial 3-D environment matched to his movements. This can provide a sense of exactly how something would look when finalized on film.

## INDUSTRY VIEWPOINTS

### Frank Foster—Vice President of Previsualization, Sony Pictures Imageworks

For Frank Foster, the previsualization of a filmmaker's ideas has been a rewarding experience in terms of enhanced creativity and saving time. While there are many different methods of previsualizing how a film set may look or be constructed, there are some specific techniques that Foster's division at Sony Pictures Imageworks has perfected. Says Foster,

> We've been able to accomplish very sophisticated previsualization results which have allowed filmmakers to try ideas before they ever get on the set. We routinely scan the dimensions for sets from blueprints and basically make the set on the computer. We also use CD-ROM based libraries which have props and figures which we can paste into the environments we are creating. The filmmaker can then dictate the focal length that is going to be used, and we can position the camera's point-of-view. So, in about 45 minutes we were able to fine-tune two shots that needed spe-

**Figure 4-1** Photo of Frank Foster. Courtesy of Sony Pictures Imageworks.

cific questions answered. The result is that the director is able to proceed with confidence.

Foster created much of the previsualization for the 1993 film *Striking Distance*. One specific example was an intricate realization of a car chase sequence. Shown in figure 4-2a is the computer-generated image of a police car in the process of flipping over. Figure 4-2b shows the actual image that was filmed. The position and angles between the computer-generated example and that of the actual live action car flip show

the precision that can be achieved with previsualization tools. Says Foster,

This was really an example of how previsualization can allow the filmmaker to technically rehearse the logistics of a complex sequence. We began by putting the city streets and tunnel in the computer as a three-dimensional model. Then taking direction from the stunt coordinator we added the cars, trucks, and bus and animated them at the correct speeds and positions. We were then ready for the second unit director to place the cameras and select the lenses. Each

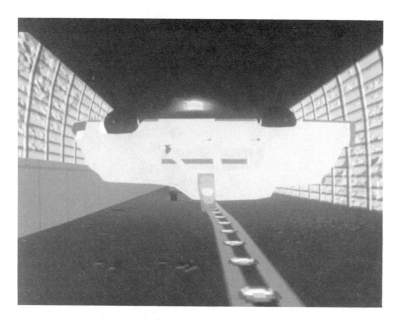

**Figure 4-2a** A computer-generated image used to previsualize an intricate realization of a car chase from the 1993 film *Striking Distance*. Previsualization done by Frank Foster at Sony Pictures Imageworks. © Copyright 1993 Columbia Pictures Industries, Inc. All rights reserved.

**Figure 4-2b** The position and angles between the computer-generated example and that of the actual live action car flip show the precision that can be achieved with previsualization tools. From the 1993 film *Striking Distance*. Previsualization done by Frank Foster at Sony Pictures Imageworks. © Copyright 1993 Columbia Pictures Industries, Inc. All rights reserved.

shot was then rendered as an animation for the first and second unit directors to review and make changes. Finally, the video was edited by the same editor that was cutting the 35mm motion picture film. As a result, the film's director knew almost exactly what the second unit was planning and had a very good idea of how it would look edited together. In fact, the final live action shots were so similar to the previsualized animation that when we later intercut between them they aligned perfectly!

Foster is also quick to point out that previsualization is invaluable because of the shrinking amount of time that a filmmaker experiences in completing a film. Continues Foster,

A director and the actor's time is so precious that if we are able to get them one image that represents what they are trying to accomplish, it is a huge positive gain. In making these sets and calculating the results of a specific camera move, we can tell if a post is in the way, and we can creatively deal with the technical challenges or physical impediments that the director would normally have had to worry about on the location or set. The more that directors are exposed to previsualization, the more that they tend to use it.

## Utilizing the Work Products of the Previsualization Stage

Traditionally, work done during previsualization was only used to give the filmmaker an idea of how to accomplish something. Little thought was given to actually using the materials created in the final film. That is changing rapidly as the ability to previsualize has gotten very precise and qualitative. Previsualization allows the filmmaker to ask "what if" questions with regard to how big a set needs to be, or if a creature can be manufactured through the use of computers, or how to plan camera angles.

## Storyboarding: Visualizing Scene Coverage

Many filmmakers utilize some form of storyboarding, which are drawings that seek to convey how action flows in a scene. These storyboards can be crude drawings on small pieces of paper, or can be quite elaborate. There have been books published solely to showcase the work of the storyboard artist. For special effects sequences, there may be many elements involved, such as miniatures, pyrotechnics, high-speed photography, and motion control, and a visual blueprint which describes the shot can be very helpful and informative.

Shown in figure 4-3 is the storyboard version of the intricate helicopter chase sequence from *Terminator 2: Judgment Day* (1991). Even when viewed in this static form, the individual storyboard frames of this sequence have an apparent and inherent motion.

Storyboarding allows the filmmaker to see how shot selection and the building of shots can combine to create a finished scene. There have been many films where, during the postproduction stage the editor has literally torn up the storyboard and chosen an entirely new path. There have also been many films where the editor could put together a specific sequence by following the storyboards and then refining the transitions between the shots.

There are really three reasons to create storyboards: first, as a strict blueprint of a scene; second, as a representation of the camera set-ups that the filmmaker feels are crucial to obtain; and third, as an exercise to help the filmmaker visualize different ways to film a scene. Storyboards for director Alfred Hitchcock were an exact blueprint of the finished form he intended. Other directors utilize storyboards simply for the sake of the mental exercise of visualizing camera and actor together.

## Electronic Storyboarding Software

There are software programs that enable the filmmaker to create storyboards with tools that offer the ability to draw, the use of predefined character sets, and a view in various film aspect ratios. While some filmmakers will present a director of photography with stick figures drawn on paper, more sophisticated drawings are preferred, and these will include screen direction and camera movement. There are storyboarding packages that alleviate some of the difficulty of not having adequate drawing skills. One such program is StoryBoard Quick. This program has been in wide use and can assist the filmmaker in realizing highly detailed storyboards.

## Storyboarding Tools and Creating an Electronic Storyboard

As tools vary from program to program, it is helpful to describe how a filmmaker would go about using an electronic storyboarding program. Many of the func-

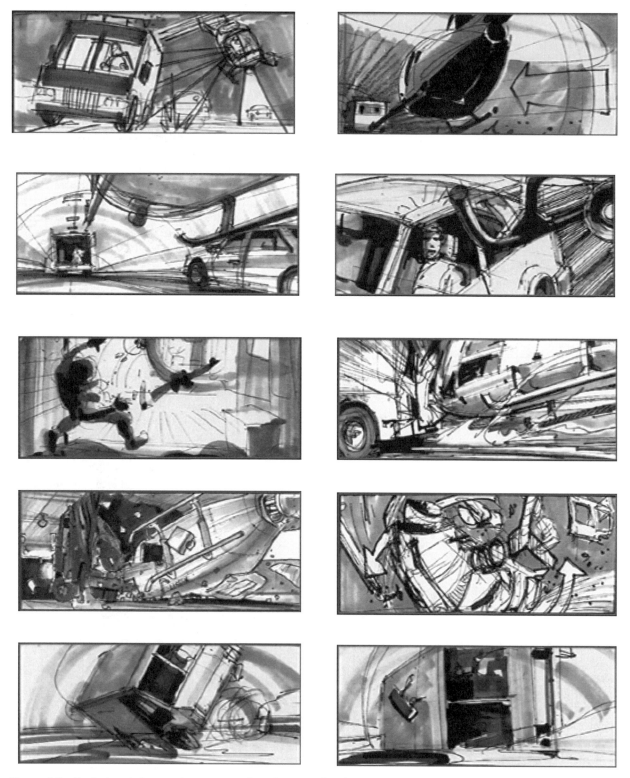

**Figure 4-3** The intricate helicopter chase sequence from *Terminator 2: Judgment Day* (1991) was storyboarded, carefully planned, and shot. From *Terminator 2: Judgment Day.* Courtesy of Carolco Pictures and Twentieth-Century Fox, Ltd. All rights reserved.

tionalities described below are specific to a program such as StoryBoard Quick, and the filmmaker should routinely seek out the specifications of the program being evaluated.

## Drawing and Pasting

Here is how an electronic storyboard can be created. First, if the user does have drawing skills, an electronic pen tool can be used to draw directly in the storyboard frame. However, if the user is uncomfortable with drawing, a series of characters and props may be available in software. If the filmmaker needs to show two characters talking, and one character is a man and the other is a woman, there may be figures that exist in a software library. In the case of StoryBoard Quick, there are libraries such as: Drama, Comedy, and Action Adventure characters. Shown in figures 4-4a–c are some of the tools and libraries that are available in StoryBoard Quick.

Next, the user is able to use the library, and the figures of a man and woman are accessed and electronically inserted into the frame. The first frame we are looking at is a shot of the woman towards camera and the rear of the man's head is facing us. She is talking to him. However, it would be more appropriate for the figures to be in a room, and a room obviously requires furniture. There are various prop (property) libraries, and the user can now electronically paste a table, a wall painting, and chairs into the frame.

Let's say the user is happy with the first frame. The frame is duplicated, and now the user wants to show the action of a camera as it would track slightly right, revealing more of the man's profile. By using software tools, it is possible to show the different angles and the camera movement required. Now the frame is duplicated to create a third frame. Here, the user wants to show the same shot, but at a different camera focal length. By using resizing tools, the user can resize characters, props, and locations. The result is that the user can very quickly see a certain setup in wide, medium, or close-up. Two-shots, over-the-shoulder shots, and spatial relationships between people and objects can easily be shown. Now the user

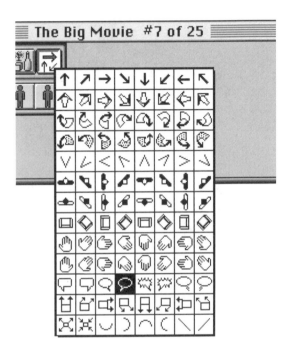

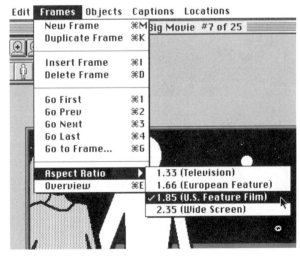

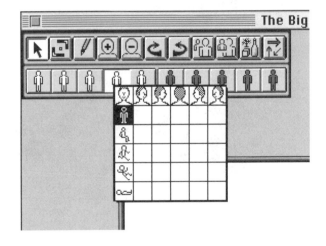

**Figures 4-4a–c** Some of the tools and libraries available from within STORYBOARD QUICK. Courtesy of PowerProduction Software.

duplicates the frame, and a fourth frame exists as the user wants to include some dialogue that will be spoken. A text tool lets the user type in the script lines. While there are many other tools, this brief example provides an outline of the ease and speed with which a filmmaker can put together a detailed storyboard.

## INDUSTRY VIEWPOINTS

### Paul Clatworthy—Cocreator, PowerProduction Software

For Paul Clatworthy, cocreator of some of the most commonly used software packages for filmmakers, the incorporation of computers and software designed to make the previsualization and planning stages more easily accomplished has been a personal goal. PowerProduction Software, makers of various programs such as StoryBoard Quick and Costume Pro, has been able to bring easy-to-use tools to filmmakers who normally would rely on creative artists with drawing abilities. Says Clatworthy,

> I started in 1986 as a consultant for the entertainment industry and occasionally directors would ask, "I really need to find a package which will let me storyboard a scene, do you know of anything that's easy to use?" So I would often direct them to painting and drawing applications, but the directors would come back and say, "But I don't know how to draw!" Well, that made it very clear that they needed a tool that was easy to use and didn't require innate drawing skills. In 1991, we came up with different ideas of how to create such a program.
>
> With the assistance of Sally Walsh and Ray Walsh, coding the program took us one year and we introduced StoryBoard Quick in 1993 and we had a wonderful reception. The program has a pen tool, caption boxes and supports different aspect ratios such as TV at 1.33:1, European at 1.66:1, US Feature at 1.85:1, and Widescreen at 2.35:1. There is a character library, and you can shuffle frames around easily to make any changes in the storyboard layout. So, with these characters, props, and locations, you don't have to draw to get an idea out of your head and onto the storyboard page.
>
> The satisfying thing for us is that people who call are amazed that they are up and running in five minutes. I had a director who was working on a movie-of-the-week and didn't get a budget for a storyboard artist. So he used StoryBoard Quick and printed his boards and gave them to the director of photography. Sometimes directors will use the pro-

gram to rough out ideas and then give the printouts to the artist for further refinement. DPs pick it up as well, and they use it on their portable computers on the set. A lot of the development of filmmaking is based on them making the movie before they actually make the movie, meaning that everyone wants to know how something will look, and having tools that help you visualize are extremely important.

The use of software for previsualization is also undergoing improvement and Clatworthy points out that a new version will support animation and sound. He says,

> Next, we'll let the user add to the library in order to create new art. The animators and multimedia artists want to use the application for presentations. Also, you'll be able to import QuickTime movies so the whole concept of a storyboard as something flat and static is going to change as motion and sound are introduced.

PowerProduction Software also creates different packages used by various departments in the filmmaking process. One such program, Costume Pro, is particularly helpful in assisting the costume department. Says Clatworthy,

> A program like Costume Pro is helpful in determining breakdown and budgeting when dealing with the various costume issues on a show. This program saves hours compared to manually figuring out who's wearing what, in what scene, how many costume changes a character undergoes, and so forth. So, everyone knows who's in what scene and what everyone is wearing. We can create breakdown pages, and when the script changes, the user can input the changes and the program recalculates everything to update the breakdown pages. It has meant a huge time savings.

## Digitally Enhancing the Storyboard with Pictures and Sounds

Some programs can import picture and sound files. A still photograph could be taken of an actual room. The picture is then imported directly into the background of the storyboard frame. Even more impressive is the photograph taken with a digital camera that creates a digital file. The storyboard process takes on an enhanced presentation through the integration of such real-life backgrounds.

The filmmaker can even create storyboards that contain sound files. Even if the filmmaker is only interested in a rudimentary sound reading of the dialogue lines, a microphone can be connected to the computer and scratch versions of dialogue can be spoken and captured. By importing snippets of sound, a storyboard can be created which contains a combination of real-life backgrounds, characters, and spoken dialogue. The order of the frames can be easily rearranged and all of these aspects provide the filmmaker with a more advanced version of the movie than a static storyboard.

## Communicating the Storyboard

In the past, storyboards were either sent via mail or fax. With a digital storyboard, a computer file can be transmitted electronically. If a filmmaker is intent on using digital technology because the previsualization artist intends to import files into the storyboards, animate the frames, and watch a cycled version of the film, sending a script electronically to the storyboard artist can start the cycle of the previsualization process. The script lines are then pasted into the appropriate sections of the storyboard and electronically sent back to the filmmaker.

## *INDUSTRY VIEWPOINTS*

### *Fred Gallo—Director*

*Pistol Blues* (1995), *Lady In Waiting* (1994), *Dracula Rising* (1993), *The Finishing Touch* (1992), *Dead Space* (1990).

For feature film director Fred Gallo, electronic storyboarding has become a significant asset to his work as a filmmaker. Gallo explains,

> The idea of storyboarding is to visualize the story based on the script's written words and to communicate those ideas and images to the film's creative personnel, including the Cinematographer, the Production Designer, and of course, the cast. Unfortunately, sketching stick figures is of little use in conveying detailed ideas.
>
> I was aware of the increased graphic abilities desktop computers were beginning to have. After StoryBoard Quick came to my attention, I purchased a Mac to specifically run the program. The computer allowed me to more fully develop ideas before preproduction even began. Until then, my previsualization process was closely connected to locations and schedule, as opposed to imagination and emotions.

> On *Lady In Waiting,* my first film to incorporate computer-aided storyboarding, before scouting a single location, I read the script, then on the computer drew the characters within the settings I wanted. I was then able to hand out the computer-generated boards to the production personnel for them to go scout locations that conformed to my ideas.
>
> Once the location scouts found the appropriate locales, I would then go out and photograph them myself looking for specific angles that were in-sync with my original ideas. I would then take those photographs and/or video and digitize them. After the images were on my computer, I would import the stills directly onto my storyboards, replacing my original drawn backgrounds with the actual locations—thus I was able to show exactly what angles and lenses we would use; everyone then knew the shot before we even got to the location to shoot it.
>
> Detailed storyboards, the kind the computer allows me to create, get everyone on the same page immediately. I am then able to solicit ideas from my key collaborators, adding to my original concepts without compromising them.

Shown in figure 4-5 is an example of the first step of previsualization using computer storyboarding software. This frame was created using StoryBoard Quick.

The next stage, shown in figure 4-6 is to replace the computer-generated backgrounds. This frame was created with StoryBoard Quick and the background was a digital photograph of the actual location. The result is a much more fully realized storyboard that better communicates the intention of the director.

## Three-dimensional Previsualization

As computers have become more affordable, powerful, and compact, they now provide functions normally not available during the preproduction stage. Sophisticated software, capable of creating three-dimensional environments which can be traversed in real time, is an outgrowth of computer-aided design (CAD) software used by professional engineers and architects.

## From Flat Storyboards to Three-dimensional Representations

Imagine you are a film director and your film has a scene that requires constructing the interior of a room where a dialogue between two characters takes place.

**Figure 4-5** An example of the first step of previsualization using computer storyboarding software. This frame was created using Story Board Quick. Courtesy of Fred Gallo.

**Figure 4-6** The computer-generated background is next replaced with a digital photograph of the actual location. Courtesy of Fred Gallo.

After the scene is finished, the camera will travel out of the room and into a street scene taking place on the studio's back lot. A simple dialogue scene such as this doesn't sound as if it should cause too many problems, but there is a unique set of objectives that may be working in the mind of the filmmaker:

For example, how big does the room have to be? Responses could be: How wide a camera angle do you expect to use to shoot the scene? Will it be done in close-up, or for stylistic reasons, in an exaggerated wide shot? And what of the layout of the room? Where is the furniture, what color scheme is being used, and where can the camera be positioned? If a television is located in a particular place, and if the camera is moved to the side of the television, what will the camera see given a certain camera lens? What would the view be if the camera was moved six inches to the left?

While a filmmaker may have no difficulty imagining how this will look, once staged, what the filmmaker cannot anticipate is the degree to which objects on-set may have to be moved in order to accomplish a shot. If a frame of the storyboard shows that a certain angle is needed of our two people talking, there may be no way to know, given the camera angle, that a refrigerator is in the way. But what can be done? The angle is needed, and time is then spent moving the refrigerator. All of these time consuming instances could have been removed had the filmmaker been able to navigate through an artificially created set.

## INDUSTRY VIEWPOINTS

### Steve Katz—Filmmaker/Digital Production and Previsualization

Steve Katz, a filmmaker for over twenty years, has been involved in digital production and previsualization for films and commercials. Katz, who has written two books on filmmaking and is a regular contributor to technical trade magazines, has created some of the most intricate forms of previsualization to be found. Currently, he is a director and head of digital production at Curious Pictures in New York City. Says Katz,

About five years ago when I was writing *Shot by Shot,* I was introduced to a software program called VIRTUS WALKTHROUGH. This was my first experience with 3-D computer graphics and I was blown away. Here were tools that accurately simulated the working space in front of a motion picture camera—motion, lighting, lens angles—it was all there. I made the decision to learn computer graphics so that I could storyboard movie projects. After a few months, I created a three minute, full motion storyboard with sound and a score. I showed the piece around Hollywood and was very surprised that only a few people were using computers for previsualization. The director Joe Johnson was particularly encouraging and I spent the next year refining the process.

Katz, who has created digital full motion storyboards for top grossing films, points out some of the advantages that previsualization provides:

Storyboard and concept art have been used in Hollywood since the '30s. They're just not very good when it comes to showing moving shots or heavily choreographed staging. Computers can simulate those things easily. With a Mac, a PC, or an Amiga you can test crane shots, sequence staging, and fast action precisely. There are a lot of directors who have purchased computers so they can design sequences at home.

On the more practical level, full motion storyboards help a director sharpen his sequences and save money. This is because most directors shoot coverage even when they are working from a storyboard. After a shoot wraps, a director gets to go look at the dailies of the previous day's work. Typically, he sees an even mix of good and not-so-good shots. Now imagine a crystal ball that lets a director see his dailies before he shoots them. Armed with that knowledge, a director could eliminate all the failed shots and spend more

time on the setups that are working. Computer storyboards come very close to providing this very kind of pre-dailies—they can be that accurate. When you add sound and music to the storyboard you actually give the director a tool that goes beyond dailies because now you are showing an edited sequence. A $20,000 digital storyboard may reveal $200,000 of dramatic or visual problems.

In *Clear and Present Danger* (1994), I was asked to previsualize a big action sequence that would be shot in Mexico. This was the "Killing Zone" scene where a street is blocked off by Colombian drug heavies who then ambush Harrison Ford and four carloads of DEA agents. The scene involved large scale pyrotechnics, stunts, extras, and a 300-foot set replica of a Colombian street. Production Illustrator, David Negron created elaborate storyboards which described the camera angles for the scene, but these were static drawings which are of minimal help in visualizing camera movement or the pace of action. The computer seemed like a good solution.

The entire computer model for the "Killing Zone" sequence in *Clear and Present Danger* was based on set blueprints given to me by the Production Designer, Terrence Marsh. I built the street, buildings, cars, and some of the actors on the Macintosh. To these I applied image maps created from location photos of Colombian buildings. This way any shot set up in the computer accurately described what the camera would see in the real set when construction was finished. It took about four weeks to complete the six minute sequence with sound effects, music, and a few lines of dialog. [See figures 4-7a–b.]

The producer, Mace Neufield, director Phillip Noyce, and Harrison Ford looked at the first digital storyboard and they all had the same reaction; the lead up to the action was too slow. The storyboard also revealed technical problems with some of the rooftop camera angles due to the narrow streets. With the shoot about a week away, Noyce had time to rethink parts of the sequence and adjust his shot list. Producer Ralph Singleton felt that the digital storyboards may have saved the production $100,000. More importantly it sharpened a key scene.

Katz sees distinct advantages to previsualization as a creative tool and as a tool that can be utilized during the production, and not only during the preproduction stage. He says,

While 3-D animation is a lot of fun, there are other, and frequently more practical, ways to previsualize shot flow with a computer. One powerful tool which I keep seeing more of is editing on the set. Taking the output from the video tap and running the data to a digital nonlinear editing system—this is a great way

**Figures 4-7a–b** Examples of elaborate previsualization for the "Killing Zone" sequence in *Clear and Present Danger* (1994), created by Steven Katz. Courtesy Paramount Pictures.

to hone your staging. Hi-8 or S-VHS is also getting a lot of use. Directors are shooting rough staging in rehearsals or with stand-ins on location before shooting actually begins. Rough sequences of this kind can be edited on the computer very economically. . . .

The tools are getting better and cheaper fast. Within a few years, digital previsualization will be standard procedure for designing movie sequences.

## Creating the Virtual Environment

Before a piece of lumber is sawed and a wall is constructed, advanced previsualization tools can specify exactly how long a set needs to be, how much lumber is needed, and what colors of paint will be required. Through the use of a software package called Virtus Walkthrough Pro, a room can quickly be created, and the user can access many different room objects, such as chairs, tables, lamps, and textures through a highly graphical user interface.

Once the basic shape of the room has been constructed, furniture is added. We can now add a table, chairs, and a wall painting. We may even want to construct a window and show various real world textures outside that window. Accurate representations of grass, stone, wood, and water are available as a visual layer in this environment.

## ART DIRECTION, COLOR, AND TEXTURING

Art direction extends to the photographic tone, the costumes, the sets, the set dressing, and the props. Clearly, how believable a story is to an audience is greatly affected by the visual look of things. What a main character's room looks like and contains, and the clothes that the character wears are integral reflections of the character. A great deal of thinking often goes into these areas.

Previsualizing a three-dimensional environment can include various methods of changing the color schemes. Let's say the director first wants to see the room with tan walls and then with a textured wallpaper. It is very easy to make these required changes and show the director the options. These choices can be applied to objects in the room. If the walls now suddenly have sand textured wallpaper, an appropriate color scheme can be mapped onto a couch in the room. One company, ModaCAD, Inc., offers software packages such as: ModaDRAPE, ModaFINITITY, and ModaSKETCH which can be used to accomplish such tasks.

Shown in figure 4-8 (see page 81) is a sofa which has a particular pattern, color, and texture. Next is the interface from ModaDRAPE which allows the shape of the sofa to be highlighted. Note the various tools which allow for specific selections. Once the sections are highlighted, a different color, pattern, and texture can be mapped onto the shape of the sofa, as shown in the bottom figure. In seconds, an art director can provide the filmmaker with many different choices for a set's look and can instantly take into account the color scheme of the costumes.

## Lighting Considerations

It is also possible to previsualize different lighting setups. This can be of great assistance to the director of photography (DP), who can make some pre-lighting decisions. Where there will be room for lights, how high up they can be, and where in-set practicals can be placed are all areas that the DP can explore. Some of these tools only cast shadings on objects in the frame while other tools are especially evident of the lighting equipment that the DP actually uses and have the same light throw characteristics as the real equipment.

## Integration of Other Media Types

One of the strengths of previsualization is that we can use other file types to create our three-dimensional environment. For example, let's say that we want to replace the blank television screen in our room with an actual moving image. Using a different software package, we could edit together a short series of images which we could layer, or paste, into the television screen, simply by being able to import different file types.

## Communicating Ideas to Other Departments

As the room is being created, various facts become known. The filmmaker is able to look at the room as if the camera had, for example, a 30mm lens, situated three feet off the ground, and shooting in Academy format aspect ratio. By seeing how the elements in the composition work together, the filmmaker is able to come to certain conclusions. For example, if it is determined that the scene will be covered with two specific camera lenses, previsualizing the 3-D model will show exactly what the camera will and will not see. We would now know how far out a set wall has to be before we are shooting off the set. Because we have the precise dimensions of the walls, we also know how much lumber to order. Since the color schemes that are used correspond to known and standard color patterns, such as Pantone scales, we are able to pre-order materials and have an exact match.

## Navigating through the Environment

Computer software that allows the user to create an environment has become very easy to use. Rooms can quickly be constructed and libraries of objects provide the various items that one expects to find in a room. Shown in figure 4-9 is a software library where the user can choose desks, tables, and chairs.

Shown in figure 4-10a is a room that has been constructed in the computer. The room can be viewed with lenses between 15mm and 500mm. Note how as the camera is repositioned around the room, we first move closer to the couch, then swing around it, and move toward the other side of the room. Figure 4-10b shows the camera moving closer to the desk, through the window, and to the outside of the building. These images can be sequenced to run on a timeline which can actually show the effects of moving from one area of the room to another. Movement can be slowed down, sped up, or frozen.

As our room is finalized, the full power of working in a digital 3-D program becomes evident when we navigate through the room. Using forward, backward, right, left, up, and down arrows, we can move around and through the room that we have created. All possible angles of the room can be viewed through different camera lenses and film format masks. If it is our goal to simulate the point of view of a character moving into a room from off-camera, this

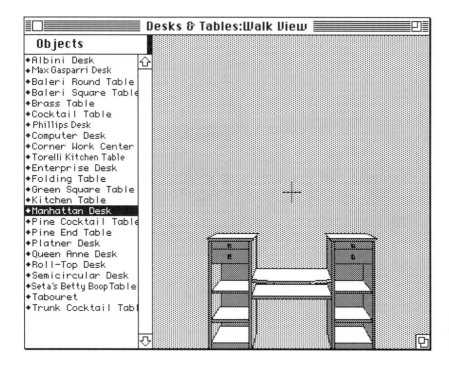

**Figure 4-9** A software screen from Virtus Walkthrough Pro from which the user finds desks, tables, and chairs.

can be programmed, and using the Play keys, a walk through of the environment is displayed.

The following example shows how three-dimensional previsualization software was used to provide a view of how a scene would work given various staging and camera choreography. In text form, the script reads:

**FADE IN:**

*EXT.—West Village BROWNSTONE BUILDING—FOLLOWING Dolly down tree-lined, West Village street. A group of HOODS hang out near a magazine stand. Passing houses, stop dolly on nice Brownstone with a homeless MAN lying in front of it.*
*(courtesy of Kyle Shannon).*

Shown in figure 4-11 are four points of the three-dimensional realization of the scene. Note how the high, birdseye view of the street scene is followed by images which move past the group of hoods to reveal a figure lying in front of the building. Previsualization in this manner provides all of the benefits stated above, but the fact that the viewer, as the camera, is moving through and around the environment is a critical aspect of this form of previsualization that, heretofore, has escaped the filmmaker.

Traditionally, if a filmmaker wanted to previsualize a film in this manner, the director would go to a location and shoot film tests. As years have passed, shooting a location has included hundreds of instant still film images, or with handheld consumer video recorders. Regardless of the method, these are forms of previsualization.

## Proof of Concept

Enhancing previsualization by using 3-D representation can show proof of concept to those investing in the film. Three-dimensional modeling software has been used for many years in the architectural industry in order to give clients an idea of how a building will look, both from the exterior and interior, as if the client was a visitor walking through the building for the first time. In recent years, 3-D software has been used by the members of the law profession to recreate situations and crimes for visual presentations to a jury. As stories are brought to the screen which are larger in scope and involve new visions, proof-of-concept meetings will continue to be a major component in convincing investors that the film can be made within the allowed budget.

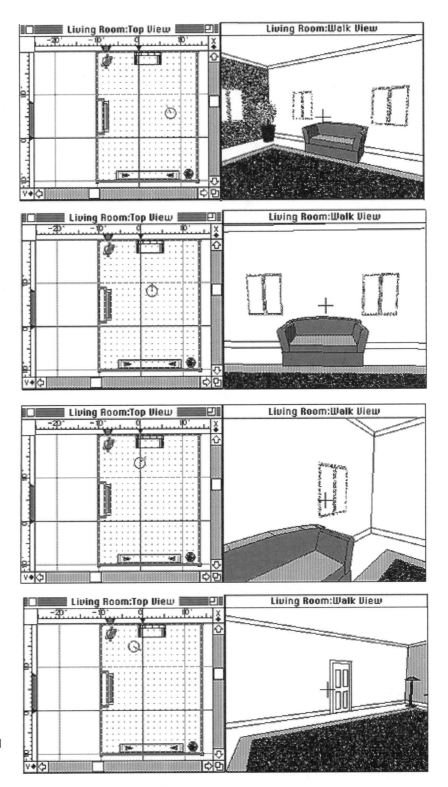

**Figure 4-10** Using Virtus Walk-through Pro software to show the actual movement through a computer-generated set and the various views and angles that can easily be previsualized.

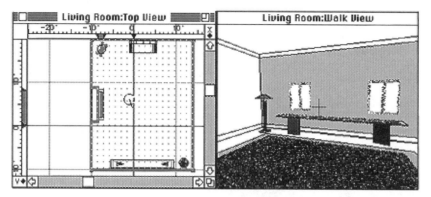

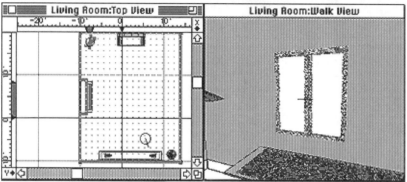

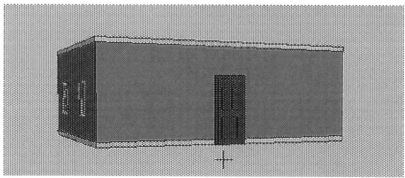

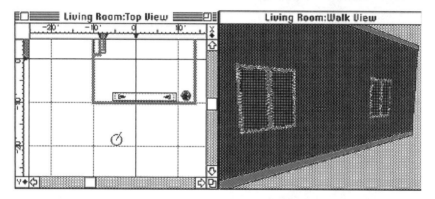

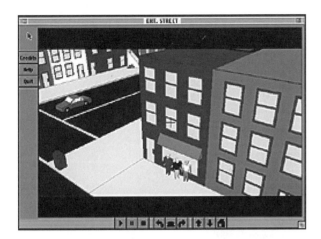
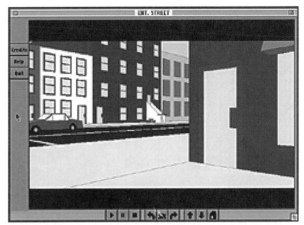
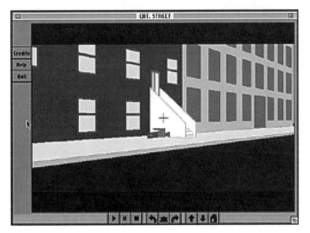
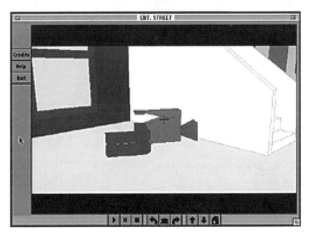

**Figure 4-11** Applying the three-dimensional software to achieve a computer-generated rendering of a scene from a script to show a group standing on a street while the camera moves past them to reveal a figure lying in front of a building. Courtesy of Kyle Shannon.

## Importing into the Editing System

Work done in the three-dimensional system can be utilized in the editorial stage. Take the example of the brownstone building which has been previsualized in 3-D. This previsualized, yet-to-be-shot sequence can be exported from the 3-D software package and into the digital, nonlinear editing system. Export options such as PICS, QuickTime, or AVI allow the previsualization artist to export the individual frames of the three-dimensional rendering into the editing system. Let's say that the director has shot the material that comes immediately before and after the 3-D previsualization and just wants to get an idea of the flow of the movie. The editor splices the 3-D rendering into the appropriate place, and the director can instantly see how the sequence works.

## *INDUSTRY VIEWPOINTS*

### *Glen Scantlebury—Film Editor*

*Bram Stoker's Dracula* (1992), *Big Time* (1988), *Spirit of '76*

For editor Glen Scantlebury, electronic, nonlinear editing and previsualization techniques have become instrumental in the filmmaking process. For *Bram Stoker's Dracula,* Scantlebury began by building the basic story line with still images and scratch narration. Says Scantlebury,

> Previsualization on *Dracula* was very extensive. We took the storyboards and shot each frame onto video. We then cut it together to a reading of the script and there were various versions that we did over the

**Figure 4-12** Photo of Glen Scantlebury. Courtesy of Glen Scantlebury.

course of the previsualization period. Some versions had just narrator and some had the full cast. We would then watch these still images playing back against the soundtrack from the start to the end of the film. This was invaluable because it told us a lot of things—if a scene is weak you catch it immediately. Because you are looking at still images and you are really concentrating on what is being said and if it's not working it tends to make you uncomfortable—you shift in your seat just as a real audience does. So we would take notes and say, "Okay, that's something we have to fix." As time passed, we would do additional versions and eventually the process was complete—we would have versions that had narration, dialogue, music, and sound effects. . . .

I knew the film intimately before it had even been shot because of the previsualization stage. It had gone from cutting storyboards—like a radio play—to a real play where Francis (director Coppola) had five or six local actors acting out the whole movie. We videotaped these rehearsals and I then cut that together and we looked at how the script played not with still storyboards but with actors. All in all, we did 47 versions throughout this pre-planning stage and with all that work we got a very good plan for shooting. When we finally did shoot, we had the best ideas going. Francis would often say, "It's not what you miss, it's the little things that you catch," and I kept this in mind because as an editor you assume the role of a writer as you start to change and rearrange.

Scantlebury, who utilized electronic, nonlinear editing for the film, advises that as long as a proper postproduction outline has been created, there need not be any surprises when using new technology. He says,

You really have to know how to work out the problems of co-existing film and video—where things get slowed down and sped up—there are a lot of technical issues that are easy to deal with if you take the time before the film starts coming in. One thing that excites me is the prospect of working in parallel, especially the sound people working with the picture people. We have experienced a huge advance over four or five years ago because we would spend hours conforming mag tracks when today we can take sound directly out of the editing system and use it for screenings, and we do this in minutes. One of the benefits is that this means that the director can continue working on a picture while sound is being worked on. Normally, you would lose so much time because the picture would have to be locked before sound work began. Now, the director can continue working on the film without having to finish earlier for the sound people. . . .

The best thing about this technology is that it has given a whole generation a chance to enter into the filmmaking field.

## Media Presentations

Particular file types, such as QuickTime and AVI, are hardware independent, media playback routines. If a filmmaker has made a previsualization of a specific sequence and has included some sound effects and temporary music, the resulting "movie" can be played on generic computers which are equipped with either QuickTime or AVI codecs. As a result, the filmmaker can send a QuickTime for Macintosh movie to anyone who needs to see the sequence. This convenient method of distributing work, while not requiring expensive and specialized equipment, will further foster the communication between filmmaker and those that need to be presented ideas and concepts.

## Previsualization's Role in Parallel Work Activities

Also important is that this sequence, in its clearly unfinished form, can be utilized by other film departments. The sequence can be sent to the sound design department which can begin working on the sequence. While it is understood that the middle section will eventually be replaced, the sound elements that are still required can be researched and created without waiting for the middle section actually to be shot.

## Representing the Actors in Previsualization

Actors can be represented in previsualization. Some previsualization artists will shoot new footage of a stand-in for the actor using a handheld video camera. Next, the head of the real actor is pasted onto the body of the stand-in. This new way of placing actors has led to the emerging term: synthespians, or synthetically created characters. A synthespian is an animated figure that is a unique combining of the real-life actions of a human (or animal) mapped onto a computer-generated figure. This is generally accomplished by placing motion sensors on various parts of the human body and shooting the required choreography from multiple camera angles. This results in data that captures where the actor is, in X,Y, Z space. The data is then applied on a frame-by-frame basis to the computer-generated figure being created. Figure 4-13 is an example of computer-generated synthespians.

## Representing the Actors in the Finished Film

There are special instances where synthetic creations can be extremely helpful to the filmmaker. This is especially true in the area of very dangerous physical effects, or stunt work. Take, for example, a sequence that calls for a car to be hurtling out of a burning building, and the lead actor is to be seen driving the car. Normally a stunt artist performs this action. Now, however, consider an additional element. Instead of the building just burning, at the moment before the car crashes through the side of the building an explosion occurs, and the building collapses. A stunt like this requires precise timing, and becomes perilous for a human. Instead, the car and the human driver can be created through computer-generated imagery. Will the car and driver look realistic? Today, the technology exists to create an accurate and realistic solution to this problem. More on this capability is found in chapter eleven, which describes the film-digital-film connection.

## INDUSTRY VIEWPOINTS

### Jeff Kleiser—Kleiser-Walczak Construction Company

Jeff Kleiser, with Diana Walczak, formed the Kleiser-Walczak Construction Company in 1987, a firm specializing in high end database construction and human figure animation. Through the intervening years of research and development, the pair developed proprietary systems for the creation of computer-generated actors, called synthespians. Recent feature film work includes *Honey I Blew Up the Kid*

**Figure 4-13** An example of computer-generated synthespians. Courtesy of Kleiser-Walczak Construction Co.

**Figure 4-14** Photo of Diana Walczak and Jeff Kleiser of Kleiser-Walczak Construction Company. Courtesy of Kleiser-Walczak Construction Company.

(1992), *The Pickle* (1993), *Stargate* (1994), *Clear and Present Danger* (1994), and *Judge Dredd* (1995). The duo has also provided high speed complex computer animation digitally composited with motion control models and live action for the Luxor Hotel in Las Vegas, designed and directed by Doug Trumbull. Says Kleiser,

> Diana is a sculptor specializing in the human form. We became interested with the idea of creating human-like characters for entertainment purposes—characters that perform actions that would be difficult for humans to perform. You can imagine a stunt that's very dangerous for a human to perform yet a stunt that the filmmaker really wants—using computer-generated forms can be successful, particularly if you can show the sequence at night, where the characters are wearing skintight clothing. Hair is especially difficult—flapping hair is really challenging.
>
> For the Luxor Hotel in Las Vegas, we created a stereoscopic dream sequence where the dancers are made of glass and these dancers change into armored warriors. We build this by first starting with a sculpture done by my partner, Diana Walczak that is encoded into the computer. We do this by taking male and female dancers and place 30 witness points on them—on the elbows, wrists, knees, and feet. Using a system of six high-speed video cameras we shoot from precisely different angles and determine where each of the reflective points are in space—for each point we get an X, Y, and Z coordinate. Now, the collection of this data can be applied on a frame-by-frame basis to our computer-generated body. It's a very involved process because we've got to animate the figures in synchronization with the soundtrack. Facial expressions are particularly difficult—I have yet to see a computer-generated animation where the facial muscles under the skin seem correct. To work around this limitation, we created a library of facial expressions in clay which emotes according to the expression we needed.
>
> For the work that we did on *Stargate* we did our animation and compositing on SGI workstations using Wavefront, Matador paint, and so forth. We composited at high resolution and then output to film so the director could see the effects on film, and cut into the workprint. I think we are seeing much more of a trend toward an integrated process—we are not just sending off elements to an optical printer. And it's just a much more enjoyable process because the creative decisions do not have to wait for the optical effects.
>
> Turnaround time is much faster. Now directors look at the graphic experts as having great insight. Credibility is everything in our industry. For *Clear and Present Danger* we created a computer-generated smart bomb that we are inserting into live action footage, where we went up in a jet to shoot the background plates and the elements that we needed. Trying to make a photo realistic bomb with motion blur so that it looks as if it's real, allows us a great deal of input and it is much more fun when people are asking you what it should look like as opposed to just being told what to do—and that's why we're in the business—to entertain and to be entertained.

Networking is also very important to this type of business. We already have distributed sharing. Many different sites that we have to talk to regularly are networked together. We can therefore distribute the rendering time, and we can tighten the feedback loop. You need to be able to discuss complex graphics sequences, and you can have greater efficiency when you have people working the way they want to work, where they want to work. We have an artist in Chicago and we send sequences there and receive the work over the network here in California. You can easily assemble a team regardless of where they are in the world.

## INTERACTION WITH MOTION CONTROL TECHNIQUES

Motion control is the means by which camera operation, camera dolly, and object movements are repeated through the use of computer guided programming. While the specific aims and operations of motion control are discussed in chapter five, it is important to note that there is the potential for the previsualization stage to interact with the motion control stage during shooting.

Let's return to the example of our room that we constructed using three-dimensional software. We have created a motion path that shows, using a specific camera lens, exactly what we would see in this room according to the X, Y, and Z axes. This is a plotted path which is repeated until we have refined exactly how we want to glide through the room.

The script calls for our actor to be walking through this computer-generated room. Clearly, we must eventually composite the two elements, the room and the actor, together, but we must first shoot the actor. Since we decided upon a particular motion path in creating our three-dimensional room, there needs to be a way to translate the X, Y, Z information to the computer running the motion control software. While this may seem like a very complicated procedure, it is actually quite easily accomplished. All that is necessary is to created a tab-delimited ASCII (American Standards Code for Information Interchange) file. This file is read into the motion control software, and the camera then exactly mimics the motion path of the three-dimensional previsualization.

By showing the actor an electronic composite of the 3-D room and the live camera, the actor can see, in real time, exactly how he needs to act as the camera seems to propel him forward through the room. It

should also be noted that this information exchange could also be reversed. For example, if the motion path was originated at the camera, this data could be imported into the 3-D program so that the original motion is preserved as an artificial environment is created around the path.

## LOCATION MANAGING AND SCOUTING

Over the last twenty years there has been a noticeable shift from studio to location shooting. The availability of faster film stocks, enabling directors of photography to expose film with less lighting equipment, the introduction of more portable cameras, and a desire to broaden the visual scope of films has led to a noticeable rise in on-location filming. For the feature filmmaker, going on-location translates into a huge array of logistical issues. When a location manager must find a specific environment, there are a variety of traditional methods that can be used.

First, let's say that one section of the script describes a scene as follows:

### EXT. DAY.

*Red Barn. A farmer exits and his breath is visible in the cold air. Wind and snow swirl around him. To the West and East there are open fields where wheat is usually growing. Now the fields lie dormant, covered with snow. To the North, there is a huge mountain. This is the Bozanich Mountain that our characters are climbing when we first meet them, where they will become trapped, and where they will not be rescued until the 21st of June—the beginning of summer.*

It is now left to the location scout, operating on considerations from the production designer, to sort out the details that will result in permission to shoot on the location. Permits, visas, and bureaucracies may be encountered. While dedicated film commissions are on the rise around the world, there is a wide discrepancy in finding the correct people to query with regard to filming in a specific locale. The effort and time that it takes to locate the right person and to receive a positive response may be considerable. Even if the perfect location is found, issues such as whether there are adequate lodgings available within a reasonable distance from the site, and whether the necessary equipment can be taken to the location must be favorably answered from a standpoint of safety and economics.

And what of weather and environmental conditions? Since this scene is taking place during the winter, the mountain must have snow on it, or at least for the wide-angle shots. Additional questions arise with blazing speed: How many hours of daylight will we have to shoot in? When the sun begins to set, where will the shadows be cast? What is the average snowfall and temperature?

## Querying a Film Commission

Normally what happens is that the film's location manager makes an inquiry of a state or country's film commission, describing and discussing what the filmmakers require. This phone conversation then leads to the searching and distribution of the images back to the location manager. When the material is received, it may not be sufficient. In the interim, a great deal of time has been lost. Similarly, narrowing the possibilities of where the location scout should be sent is another step. For a state film commission faced with trying to be as competitive as possible with other commissions, the ability to provide as many answers as possible in a timely fashion becomes crucial.

## Previsualization of Locations

While no technology will ever eliminate the need to actually visit a location and see it first hand, digital filmmaking methods can facilitate a solution to one important item that the location manager must contend with: narrowing down the possibilities and making the best use of the limited time to successfully find and secure a required location.

## Locating Stock Footage

Not all films have original material shot for the film. There are many instances where films will include material that is referred to as stock shots. Consider the horror film that features a cutaway to a perfectly framed, perfectly exposed shot of a full moon. Or, the film that has a sequence which features ominous looking time-lapse photography of circling clouds. Footage falling into these categories are usually purchased from stock footage houses, and this footage must be located.

## The Digital Backlot

In addition, consider when a filmmaker requires a location that no longer exists and cannot be easily recreated. Let's say that a filmmaker wants to composite a character into a San Francisco street of 1922. There is an abundance of film that exists from this time period, but it must be located, viewed, and rights must be obtained. In the early days of filmmaking, street scenes would be recreated on the studio backlot. Now, however, through digital technology, footage which is many years old can be reconstituted and utilized. Locating the footage is the first problem to overcome as these digital backlots are reformed and made available to today's filmmaker.

## Computer-based Queries

Through the use of digital storage, computers, and telephone lines, a location manager is now able to query a database using a certain set of characteristics, then to be presented with visual information, such as actual photographs and even possibly moving video. In addition, a range of ancillary data, such as seasonal environmental conditions, lodging, etc., may complement the visual information.

## Converting Photographs and Location Information into Digital Form

Increasingly, local film commissions are converting their store of photographs and in some cases, video, to a digital format that can be accessed more quickly than if a commission employee had to manually rifle through the various files. The conversion to a digital format can be very inexpensive, and there are two types of files that are being used for the conversion: the Eastman Kodak Corporation's Photo-CD format for still images, and either QuickTime or AVI for moving video.

## Still Images: The Photo-CD Format

A Photo-CD, photo compact disc, is in the same form as an audio compact disc. A Photo-CD can store pictures as well as sounds and these pictures can be viewed on a television screen or can be accessed via a computer. It is a very straightforward process to place images on a Photo-CD. First, a roll of film is developed into either negatives or slides. These negatives are then electronically scanned and the data is used to digitize the images at five different levels of resolution. Next, the data is processed by a Photo-CD writer, which takes the five images, now known as a pack, and writes the information onto the compact disc. Last, a catalog of what images are on the disc is created in the form of an index, also called a thumbnail. This thumbnail is a small image with a corresponding number. The result of this process is that still images can be preserved in digital form and at various resolutions.

## Moving Images: QuickTime™ or AVI™

Location scouting has always relied on still images, but a two-dimensional picture often does not tell the full story of a location. Wouldn't it be convenient if there was a way that the local film commission could provide some moving video, however short in duration, which the location manager could review? In the past, integrating moving footage into a computer database was quite expensive. However, it has become very easy to integrate moving footage into a computer presentation. Here is how a QuickTime file can be created.

QuickTime is an extension of the Macintosh from Apple Computers. It allows the computer to display time-dependent media such as video, audio, and animation and to combine these media with time-independent media such as text and graphics. AVI (audio/video interleaved) is the corresponding extension to Intel-based CPUs.

Using a video capture board, a videotape player, or even a live video camera connected to a computer the images and sound can be captured and stored on the computer's disk drive. A variety of picture resolutions is available, and the display format can be quite small, such as $64 \times 96$ pixels, or a full screen $640 \times 480$ pixels. Additionally, while the video standard in NTSC is 30 fps, the QuickTime file could be compressed to play at anywhere from 5 to 30 fps and either single or dual field.

The attraction that QuickTime and AVI files have is that they can be played on any computer that is compatible with the codec (encoder/decoder) required to play the file. In the case of QuickTime, it means that a Macintosh computer, regardless of where it is in the world, is capable of playing a QuickTime file as long as it can run the QuickTime extension and player software. The ramifications that

this has in accessing databases of film commissions and stock footage houses is quite significant.

By storing information digitally, a film commission could therefore not only include a photo of "the red barn with open fields which faces a mountain" but could also include a short snippet of moving video. Suddenly, the location manager and the entire filmmaking team have much more information than ever before.

## Accessing the Information: Central versus Local Databases

Whether it is a stock footage house or a film commission, both parties have the same question to ponder: how to get their images to the filmmaker in the most timely and cost efficient manner. Stock footage houses are rapidly pursuing the idea of a central database which can be accessed by the world's filmmaking community, and which facilitate inquiries to their abundant catalog of both still and motion images. Those film commissions that have chosen to offer their images in digital form can decide whether to mail the filmmaker a Photo-CD, or allow the filmmaker to remotely browse the disc(s).

## Kodak™ Picture Exchange

One remote database system is the Eastman Kodak Corporation's Kodak Picture Exchange (KPX) which offers digital images from stock footage houses as well as still images from various state film commissions. Additionally, image suppliers such as news organizations, museums, and universities are participants. Photos are stored in variable pixel sizes: small thumbnails ($32 \times 48$), medium thumbnails ($64 \times 96$), large thumbnails ($128 \times 192$), and design proofs ($256 \times 384$).

Film producers and location scouts using either Macintosh or computers using the Windows operating system connect to the KPX via modem and can research images using key words and phrases; if more detailed search criteria are required, over forty image descriptions can be used (figure 4-15). The location scout can review, browse, and print low resolution images. For example, let's resume our search for the red barn. The various key words that narrow the search are entered, and the screen is filled with various images. Each image will have with it associated data that is deemed important by the image supplier. Data such as sunrise and sunset for each month, aver-

**Figure 14-15** A representative screen from the Kodak Picture Exchange that provides a database of digital images from stock footage houses as well as still images from various state film commissions. Courtesy of Eastman Kodak Corporation.

age rainfall, major highways, and road access are included.

Once the user has chosen specific images, the files can be downloaded via modem to the user's computer at a resolution of 256 × 384 pixels. These images can be used to decide if a location is worth pursuing. If the image is stock footage that must be purchased from the stock footage agency, the user fills out a form while online, the form is transmitted electronically to the stock footage company, and the user negotiates directly with the agency for use of the full resolution image. Not only can the cost of image searches be reduced, but the number of locations that a filmmaker can access expands greatly while remaining cost-effective.

## Image Providers

Clearly, a database of data, still images, and motion video is only helpful if it can provide a range of information. Six months after its introduction, KPX lists over 24 providers with an initial commitment of between 5,000 and 20,000 images. Among the providers: Archive Photos—over 5,000,000 images; Ewing Galloway—over 2,000,000 images; and FPG International—over 6,000,000 images on a variety of subjects, from wildlife and nature, to historical personalities, to computer graphics.

## Databases with Moving Video

Motion video that has been digitized and stored on either Photo-CD, CD-ROM, or on optical or magnetic computer disks can be cataloged in a database that permits viewing. The usual reason that moving video databases are not yet commonplace has to do with the amount of storage that motion video requires. The file sizes are much larger than the still pictures of thumbnail size, and it takes much longer to download the motion video. All of these issues are being addressed by more powerful image compression algorithms and high-speed data lines.

## Related Filmmaking Databases and the Previsualization Artist

As computer databases grow, their influence will extend to other areas of digital filmmaking. For example, while the location personnel are more interested in finding specific locales, the actual quality of the pictures are not that important; they are used for reference and to generate debate and interest. However, there are other crafts people for whom the locating of images can be a significant time-saver. Many of the types of images that are related to the digital backlot, images of events, people, and places long since unavailable to the filmmaker, have been preserved on film. Let's say that the film contains a scene where a character reads a newspaper and sees a younger version of himself standing amidst a crowd on New Year's Eve in New York's Times Square. Since this prop must be created, it is left to the previsualization artist to ensure that the filmmakers will have the necessary materials. To do this, the entire composite can be created in the computer. Here is just one way to proceed:

Since the actor is now made up to look much older, the previsualization artist will photograph the actor sans make-up and in the correct costuming. This photograph can be done with an ordinary 35mm camera, or with a handheld consumer camcorder while the actor is standing against either a blue or green screen. Next, the 35mm negative can be stored on a Photo-CD and then scanned into the computer, or the videotape can be digitized into the computer.

Next, the artist looks for the correct background shots of Times Square during New Year's Eve. The artist connects, via modem, to an image database and enters search criteria to locate the desired material. A series of choices appears on the screen and the artist finds an image that is perfect for the composite. Next, a full resolution version of the image is downloaded from the image database into the artist's computer. Depending upon the resolution required and the network connection, this transfer can be complete within a few minutes. The actual use of the image must be negotiated with the owner of the material, but this can be set up in advance.

The next step is to begin compositing the materials. Since the background shot, or plate, is already in digital form, it is opened from within the graphics program that the artist is using. There are a number of different types of programs that can be used, and they range in price from US $50 to several thousand dollars. The artist then opens the file of the actor standing in front of the blue screen. Through digital keying, the blue color is removed and replaced with the background of Times Square. This technique is referred to as blue screening, or chroma keying. By using software tools such as magnifying glasses and paint brushes, the artist can zoom into the digital composite, down to the level of one pixel, and can smooth out the edges where the actor has been "pasted" into the background. This smoothing, or anti-aliasing, lends a softer look to the two images and results in a more realistic composite. There are even filters that can impart specific film-related qualities, such as grain, flicker, and even scratches!

## Linking Location and Previsualization

Previsualization assists the interaction between the on-location crew and various departments. Normally, photographic stills are taken by the location manager and passed on to those people who need to see the various locales. However, consider the time factor involved—a photograph is taken using a self-developing film, and the package of photos is sent back. It becomes difficult to pass along this information, and the result is that usually not just one Polaroid, as these photographs have become known in the generic sense, but several are taken for the various departments that require the images.

There are a variety of problems when working this way. There is the inefficiency in not being able to communicate visually with the departments that may be very far from the location; there are multiple copies required, and this takes time. There is also the expense; in this case, three or four "instant" photographs may cost less than $1 in the United States, but may cost $4–5 in other countries.

## DIGITAL PHOTOGRAPHY AND DIGITAL INFORMATION GATHERING

One solution is to gather information digitally. Instead of taking snapshots of locations (or, for that matter, props and potential actors and actresses) the on-location crew can communicate visually and digitally by sending digital files. One way that this is accomplished is through the use of digital photography.

A digital camera resembles a handheld still image camera and is portable and lightweight. However, this camera is not loaded with film. Instead, the user points this camera at the subject and through the use of a CCD (charged-coupled device) array, the image is captured in digital form. Generally, full resolution, 24-bits per pixel, color images are provided, and approximately 32 images can be stored. The camera is connected to a computer, and the images are downloaded into the computer's storage disk.

One such camera is the Apple QuickTake 100 (figure 4-16). This camera provides 24-bit color, and its one megabyte of flash eprom stores up to 32 standard resolution ($320 \times 240$ pixels) images, eight high-resolution ($640 \times 480$) images, or a combination of these. The camera connects directly to the computer via a standard serial cable. Using the Quick-

**Figure 4-16** The Apple QuickTake 100 camera, a 24-bit digital camera for the Macintosh computer. Courtesy of Apple Computer, Inc. Photograph by John Greenleigh.

Take application, pictures can be rotated, cropped, scaled, zoomed, and saved in PICT, TIFF, or Quick-Take file formats. The images can also be compressed using QuickTime software.

Now that the material is in the computer, it can be manipulated and sent elsewhere. In the earlier example of the artist who had to shoot the actor with a handheld video camera, a digital camera would be a proper replacement for the video counterpart.

Let's say that a crew is on-location and a scene is being filmed that will eventually require digital matte paintings composited with the live action material. It is a very easy process to communicate visually with the postproduction departments. On-location, several different angles can be captured through the use of a digital camera. These files can then be loaded into the computer and, using an ordinary modem, the images can be sent to any location in the world. Within minutes, the files can be viewed and commented upon.

If the live action being shot shows three actors riding away from the camera on horseback, a series of digital frames can be shot that provides various departments with almost instant feedback: the horizon line is here, the sun is setting in this direction, the environment is bare. Therefore, the sunset will have to be enhanced to make it appear fuller, shrubbery will be added to the landscape, and so forth.

Various contributors, such as the music composer, could also be on the receiving end of these files. A few representative shots sent to the composer that provide the feeling of how the film is going to end are often appreciated, rather than having him compose with only the printed script in mind.

These new methods of working most importantly translate into work beginning earlier, even before the film has been processed. Now that the incoming images from the field are in digital form, they can be sent to many different departments, and each department can also view what previous users accomplished with the images.

## Searching Digitally

There are many filmmaking areas that can use digital image databases. For example, films require certain props, which can range from an antique sewing machine to a bowling trophy. Not only do many film studios have extensive property departments, but there are also specialty houses. If the research stage of assessing what props are available can be enhanced through the use of digital searches, there are certainly benefits to be realized. There are now Photo-CD methods that can store thousands of images, such as the Kodak PROfiLE CD Catalog that provides a maximum of 4,500 images on one disc. Imagine a library of discs that have been created to provide the user with access to thousands of props for films.

## Talent Databases and Remote Casting Sessions

Those casting a film can benefit from digital technologies and digital filmmaking methods. Supporting members and bit players certainly are under the domain of the casting director. Casting sessions can take a variety of forms. The casting director and director may have a series of choices in mind for a particular role. These actors are contacted via their agents. Or, rather, the director may be interested in having less well known actors in the role. Last, there are a variety of bit roles that may be limited speaking or non-speaking roles. It is left to the casting director to locate these individuals.

## Talent Casting

Since 1988, there have been at least eight different companies that have formed to provide different types of database services for casting directors. The capacities of these services will vary, as some provide still image capability with text, while others provide full motion video, audio, text, and graphics. If used properly, these capabilities can provide the casting director with a solid form of research.

One such system is the Global Talent Guild's Interactive Talent Directory. A CD-I (compact-disc interactive) disc and a graphic menu display allow the user to search a comprehensive database using such qualities as: hair color, eye color, ethnic portrayal type, character portrayal type, language, dialect, and accent proficiency (native, trained, limited, moderate, fluent), vocal abilities, stunt skills, credits, and many other important characteristics. Shown in figure 4-17 is a representation of the GTG casting system, where the talent profile, consisting of a head/body shot, resume, and options for both a full motion video clip

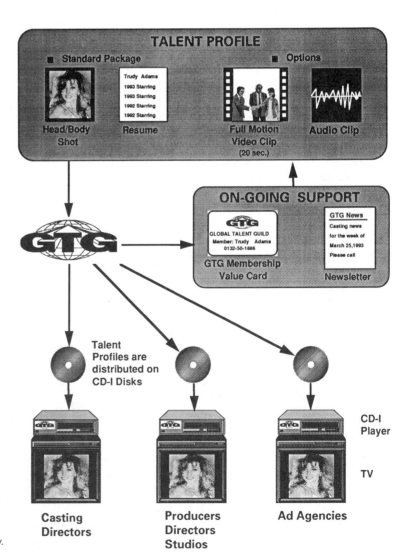

**Figure 4-17** The GTG casting system. The talent profile, consisting of a head/body shot, resume, and options for both a full motion video clip and an audio clip are distributed on CD-I discs, accessible by casting directors, producers, directors, studios, and advertising agencies. Courtesy of Global Talent Guild, The Interactive Talent Directory.

and an audio clip are distributed on CD-I discs and can be accessed by casting directors, producers, directors, studios, and advertising agencies.

A casting director, faced with the normal methods of research, such as resumes, glossy photos, and casting calls, may find a digital methodology beneficial as an additional source of casting. After the casting director has chosen a set of criteria, a "proof sheet" or "slide show" presentation is shown on-screen of all the available artists that meet the casting criteria. These photos can then be viewed full-screen, along with text of such material as the artist's resume. Optional information includes a twenty second full motion video clip and an audio clip for judging voice-over talent.

## Digital Transmission of Live Casting Sessions

When a film is being actively cast, it may become necessary to hold open casting sessions in one or more cities. Indeed, there are many instances when world-wide searches are undertaken to fill a specific role. This is often an expensive and time-consuming undertaking. However, an alternative to attending a casting session in all of the different cities is the digital transmission of the casting session. When it has been determined that the casting session does not require that the director be present, the casting session can be digitally transmitted. By shooting the casting session with a video camera, the live pictures and sounds can be sent over telephone lines to another location, and the transmission can be made in real time. For the director, being able to agree upon the casting of these roles without having to travel to all the locations can be very beneficial.

## Digital Previsualization with Actors

There are some very unique and exciting possibilities for previsualization. Consider the following scenario: A location scout could take a photograph with a digital camera and, using a modem, send the file back to the production center. A director could remotely evaluate locations and these digital backgrounds could be used to composite a live action shot of an actor who is taking part in a casting session. In only a few minutes, the director is able to not only see a remote location, but is even able to see a possible role candidate composited into that location!

## COSTUME DESIGN

Costume design and pattern creation can also benefit from previsualization. Using computers to accomplish what previously would have been difficult or altogether improbable, the filmmaker is able to see exactly what a character would wear, and what the color schemes would be by seeing the character photographed against particular backgrounds. The digital compositing provides a greater efficiency to the design and review process.

For the filmmaker who must be attuned to every nuance of how the story is presented, it is no small matter to determine what type of clothes a story's characters wear during the course of the film. There are two core issues when considering what type of costumes will be created: first, how do the costumes fit into the lives of the people; and second, how does the clothing further the realism sought by the film to portray a certain period? When the costume design succeeds, it is rarely noticed by the viewer. In the words of costume designer for theater and multimedia, Diane Shapiro, "A good costume design doesn't stand out at all, it just looks like it belongs and it supports the story."

## The Research Phase

Basic theater and film costume design techniques begin with meetings between the designer and the director. Having read the screenplay, the designer then attempts to determine any special motifs, concepts, or feelings that the director may have in mind, and which the costumes must convey. Additional questions will arise: Is the film a period piece? Will it be photographed in black-and-white or in color? Are there backgrounds that the characters will be photographed against which will be in harmony or contrast with the costumes?

The designer then begins basic research, necessary before any sketches or renderings can be done, that outlines the type of costuming that will be offered for the filmmaker's review. If the designer is creating for a film that takes place in 1895, and the designer needs to know the types of shoes that were worn during that time, photographs and books can be located and examined. Usually, a designer will concentrate research in three areas: photographs, books, and works of original artists. If possible, the designer will seek out the artist or the originator of a style. Photographs of clothing styles, how clothes were worn, and even the physical shape of people during a certain period are all important aspects that the designer must verify.

Throughout this research phase, the designer will most likely be creating sketches, hand drawings, and silhouettes. Next, fabric swatches can be attached to the hand drawings. The next stage may involve creating mock-ups of the costumes. These mock-ups are often done in muslin, and the goal is to obtain the lines and shapes of the design. If the actors have been cast for the film, they may be brought in at this time for an initial fitting.

At this point, sketches, and the all-important sketch notes, which outline exactly where everything is to be located on a garment, are shopped around to costume houses. Competitive bids may be made on a batch of sketches, and the designer will work with the house's draper. More mock-ups are created, followed by a second fitting, then alterations, and then, finally, the garment is finished. With slight variation, this is generally the manner in which the costume designer will operate.

## Previsualization for Costume Design

There are a variety of ways that costume design can make use of digital filmmaking techniques. A great portion of the costume designer's time is spent doing research, for only with proper and comprehensive research can a truly accurate and lasting rendering of a period in time be recreated on film. There is nothing more unfortunate than to have a worthy script, cast, and crew all betrayed by inaccurate or obtrusive costuming.

## *INDUSTRY VIEWPOINTS*

### *Maurizio Vecchione—Executive Vice President, Advanced Technology, ModaCAD, Inc.*

Software which is used to visualize how different fabrics, wood treatments, and so forth will look on pieces of furniture is among the innovative offerings of ModaCAD, based in Los Angeles, California. Through the use of specialized software, designers working on costuming fashions and furniture concepts can quickly see the effects of how different patterns, colors, or styles will look. The ability to previsualize not only how a costume will look, but how,

**Figure 4-18**  Photo of Maurizio Vecchione. Courtesy of ModaCad, Inc.

after constructing a set, the look of the furniture within the room can be changed, are powerful previsualization tools. Says Maurizio Vecchione,

The idea is to visualize pieces before they are made, whether the piece is a costume or a piece of furniture. Normally, when people create a fabric for a costume, they can create as many as fifteen samples, but by using our technology, they have eliminated the need for making these samples. Many of our designers come from the entertainment industry, so they know the processes that can be replaced or done better by using computers.

With our software, ModaFINITY, using either the Macintosh or a PC with Windows, you can take a fabric swatch and apply it to a picture of the actual furniture or any item in a room setting. In this way, you can quickly change the entire look of a room. We've done many different types of rooms, such as bedrooms where we can show exactly how a different floor would look, or different drapes, or different bedspreads, and we can offer the client different looks depending upon how they need the pieces to be put together. You can design and apply fabric to a garment, tile on a floor, wallpaper on a wall, and so forth. You can even access multimedia clips via QuickTime.

Another program we have developed is Moda-DRAPE, which is capable of taking a 2-D image and recognizing 3-D surfaces present in the model. It turns out to be simpler to model 3-D images with this technology than using 3-D imagery. This allows you to map a texture onto the contortions of a 3-D model. We gives clues to the program about the surfaces of the texture. You can think of these as control surfaces where you are biasing the material so that you are draping the fabric directly onto the model, and you see how the fabric would look as if it were actually being worn, and not just hanging there lifeless. The software also has animation capability so that you can simulate movement—such as how cloth clings to the form underneath. . . .

For the garment industry, the computer represents an electronic cutting table. You can simulate three incident lights and ambient light, and it not only casts shadows but it can change the color cast of the garment itself.

Libraries are very important to us. We have the history of fashion design on CD-ROM where you can see period pieces and scenes. You can find, access, and modify as you require.

## Computer-assisted Research

Research is often limited by the amount of material that can be located, retrieved, and perused. Short and long distance communications, the necessity to travel to different locations, and the time involved in getting adequate samples all can prolong the research phase. The emergence of CD-ROM (compact disc, read-only memory) as a means for encyclopedic retrieval of information allows the costume designer to find material much more quickly. CD-ROM titles that are created around costume libraries are of great assistance to the designer who is searching for, say, the manner in which women's dresses were pleated in the early 1930s in Rome, or the style of boots worn by soldiers in war-torn Paris during World War II. Further, fabric types can be stored off on CD-ROM and accessed by the designer. Many modern museums are creating CD-ROM versions of their various exhibition wings. Clearly, the vast amount of information, heretofore available to the designer only by laborious and time-consuming research, is now becoming available digitally, and is accessible quickly by computer.

Through the use of a modem and ordinary telephone dial-up service, it is possible to access a great deal of information from the home. Further, through communications networks, the designer can query individuals with like-minded goals. One of the networks that has emerged is known as the Internet, and it allows people to communicate with one another. By posting one's message on an Internet-type server, the possibility of one's message being seen jumps dramatically.

## Location Backgrounds

Tapping into networks can be quite promising. Imagine you are a costume designer who has never been to a particular country and portions of the film have characters photographed in front of certain buildings. The settings in which the story takes place play an important role for you, so it is helpful to see the backgrounds that will be used. Consider that you are about to finalize your designs and swatches for scenes that will be filmed near the Pantheon in Rome and you are now able to do so with the background shots of the on-location settings that will be used. If you could tap into multiple databases and find the types of clothes worn during the period, how they were worn, fabric swatches, and even generic backgrounds from the area that will be used for filming, you would be much closer to completing the research phase of design.

## Computer-assisted Design

Using several different computer packages, we can accomplish many of the more laborious design tasks digitally. One manner of working is to create the sketches and more elaborate drawings by hand, through the use of a stylus and a pressure-sensitive pad. These drawings become individual files and can be easily duplicated, whereas if a designer needed to change a design, an entirely new drawing could be made. Within the computer, however, a copy of the original drawing can be easily changed. The benefit is that if the change is minor, it can be made quickly and with less effort.

## Three-dimensional Views

Once a sketch is present in a computer, it can be augmented to include views from different perspectives. By assigning the drawing values on different axes, the shape can be viewed not from a 2-D perspective, but rather in 3-D space. This will most likely be as a wire frame, but this visual can be invaluable in giving the designer an idea of how a garment will look with, say, flared pants legs when viewed from a side angle.

## Applying Swatches and Colors

Now that the drawing is in digital form, a collage can be created in 2-D. The designer can apply color to the drawing (or to the wire frame). When a designer tells a director, "Here the dress will be red, with stripes of black interwoven," it may be difficult for a director to envision the look. To solve such problems, the designer can scan the actual fabric swatch that was gathered. The color, detail, and texture of the swatch are preserved, and this fabric swatch is applied to the drawing. Through the use of high quality color printers, the designer can create a portfolio of items to present to the director.

## Sampling the Background

It is easy to sample the exact background, or a reference background, that will be used during the actual shooting process. In our earlier example, a CD-ROM drive can be part of the designer's system. From a disk, for instance, old photographs of the Pantheon can be imported into the computer. This background can then be scaled appropriately, and the costume design can be manipulated given the background. How do the designs change if the background is in color versus black-and-white? All of these things can be tried quickly in the computer and the options can be judged visually as a 2-D or 3-D collage.

## Computer Processing Power

As computers become more powerful and more affordable, working in real-time 3-D space will become more prevalent. One can envision a program that, when the designer applies the actor's dimensions to the design, will calculate the pattern and estimate the fabric yardage required for costumes. This is a task that has traditionally been accomplished by individuals known as drapers, but the number of individuals training in this discipline has consistently been on the decline.

## Communicating the Design

Not to be overlooked is the flexibility that the filmmaker now has in being able to take this digital information and to communicate it in different ways. The files can be sent electronically to the director who is scouting locations. Also, a collage can be created, and the designer could send this digital file, over a mo-

dem, to an expert in a particular field to check for historical accuracy.

Shown in figure 4-19a is a computer scan of a line drawing. A fabric swatch is also scanned (figure 4-19b), and then highlighted areas of the drawing are filled in with the fabric (figure 4-19c). The final result, as shown in figure 4-19d, provides the designer with the ability to quickly previsualize different patterns and colors.

## INDUSTRY VIEWPOINTS

### Diane E. Shapiro—Theater, Film, and Multimedia Designer

For Diane E. Shapiro, computer imaging and traditional costume design media are merging to create new tools and methods for her to use to enhance her effectiveness as a designer working in theater, film, and multimedia. Says Shapiro,

> A designer can use an application such as ADOBE PHOTOSHOP, along with a Wacom drawing tablet on a Macintosh Quadra, or a Power Macintosh to create renderings with patterns and textures in full color. It is very easy to scan a line drawing into the computer, or in some cases, to draw directly into the computer—which is a skill one can learn just as one

**Figure 4-20** Photo of Diane E. Shapiro. Courtesy of Diane E. Shapiro.

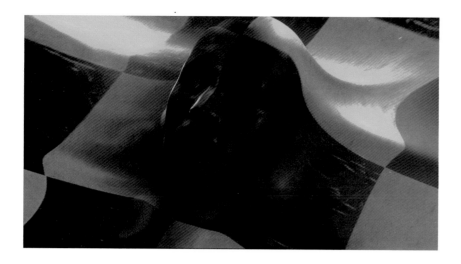

**Figure 2-1** This 3-D computer-generated model with realistic texture mapping of the surrounding environment is an example of one of the fantastic images contained in the 1991 film, *Terminator 2: Judgment Day*. Courtesy of Carolco Pictures and Twentieth-Century Fox, Ltd. All rights reserved.

**Figure 4-8** Changing the pattern, color, and texture of a sofa for previsualization purposes using ModaDRAPE software. Once the sections are highlighted, a different color, pattern, and texture can be mapped onto the shape of the sofa. Courtesy of ModaCAD, Inc.

**Figure 4-19a–d** Stages that illustrate how a computer scan of a line drawing can be filled in with a fabric swatch in order to quickly previsualize different patterns and colors. Sketches and graphics by Diane E. Shapiro © 1994. Used by permission.

might learn to paint with a watercolor brush—and then create colors or patterns from within the computer to apply to the drawing. Design elements such as color balance, harmony, and contrast can be played with in a very flexible fashion and can be quickly and easily edited. A designer can collage together 2-D images, and with systems such as the ALIAS software on a Silicon Graphics Workstation, can move these ideas into 3-D visualization.

This computer imaging approach to creating renders can facilitate working relationships between designers and directors. It allows the designer great flexibility in the creative process and the ability to explicitly communicate visual ideas to a director from multiple and diverse perspectives, such as 2-D fabric collages, 3-D computer rendered models, and so forth. . . .

In a typical design scenario, a designer reads the play or the script, develops an emotional response to it, discusses his or her responses with the director, and then begins to collect research. When a costume designer begins to do research it is helpful to know as much about the other production elements as possible. For a film, having pictures of the location can be quite important. Good costume design will be influenced and inspired by the visual elements of the location—the atmosphere, the quality of light, the buildings, etc.

In creating a film, all of the designers must communicate and work closely with each other and with the director during the initial stages of the production's development. When all of the designed elements evolve together simultaneously and successfully—art direction, costumes, lighting, and so forth—a special visual impact can be created. About recent films Diane continues,

*The Age of Innocence* (1993) certainly had gorgeous costume design as part of an overwhelmingly sensual attention to details about social life. Yet, the one film that especially impresses me is *The Unbearable Lightness of Being* (1988), which was very well designed in every aspect—it combined the creative use of mirrors, fog, costumes, cinematography, and various other elements. Also, one of the best examples I've seen where a real understanding of good design is evident is in *In the Name of the Father* (1993). This movie is absolutely correct in its representation of the period. At the outset of the story, the film takes place in a period where women wore their hair very long and straight, which is for the most part how it was portrayed in the film. Often times there may be a situation where an actress either can't, or won't wear her hair, or some other costume element in a particular way. This

brings up stylistic issues that the designers have to deal with. Many period films are created through the eyes of the current period or date in which they are produced. For example, *Cleopatra* (1963) is the Egyptian period as seen through the eyes of the early to mid-1960s.

The design for *In the Name of the Father* really made choices that supported the story. As a viewer, I felt I was watching a story which took place in the 1960s as if I was in the 1960s, not as if I was watching a film done in the 1990s about the 1960s. Daniel Day Lewis wore his clothing appropriately. He didn't just have the right clothes, he also wore the clothes the way that kids from that period would wear them. He had a typical body structure of a young man from that period. Young men look quite different now, many work out and thus have a different, a real muscular, physical structure.

These are all visual elements that the designer must consider and work with. Similarly, the way women wore bell bottoms in the 1960s is quite different from how they are usually worn in the 1990s. There has been a sort of retro phase going on now where women will wear bell bottoms in a high fashion way. Bell bottoms in the 1960s were worn very low on the hips, and were made mostly of denim and corduroy—non-stretch fabrics, making them look bulky and slightly uncomfortable. The 1990s bell bottoms are usually garments made from stretch fabrics which are worn more at the natural waist line, thus being more tight fitting and somewhat more comfortable garments. A good designer will notice these types of subtle visual differences and take them into consideration when creating costumes for a period film, thus helping to create the appropriate visual illusion for a particular period. . . .

With the rapid emergence of new media such as CD-ROMs, there is a need for multimedia designers as well as traditional fashion, theater, and film designers. The premise of successful design is the same whether one is designing costumes for an opera, art direction for a film, lighting for a 3-D animation, or a photo-collage on a computer screen for a CD-ROM. Good design will really support the story.

## MAKEUP

Throughout the course of this chapter we have explored the various traditional filmmaking disciplines and how digital technology has affected standard techniques. Makeup, character and body shaping, and creature design can also benefit. Makeup is a craft that draws upon the makeup artist's feel for how a character should look and must support the creative visions of the filmmakers and the actors. Prior to digital techniques, traditional character treatments began as drawings and quick pencil sketches done to get an idea of what a character should look like and to present these visual thoughts to a director or actor. From these drawings, it might have been necessary to make a casting of an actor's face. This casting is then used to create prosthetic devices that could be attached to the actor's face to allow the actor's natural expressions to be preserved through the makeup.

While hand drawings and sketches may characterize the initial stages for a character concept, it is often difficult to give filmmakers a full idea of how a character could really look, present many options, and hone in on the treatment of makeup design for the film when the previsualization stage is largely a manual process.

## Digitization, Painting, and Image Manipulation Software

Previsualization of makeup can be greatly enhanced by using software programs that allow the artist to scan either hand sketches or actual photographs of an actor's face and then to electronically paint over the face or manipulate the image to achieve a particular look. By using the computer as a canvas, remarkable tools become available. Such items as being able to create particular colors, blends of colors, swatches of hair, various nose, lip, and mouth sizes, and so forth allow the artist the creativity to take an actor's image and show how the actor would look in character. Often, software such as ADOBE PHOTOSHOP and META FLOW, FLO-FREEFORM PLASTICITY are used to create such effects.

For the feature film, *Wolf* (1994), makeup artist Rick Baker utilized traditional makeup skills enhanced by software programs to present director Mike Nichols and actor Jack Nicholson with various visual examples that showed how a character would be transformed during the different stages of the script. After artist Baker created the images showing different transformations using software, the files were then printed by a color printer and viewed by the filmmakers. By presenting, in essence, a chronology of how a character would change, designs were able to be discarded, or enhanced and ultimately accepted. It was then left to Baker to realize the makeup in 3-D which then became applications for the actors.

While much makeup work is still accomplished traditionally, the growing use of computers and so-phisticated software that allows makeup crafts people to try new designs before committing ideas to three-dimensional appliances is a great advantage in fostering further creative growth.

## INDUSTRY VIEWPOINTS

### Rick Baker—Special Makeup Effects Artist, Cinovation Studios, Inc.

*Little Panda* (1994), *Ed Wood* (1993), *Wolf* (1993), *Harry and the Hendersons* (1987), *An American Werewolf in London* (1982).

For makeup artist and designer Rick Baker, a three-time Academy Award winner for best makeup, the use of digital technology has been a successful adoption of new techniques that have allowed Baker to design and realize some of the most memorable makeup creations in film history. Explains Baker of the basic methods of makeup creation,

> Traditional design begins with perhaps a quick pencil sketch. The next stage could be an overlay on a photo of an actor, and onto the overlay I would draw or paint the design that I had in mind. We'll also do casts and three-dimensional sculptures.
>
> About five years ago I wanted to learn more about computers and how I might use them. I wanted to take an image and do an overlay and paint on the overlay and then output it to video or print. The very first program I used was called PHOTO MAC and I instantly fell in love with it. What I instantly loved was that you could try different things. So many times you are afraid to paint something—you get something you like and you want to do more—but you don't want to lose what you have. But on the computer, you do variations on a theme.

Baker, who now uses various software programs for painting, image manipulation, and compositing, counts experimentation as an important factor in the creative process. Says Baker,

> Just the idea that you could create a whole new palette of facial tones by clicking on different sections of a photo is great. Once I learned how to use the software, I could do so many similar things in such a short amount of time. It's one thing to take a person's face and make it older, but when we are designing a creature, sometimes what I'll do is make a little sculpture and then digitize a frame of it into the computer.

**Figure 4-21**   Photo of Rick Baker. Courtesy of Rick Baker, Cinovation Studios, Inc.

Then I'll paint it and do things like an asymmetrical head or if I really like the eyes on this example and the head on another example, I can easily combine those elements into one design. I've come up with designs that I may never have tried before.

Baker also credits previsualization software for makeup as being extremely helpful in assisting filmmakers in realizing what a design will look like. Continues Baker,

So many times we show a little clay model when what the filmmakers were expecting was a larger size example. But now it is so easy to take the model, digitize it into the computer, and make it look ten feet tall. This has been really helpful, and our initial ideas have been more refined. It has also helped me because normally I'll read a script and have a vision in my head and the computer helps bring that to reality. Still, everything I do is two-dimensional and I eventually want to work in the 3-D world.

Interestingly, Baker has used computer technology to create some last minute set dressing that filmmakers have requested. He says,

On *Gremlins 2* (1990), I instantly found uses for the computer. In the film, there's one scene where Gizmo

is supposed to get photocopied to death. So I grabbed some images of Gizmo and digitized the images into the computer. Then I took people at work and had them make strange faces as if their faces were pushed up against glass. I composited them together and printed it up. There's also a scene in a dentist's office, and the director said that it would be great if there was a gremlin X ray on the wall. So I said, "Give me a half an hour and I'll do it on my computer." So I took an image, made it into a negative, and stuck it on the wall. We even did a front view and a side view!

Baker, who created the makeup worn by actor Jack Nicholson in *Wolf* (1994), credits digital technology with providing the ability to hone in on the treatment for the makeup realization. Says Baker,

When I first spoke to (director) Mike Nichols, I said that it is really a different kind of werewolf—a very subtle change. I took a photograph of Jack Nicholson and digitized it and did a series of designs—some subtle and some more extreme. I went to his house with about 25 different examples that I had all done on the computer. Jack basically said, "This is the first werewolf movie without any makeup." And this was what I had felt all along so by looking at the different examples I had created, he instantly saw that I was right for the job. . . .

We could see what Jack would look like during different stages of the script—here's what he'll look like in Central Park—here's what he'll look like by this point in the script. This became very valuable for (director) Mike Nichols. . . .

The biggest benefit for me is that I really try to make art out of what I do. It takes a lot of time to make these things and if you put six months into a design and create the makeup that someone is going to wear and it doesn't work, you've got big problems. By using the computer, we can show people what they'll get and then you can really commit. I can do more in less time, and I think my work is better and more fully realized.

## FEASIBILITY TESTING AND FINISHED WORK

When one examines the vast number of tools that are available to the filmmaker during the previsualization stage, the aggregate conclusion is that previsualization methods seek to answer questions. "What will it look like?" "Will we be able to do it?" and "How do we know when we've got what we need?" are some of the questions that have been known to cause filmmakers fitful sleep. As digital technologies become more common, less will be left to the unknown, filmmakers will be more prepared, and more and more work done during previsualization will find its way into the finished film.

# Production

# 5

# The Technology of Film: Timecode on Film, Computerized Cameras, Motion-control, and Pre-editorial during Production

Digital processes are being introduced to the production stage of filmmaking. Generally, the capture of images has remained unchanged through the years—light enters through a lens and strikes a piece of film negative that is moving through the camera at 24 fps. One of the earliest developments where technology has changed image capture is in the application of timecode to the negative during shooting. Aaton Corporation has had such an application in their cameras for over fifteen years. The codings support film-to-tape transfer, have been the advent of digital, non-linear editing (DNLE) systems, and productions are just beginning to reap the rewards of in-camera timecode.

## IN-CAMERA TIMECODE

Each film frame can be uniquely identified by an in-camera timecode system. This is accomplished by exposing the timecode data onto the film negative between the perforations. The timecode rate is established by the running speed of the camera. Therefore, the timecode rate is a SMPTE 24 frame timecode when running at sound speed. Unlike latent edge codes or keynumbers, the timecode is exposed on the edge of each and every frame of film. There are two types of in-camera timecode on the market today. One was developed by Aaton, and the other by Arriflex. They both perform the same function but are created and read differently. Arriflex employs a barcode method of encoding while Aaton employs a matrix of dots. Aaton timecode also provides man-readable information on the negative that corresponds to all the information available within the dot matrix. Shown in figure 5-1 are examples of film timecode as it appears on the latent film negative.

In addition to timecode, the date in the user bits is also exposed on the negative. In the remaining unused users bits, either sound roll or camera roll can be encoded. Aaton code is also capable of encoding production number, camera number, and camera magazine ID, as well as man readable timecode, date and roll identification. While there may be opinions that in-camera timecode and encoding data into user bits are both very technically advanced compared to using edgenumbers and slate information, the overwhelming reason for using these new forms of technology is

**Figure 5-1** Clockwise from left. Aaton generated timecode on 35mm negative film. Courtesy of Aaton. Aaton generated timecode on 16mm negative film. Courtesy of Aaton. Arriflex generated timecode on 16mm negative film. Courtesy of Arriflex Corporation. Arriflex generated timecode on 35mm negative film. Courtesy of Arriflex Corporation.

that information is not transcribed manually, which always introduces the possibility of error.

## The Technology of In-camera Timecode

It is helpful to understand the integration of in-camera timecode. On the Arriflex 535 camera there is a timecode module, and timecode is recorded between the perforations and the exposed frame on the camera right side of the film (when standing at the rear of the camera). The timecode on the 535 runs at four different speeds: 24, 25, 29.97, and 30 fps. The 24, 25, and 30 fps recordings are non-drop frame timecode, while the 29.97 fps is drop-frame code. The timecode module has an LED (light emitting diode) that optically records a barcode version of the timecode signal that is created by the internal SMPTE

timecode generator. The timecode module only exposes timecode on the negative and is not capable of generating timecode. This timecode and the film's keynumbers will later be read by a keynumber/timecode reader head, housed on the telecine unit.

The timecode can be set by either using the Arri CCU (camera control unit) or by another master clock such as a Nagra IV-S TC 1/4″ audio tape recorder. The module must be set based on the sensitivity of the negative. As the timecode module is actually exposing the negative, depending on the stock being used, the assistant camera person can refer to a manual for the settings, which are based on film ASA and manufacturer recommendations. In this way, the timecode exposure will not be under- or over-exposed when the negative is developed. If not exposed correctly, the reader head may have trouble decoding the timecode and this will defeat all benefits of using in-camera timecode. Shown in figure 5-2a is an example of the Aaton OriginC+ master clock used for the Aaton in-camera timecode system. The Arriflex computer control unit (CCU) is shown in figure 5-2b.

**Figure 5-2a** The Aaton OriginC+ master clock. Courtesy of AbelCineTech.

**Figure 5-2b**   The Arriflex CCU. Courtesy of Arriflex Corporation.

## The Accuracy of In-camera Timecode

It is critical to note that the timecode is accurate to +/- one frame over an eight hour period and it is recommended that an update be performed halfway through the shooting day. Normally this is done during a lunch break as part of normal camera maintenance. As user-bit information is user-selectable, this data is sent separately from the CCU to the camera. The user-bits will normally contain date and reel ID, but any data that the user wishes to enter can be contained in an eight bit field. This information will remain unchanged, unless changed by the operator. The only information that updates is the running time-of-day timecode (TOD). TOD is a timecode that runs from midnight to midnight, and the range is from 00:00:00:00 to 23:59:59:23 or 23:59:59:29 and then rolls over to 00:00:00:00 with the new day's date attached.

Since each day has the same time, that is, a take may be shot exactly at noon every day for the length of the shoot (12:00:00:00), the TOD timecode also has a date encoded into the user bits of the timecode. When both date and timecode are used, each sound element is made unique by that stamp. Productions that shoot both in the United States and Europe may use a military dating system so that no confusion of dates occurs. For example, if the production is shooting late in the year, say on October 9, 1993, the date is written in the U.S. as 10/09/93 while in Europe, the day and month are reversed: 09/10/94. Problems may also arise if the film is a very long shoot and there are already sound reels with a September date. By using a military dating system, one would always expect to see year/month/day making the above example 94/09/10.

The date and time of day timecodes ensure that each exposed frame is unique. The synchronization of other devices is accomplished by slaving one or more machines to a master clock. This is done by jam syncing the slave to the master. There are two types of jam syncing. One-time jam sync is when the starting timecode is sent from the master clock to the camera's control unit and they are then disconnected. The camera then locks its internal clock to the master time and will not accept any other timecode until the master clock is re-introduced and instructs the slave to rejam itself to a new time. Continuous jam sync refers to timecode always being available as a data stream from the master clock. The timecode is sent from the master clock in a continuous flow and the master clock is not removed.

## *INDUSTRY VIEWPOINTS*

### Jean-Pierre Beauviala—President, Aaton®, France

For Jean-Pierre Beauviala, creator and founder of Aaton, a maker of cameras for motion picture pho-

**Figure 5-3** Photo of Jean-Pierre Beauviala. Courtesy of Jean-Pierre Beauviala.

tography, the improvements he has created in the area of in-camera timecode systems have helped to define camera and film coding principles in the digital filmmaking process. Says Beauviala,

We first received a patent for in-camera timecode in 1968 and we proposed the idea to the Eclair company, who had the first crystal controlled camera, but they were not as interested in timecode. So in 1971 I founded Aaton because we needed a camera to show the concept of in-camera timecode. We made a modification to the Nagra because all of this was prior to having SMPTE timecode, and we designed it so that there was no cross-talk onto the audio tracks. By 1977 to 1981 we had quite a few users who were using the system. . . .

AatonCode consists of both a dot-matrix and a man-readable code and we introduced this in 1984. If all of the dots are illuminated there are a total of 91. Eighty bits are for SMPTE timecode, eleven are for vertical and horizontal sync and parity so that the SMPTE timecode is protected. We utilize user bits for date, camera, negative numbers, and so forth and we can increase the number of information when necessary. In general, we found that barcode systems alone do not resist the processes that the film must undergo. The matrix, on the other hand, is abuse resistant.

With Aaton, a master clock is used to generate the timecode and synchronization between camera and recorder. Says Beauviala,

We introduced the master clock from the very beginning so that we could have a very friendly interface between the clock and the other devices in the system. The clock is very precise—plus or minus one-half frame in eight hours. We were the very first manufacturer to incorporate a microprocessor in a film mechanism.

Equally important to Beauviala's vision of the role of digital technology in film production is the necessity to capture as much information as possible, as early as possible in the shooting stage. Continues Beauviala,

We created "Script Scribe" in 1979 and it was used to enter all scene and set information correlated into time and real-time related to the machines on the set. When we invented the first machine, there were no portable computers, so we had to design our own box. Now, of course there are affordable portable computers but they make too much noise on the set. What we are really waiting for is the pen-driven computer, so that you can write on set and develop the database.

Continued developments and advancements in video tap technology will, in Beauviala's opinion, change the methods of film production. He says,

In 1980, we introduced the first video tap with timecode burn-in windows. We had a black and white vidicon camera which we made and we included a time inserter. But it was very early and no one was thinking about using the tape to edit from. So we reintroduced the system in 1994, also in PAL, along with white flag capability. The white flag starts the video recorder automatically, so there is no start cable and you can start the recording machine simultaneously with camera or even before the camera is up to speed.

With the improvements in video taps, you can theoretically make a rough edit, pull the selected film via timecode, transfer the film via timecode, and then pull the negative to complete the film. There are things to be aware of, however—you may have 1/48th of a second of a delay and you many not know if the negative is fine—it may be scratched but you are using the video tape version of it in the edit. I think the beauty of editing on the set is the immediate access to the work of the day and in checking continuity, but not to actually use this time to edit creatively—there are probably too many distractions. . . .

Digital, nonlinear editing is the real trigger for requiring timecode recording during production. Before, people were reluctant to use in-camera timecode systems, but now because of digital editing, you can sync sound on the editing system itself and save time and money syncing in the telecine room or on the VTR prior to digitization and this is pushing people towards using timecode on film. Now, a lot of television series and documentaries are transferred from film to video, and they are asking for timecode on film. They can use the double system all the way from production to postproduction and even on to the actual showing of the film.

## RECOMMENDED PRACTICES FOR FILM RATE AND AUDIO TIMECODE RATES

There is always confusion when trying to determine what speed and frame count should be used for the sound elements when shooting double system. Since there are two elements involved, picture and sound, both film speed and timecode stamp need to be addressed. There are four combinations that can be used during a sync sound shoot:

| Speed (fps) | Timecode Stamp |
| --- | --- |
| 30 | NDF |
| 30 | DF |
| 29.97 | NDF |
| 29.97 | DF |

It is the relationship between sound speed, film rate, and timecode stamp in conjunction with the telecine process that needs to be correctly set and referenced for all elements in order to remain in sync throughout the postproduction process. Specific information on the telecine process can be found in chapter seven.

Speed refers to the speed of the audio recorder (Nagra or DAT), and Timecode Stamp is the type of timecode used at that speed.

| Speed(fps) | TC/Stamp | Used For |
| --- | --- | --- |
| 30 | NDF | Sync sound recording for film shot at 24 or 30 fps for a telecine or mag transfer. |
| 30 | NDF | Shooting sync playback with film at 24 or 30 fps using master 29.97 fps audio for the telecine. |
| 29.97 | NDF | Sync record for film shot at 29.97 fps and telecine at 29.97 fps. |
| 29.97 | NDF | Sync playback for film shot and telecine at 29.97 fps using master 29.97 fps audio for telecine. |
| 25 | n/a | Sync recording of film shot at 25 fps and telecine to PAL or SECAM 25 fps video. |
| 25 | n/a | Sync playback of 25 fps master audio with film at 25 fps. |
| 25 | n/a | Sync sound recording to film shot at 24 fps.* |
| 24 | n/a | Sync recording to 24 fps film.** |

*The Aaton keylinker can reference 24 frame timecode on film to the 25 frame timecode on the audio. Perfect sync is referenced at the top of every second. Refer to chapter seven.
**In NTSC, this timecode rate is usually at the demand of the post facility. With the use of digital audio workstations, 24 fps timecode may be of more use in the future for sync purposes in postproduction environments. This frame rate is common for PAL transfers when film is shot at 24 fps. This creates a one-to-one relationship between each frame of film and its sync sound element.

## IN-CAMERA TIMECODE AND LOGGING ON SET

As in-camera timecode information is available on the set, it becomes a very interesting way of approaching logging while shooting. This forms the initial stages of creating a database of scenes and takes, before the negative is developed. Once the negative is developed, the keynumber relationship will be added to the database of the in-camera timecode, and the negative conform can use either keynumbers, timecode, or both.

### Logging on the Set

The BVE Logger is a wireless timecode reader that attaches to the camera, or to the camera operator's belt. The logger can detect camera start and stops, for automatic logging of takes. The operator can add extra data at the push of a button. There is no keyboard for data entry as each of the entries have been predetermined prior to the shoot. The display on the front of the unit can indicate camera roll, scene, take, timecode start, timecode out, duration of take, time of day, date, user-bits, shot status, and labels. An addi-

**Figure 5-4** The BVE Logger unit. Courtesy of BVE.

tography, cameramen, and assistant cameramen. One company, dSam, Inc., produces an integrated circuit (IC) card that easily slips into Sharp and Wizard electronic organizers. These IC cards contain different applications on a surface smaller than a credit card. The variety of calculations available on the Cinematographer's IC Card is quite extensive and include:

## Color Control

Given the requirements for color temperature and the color temperature available in a specific lighting situation, the card calculates color temperature mired shift and lists suitable filters for both cameras and lights. Mired is an abbreviation for micro reciprocal degrees and is a system that is used to handle the conversions when it is necessary to adjust from one color temperature to another.

If the mired shift is greater than that which can be corrected by a single filter, the program will suggest additional filters for both camera and lighting. The program can also convert between Kelvin temperature and mired. A list of the colors of the light spectrum and their respective wavelength in nanometers is also available.

The program lists the CC filter when using fluorescent and high-discharge lighting schemes for use with both daylight and tungsten-balanced films. Once the CC filter is selected, the program also gives the exposure adjustment required for a specific filter, or for a set of filters. Since each filter reduces the amount of light that enters the lens, the exposure must be adjusted. When several filters are combined, the program calculates the total adjustment that is required and also calculates additive and subtractive colors by listing the resulting colors when primary colors are added and complementary colors are filtered out.

## Diopters

Given the diopter power length of a supplementary lens, the program on the card calculates the focal length. Or, given the focal length, it calculates the diopter power. It can calculate based on focal length and diopter, and when both values are known, it returns the combined focal length.

## Distances

Conversions can be done between feet and meters as well as the addition of distances to arrive at total dis-

tional five buttons have eight default attributes for automatic logging of the take. In addition, at the push of a button, an indication of whether the take was good, bad, or fair can be tagged to the clip. The default attributes can be changed via software running on an external computer to customize the logging to the particular style of shooting. Once the day's shoot is completed, the contents of the logger are exported into a master logging software program where all events and attributes are easily manipulated, sorted, and exported in several popular formats for importing into other database programs or DNLE systems.

Shown in figure 5-4 is the BVE Logger unit.

## HANDHELD ELECTRONIC TOOLS FOR CAMERA AND LIGHTING

Handheld electronic equipment that assists production issues is available and is used by directors of pho-

tance or to calculate triangulated distances when given the distance of any two sides of a triangle.

## DX Codes

DX codes are the manufacturer markings available on a film that automatically set the exposure index in the camera to match the film rating. These are found on rolls of 35mm still film used on the set to create backgrounds or for publicity stills. Given the exposure index, the calculator displays the DX coding for that film.

## Electricity

This capability is of great use to both the DP and the best boy. It can be of particularly great value when on location, and the electrical source is indigenous and does not offer the same precision control as that found on a sound stage. This portion of the program recalls previously set voltages, phases, maximum acceptable voltage drops, number of conductors, cable types, conductor materials, and maximum ambient temperatures, so that they need not be entered each time.

For comparative cable size it converts between AWG size, circular mile, inch, or millimeters. Given the material of the conductor, its size, length, the number and type of conductors, and the maximum ambient temperature, the program calculates the resistance of the conductor. It also rates the conductor current carrying capacity, given the cable material and size. Given the voltage, the maximum voltage drop in percent (%), the total load, the length of the cable run, the number of conductors and how they are arranged with the maximum ambient temperature, the program calculates the minimum cable size needed to carry that load. The total cross-sectional area can be calculated, given the number of strands and their diameter.

Once the conductor material, size, length, number of conductors, and how they are arranged along with the maximum ambient temperature and the maximum load are available, it calculates the anticipated voltage drop, the resistance, and the power loss. When given amps, or kVA (kilo × Volts × Amperes) or KW (kilo × Volts × Amperes), together with the volts, the number of phases and the power factor, it calculates the available power and the needed power to achieve that power output. Ohm's law is supported when any two selected factors selected from current, power, resistance, or voltage results in a calculation of the remaining two factors.

## Exposure

The factors that affect exposure include preset apertures, exposure times, frames per second and shutter angle, film speed, filter factor, light level, and ND filter (a neutral density filter which affects exposure level but not color value). Whenever any one of these factors is changed all others are recomputed by the card based on that change. Incident light and exposure levels are also calculated: given a standard light level, a standard aperture, and a new lens aperture it will compute a new light level. It also calculates the reverse: given a standard aperture, a standard light level, and a new light level, it computes the new aperture. Key light and fill light ratios are also calculated given the key plus fill light level. The level of the fill light alone is used in computing the lighting contrast ratio and difference in stops.

## Film Time, Length, and Timecode

The program automatically recalls the last settings of film gauge and frames per second so these data need not be entered each time. It also converts between feet plus frames to meters based on the film gauge being used. Given the number of feet or meters and film gauge, it can compute the estimated weight of the film in film cans, which will determine shipping costs.

This part of the program can compute film length, if given the diameter of the film type being used as well as the film type and the diameter of the core. The roll diameter can also be computed if all other parameters are present. Film running times are displayed in both minutes and seconds and in timecode format; the times are based on film gauge, length, and running speed; and the program will also total several entries into a cumulative running time.

Remaining running times are also computed based on total length of roll and full running time. A full timecode calculator is also available that will calculate "in" and "out" durations. The differences in percentages and frame change rates are also computed, and timecode values can also be expressed in total frame count. Frame counts are useful when shooting stop motion and animation.

## Focus

Perhaps the most important factor to a camera person and the focus puller is the depth-of-field (DOF) calculations. DOF refers to an area in front of and behind the main plane of focus where the subject can be captured as an image of acceptable sharpness. Depending on the blocking set forth by the director, the DOF will allow the focus puller to place appropriate markers on a lens and to judge the amount of focus needed to separate foreground from background.

Given the point of focus, the lens aperture, focal length, and lens type (fixed or zoom) and the circle of confusion, the card computes the near and far distances which will be in acceptable focus. Circle of confusion refers to the circumference of a point of light on the exposed film that is within acceptable focus. Acceptable sharpness, according to the American Society of Cinematographer's Manual, is calculated as a .001 inch image of a point (circle of confusion) for an image on 35mm film.

The hyperfocal distance is also computed, given the lens aperture, focal length, and the circle of confusion where the limit of the DOF will calculate to infinity. If a lens is at the hyperfocal distance, the DOF will be one-half the hyperfocal distance to infinity. Given the film gauge and format, the program calculates the image size, the diagonal, the area, and the aspect ratio of approximately 30 motion film and video, and film, video, and still video formats.

## Light

Light measurement conversions are computed between foot candles and the measure of light or lux (lumens/square meter). The program computes lamp beam width and distance, based on lamp brightness values and beam angle. This helps determine the number of lamps needed to cover an area of a set.

## Macro Photography

For close object focusing, given the object and image widths, the lens focal length and the exposure meter reading, the program computes the lens-to-subject distance, the lens extension required, the magnification, the corrected exposure, the overall depth of field, the optimum lens stop for maximum depth of field, and what the optimum exposure meter and maximum possible depth of field would be to achieve that stop.

## Speeds

If a certain shot must take a specific amount of time on screen, the program computes the camera frame rate and the number of film frames required to achieve that effect. It also calculates panning speeds at a normal 24 fps projection time for an object to clear the frame from one side of the frame to the other. In addition, when shooting a moving object, for example a car, the vehicle will appear to move faster when shot at a 90° angle than, say, a 45° angle. If the filmmaker wants the car to appear as if it is traveling at 30 mph, the program calculates the recommended speed for the vehicle when combined with an already chosen camera angle and focal length, given a playback of 24 fps.

This program is capable of calculating sunrise and sunset times given a choice of country and city or via latitude and longitude for true north and magnetic north. The sun's position can be learned when the geographic location, date, and local time are provided. Both magnetic and true north directions are given as well as the magnetic shadow direction as there is usually a difference of approximately 10° between the two.

These digital technologies are of great benefit to the DP, camera person, assistant camera person, and gaffer. These tools can assist in the more reliable creation of an image before that image is committed to negative. While digital technology is used for creating film databases, computers are also being used for many phases of production. One specific area is to enable the repeatability of camera moves for creating special visual effects shots and to facilitate integrating camera moves with digital imaging systems during the postproduction process.

## COMPUTERIZED CAMERA SYSTEMS

Recent developments in cameras have allowed filmmakers to begin a scene by shooting it at 24 fps and, midway through a take, change the filming speed to 48 fps, effectively sending the scene into slow motion. Further, the scene can progress and be returned to the normal 24 fps. Normally, this effect would have to be created during the postproduction stage.

There are a variety of camera manufacturers who supply equipment for filmmakers. Aaton, Arriflex, and Panavision cameras are shown in figures 5-5a–c. A great deal of work has gone into providing very sophisticated remote camera operations through computer control units (CCUs). These CCUs allow a filmmaker to make very specific camera operations occur at critical times. The Arriflex LCC, for laptop camera controller, is a software program that an assistant camera person uses to control the Arriflex 535 or

**Figure 5-5a** The Aaton 35mm film camera. Courtesy of AbelCineTech.

**Figure 5-5b** The Arriflex 535 35mm film camera. Courtesy of Arriflex Corporation.

16SR3 camera from a Macintosh Powerbook portable computer.

## Remote Camera Operations via Software

Some of the operational capabilities that can be controlled by a laptop computer are, in the case of the Arriflex LCC, multiple step speed/shutter programs, frame accurate rewinding or fast forwarding, and running the camera at the speed of 1 fps and at negative speeds from 3 to 30 fps. Informational capabilities include reading camera status, changing camera settings, making automated film inventory logs, and automated camera reports.

## Database Functions

Shown in figure 5-6 are screens from the Arriflex laptop camera controller software program. The upper

**Figure 5-5c** The Panavision Panaflex 35mm film camera. Courtesy of Panavision, Inc.

screen is the camera report database created for one roll of film. This report is normally handwritten. Note that all the essential pieces of information are present and viewable, such as: roll number, emulsion type, printing notes, film stock count, and scene/take comments. There are additional tools for seeing all the received, available, and exposed film logs so that all film that passes through the camera person's hands can be accurately accounted for.

## Software-based Camera Operation

Also shown in figure 5-6 is the edit program window of an Arriflex laptop camera controller. This function allows the filmmaker to precisely control when certain functions of a camera should occur. Notice in the graph that in 68 seconds the camera will go from operating at 50.00 fps to 6.25 fps and that the camera shutter will change from 180 degrees to 22.5 degrees. Note that there are also intermediate positions; for example, at approximately 21 seconds, the camera will be operating at 25.00 fps with a shutter of 90 degrees. Precise operation such as this can be very helpful in creating a shot that requires many different changes in speed and shutter. It is also helpful in providing the resulting screen time that the shot would consume when finally running at 24 fps.

## Integrating and Sharing Information

The ability for a camera to be controlled via computer, the storing of information about what the camera is doing, and the database being created are essential pieces of information to be used in other aspects of the digital filmmaking process. For example, since the camera can be controlled through a software program, precise filming speeds can be dictated by the speed at which characters in a computer-generated environment are meant to interact with a live action figure. Consider if we have computer-generated characters whose movements are meant to be exactly 24 fps, but at one stage they begin to jump up and down at 48 fps, slowing down their actions by a factor of two. We may want to rehearse what it would look like if our actor, being shot on blue screen, were to interact with the characters at precisely the same moment and at the same speed. By creating a time plot for the camera operation—a time plot that is linked to the computer animation—we could see the results of this real-time composite through the use of a camera video tap and an electronic video switcher.

By importing the database from the camera report into the digital, nonlinear editing system, the editor no longer needs to search through camera reports to find a piece of information that is desperately required.

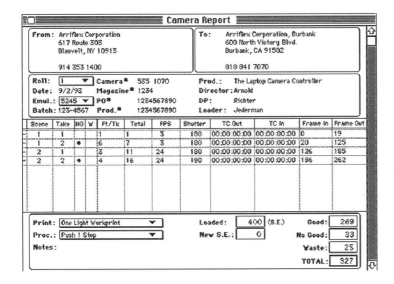

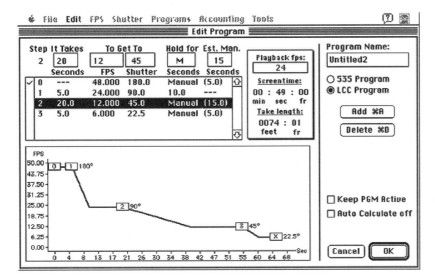

**Figure 5-6** The camera report database and the edit program window from the Arriflex laptop camera controller software program. Courtesy of Arriflex Corporation.

## COMPUTERIZED MOTION-CONTROL

Computerized motion-control refers to the ability of a camera to perform repeatable movements. There are many reasons why this capability is desirable and necessary. Whenever a filmmaker must create a composite shot that contains many elements, it is necessary to devise some way to ensure that each element can be shot in exactly the same fashion. Consider the visual effects shot that shows a spaceship traveling through a series of asteroids. There may be many elements to this shot. There would first be the background shot, and then the model of the ship would be photographed. There may be another pass where the lights of the ship are illuminated. Next, there may be a pass where ambient light passes along the ship. Regardless of the amount of layers, it is necessary that each photographic pass be made exactly as the previous pass to ensure that the elements line up accordingly.

Another example where computerized motion-control is critical is for scenes that involve one actor playing two roles while both are simultaneously on screen. In the past, these shots were quite static with a camera being locked off—first the actor stood on one side of the screen and then stood on the other side. Motion-controlled photography has enabled the camera to move, allowing the director to follow a character and then to repeat the same move while the actor, as a different character, follows the first character. Being able to move the camera and to exactly re-create every movement of the camera has been a great liberator in the creativity that filmmakers can now enjoy when considering a motion-control shot.

Motion-control systems have been used since the 1920s and enabled multiple-pass photography where an action would be photographed, the film would be wound back, and another action would be photographed on the same piece of film. Modern motion-control systems are comprised of several items. First, there is a motion-control rig, along which the camera moves (figure 5-7). The guide rails and boom arm that suspend the camera are responsible for movements such as panning, tilting, dollying, booming, and tracking. Second, there are the camera head controls which control items such as camera rotation, tilt, pan, focus, and zoom. Last, there may be computerized control over peripheral elements. These

other elements could be lighting setups which turn on lights at specific frames in a shot's duration, an operation which heretofore would have had to rely on a grip trying to move and match a lighting effect at the precise moment on each take! Other elements could also be the actual items being photographed, such as robotic elements that must behave in the same fashion time after time.

The result of such a setup is repeatable control in X, Y, Z axes. Each component is then processed by various motor drivers, either micro stepper motors or DC servo motors. The data that is created by these motors is captured and stored in a computer. Thus, for every film take, there is a corresponding data file. If a human operates the camera controls, hand cranks connected to encoders are used and pass data to the computer, and the movements that were made are stored as information that the computer will use to create a fully automated camera movement.

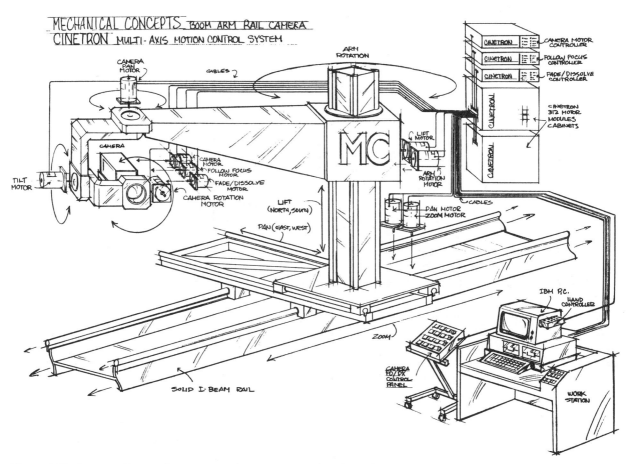

**Figure 5-7** Design and layout of a motion-control setup. Courtesy of Mechanical Concepts, Inc.

In David Cronenberg's *Dead Ringers* (1988), motion-control photography was used to allow actor Jeremy Irons to simultaneously play dual roles. By filming a take and then having the computer recall the data file for that take, repeated camera movements were possible. It then became a matter of filming the A side of a shot, loading the data file, and then filming the B side, with Irons playing the role of the second character. Further, by using an electronic video switcher, director Cronenberg could see the resulting interaction between the two characters. Shown in figure 5-8 is a video split-screen showing the two sides of a motion-control shot from *Dead Ringers*. The resulting composited image is shown in figure 5-8.

**Figure 5-8** A video split-screen showing the two sides of a motion-control shot from *Dead Ringers*. Courtesy of Balsmeyer & Everett/Syzygy Digital Cinema. The composited image as a result of using motion-control photography.

## Motion Control and Digital Compositing

Motion-control photography and the use of motion control are undergoing rapid change. The need for motion control is diminishing in light of the rapidly evolving combination of computer-based motion tracking and digital compositing. Whereas a model would normally be filmed several times in order to generate several different pieces of film, and then be optically composited, digital technology is being used to replace these traditional methods. In recent years, filmmakers working in the area of special visual effects have found that tracking backgrounds and performing digital rotoscoping have provided a successful alternative to motion-control photography.

A basic example is a visual effect that requires that an actor be placed in a computer environment with movement defined by a camera. This is a combination of live action and computer-generated 3-D animation. Typically, the live action of the actor would be shot, and the actor would be given visual clues as to the layout of the environment that will be computer-generated. These clues also act as plot points for X,Y, Z axes.

Next, a scale relationship is made between the live action stage and the computer environment to be created. As the motion-control camera provides data for each and every frame in the form of simple ASCII text, the result is a camera move that the computer can map. Whether the item being photographed or created is in a studio or in a computer, there is no doubt as to where an object is in relation to X,Y, Z axes and rotational space. The result is a 3-D model which is coordinated to the camera move.

For the digital filmmaker, after shooting the live action element, in this case the actor against a blue screen, the next stage is to design the 3-D computer environment by importing the data as to where the actor is in X,Y, Z space. Next, mattes are pulled from the live action blue screen and compositing is done digitally. A multi-layered composite effect can be created with all the elements tracking the original blue-screen shot. Finally, the composite is recorded from the digital disks back to film and is projected.

## Starting in the Computer

It is also possible for work to begin in the computer. In this case, an environment is created and the movement through the environment is accomplished in

3-D. These data files are then imported into the computer that runs the motion-control system. The result is a camera move that matches the motion path of the 3-D environment. The ability to precisely trigger camera movement or other devices that are slaved to the camera, has been easier to accomplish with advances in film cameras that are capable of reading and generating timecode. For example, a camera's movements could be dictated by an external controller unit running timecode, or a computer could be instructed by a camera to play a file. One possible result is that a composite effect could be rehearsed in real time on the stage.

The integration of digital techniques within motion-control photography has created new ways of combining elements. These new methods form the link between traditional motion picture photography, and digital environment and creature creation. The result is further control over the motion paths of various objects in the frame, and a greater degree of quality as made possible by digital compositing methods.

## INDUSTRY VIEWPOINTS

### Randall Balsmeyer—Designer, Balsmeyer & Everett, Inc./Syzygy Digital Cinema

Film audiences have experienced a great deal of motion-control photography over the last decade, and in so doing have likely witnessed the artistry of Randall Balsmeyer, an accomplished filmmaker and visual effects designer. Balsmeyer, who has created visual effects, digital title sequences, and motion-control shots in films such as *The Hudsucker Proxy* (1993), *Sleepless In Seattle* (1993), *Ghost* (1990), and *Dead Ringers* (1988) has a long history of traditional motion-control methods along with a new emphasis on combining live action, 3-D animation, and digital compositing to ensure that filmmakers have as much flexibility as possible during the production stage. Says Balsmeyer,

Directors typically don't want anything to interfere with or hinder their options. And a director likes to reserve the right to change his or her mind. They don't necessarily want to think about the technical items—although some directors have a good grasp of what needs to happen technically—and we now have

tools that allow for more flexibility, especially in letting a director move the camera within a shot.

When we worked on *Dead Ringers* (1988), the director, David Cronenberg, wanted to be able to shoot the movie as if he really had two actors who were interacting with one another. By using motion-control, we were able to have the camera move which lent believability to the story. For the "twinning shots," we would first shoot the A side of a twinned shot and we would play back, on video, each take for David. He would pick the take that he liked best and we would call up the computer file that had the motion-control move. We then shot the B side and, using a video switcher, we would show David the A and B shots composited together using a follow-wipe. The result was that he could watch the action "live," as the actor performed, as well as on video playback.

Most people, when they think about motion-control think about using it only for twinning, and I think the best examples of twinning are in the *Back To The Future* series by Industrial Light and Magic. For *Ghost* (1989), we did the motion-control shots for the scene where Patrick Swayze tries to stop the criminal from hurting Demi Moore and passes through the actor. This was created by combining the two film elements and carefully coordinating the actor who plays the criminal.

Balsmeyer, who has experienced the manner in which the increased use of digital technology has changed the nature of motion-control photography, has begun to employ a vast array of computer technology in creating visual effects and title sequences in films as varied as *Crooklyn* (1994), *M. Butterfly* (1993), and *Fresh* (1993). Continues Balsmeyer,

Ten years ago you would have used matte paintings to create the types of composites that we are digitally creating today. When combining live action and 3-D animation, you'll have your live action shot which has witness points in it—something that you can see very clearly in the shot and in the area that is going to be replaced; something precise and measurable that you can track. And now you'll have a computer generated background that now has to track digitally with the live action. Before, it was a very tedious process, but now you can see the composite in real or close to real time. Of course, you still have to line up the shots and make sure the pieces track together correctly.

It is this motion-control–CGI connection that Balsmeyer points out as being representative of how the traditional motion-control techniques are being redefined by digital technology:

> My partner in Syzygy, Michael Arias, has worked out a method whereby moves can originate in either the real world (motion-control/motion capture) or the digital world (3-D computer animation) and be transparently ported to the other, so that characters, objects, and environments can be seamlessly combined. A very simple example of this is when you see a logo where the follow focus on a live action hand is duplicated in a CG background.
>
> Most of the time you aspire to not having anyone notice what you are doing—you are trying to accomplish something that you would have shot in real life. When we create these shots, we are trying to be invisible. Of course, every once in a while, you want to do a "show off" shot, where you are calling attention to the effect. Such a shot is found in *Dead Ringers* where the camera moves down the clinic hallway, watching the twins through a series of doors.

## Tracking the Environment

If a film is being shot on location, it is very important that the crew know exactly where the natural lighting of the sun will be at specific moments of the day. By utilizing equipment such as the Global Positioning Satellite (GPS), a DP can tell a director that a scene must be shot by noon as the sun will be in a prime location for the shot. In addition, a director may ask the DP what time the sun will be in a certain position in order to shoot a scene that has certain shadows. By using a system such as the GPS, the DP is able to determine exactly when the sun will be in the desired position.

## SOUND ON SET

Sound is captured on set using analog equipment such as a Nagra or another tape system that is in crystal or pilot tone sync with the camera. The quality of these recordings is very high and tape manufacturing and sound enhancing techniques have prolonged the use of analog recording. Timecode has been added to the sound equipment to allow easier syncing of sound and picture, and to more easily conform the original sound elements after the editing process is complete.

## Recording on DAT

The use of DAT, digital audio tape, for on-location recording has grown in recent years, primarily as a backup to the traditional Nagra. As with any new technology, it will take some time before DAT or another digital audio recording technology has proven its reliability and is used in place of the traditional analog recorders. DAT offers some distinct advantages over analog systems, primarily in sound quality, size, recording time, and portability.

DAT sound is 48 KHz, superior to even the audio compact disc, and has no tape hiss associated with it, so that even the softest sounds can be recorded without fear of hitting the "floor" of analog tape. Where DAT does suffer is in the area of "headroom." If a sound becomes too loud and peaks, the recording will be nothing but hiss and cracks. Analog is much more forgiving when dealing with headroom. But as technology advances, these drawbacks are being eliminated and Nagra currently markets a digital Nagra that is four-track (DAT has just two tracks), has 20-bit sampling instead of the more common 16-bit sampling, and provides headroom in a digital format. DAT tapes can have recording times of up to two hours in a tape size that easily fits into a shirt pocket. Headroom is overcome by sending the audio signal to both channels of the DAT where one of the channels is set 10 dB lower than the other channel; if one channel is overwhelmed, the other can be used to compensate.

Portable DAT machines are also capable of recording in several timecode formats, making them very stable for sync recordings. Once the audio signal is digital, transfer from the original reels to the editing system and throughout the post-process can be accomplished with no generational loss, as all transfers are accomplished via the AES/EBU protocol.

## Digitizing on the Set

Methods of postproduction are becoming more prevalent during production. The most obvious trend is to begin the editing process on the set. Video taps, which provide a video signal from a film camera, have been available for some years and video playback can be quickly reviewed on the set. While this accelerates the dailies screening, it still does not allow a director to clearly see continuity and pace.

New video taps introduced by camera manufacturers that allow the capture of only the real film frames from the 30 frame video signal are a significant development. This is accomplished by the insertion of a white flag into the vertical interval of the picture signal. A white flag is a single line of 100% white across the entire width of the picture. This white line is usually inserted somewhere between lines 10 and 20 of the video frame. The white flag is created when the shutter is closed and the film frame is being advanced. During this time, the light from the lens is being diverted to the video tap and to the viewfinder. As the shutter turns, a white flag is inserted into the picture. At sound speed, there will be 24 white flags for each second. Since the film frames are at 24 fps, and the video signal is at 29.97 fps, there will be a "beating" of the image since there isn't an even ratio between film rate and video rate. The telecine creates an even relationship by reducing the film rate by the same ratio of 0.01% to 29.97, thus playing film at 23.976 fps. Since this is not possible in the video tap, this uneven adjustment of the film speed to video speed appears as a flicker in the picture.

When an in-camera timecode is used, each white flag is tagged with a SMPTE 24 frame timecode. This timecode can now be used throughout postproduction, for identification of the exact film frame, and for syncing sound during the telecine process.

By digitizing picture and sound on the set, an editor can assemble the takes into a rough cut of the sequence. The director can quickly review a specific take as it is edited into the sequence and determine that extra takes are either necessary or unnecessary. Also, if the production unit is leaving a location and the dailies will not be available until after the move, the director can avoid having to return in order to shoot pick-up shots. Instead, by viewing a version of the scene, the editor and director may already have established that an extra shot such as a close-up or an establishing shot is not needed. Another savings is that the audio being digitized on the set does not need to be redigitized for the video dailies. It does not even have to be synced during the film to tape transfer. The transfer can be done MOS and the DNLE system can sync the telecined picture back to the original audio already digitized on set. This syncing is based on the common timecode between the negative and the sound elements. MOS transfers of negative are considerably cheaper and faster.

**Figure 5-9** Photo of Edmund M. DiGiulio. Courtesy of Edmund M. DiGiulio.

## INDUSTRY VIEWPOINTS

### Edmund M. DiGiulio—Founder, Vice-Chairman, Director of Research and Development, Cinema Products Corporation

Before founding Cinema Products in 1968, Ed DiGiulio was vice-president of Mitchell Camera Corporation. Prior to Mitchell, he applied his inventive talent to the development of the Craig Reader, a teaching machine that involved him in film and optics research. This activity brought him into the motion picture industry via his post at Mitchell, and from there to the founding of Cinema Products.

DiGiulio has always been at the forefront of camera design and engineering. Perhaps the award that has gained the most attention from the motion picture industry was the Class 1 award for the invention and development of the Steadicam. For their invention and development of the Steadicam system, the Academy Award in 1978 went to inventor Garrett Brown, DiGiulio, and to the Cinema Products engineering staff.

As befits DiGiulio's interests in engineering, one current project is the Vidiflex (with Ron Goodman of

Spacecam Systems)—a video viewing system which replaces the traditional ground glass optics with a tapered fiber bundle. According to the Vidiflex viewing system technical document, the conventional ground glass is replaced by a coherent fiber optic bundle in which the front face is at the reflex image plane, and the bundle tapers down to a rear face the size of the imaging surface of a high-resolution CCD chip camera. These cameras are reflexed using a thin (.010″) beam split mirror, or pellicle, fixed in position at 45° between the taking lens and the film plane. Says DiGuilio,

> A further benefit from pellicle reflexing is that video record can be phase-synchronized with film record. Due to the spinning mirror, the video record is always 180° out of phase with the film and this is annoying to editors.

DiGuilio states that the device could be utilized on multicamera film-based shows.

> Not only would the color image provide the studio audience with a more pleasing presentation, but more importantly, an image that could be fed directly to a video offline editing system. With the quality of color image produced by the Vidiflex system, the editor has the confidence to make a final edited tape version while the film is being processed and before it is transferred to videotape. This would result in a tremendous savings in time and money. Negative would be cut to conform directly with the video edited version and only that film would need to go through the telecine process for final video release.

This technology is also applicable to feature film work. DiGuilio continues,

> By using timecode in the film cameras, you could take the imagery and feed it directly to a digital, non-linear editing system and have a rough cut even before the negative is processed, which would allow you to save time by transferring only the good takes.

DiGiulio is a member of the Academy of Motion Picture Arts and Sciences and currently serves as Chairman of its Scientific and Technical Awards Committee.

## PREVISUALIZING ON SET

On set, the director and editor can preview many optical effects during shooting, especially for shots involving special effects such as blue screens. Let's imagine that the special effects crew has already created the background for a fifteenth century castle. The knight in faded armor needs to run up to the front gates and jump off the edge of the drawbridge. The special effects crew provides the blue screen shot of the actor to the editor and the shot is then digitized into the DNLE system. As each take is shot, it can be keyed in place over the background castle element and checked to see if both timing and placement are correct. If the shot doesn't precisely work, there are other tools that the editor can use such as flop, image re-size, and cropping. Other effects such as superimposition, matte keys, and title sequences can be previewed as the intended shots are being photographed. Such immediate feedback about how the shot will look in context with other shots has never before been available to the filmmaker.

Once the original negative is developed and processed, the new picture dailies, using their keynumber references, can now be linked to the sequence that was edited on the set. This is done based on the 24 frame timecode that was generated and exposed onto the negative on a per-frame basis.

As the negative and sound elements move through the postproduction process, additional database information is introduced. The database started with just the information that was available for the picture and sound elements from the shoot on location, being a 24 frame timecode on the negative, and sound timecode on the 1/4″ reels of DAT. During the telecine process, the corresponding keynumber was added to the database, which could also include film timecode, sound timecode (the same as film timecode but interpolated to a 30 frame and not a 24 frame count), and the videotape timecode of the dailies tape. If a playback timecode was used, as in the case of a musical sequence, this code can also become an entry in the database. Other data that already exists from the continuity person's database, or from the on-set digitizing system, can then be merged into this database—items such as the different camera, sound, and continuity reports. Add to this timing lite information, comments, and descriptions, and the database becomes quite a powerful tool. It can be viewed in different modes depending on the information desired. In essence, this database becomes the master log book, accessible to all.

**Figure 5-10** Photo of Tony Westman. Courtesy of Tony Westman.

## INDUSTRY VIEWPOINTS

### Tony Westman, CSC—Director of Photography

Director of Photography: *Horseman* (1994), *Needful Things* (1993), *Personal: Evelyn Lau's Diary* (1993). Director and Director of Photography: *Charlton Heston Presents The Bible* (1992).

For Director of Photography Tony Westman, the use of digital filmmaking methods has influenced his vast repertoire of traditional cinematographic skills. Westman, who has photographed feature films, documentaries, and television shows, comments on the myriad ways that the director of photography is increasingly making use of the tools that digital filmmaking provides. Says Westman,

> The opening of the film that I am working on, *Avalanche* (Fox) has a scene which shows a plane crashing into the side of a mountain. This sets off an avalanche which sets the stage for the story. The producers took a traditional view of approaching how the scene would be filmed—by creating models and miniatures, blue-screen work, and using methods which would be very complicated and expensive to

pull off. We did not have the time nor the budget to approach the scene in the traditional filmic way.

> So you start to draw upon your experience of what's possible using digital compositing. I found myself providing a proposal for the producers—where we would use digital compositing instead of creating conventional models—effectively finding a way to crash the plane into the mountain by using the computer. We went up and shot aerials, some explosions in miniature, and a crash site in the mountains, and we sat in a small dark room and started to put the pieces together in the computer and we got a very effective plane crash. By compositing fly bys and background plates, we wound up with a sequence where you see the fuselage break apart, a huge explosion, and blowing snow. To put this composite sequence together cost about $5,000 as opposed to $50,000 for 3-D animation or $500,000 to $5 million for mechanical models and miniature mountain landscapes.

> The scene was so effectively done that the producers were very pleased with how it worked out. If I hadn't had the experience of what's possible with digital technology, I would never have known what the options were to the traditional way of shooting a scene like this on the budget we had. The funny part is that when we made the presentation to the client, they complained that the real airplane looked phony, while the composite (fake) crash looked real!

For Westman, the use of digital filmmaking methods is further defining his craft as a cinematographer. He continues,

> You start to combine the known camera techniques and tricks and what you can control in traditional photography with how you can use digital to change or augment the reality you captured. Now, I have got a whole array of tools and a list of experts that I can call upon. It gives you a whole new sense of authority on making an image that is not all a photographic image—it becomes a combination of techniques.

As eager as Westman is to praise the use of digital technology in creating motion pictures, he cautions that the artist must not rely solely on the capabilities of digital and electronic equipment. Says Westman,

> Normally the last thing you'll do for a film is to time the picture, and six points is a stop in terms of light values. But the power in a digital color correction system is astounding. If I'm printing film and I want my printer lights to be at 29, 30, 34, etc., I know that every single day of rushes is going to come out looking the same. But with digital and electronics, you

may see a little bit of difference from day to day—there are different knobs, settings, electrical loads—so you can't rely on a machine—it's your own brain and eyes that tell you if you are on the right track.

Westman recounts the use of digital, nonlinear editing during the production of *Needful Things* as a particularly useful approach that assisted the filmmakers in exploring options during the shooting stage:

> We used a digital, nonlinear editing system on *Needful Things* and we had 40 hours of rushes that were live access and we are rearranging three versions of a scene and the power to explore options was very powerful. When we started the film, we began to plan how we would apply the nonlinear approach to a large feature film. By cutting at 24 fps and tracking edgenumbers, we were able to assemble the workprint and do a screening. And we never touched the negative and instead it became a lovely hand-in-hand marriage. We screened the workprint once and it looked wonderful because it had not been touched except for the assembly.

Perhaps the most telling episode Westman relates in terms of the capabilities of digital filmmaking methods to be used simultaneously with the filmmaking process is evident in planning and executing the film's conclusion. Continues Westman,

> Fraser Heston, the director, Rob Kobrin, the editor, and I worked through all the ideas for the end of the film. We had a very complicated scene which required us to blow up the town and we had to answer the question, "How are we going to unravel it?" So we would go up and see Rob's assembly of the scene as it had thus far been shot. Since he had been editing while we were shooting, we could see how things were working up to this point. And the use of digital editing and having options was so important on this film.
>
> Because there we are—we had already blown up the town and we have smoldering ruins and people are lying around with injuries and we have reached the definitive end of the movie. We had been night shooting for two-and-a-half months and Rob's been assembling and editing—so we have a very clear sense of the characters—their fears, their battles—and we look at each other and say, "The ending that is written is not going to work."
>
> Because we had the opportunity to edit so quickly and see how all the scenes were developing, Fraser and I could step out of it and we decided that

we had to film a different ending—which is not something that you take lightly. That's a difficult thing to decide when you have a producer who is wondering why you just can't go with what's in the script. But the ending that is in the movie works—which is where Max Von Sydow as the Devil gets into his car and the car de-materializes. The original ending as written did not take into account what happened once the actors took the characters and made them real characters—they became different from what was on the page. But Rob had cut a sharp and polished piece, not just a rough assembly . . . complete with step frame optical effects that he had generated in his Avid. So we could really tell what was going to work because we were seeing the movie and all the interactions among the characters.

> The power of these digital editing tools helped give us the insight . . . and the confidence, to successfully deal with the abstractions of the filmmaking process.

## INDUSTRY VIEWPOINTS

### Walter Murch, A.C.E—Editor, Sound Designer

*The Conversation* (1974), *Julia* (1977), *Apocalypse Now* (1979), *Ghost* (1990).

For Walter Murch, A.C.E., winner of an Oscar from the Academy of Motion Picture Arts and Sciences for best sound for 1979's *Apocalypse Now,* the use of digital technologies has always been tempered by a desire to create the best possible treatment for a film. Says Murch,

> Any new introduction of technology is a point of departure and whether it's Eastman Kodak with a new type of film or Lightworks or Avid in nonlinear editing systems, they all enter the marketplace under the camouflage of saving time. But, in fact, once you start to use them, that explanation becomes irrelevant—all the technologies allow you to delay the irrevocable time and moment of commitment, at which point it becomes very difficult to make changes.
>
> For example, I was reading a biography on (filmmaker) Jean Renoir where he detailed one film he made. He wrote the film in a week, shot it in a week, and edited it in a week, and three weeks later it was in the theaters making money. Today, there is a tendency to squeeze postproduction time. One of the focuses that we had at American Zoetrope was to get more time for postproduction and we structured the

time in postproduction in order to afford more creativity.

Editor Murch points out the growing pains that are apparent when traditional film postproduction and digital postproduction methodologies merge. Continues Murch,

> There are great benefits to using digital editing. For example, I used a digital, nonlinear editing system to create a five level montage of images in a four minute sequence in *I Love Trouble* (1994). I took the video output and we showed it to the director and producer. We discussed the changes that they had and we quickly fixed it. . . .

The main thing is not to use digital for the sake of being digital. When zoom lenses appeared, people began using them gratuitously, and a zoom lens should only be used in specific instances. There are things that you learn from the mechanical side of filmmaking that the digital tools have not yet provided to me. For example, I've learned a tremendous amount when I'm editing from watching the film going through the head backwards at five times speed rather than at 24 fps, just seeing the film going back, and hearing the pacing. You deny yourself that on a digital system because you can get from one point to another instantly and you may not have the opportunity to think about some decisions that you need to make while the film is running backwards.

# Postproduction

# 6

# The Traditional Filmmaking Postproduction Process

Digital filmmaking techniques are changing the methods by which the laboratory prepares film for the postproduction process. In later chapters, we will explore in depth the areas of digital, nonlinear editing for picture and sound, digital video compression, and the transmission of a scene from one editing system to a viewing station thousands of miles away. However, now it is beneficial to describe the traditional filmmaking postproduction routines—the manner in which films are put together, screened, changed, and released. Only by being exposed to this history can we ascertain just how significant an impact digital filmmaking methods will have on postproducing a film. What follows then is a very basic, but thorough explanation of the traditional filmmaking postproduction process.

## DIFFERENT FILM CATEGORIES

As we know, there are feature films, documentaries, animated films, and so forth. Overall, how a film is put together and delivered is the same regardless of the type of film being made. There are obvious differences along the postproduction route—one example is in the form of changes. For the feature film that must be previewed before an audience, it may be necessary to make changes. For the documentary film, the process of previewing the film and making changes based on audience reactions is extremely rare.

## A HISTORY OF IMAGE AND SOUND EDITING

Given the history of film editing, the incorporation of digital techniques for picture and sound editing is extremely recent. This chart shows editing chronology:

| | |
|---|---|
| Film Editing | c. 1900 |
| Analog Audiotape Editing | c. 1945 |
| Videotape Editing | 1956 |
| Videotape Editing with Timecode | 1970 |
| Digital Disk-based Audio Editing | 1985 |
| Digital Disk-based Picture Editing | c. 1989 |

As the chart shows, digital disk-based audio and picture editing are relatively new techniques. For almost 100 years, film editing and the film editorial process have been the quintessential low-tech method of completing a film, basically using scissors and glue or splicing tape.

## Standards

Film, running in a film projector at 24 frames per second, is a unique standard in a world where standards are often difficult to achieve. A feature film or a documentary can be shipped to any country and played on a projector without any special modifications. True enough, if the film offers multi-track digital sound, a specific theater may not be equipped to take advantage of this capability; however, the pictures will play back and analog soundtracks will be used.

The issues of standard formats and display areas are classical areas of difference between delivering a program on film or on videotape. There are various film gauges such as 35mm four-perf (perforations per frame), 35mm three-perf, 16mm, Super 16mm, even Super 8mm. There are also different ways of utilizing the display area of the film frame, such as using 35mm four-perf film in Academy, Cinemascope, or Super-35mm format. Regardless, it is the 35mm four-perf Academy format film that has become the standard of projection across the world. This unique advantage ensures that the product created by one filmmaker in Los Angeles, California can be played on a projector in Bombay, India or in Rome, Italy. This country to country interchangeability that film enjoys is not experienced by videotape.

There are many different types of videotape formats, such as 3/4″ Umatic, 1″ Type C, MII, Betacam, Betacam SP, D1, D2, D3, D5, Digital Betacam, DCT, and formats which tread a line between consumer use and professional use—VHS, Hi 8, and S-VHS. A dizzying array of new videotape formats are introduced each year. Which format to invest in is a difficult and frustrating decision for many facility owners and program creators.

There are also different display methods for video. Some countries display video at NTSC (National Television Standards Committee) rates of 29.97 fps, 60 Hz, with an interlaced scan of 525 lines; other countries utilize PAL (phase alternate line) rates of 25 fps, 50 Hz, scanned at 625 lines (or in some cases, 525 lines). A film-originated program that has been transferred to NTSC videotape cannot be played on a PAL television. Along with NTSC, PAL, and a SECAM (*séquential couleur à mémoire*; used primarily in Eastern Europe and France), there are new display formats such as High-Definition Television (HDTV).

Faced with these decisions, it is no wonder that program makers have relied on originating on film and transferring the completed film to the videotape format of choice, in the display format endemic to a particular country. The importance that a foreign market has to a film's earning potential requires that the distribution medium be easily transportable and displayable. Film offers this, videotape does not, and it remains to be seen whether a digital medium can compete with film on this issue.

## Standard Practices

Standard practices have developed within the film postproduction process. In general, the manner in which a film is finished is the same from country to country. The actual equipment and personal tastes and techniques may differ, but the gross processes of how film is developed, workprinted, synchronized, edited, screened, changed, and finalized are remarkably similar around the world. Contrast this to the world of videotape editing, where the capabilities of one editing room can be greatly different than another room.

Given this history, there has been no great impetus for filmmakers to change the way they go about postproducing a film. This is changing as digital filmmaking techniques enter and permeate the postproduction process; a redefining of these principles and methods will be necessary. Just what will be the responsibilities of the assistant editor? How will the responsibilities of the optical house change, now that a computer disk and not a film workprint are delivered? Large scale changes are taking place in the areas of defining responsibilities given the long history of film postproduction.

## THE TRADITIONAL FILMMAKING PROCESS

### On-location or In-studio

Let's assume we are shooting 35mm four-perf film. A roll of film is loaded into the film camera and these camera rolls are usually ten minutes in duration when running at 24 fps. Sound for the film is recorded on a separate 1/4″, reel-to-reel audio tape recorder. While there are different types of recorders, the most common is the Nagra. By utilizing two different systems, one for recording picture and one for recording sound, film shooting is often called a dual-system approach.

### Processing the Film

Each day, when shooting has been completed, all of the exposed camera rolls are taken to the film laboratory for processing. This may be a lab in the same city or in an entirely different country. It is now routine procedure to shoot a film on location, say, in Eastern Europe, to process the film in London, and to edit the film in Los Angeles. This division of tasks will become far more prevalent when it is digital data moving over communications lines and not film cans being delivered by overnight airline carriers.

Continuing, the exposed negative is processed, and then a positive, or workprint, is created. It remains to the filmmaker to decide if all of the negative will be workprinted and this decision depends upon the sheer amount of film being shot. Most often, less film is printed than was shot. Only in the case of an extremely small shooting ratio will all the film be workprinted. A guideline for the average shooting ratio for a feature film in the $10–13 million dollar range (the budget for a feature film considered to be average in Hollywood terms is approximately $18 million) will be approximately 20:1. This ratio refers to the amount of film shot to the amount of film used in the final presentation. A two hour film will have forty hours of original material.

Of course, there are many exceptions. Some two hour films with tiny budgets will have been shot with one or two takes yielding a 2–3:1 ratio. For these films, perhaps all of the film will be workprinted. Other films, involving scenes covered with multiple cameras and intricately choreographed action sequences, could have a million or more feet of film. If from the million feet, the filmmakers choose to print 500,000 feet, the editor still has a staggering ratio of 454:1 to wade through as the final two hour movie will only consist of about 11,000 feet of film!

To conserve time and expense, the takes that the director wants workprinted are usually referred to as circled takes. These takes are noted, commented, logged, and this log is used by the lab so that the proper portions of the film negative are printed. The quality of the print is minimal, since this workprint will be physically handled, cut, and recut. The critical film timing stage occurs much later where attention to picture quality is of major importance. The original camera negative is stored under appropriate environmental conditions, and will not be utilized (unless another print is required) until the time arrives for the negative to be actually cut and assembled together.

Thus far, our film has been shot, developed, and transferred to positive, yielding a workprint. This workprint can be in either color or black-and-white; budgets may require that less expensive black-and-white film be used for the workprint.

## Transferring the Sound

The next stage is to put the sound into a proper format for editing. In the same way that the original film negative is not used for editing, the original audio recordings are first transferred to another format and then stored away. Each of the 1/4″ reel-to-reel audio tapes is transferred to 35mm magnetic track (mag track). Since 35mm film editing requires that picture

and sound ultimately be edited together, sound must exist in the same format as the workprint. Each circled take for picture yields the corresponding circled take for audio. These audio takes are then transferred to 35mm mag track (figure 6-1).

Note that there are various forms of sprocketed film for sound work. Single stripe contains a single sound channel while full coat track stock is completely coded for multiple sound channels.

There are also various logs, such as the script supervisor's log, camera reports, and sound transfer reports. On a feature film, one with hundreds of thousands of feet of film, wild track audio (audio that was not captured at the same time that the picture was captured) arrives on 1/4″ and is transferred to mag track. At any moment, the editor may require a very specific wild track, and it is left to the assistant editor to locate the material as quickly as possible. Absolutely essential to the filmmaking process is meticulous record keeping. One of the great promises of digital filmmaking is that the computer provides the ability to create and maintain large databases of information which can be quickly sorted, sifted, and cross-referenced.

## Synchronizing and Viewing Dailies

Thus far, we have solved the first problem: picture and sound now exist on the same media type, sprock-

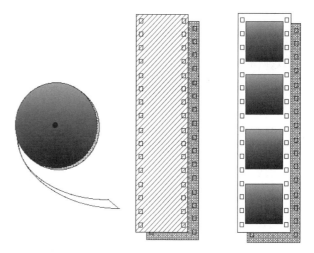

**Figure 6-1** The quarter-inch sound roll is first transferred to 35mm magnetic track. This magnetic sound track is then combined with the 35mm picture track. Picture and sound now exist in the same 35mm format, and editing can begin. Illustration by Jeffrey Krebs.

eted 35mm film and sprocketed 35mm mag track. Dailies are viewed and editing begins. Using a chinagraph (china) marker, each take is located on the mag track, and a mark is made at the sound of the striking clapsticks. The printed takes, also called dailies (or one-lites) are marked with an X at the visual point of the clapsticks hitting.

These marks provide the references to synchronize, or sync, the soundtrack to the picture. By lining up both reference points for picture and sound, both 35mm pieces are in sync. If we watch an actor delivering lines, we will see and hear perfect synchronization. Great fanfare is given to the watching of dailies and this ritual is usually done at scheduled daily times during the course of shooting. Who attends dailies is open to review, but typically the director, editor, and producer will screen dailies. It is important to judge how new material looks on film and how it will affect previous material.

## Identification Numbers

As we begin the process of editing the film, we are editing workprint and this is a disposable form which is used as a guideline to match the original film negative. For this reason, there must exist some correlation between the film workprint and the original negative. Traditionally this was done by punching a hole in a common frame between the workprint and negative; lined up in parallel, each roll would share a similar starting point and be of a similar length.

Thirty-five millimeter film contains identifying codes spaced at constant intervals. These are edgenumbers, and they are essential in being able to describe, numerically, what frames are being used in the project (figure 6-2). These edgenumbers are on the latent film negative. When a print is made from the negative, the corresponding and exact numbers from the negative print through to the workprint. These numbers become extremely important for digital filmmaking because a workprint may not be made. In that case, the digital editing system must track the edgenumbers exactly so that a list can be generated that will instruct the negative cutter to cut and assemble the proper pieces of film negative. Since 1987, these edgenumbers have also appeared on negative in machine-readable form, and classified under the generic term, keycode.

For our 35mm mag track, however, there are no identifying edgenumbers at the time that the original sound is transferred to mag track, because there are no latent edgenumbers on mag stock. To solve this, the process of coding stock (also known as inking) places ink numbers along the edge of the mag track. A machine is used to stamp these new ink numbers on both the workprint and the mag track. By doing this, now both picture and sound share identical reference numbers.

Consider what would happen if these numbers did not exist. If the film editor decided to remove a few frames from the picture track of a take and forgot to remove the same number of frames from the corresponding mag track, the take would now be out of sync. Now let's say that some time has passed, and the editor returns to the scene and finds that it is out of sync. The editor must, through trial and error, resynchronize the material by pulling out the correct number of frames from the mag track. By inking, the editor can easily put picture and sound back in synchronization if sync is lost. Do the numbers agree? If so, the material is in sync. Are the numbers different? Then the material is out of sync.

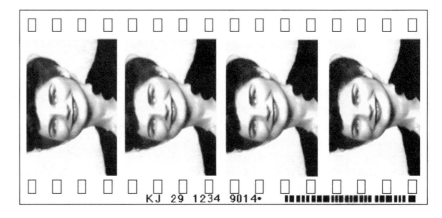

**Figure 6-2** Film negative has edge numbers that identify the film frames. When a print is made from the negative, the exact same numbers are printed through from the negative to the positive. In this way, the same frames have the same numbers. Illustration by Jeffrey Krebs.

Just prior to editing, workprint and mag are separated according to the method that the editor prefers. Most often, dailies are broken down into one roll that combines the film and mag track for one take. This roll is labeled with the scene and take number (Sc 5, Tk 1) and some editors even include a brief shot description on the label.

## Shooting and Editing Simultaneously

Most often, editing occurs simultaneously with shooting. As each day of shooting is completed, the editorial team will aim to keep "up to camera" by trying to have edited scenes for which all the footage has been delivered. By keeping up to camera, the goal is to deliver a complete first cut as quickly as possible after the production is wrapped, or completed. Further, as the cost of making films has increased over the years, it is important to minimize the amount of time that it takes to get a film into theaters so that costs can be recouped.

## EDITING THE FILM

### Linear versus Nonlinear Editing

Film editing is a nonlinear process. Linear means straight, and in the context of putting a film together it means that the editor would have to decide exactly how to put a series of shots together and would not be able to easily change the order of these shots. Videotape editing is a linear process. With videotape, the editor must first record shot 1, then shot 2, then shot 3. If the editor then decides that the order should be shot 2, shot 3, and finally shot 1, all the work that had been done must be redone. Because videotape cannot physically be cut and edited together, a re-recording process is necessary. This is the linear nature of videotape editing.

Film editing allows the editor to easily rearrange shots simply by removing the appropriate tape splices, moving the pieces of film into the new order, and resplicing the shots. This allows a particularly difficult scene to be constructed, pondered, and reconstructed. Entire sections of a sequence can be lifted and placed elsewhere. Film editing is the essence of nonlinear editing, but the process involves much physical labor and while nonlinear, film is not technically random access. Not being random access means that the film editor cannot get to a shot on the middle

of the roll without winding through all the intervening material. If film were a random access medium, such as a laserdisc, a shot could be located without having to proceed linearly through the unwanted material.

## Editing Systems

For the film editor, there are various types of editing systems. They fall into the category of Moviolas and flatbeds. There are different forms of flatbed editors with the two most popular being Steenbecks and KEMs. If a Steenbeck is being used, the editor begins by threading a segment of film and its corresponding mag track. If the editor requires more picture or sound tracks, there are flatbeds which provide multiple picture heads and additional sound plates. Some editors work on four plate flatbeds, others on six plates. Some editors who work on filmed musical concerts may require a three picture head system.

At sound speed, 24 fps, picture and sound are in sync. Working from left to right, that is, from feed reel to takeup reel, the editor reaches a frame where the shot should start and marks the frame with the china marker. The end frame is also marked. The film and mag tracks are placed in a sync block or synchronizer (figure 6-3) and a film splicer (butt splicer) is used to cut the film on the line between frames and to cut the mag track. The same occurs for the end frame.

This newly cut film segment represents the first shot that will be used in the sequence. Leftover material from this take occurs before and after the segment that was just cut. This leftover material is called the trim. Further, material before the start frame we used is called head trim. Material after the end frame that was marked is called tail trim. It is critical to keep track of these trims because they are often needed again. These strips of film are hung from a hook in a trim bin. Very short sections of trim are placed in a box.

Eventually the editor will have chosen all the shots that are to be used in cutting the scene. A flatbed editor is able to hold one roll, or roughly ten minutes of material, at one time. Note, however, that if a particularly intensive scene has hours of material, there may be quite a number of select rolls. It is not unusual for an action sequence lasting only a few minutes on-screen to be created from twenty hours of material. Building select rolls in this instance is not only time consuming, it might be next to impossible.

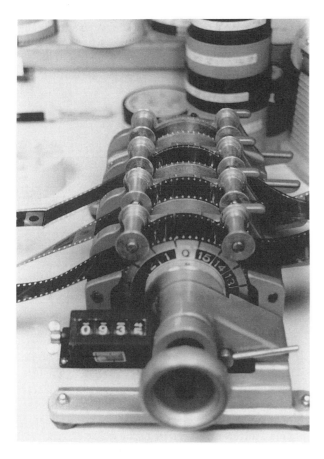

**Figure 6-3** The film and mag tracks are placed in a sync block or synchronizer to help keep picture and track in sync. Photo by Michael E. Phillips.

## Editing

As editing continues, the amount of film in the trim bin will most likely increase and the rough assembly of the scene will be on the takeup reel. The editor plays back the scene to decide where to make changes. Splices are removed, changes are made, and the viewing continues.

## Trimming Shots

Once a scene is put together, the editor will review and tighten the shots accordingly. At this point, the transition between two shots is a cut, where one shot rapidly switches to the next shot. If one or both of the shots that transition into one another must be shortened, the editor will usually play back and forth over the splice point and determine how many frames must be removed or added. If frames are to be re-

moved, the film and mag track are placed in the splicer, and those frames are cut out and are put into the trim bin. The film is respliced and the new cut is viewed. This process is repeated until the cut is exactly how the editor wants it.

Conversely, if a shot in the scene ends too quickly, the appropriate head or tail trim must be located in the bin. If the editor feels that 16 frames (one foot in 35mm four-perf) must be added to the tail end of a shot, the trim is located in the bin and spliced into place. As this shaping becomes more exact, the trims become smaller. This is one of the reasons for film editors to joke about having to find a trim at the bottom of the bin!

## Overlapping Cuts

While editing continues, it is important to realize what is going on in the editing room. The editor is up and about, retrieving rolls from the shelf, winding down to the needed sections, and working away at the trim bin. There are essentially two type of transitions the editor can accomplish on the flatbed. This stage limits the editor to transitions that are either straight cuts or overlapping cuts. A straight cut is when both picture and mag tracks are cut at the same point, in a straight line. An overlap occurs when picture and sound tracks do not transition together. For example, if we have a scene where two people are talking, and we cut from one person talking to the other person talking, this is a straight cut. However, if we edit the scene so that we continue to see the first person while we are hearing the second person talk, we do not have a straight cut; instead, we have an overlapping cut where the picture of person one has been overlapped onto the audio of person two.

## Optical Effects

The film editor cannot immediately view optical effects such as dissolves, fades, or wipes. Instead, when any transition other than a cut is required, the editor must provide directions to the optical laboratory (optical house). These directions instruct the optical house in the manner in which two pieces of film should be transitioned together. For example, when the editor wants to indicate where a dissolve will occur, a china marker is used to mark the workprint. While the dissolve cannot be seen, the markings will show the filmmakers that the two shots are not intended to transition as a straight cut, but rather, as a dissolve.

## The Rough Cut and the Final Cut

The goal of any editor during the rough cut stage is to show the director all the material that was shot while forming the best possible assembly, based on the editor's interpretation of the script and conversations with the director. This is the first complete viewing of the entire film. There may be only china markings to indicate transitions and black film leader to indicate missing special visual effect composite shots. Changes and re-editing may be minimal or extensive, and editing continues until the final cut is achieved. This final cut is the point where the picture portion of the film is complete. This is called "locking the picture."

## *INDUSTRY VIEWPOINTS*

### *Mia Goldman, A.C.E. Editor*

*Flesh and Bone* (1993), *Untamed Heart* (1993), *Crazy People* (1990), *The Big Easy* (1987), *Choose Me* (1984). Member, Academy of Motion Picture Arts and Sciences.

For Mia Goldman, A.C.E., making use of a digital, nonlinear editing system has allowed her to put aside much of the manual labor usually associated with film editing and has left her free to experiment in any way she desires. It is a particularly important tool when determining and creating the best possible performance. Says Goldman,

> The most important aspect of nonlinear editing is that it frees your mind to do your work as fast as you can think it. You can experiment a lot faster and compare takes. These are things that I did when I was working in film—I would take every single reading and break it down and if you have a three page scene, you may have fifteen interchanges, or seven interchanges per character for a two-character scene. Now, say you have three takes—that's 21 different comparisons on each exchange. In film, I would pull out the whole section and splice the pieces together. I would carry those exchanges until I could see the other character's exchanges.
>
> I'm currently working on a film where I have a lot of takes—sometimes as many as seven takes. I just finished a dance sequence where I had 280 takes. I spent four days cutting the scene using a digital, nonlinear system and it would have taken three weeks if I were working on film. I simply mark in and out on my takes and narrow from seven down to three takes. The process of elimination becomes so much easier. Many people say that editing is taking out the bad stuff, but that's not true—it's molding—creating something.
>
> With digital nonlinear, your work is that much more concentrated, but you don't get exhausted. I find that the speed with which you can change cuts or create a montage and transpose shots is amazing. Editing has gotten much more complex and the idea of montage is now hitting its zenith. The ability to instantly create an optical, and the sound capabilities that you find in digital are just incredible—it just blows away film editing. It's giving people the illusion of a better product, meaning a more complete product because now I mix while I edit and it's making a better cut.
>
> The director I'm working with is one of the first who used a nonlinear editing system, so he expects it to be fast. When you have many things to cut or explore, it's important not to feel pressured to try things. There's always a factor of exhaustion and you can try infinite things and feel it's not been a waste. Exploring the material is so much more complete—it gives you a sense of going over it inch-by-inch. When you do have the correct time and you have something subtle that you have to accomplish, the sense of completion is wonderful.

**Figure 6-4** Photo of Mia Goldman, A.C.E. Courtesy of Mia Goldman.

## INDUSTRY VIEWPOINTS

### Sylvie Landra—Editor

*Lèon (The Professional) (1995)*

Sylvie Landra, editor of the 1995 Luc Besson directed film *Lèon*, is exuberant about the capabilities afforded by editing on a digital, nonlinear system. Says Landra,

> The most obvious benefit of the editing digitally, in my case on the Avid, is an incomparable savings in time as well as its tremendous flexibility in usage. The range of available commands is represented simply and directly. Editing is done in real time, by which I mean that any change you want is made instantaneously. On the one hand, while the method of editing remains intrinsically the same, sorting and searching, as well as archiving are now carried out immediately. The fact that you're working at true 24 fps conveys not only a real sense of confidence while pacing shots, but most importantly, there aren't any "surprises" during projection of 35mm dailies . . . So what may at first appear to be a system geared up primarily to save time, in fact is a major boost to the creativity of editing; to be able to access and display as many different versions of a sequence as I want, in real time, allows the Producer and Director to explore the full width and breadth of their creative desires, doubts, and questions.
>
> Also, it often happens when we're fine-tuning a version of a sequence, we find it either a bit too long, or not enough, and feel it would take just an infinitesimal "tweaking" to really capture the appropriate rhythm—this is especially true of action sequences. There's not that much difference between a well-timed scene and another which comes across "mushy." With the Avid, we get a remarkable transformation very quickly. [Translated from the French by Howard A. Phillips]

### Sound Editing

Usually, the amount of sound work that the editor does is kept to two-track work and focuses on two things: first, overlapping dialogue edits, and second, the replacement of dialogue with dialogue from a different take(s). Depending upon the complexity of the film, and the delivery date, sound work could begin in parallel with picture editing, but in the traditional film postproduction process, audio work, such as sound effects editing, music composition, and dialogue replacement, begins after the picture portion is finished. Shown in figure 6-5 is an vintage photograph of a sound editor at work.

Somewhere along in this time, optical effects begin to be delivered by the laboratory. These effects are spliced into their already determined position in the workprint. Next, the entire film, usually broken down into twelve ten-minute reels (for a two-hour film) becomes available for final audio dubbing. Each of the reels is projected while the different sound elements are mixed together. Original music scoring and orchestral recordings are undertaken. Figure 6-6 is a vintage photograph that shows the recording of an orchestra for a film.

## Conforming the Negative

Now that a complete workprint is available, original camera negative can be conformed. This first generation material, the camera negative, is cut in the exact manner, frame for frame, as was the final version of the workprint, and the newly created film opticals are

**Figure 6-5** A vintage photograph of a sound editor at work. Courtesy of The Academy of Motion Picture Arts and Sciences.

**Figure 6-6** A vintage photograph which shows the recording of an orchestra for a film. Courtesy of The Academy of Motion Picture Arts and Sciences.

cut into the assembled negative. Negative cutting is the final aspect of preparing the film for mass delivery, and if a change is made to the workprint after the negative has been conformed, it is not impossible to make the change, but it can be an expensive process.

Note that splicing negative to negative does require that a portion of the adjacent frame be used, thereby rendering a portion of the next frame unusable (this portion is usually one frame, depending upon the film gauge, splicing method, and whether the film will be blown up to a larger film size). One item that has traditionally plagued filmmakers is how a film can be changed once the negative has been cut. If suddenly a frame must be added back and the frame does not exist anymore because it has been removed for splicing purposes, either a similar but not exact frame can be used (this works particularly well in static situations), or new digital techniques can be used to repair or recreate fractured or missing negative.

## The Answer Print

When film mixing is complete, a mixed magnetic master tape is used to create an optical soundtrack. The conformed negative is then color-graded, to create a continuity of color from scene to scene, or to add any required color effects, such as making scenes shot during the day take place at dusk (Day for Night). The first version of the film that contains optical effects and the complete and mixed optical soundtrack is called the answer print. Here is a last-minute opportunity to check everything, the quality of the mixed soundtrack, with particular attention to the quality of the soundtrack mix.

## The Release Print

Once the answer print has been finalized and approved, a release print is created. Additional print copies are then made from a copy of the original negative, and these copies are distributed to theaters. When a film is shown on television, or sold on videocassette, the videotape copy can be made either from one of these prints, from the release print, or from a copy of the original assembled negative.

## THE PROMISE OF DIGITAL FILMMAKING METHODS

The manner in which a film is edited offers the editor great flexibility, but there is time involved to make even the most simple change. An operation that may take several minutes on film can be done in seconds on a digital, nonlinear system. When one examines the various steps of the traditional filmmaking postproduction process, it is apparent that using digital techniques and methods can provide vast improvements to both the artistic and economic concerns of making a film.

New methods of working with multiple channels of digital sound are obviating the need to have mag track in the cutting room. Being able to instantly see optical effects such as dissolves without waiting for the optical house to create and deliver the effect changes the experience for the editor as well as the director, who can now get a closer idea of what the final film will be than ever before. Not only does the postproduction process become more efficient, but it becomes possible to effect changes along the way without getting behind in schedule, thus greatly relieving a filmmaker's anxiety.

## INDUSTRY VIEWPOINTS

### Steven B. Cohen—Director, Digital Picture Editorial, Sony Pictures Studios

Member: SMPTE, AES, CAS, ACE

For Steven B. Cohen, the Digital Picture Editorial division of Sony Pictures Studios has brought with it the challenge of designing an entire postproduction facility that seeks to make the best use of digital methods over the entire range of filmmaking. Says Cohen,

> As far as the technologies that are growing in filmmaking, I believe that the digital storage and retrieval of media files will continue to grow. We've chosen to store sound files on DAT, DASH, Exabyte, Magneto-Optical, hard disk, and RAM. Picture elements are currently being stored on hard disk only.
>
> I believe that there will be tremendous growth in sound and picture editing workstations. They will be integrated, trading files across a network and this network will have the ability to travel well beyond the studio walls. It can extend to anywhere that can receive satellite or telephone communication and this will allow filmmakers to access the studio's support system throughout production and postproduction.
>
> Sony Pictures Studios has chosen to use digital audio and picture workstations to give the editors increased flexibility, speed creativity, and accuracy. These workstations promote an easier interaction

**Figure 6-7** Photo of Steven B. Cohen. Courtesy of Sony Pictures Studios.

> with the directors and producers and enables them to have subtle control of the editing process. Sound effects and visual effects can be digitally incorporated in the first cut of a film.
>
> Sony Pictures Studios is currently building the full service integrated digital postproduction facility of the 21st century. This facility will be able to link to filmmakers anywhere in the globe during the production and postproduction process. The audio component of this system will be: digitally recorded production sound dailies, direct digital transfer to nonlinear, digital audio workstations, all production tracks available to editors, a huge digital sound effects library, Foley and ADR recording studio with hard disk recorders. The playback and approval of all sound editing at the audio workstations, the recording on 100% automated consoles with digital and analog signal processing simultaneously. The direct digital transfer to a digital optical sound negative completes the process.
>
> The picture component of this system will offer filmmakers the choice of originating on film or High Definition Video. Prior to production, projects would be pre-visualized on computer systems with CAD sets inserted. Dailies would be available to anyone over a digital file server on the lot or they could be modemed anywhere in the world. Film will be telecined to hard disk on site and then modemed to the nonlinear picture editing system at any location. The early cuts could be modemed back to the studio for

review. CGI backgrounds, temp visual effects, and sound effects can be sent to editors on location for insertion into dailies. The editors will be able to create a temp digital soundtrack while editing the picture. First director cuts will be achieved on the digital picture workstation and then film will be conformed to preview. Our on-site visual effects company, Sony Imageworks, will complete all titles, opticals, and composites and output to 35mm negative. The release print will be single inventory with standard analog optical track and Sony Dynamic Digital Sound 8-track, digital optical track.

There are several reasons why new technologies are being incorporated into filmmaking. Basic filmmaking has worked for over 50 years. It is ripe for technological change. It has to accommodate the current economic environment and to provide for the increased need of software in the global marketplace. The increased markets of home video, cable, CD-ROM, and online services will need sophisticated software produced by current filmmakers. In many cases it will be resourced from film production elements. The repackaging to other markets will require a more streamlined production and postproduction system.

**Figure 6-8** Photo of Ed Granlund. Courtesy of Ed Granlund, Lucasfilm, Ltd.

## INDUSTRY VIEWPOINTS

### Ed Granlund—Postproduction Supervisor, Lucasfilm, Ltd.

For Ed Granlund, a postproduction supervisor working in the ever changing environment that is Lucasfilm, Ltd., created by filmmaker George Lucas, the digital filmmaking methodology is not only a reality, but is being defined and enhanced each day. Granlund, who has managed a vast array of projects at Lucasfilm, is particularly driven by a desire to augment the film postproduction process with new digital tools. Says Granlund,

I work with the Producer, Director, and Production Designer during the early stages of production, looking at a shot, or series of shots, and seeing what the intended and required results are. We always ask, "Is this the best approach?" and then proceed to evaluate options. The spirit of Lucasfilm is to not only look at conventional techniques, but to combine them with new technology—experimenting and learning new tricks. Sometimes the best solutions involve combining existing hardware and software products in ways that yield previously unachievable results.

One of the things that affects the cost of making films is the duration of the shooting and postproduction schedule. If you can collapse the schedule in any

way, huge savings can be realized. Generally, filmmaking is a linear process—as one aspect is completed, the next can begin. We are developing ways to make the filmmaking process more interactive, allowing crew members from varying disciplines to work on the film at the same time. This not only eliminates time from the schedule, it affords the opportunity to head off problems that formerly would have been passed down the line.

This process is achieved by electronically connecting the various craftspeople, who may be miles apart, and creating what we term the "virtual studio." As an example, while filming *Radioland Murders* (1994), in Wilmington, North Carolina, postproduction personnel in Marin County, California were able to view shots live from a video tap on the camera, and instantly feed back valuable information to the set that eliminated the need for expensive rotoscope work on a series of shots.

We have also utilized these long distance networks to speed up the visual effects process. By being able to look at a shot or sequence in phases, as the artist is working, no turn-around time for shot approvals was lost whatsoever. Using new technologies, like Avid's OMF (Open Media Framework) over fiber optical lines, effects shots have instantly been sent straight from Industrial Light & Magic in San Rafael, California, right into Lucasfilm's electronic editing suites at Skywalker Ranch, some 25 miles away. Effects shots can be immediately cut in and approved, often eliminating the need for expensive "handles" as well.

Our ultimate goal is to bring the cost of making films down, while at the same time improving the films that we are making. Digital filmmaking technology is key in achieving that goal.

## INDUSTRY VIEWPOINTS

### Joel Cox—Film Editor

*Bird, White Hunter Black Heart, Unforgiven* (Academy Award, Film Editing, 1992), *A Perfect World, The Stars Fell on Henrietta, The Bridges of Madison County.*

For Joel Cox, Academy Award winning editor of Clint Eastwood's *Unforgiven,* 1994 brought his first foray into using a digital, nonlinear editing system for the Malpaso production *The Stars Fell on Henrietta.* His outlook and observations are particularly significant as a first time user of digital picture editing technology.

Cox has a deep sense of the tradition of learning the entire filmmaking process. Not sure what his aspirations in the film world would bring, Cox was eager to be exposed to the many different jobs that could be found on a busy studio lot. Says Cox,

**Figure 6-9** Photo of Joel Cox. Courtesy of Joel Cox.

I started in the mail room at Warner Brothers in 1961 and worked with many people in various departments for three years. I got my break when Rudy Fehr, head of editorial, gave me the opportunity to become a member of the department. I worked as an apprentice film editor for a few years until I was given the chance to work as an assistant editor on the picture *The Rain People* directed by Francis Ford Coppola, starring Robert Duvall. After that, I was a sound assistant on the feature film The *Learning Tree.* Following that I was a sound effects/music assistant on the television series "The FBI Story" starring Efrem Zimbalist, Jr. While working on this show, I discovered a large amount of sound effects and music takes that were going to be destroyed. On my own time I went through the material, logged it, and created a library for the show's use. After that, I returned to editing on the feature *The All American Boy* and have been editing feature films ever since.

For Cox, the editorial process is where the film comes together, choosing shots and cutting them together with technical expertise and the creativity of a master storyteller.

Editing is storytelling. What I generally do is read the script once and then put it away. When I watch dailies I'm looking for basic timing and movement as well as performance. An editor can't alter the basic story but he can construct the scene the way he feels the director wanted it. In my first cut, my job is to put everything in the scene that was shot by the director, then we watch it, discuss what works and what doesn't and then make our changes.

Cox has edited all of his films on a Moviola and Kem for years with only the help of his film assistant Michael Cipriano. To make his transition to digital he added Patrick Flannery, a veteran of digital film editing, to his team.

You really need to be receptive to where things are going in your field and ask "Is this technology a good direction for film?" Digital, nonlinear editing may cost more money, but it allows you to do a lot more than before . . . as fast as you can think, you can do . . . If a producer or director wants to see a different version of a scene, I can show it to them without losing the work that I've already done.

The ability to work with multiple versions and have instant access to all the film that was printed has allowed Cox to experiment when necessary. When working in film, this flexibility is available but usually at a cost, elaborates Cox.

> For instance, if your director says, "Let's cut this scene a different way," you talk it over, find out what he's looking for and then try the changes. On film if you want to put the cut back the way it was you can get close, but it may never have the same flair it had the first time. With digital I can instantly duplicate my original cut and start making changes to the copy. I have the entire film online. I can bring footage up so fast I don't lose my flow of concentration. If I have multiple takes, I'll splice them all together, watch them one after another, then select which one is best. You can work a scene much faster and to me that's a big plus. . . .
>
> Where you used to have the grind of handling all the picture and track, you now have instant access to all the material at the touch of a button. When I worked on *Bird,* it was a big job . . . I had film all over the room. Some music scenes were five minutes long, with multiple takes, with multiple cameras. There were 500-foot rolls of film that you'd be constantly winding through. With digital editing all I have to do is scroll through the timeline, mark new in/out points, and hit the splice button.

An added benefit of editing digitally is the ability to pre-build optical effects, such as dissolves and fades, instantly. Says Cox,

> It's amazing, I have complete control! When I worked on . . . *Josey Wales,* I put in a 20-foot dissolve going from a black-and-white shot to color. Anytime you go from a light scene to a dark scene you have to make a very slow dissolve; on film it's difficult to get it just right. On *Bird* we had many opticals and in film it costs a lot of money to make test dissolves. There's a cymbal that was shot at 120 frames, I double printed it to 240 frames which made it look like it was floating down in mid-air. On the Avid system I can do slo-mo, dissolves, fades, etc., and see the results right away, this saves a lot of money and time.

A new area that Cox is exploring is the use of multiple tracks of digital sound to make his editing more complete.

> It's hard to put in sound effects on film. Since I only have one track of mag to work with, I can only sneak in things between the dialogue. Now I can add a track anywhere I want. I can add music or effects from CDs or DAT, add background fx, and really smooth out the tracks. If I want to, I can dub the

mixed output to mag and use that for previews. This also saves time and money.

Cox sums up,

> It's working very well for me, and I continue to learn the advantages and benefits of the Avid Film Composer. Each day I get faster and better; I won't have to go back to editing manually because this system offers me a lot more flexibility.

## INDUSTRY VIEWPOINTS

### *Pietro Scalia—Editor*

*Stealing Beauty* (1995), *The Quick and The Dead* (1994), *Little Buddha* (1993), *JFK* (1992, Academy Award for Best Editing), *The Doors* (additional editor, 1991), *Megaville* (1990), *Born on The Fourth of July* (additional editor, 1989).

For editor Pietro Scalia, digital nonlinear editing systems offer the ability to entertain his creative ideas without exception. Says Scalia,

> I consider creative flexibility and technical versatility the most attractive tools that a digital nonlinear editing system can offer.

**Figure 6-10** Photo of Pietro Scalia. Courtesy of Anthony Bozanich.

In productions where original shot negative is printed, screened, and telecined with 35mm magnetic, the benefits are not necessarily in saving lab and personnel costs, but in giving the director and editor the tools, like Avid or Lightworks systems, in order to maximize the creative process in "the third phase of writing of the film" and reduce the time consuming physical labor associated with the actual construction of a finished film.

The ability to store and save all previous cuts of scenes and sequences and to later compare them with more recent ones, enables the director and editor to see the evolution of the film and have at their fingertips the options to restructure, rewrite, and experiment with the material with more ease, which ultimately enriches the finished film.

# 7 The Film Laboratory

## EDITORIAL PREPARATION AND THE TELECINE PROCESS

In this chapter, we discuss new technology used to redefine the methods of a digital filmmaking laboratory.

Once the shoot is finished, original camera negative is sent to the lab for developing. The negative is then printed to create a workprint. There are two types: one-lite and color-corrected workprints. A one-lite workprint is based on a set of timing lights predetermined by the DP and the lab, and it takes into account the emulsion and exposure of the negative. Any type of push or pull in either the exposure or developing stages will affect the look. A push during exposure varies the amount of light that strikes the negative relative to the index rating of the emulsion. For example, a film rated at 200 ASA can be shot as though it was 400 ASA, in effect, doubling the amount of light that strikes the negative. This is an example of pushing exposure. Processing can also be pulled or pushed depending upon the amount of time the film spends in the developer.

Once a set of lights has been determined by the DP and timer, these printing lights are used for the remainder of the shoot. It is possible that a secondary set of one-lites may be established for interior versus exterior shots, or for day versus night shoots. Timing light information is stored on a punch tape, based on a total footage count of the camera roll. This punch tape is used as a starting point for the answer print stage after the editing stage is finished. This information is stored for later use and data are kept for each camera roll. Timing lights can also be based on the average look of a certain emulsion, and these lights will be used for the initial answer print.

Color-corrected workprints are prints that are corrected based on the RGB value of the picture. RGB are the red, green, and blue values of light value(s) in the printer. These lights are expressed in values generally in range of 0–50. When working with negative or a positive print, each light component refers to the complementary color of the print. For example, increasing the printer value for red makes the workprint more cyan. Printer values are also known as CMY or cyan, magenta, and yellow. If you increase all RGB values evenly, the print will become darker with no effect on color. Decreasing all the lights evenly will lighten the print while also having no effect on color. Printer reports are prepared describing the timing light relationships for each roll. These values are also stored on a punch tape for use during the answer print stage. They provide the color timer with a starting point with regard to the overall look of the picture.

While punch tape technology is quite old, it is quite commonly found in timing situations. Increasingly, punch tape is being replaced by floppy disk technology for digital information exchange. Shown in figure 7-1 is a sample of a color timing printer report.

There are systems available that will generate film timing values when there is no workprint involved. Excalibur from Filmlab Systems analyzes the

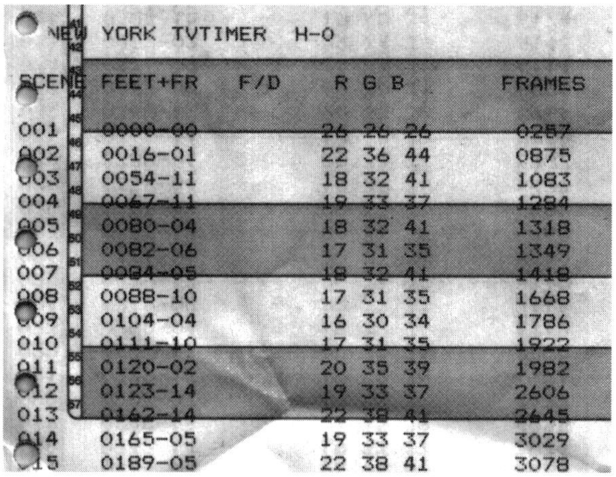

NEW YORK TVTIMER H-O

| SCENE | FEET+FR | F/D | R | G | B | FRAMES |
|---|---|---|---|---|---|---|
| 001 | 0000-00 | | 26 | 26 | 26 | 0257 |
| 002 | 0016-01 | | 22 | 36 | 44 | 0875 |
| 003 | 0054-11 | | 18 | 32 | 41 | 1083 |
| 004 | 0067-11 | | 19 | 33 | 37 | 1284 |
| 005 | 0080-04 | | 18 | 32 | 41 | 1318 |
| 006 | 0082-06 | | 17 | 31 | 35 | 1349 |
| 007 | 0084-05 | | 18 | 32 | 41 | 1418 |
| 008 | 0088-10 | | 17 | 31 | 35 | 1668 |
| 009 | 0104-04 | | 16 | 30 | 34 | 1786 |
| 010 | 0111-10 | | 17 | 31 | 35 | 1922 |
| 011 | 0120-02 | | 20 | 35 | 39 | 1982 |
| 012 | 0123-14 | | 19 | 33 | 37 | 2606 |
| 013 | 0162-14 | | 22 | 38 | 41 | 2645 |
| 014 | 0165-05 | | 19 | 33 | 37 | 3029 |
| 015 | 0189-05 | | 22 | 38 | 41 | 3078 |

**Figure 7-1** An example of a color timing printer report. Courtesy of Technicolor.

```
000 Manufacturer FSI          No. 020 Equip Excalibur  Version 2.10      Flex 1001
010 Title TALES OF YORE
100 Edit 0001                  Field A1  PAL  Split              Delay
110 Scene 1A        Take 2          Cam Roll          Sound
120 Scrpt        Comments ON THE ROAD
200       35 25.00 1                    000005+05 Key EASTM KJ121252 009912+00 p1
950     Red 23.0  Green 27.0  Blue 25.0
300              1          At 01:00:00:00.1 For 00:00:03:10.0


100 Edit 0002                  Field A1  PAL  Split              Delay
110 Scene 1A        Take 3          Cam Roll          Sound
120 Scrpt        Comments ON THE ROAD + TRAFFIC
200       35 25.00 1                    000013+00 Key EASTM KJ121252 009917+07 p1
950     Red 27.0  Green 32.0  Blue 31.0
300              1          At 01:00:03:10.1 For 00:00:08:08.0


100 Edit 0003                  Field A1  PAL  Split              Delay
110 Scene 1B        Take 1          Cam Roll          Sound
120 Scrpt        Comments INSIDE THE CAR
200       35 25.00 1                    000002+14 Key EASTM KJ121252 009956+06 p1
950     Red 11.0  Green 09.0  Blue 14.0
300              1          At 01:00:11:18.1 For 00:00:01:21.0
```

**Figure 7-2** This example of a timing report shows the timing light values for each take in relationship to timecode and keynumbers. Courtesy Filmlab Systems.

negative and allows the same type of color correction that a timer finds when correcting a workprint. These values are kept in a database that can be used for the creation of an answer print. This system obviates the need for punch tape as all information is available via an ASCII (American Standards Committee for Information Interchange) file. Excalibur printing systems are able to import the ASCII information for the answer and release print stages. Shown in figure 7-2 is an example of a timing report.

The system can also be equipped with a keycode reader and the color values can be based on a keynumber reference rather than on a footage count from a sync point at the head of each reel. The advantage is that this allows select takes to be transferred,

with color correction, without having to establish sync points for each and every camera roll. Once these values are referenced to a keynumber, the editing process can take place, and these values are available when it is necessary to create cut lists. Once the film has been developed, with or without workprint, the picture and sound elements are readied for the film-to-tape transfer process. (Note that keycode spelled with a "c" is used in reference to all edgenumber formats that can be read by a barcode reader. KeyKode™ is the official name of the Eastman Kodak Corporation's offering of machine-readable edgenumbers.)

Shown in figure 7-3 are two keycode reader heads, one for 35mm and one for 16mm film.

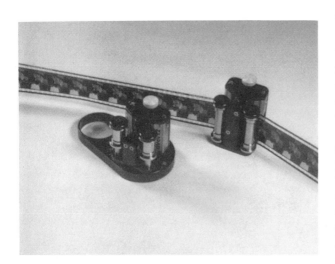

**Figure 7-3** Two keycode reader heads for 35mm and 16mm film. Courtesy of Evertz Microsystems, Ltd.

## THE TELECINE PROCESS

To prepare for digital, nonlinear postproduction, the film image is converted into a video signal and then digitized. This process involves a telecine unit that converts the film image into a video signal, which is then recorded onto either analog or digital videotape.

The film-to-tape process can be organized using several different methods depending on the type of project. When working with feature films, there is usually a workprint, and selected takes have been combined into reels of 1,000 feet. These takes can be combined in either scene/take order, or perhaps slate order, so that the editor is able to easily find shots. Each of these rolls has an accompanying mag roll synced to picture.

These rolls, once transferred to videotape, will later be used for the dailies screening. The resulting video daily is an exact replica of the film rolls. When transferring for a television movie or episodic, a workprint is usually not made. Instead of creating a workprint, the negative is transferred directly to tape.

Either selected takes, or entire uncut camera rolls, are transferred to tape. Increasingly, either workprint is being eliminated entirely, or it is being introduced after the first cut on the DNLE system, and then only the selected takes are printed. As video technology improves and projection of the video medium gains acceptance by the film community, workprint and mag will be removed entirely from the postproduction process.

Increasingly, there are film-to-tape transfers to digital betacam videotape in the $16 \times 9$ format. This means that the film image from a wide screen format is transferred ("squeezed") to the digital videotape. Normally, the image is "un-squeezed" during the transfer process leaving bands of black bars at the top and bottom of the picture. Shown in figure 7-4 are examples of the different aspect ratios when transferred to video at a 1:1.33 ratio.

## THE NUMBERING SCHEME OF FILM

An important aspect of the digital postprocess has been the development of machine-readable edgenumbers. This was first made available by the Eastman Kodak Corporation in 1988 with the introduction of KeyKode. Barcode is the machine-readable edgenumber that is placed on the negative at the time of manufacture. These machine- and man-readable numbers are latent numbers. This means that they are not readable until after the negative has been developed. The Agfa, Fuji, and Kodak Corporations offer machine-readable edgenumbers on their film stocks.

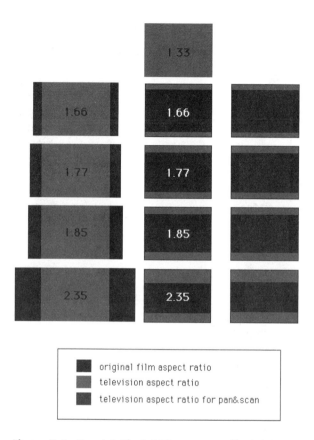

**Figure 7-4**   From L–R. The 1:1.33 aspect ratio. The 1:1.66 aspect ratio. The 1:1.77 aspect ratio (16 × 9). The 1:1.85 aspect ratio. The 1:2.35 aspect ratio.

KeyKode is encoded using type USS-128 barcode (figure 7-5). The barcode is detected and read by KeyKode readers, which are available from several manufacturers. The readers detect, read, and transmit the keynumbers from the edge of the negative.

## KEYKODE™ Number Information

0 2 9 6 2 3 1 2 3 4 5 6 7 7 0 0

Start Character | Mfg. ID Code | Film Type | Prefix | Count | Offset in Perfs. | Check Sum | Stop Character

Encoded in USS-128 Barcode

**Figure 7-5**   An example of KeyKode using type USS-128 barcode. Courtesy of Eastman Kodak Corporation.

## How KeyKode™ Is Arrayed

Shown in figure 7-6 is an example of KeyKode. Along one side of the negative is a series of barcodes, keynumbers, data, and symbols. The dot (•) symbol refers to the zero frame reference mark. It is from this perforation (perf) and frame where the 64 total perf count between each keynumber begins in 35mm film. This zero frame is also the beginning of the footage counting cycle and appears in the format: KJ 23 1234 5677 (+00)

Although the +00 is not part of the keynumber as seen on the negative, it is inferred from the zero frame reference mark. All subsequent frames are counted as an offset from that point: +01, +02, +03, and so forth. There is a mid-foot marker halfway between the zero frame reference points. In 35mm, the midpoint appears 32 perfs after the reference dot and will be frame +08 of the keynumber. The mid-foot marker uses a smaller type size and is useful in identifying short scenes.

Different film gauges will have different marker demarcations. For example: 16 mm has 40 frames per foot with a keynumber (•) every 20 frames. There is a mid keynumber reference every 10 frames. 65mm has 80 perfs per keynumber, and depending upon the format being shot, the frame will be either 8, 10, or 15 perfs wide.

Between the foot and mid-foot barcode/keynumbers are other bits of information. They are the manufacturer's information: year code, printer number, roll and part number, emulsion number, product code, and film manufacturer. There are also frame index markers which appear as a hyphen (-) every four perforations to aid in locating the position of the frame line. This is useful when editing low light level footage and the edge of the exposed frame is difficult to detect. To use this specific information, it is helpful to find a frame that is detectable from the exposed frame line and locate the hyphen symbol offset to that frame line. All other frames within that take will always have the same offset.

## Barcode

When the barcode is decoded through the use of a reader, the decoded numbers will match the man-readable numbers. The barcode version of the keynumber does not contain the alpha characters which are present on the man-readable version. For example, the prefix "KJ" is represented by 0296. These numbers are translated through the use of look-up tables in the hardware and software systems used with the KeyKode reader head.

Hardware support for these heads is available from several manufacturers, including Aaton, Alperman + Velte, Evertz, and Skotel. Sometimes KeyKode readers or keynumber software-capturing databases will not decode the first four characters of the keynumber, or they may only display the underlying number. This usually happens when a film manufacturer develops a new emulsion, and the readers are not yet aware of the barcode reference to that new stock number. Depending upon the reader being used, the prefix of the keynumber may appear as:

?? 32 1234 or as

0287 32 1234

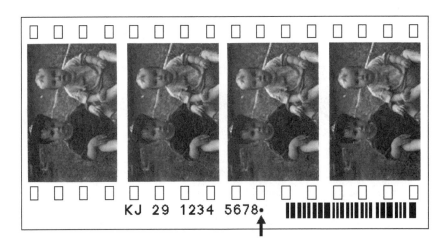

**Figure 7-6** An example of Keykode. Illustration by Jeffrey Krebs.

By using a lookup table, one can reference the proper man-readable keynumber as it appears on the negative. The first four characters are the manufacture and film type of the negative. Below is a listing which shows the translation of these characters:

| Manu-facturer | Emul-sion | Film Type | Code | Letter | Code | Char |
|---|---|---|---|---|---|---|
| Agfa | 01 | A | 20 | N | XT | 100 |
|  | 11 |  | 24 | M | XTR | 250 |
|  |  |  | 83 | F | XT | 320 |
|  |  |  | 84 | S | XTS | 400 |
| Fuji | 03 | F | 01 | I | FCI |  |
|  | 13 |  | 10 | N | F-64 |  |
|  |  |  | 13 | N | FCI |  |
|  |  |  | 14 | N | F-500 |  |
|  |  |  | 20 | N | F-64D |  |
|  |  |  | 30 | N | F-125 |  |
|  |  |  | 50 | N | F-250 |  |
|  |  |  | 60 | N | F-250D |  |
|  |  |  | 70 | N | F-500 |  |
| Kodak | 02 | K | 22 | E | 5222/7222 |  |
|  | 12 |  | 24 | L | 5224 |  |
|  |  |  | 31 | H | 5231/7231 |  |
|  |  |  | 34 | D | 5234/7234 |  |
|  |  |  | 43 | A | 5343/7243 |  |
|  |  |  | 44 | V | 5244/7244 |  |
|  |  |  | 45 | K | 5345/7245 |  |
|  |  |  | 47 | B | 5247 |  |
|  |  |  | 48 | M | 5248/7248 |  |
|  |  |  | 49 | O | 5249 |  |
|  |  |  | 72 | S | 5272/7272 |  |
|  |  |  | 74 | R | 2374 |  |
|  |  |  | 87 | W | 5287/7287 |  |
|  |  |  | 92 | N | 7292 |  |
|  |  |  | 93 | L | 5293/7293 |  |
|  |  |  | 94 | G | 5294 |  |
|  |  |  | 95 | F | 5295 |  |
|  |  |  | 96 | J | 5296/7296 |  |
|  |  |  | 97 | C | 5297/7297 |  |
|  |  |  | 98 | T | 5298/7298 |  |

## Testing Keynumber Reading Capabilities

The Eastman Kodak Corporation has introduced negative test films that allow a telecine operator to adjust the keynumber acquisition at time of transfer. Since the KeyKode reading head is not at the gate, an offset must be entered into the KeyKode reader timecode gathering system. This transfer verification film includes a 70-foot piece of film, and in the picture area of the negative is the keynumber that is being read by the head. When the operator burns-in the

keynumber being read by the head, the two numbers can be read simultaneously and adjusted to compensate for any frame offsets. Shown in figure 7-7 are four frames from the Kodak test film.

Once this test has been done, all timecode-to-keynumber relationships will have been correctly established and will also calculate reader delays that can be introduced by noise reduction equipment, Electronic Pin Registration (EPR), and timebase correctors, as well as adjust offsets when switching between 16mm and 35mm negative. It can also be determined how quickly the reader should update at

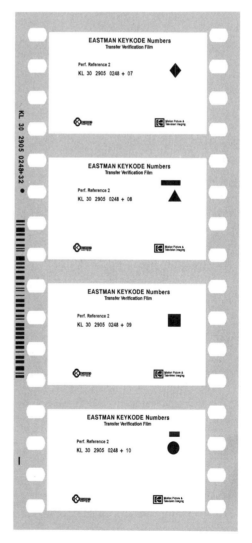

**Figure 7-7** Four frames from the Eastman Kodak Corporation's transfer verification film. Courtesy of Eastman Kodak Corporation.

splice points when a break in KeyKode is detected. The entire keynumber and frame offsets are prominently displayed in every frame of film. Five different KeyKode number sequences are included in each test film. Segments 1–4 (76 feet each) have ascending KeyKode numbers in the normal read position. Key-Kode numbers in segment 5 (48 feet) are descending and on the opposite side of the film, just as they would appear on negative that has been rewound prior to shooting.

The zero frame perf reference changes with each of the first four segments and is indicated in every frame of the 35mm test film. Perf reference is indicated in segment five of the test film. If the KeyKode reading system identifies the zero frame perforation, the test film will confirm if the indication is accurate. Perf identification is needed when transferring 3-perf film. The lower half of each frame is left open in order to burn-in the timecode and KeyKode. The information burned-in to the bottom portion should match the picture information in the picture.

## Capturing Timecode and Keynumbers into a Database

As the film transfer occurs, hardware devices are used to capture the timecode and keynumber references. This information can be stored in two different places: either in a database, later retrieved as an ASCII file, or inserted as VITC in the video signal. One method does not omit the other from being used, and often both methods are simultaneously utilized.

For example, the Keylinker system from Aaton uses a series of tags that are generated for each start and stop of the telecine. Each tag is unique to the transfer. These tags are stored in the user-bit data of a single line of vertical interval timecode or VITC. The time-bits store the VTR timecode being generated at the time of transfer. For every new tag detected in the VITC, a new entry is generated in the database. By merging the correlating tag number from VITC to the database, the user can retrieve the entire information set for that single film element—information already mentioned such as camera, shoot date, magazine number, scene, take, as well as facility, operator, comments, and descriptions.

The ASCII file version can be imported into non-linear editing systems to create the database to aid in generating lists for the final film conform. Shown below are two examples of ASCII files created during the telecine transfer. If an import process is not used,

then the information stored in VITC can be decoded as it is being played. Any single image or sound element can now be tracked back to its original elements for a final conform.

Example 1:

```
#GLOBAL
TRANSFER_FACILITY AATON LAB-GRENOBLE-FRANCE
AATON_KEYLINK Eq#069 Version 5.17
FILM_TITLE PEPIN MERHI HOLOGRAM MAN
TELECINE_SPEED 23.98
VIDEO_REEL HOUR0010 (30 ndf NTSC)
FILM_GAUGE 35mm 4perf 24fps
AUDIO_FPS 24
AUX_TC_FPS
#EVENTS
video tc audio tc aux tc keycode date/tag cam/lr
001 10:00:00:24 14:04:17:05 KL162518 4956+03
94 10 10 A
 10:00:47:19 14:05:04:00 KL162518 5026+07
51469 551597
 Scen 86E Take 1 CmR A48 SnR 14

002 10:00:47:23 14:05:27:05 KL162518 5026+10
94 10 10 A
 10:02:02:18 14:06:42:00 KL162518 5138+14
51472 551597
 Scen 86F Take 1 CmR A48 SnR 14

003 10:02:02:23 14:06:53:13 KL162518 5139+01
94 10 10 A
 10:02:26:28 14:07:17:18 KL162518 5175+05
51475 551597
 Scen 86G Take 1 CmR A48 SnR 14
```

Example 2:

```
000 Manufacturer Aaton No. 63 Equip Keylink Version
5.12 Flex 1001
010 Title DAISY PROD INC
011 00000100.FLX 348647
012 Shoot Date 94-04-04 Transfer Date 94-04-05
100 Edit 0001 Field A1 NTSC
110 Scene Take Cam 1 Sound 00:00:07:01.0
200 35 23.98 000001 000002+05 Key EASTM
KL481712 000426+00 p
300 1 At 01:00:00:00.0 For 00:00:01:16.0
400 Conv 30.00 Fps At 00:00:07:01.0
400 Cam 24.00 Fps At 00:00:07:01.0
100 Edit 0002 Field A1 NTSC
110 Scene 13 Take 1 Cam 1 Sound 1 00:00:08:21.0
200 35 23.98 000001 000045+05 Key EASTM
KL481712 000428+08 p
300 1 At 01:00:01:20.0 For 00:00:30:06.0
400 Conv 30.00 Fps 1 At 00:00:08:21.0
```

400 Cam 24.00 Fps At 00:00:08:17.0
100 Edit 0003 Field A1 NTSC
110 Scene 13 Take 2 Cam 1 Sound 1 09:40:42:21.0
200 35 23.98 000001 000058+05 Key EASTM
KL481712 000474+00 p
300 1 At 01:00:32:00.0 For 00:00:38:26.0
400 Conv 30.00 Fps 1 At 09:40:42:21.0
400 Conv 24.00 Fps 1 At 09:40:42:17.0

## Three-Line VITC Proposal

How to encode information into VITC must become standardized in order to ensure that essential data are not lost. Shown in figure 7-8 is a VITC encoder.

One proposal before SMPTE is a three-line proposal, as follows:

*Line 1:* Within the time bits, VTR timecode being generated at time of transfer.

*Line 1:* Within the user bits, space is open for the use of the manufacturer. For example, Aaton will use their tag identification relationship to the Aatonbase database while Evertz Microsystems, Ltd. and others may use this line for video reel ID, or a playback timecode.

*Line 2:* Within both time bits and user bits, the entire keynumber and pulldown phase of the transfer sequence.

*Line 3:* Within the time bits, location timecode or sound timecode from the set (usually time-of-day, or TOD, timecode).

*Line 3:* Within the user bits, date of location timecode and sound roll ID.

## Decoding the VITC Information

When decoding VITC, the following example illustrates the type of information that can be accessed during playback on a per-field basis:

1. VTR timecode        01:00:00:00
2. VTR reel ID         001
3. Keynumber           KJ 12 123456 1000 + 00
4. Pulldown            A
5. Sound Timecode      15:30:45:00
6. Date                94 03 08
7. Sound roll          23

## Alternate Shooting Formats and Keynumbers

Recent developments in filmmaking have included a return to shooting 35mm with a frame only three perfs in size. This is done to reduce costs during production as each film frame is only three-fourths the size of the normal film frame (figure 7-9). Since the frame is 25% less, there is a gain of 25% of negative stock for the entire film. A standard thousand-foot roll can now be considered to be 1,250 feet long when using cameras that have been converted to the 3-perf format. Television shows shot on film were the first productions to utilize this format. Since film resolution is superior to video, a slightly smaller 35mm film frame will not be noticed in the video image. Feature films may use this format since the full image area of the 3-perf format very closely approximates the aspect ratio of 1:1.85. When the film interpositive is created, a reduction print is actually created with black bars across the frame in order to

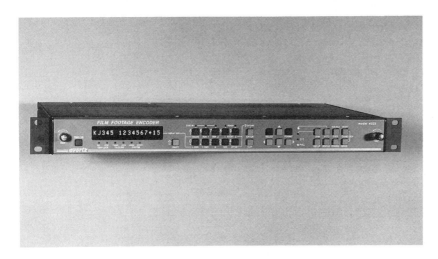

**Figure 7-8** A VITC encoder. Courtesy of Evertz Microsystems, Ltd.

**Figure 7-9**  An example of a 3-perf frame. Courtesy of Aaton.

return to the screening format of four perfs-per-frame.

## 3-Perf and Keynumbers

Conforming by keynumber is very straightforward and accurate when the perfs-per-frame divide equally into the perfs-per-keynumber. For example, a standard 35mm frame of four perfs divides evenly into the 64 perfs per keynumber that exist on the negative: $64 \div 4 = 16$ frames per keynumber. Vistavision, with its eight perfs per frame, also divides evenly into 64: $64 \div 8 = 8$ frames per keynumber. When the keynumber dot reference (•) is under a perf, for example perf 2 of a 4-perf frame, it remains under that perf throughout the run of that take no matter how long the take is. If the negative was never removed from the gate while shooting for cleaning purposes, the perf described in the example would remain under perf 2 for the entire roll.

However, since the 3-perf format does not divide evenly into the 64 perfs per keynumber ($64 \div 3 = 21.333$), a different footage counting scheme is given for this type of shooting format. There is only an even amount of frames every three keynumbers (per yard, one keynumber every foot and 3 feet = 1 yard). Counting in yards can be confusing since there are 64 frames per yard. Carrying around so many frame offsets can be confusing and lead to errors when conforming the negative (figure 7-10 illustrates the frames-to-keynumber relationship). Also there is a

problem in Europe where feet and yards don't exist and film is measured in meters. In Europe, the keynumber is used as the foot portion of the counter so instead of feet + frames they use keynumber + frames. This is especially useful when conforming 16mm, where there are two keynumbers per foot.

Since the 3-perf format is not an equally divisible format, let's examine a little closer what happens to the frame/keynumber relationship.

The first frame of the count has the reference dot (•) of the keynumber zero frame under the first perf of the frame. By the time we get to the next keynumber reference dot, 21 frames later, we see that the reference dot is now under perf 2 of the keynumber reference frame. Twenty-one frames later, we get to the third keynumber reference frame and the reference dot is now under perf 3 of the frame. The problem occurs when the next keynumber reference dot rolls around: the reference dot is back under the first perf of the frame but this frame is 22 frames away from the previous keynumber reference. Instead of a continuous 21 frames for every keynumber, the pattern is

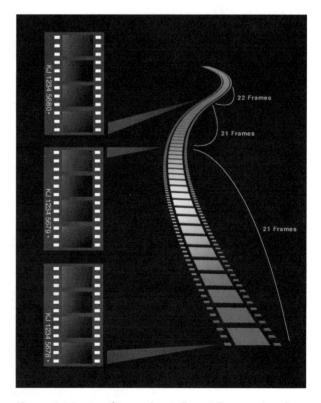

**Figure 7-10**  3-perf keynumber "rollover." Illustration by Jeffrey Krebs.

21, 21, 22. This pattern repeats itself throughout the 3-perf shooting configuration. This is due to the remaining one-third of the frame of the division (64 ÷ 3 = 21.333). For each new keynumber, the one-third of a frame has been accumulating until a full frame is created. The addition of one additional frame happens every three keynumbers. The three keynumbers within the yard are known as the short foot and the long foot. There are two short feet of 21 frames and one long foot of 22 frames before the pattern repeats itself again.

When dealing with 3-perf, the perf relationship must be carried in the database and throughout the editing process to reference the correct film frame. Durations can be expressed in absolute frame counts, or the duration can always assume the perf being on the first perf and then counting from there on. This establishes a standard upon which the durations and cumulative counts can be established. Shown below is an example of a 3-perf cut list which shows both total frame count and the 3-perf counting scheme.

Avid MediaMatch™ version 4.3 Fri Jun 30 14:35:46 1995
Project: Galatée 3perfs
Assemble List for edl file NEPAL:

| Seq | First Edge Number | Last Edge Number | Length | Total | Conform |
|---|---|---|---|---|---|
| 001 | KK 08 3924-1633+15•2 | KK 08 3924-1633+15•2 | 0 | 0 | 0.0 |
| 002 | LEADER-0000+00•0 | LEADER-0001+02•0 | 23 | 23 | 0.0 |
| 003 | KK 08 3924-2969+15•3 | KK 08 3924-2990+13•3 | 429 | 452 | 0.0 |
| 004 | KK 08 3924-3068+04•3 | KK 08 3924-3074+09•3 | 128 | 580 | 0.0 |
| 005 | KK 08 3924-3117+05•1 | KK 08 3924-3122+19•3 | 116 | 696 | 0.0 |
| 006 | KK 08 3924-1249+13•2 | KK 08 3924-1262+04•3 | 258 | 954 | 0.0 |
| 007 | KK 08 3924-1439+08•3 | KK 08 3924-1446+04•1 | 141 | 1095 | 0.0 |
| 008 | KK 08 3924-1352+06•3 | KK 08 3924-1357+05•2 | 102 | 1197 | 0.0 |
| 009 | KK 08 3924-1305+08•1 | KK 08 3924-1318+19•2 | 277 | 1474 | 0.0 |
| 010 | KK 08 3924-1330+09•2 | KK 08 3924-1336+14•2 | 128 | 1602 | 0.0 |
| 011 | KK 08 3924-1976+18•3 | KK 08 3924-1989+13•1 | 263 | 1865 | 0.0 |
| 012 | KK 08 3924-1872+06•1 | KK 08 3924-1886+04•3 | 285 | 2150 | 0.0 |
| 013 | KK 08 3924-2374+07•2 | KK 08 3924-2377+05•2 | 60 | 2210 | 0.0 |
| 014 | KK 08 3924-2107+20•2 | KK 08 3924-2109+12•1 | 34 | 2244 | 0.0 |
| 015 | KK 08 3924-2139+15•1 | KK 08 3924-2146+14•2 | 143 | 2387 | 0.0 |
| 016 | KK 08 3924-1545+14•1 | KK 08 3924-1562+16•3 | 350 | 2737 | 0.0 |
| 017 | KK 08 3924-1642+07•2 | KK 08 3924-1643+11•3 | 24 | 2761 | 0.0 |
| 018 | KK 08 3924-1657+05•2 | KK 08 3924-1659+15•1 | 51 | 2812 | 0.0 |
| 019 | KK 08 3924-2539+17•2 | KK 08 3924-2550+03•1 | 213 | 3025 | 0.0 |
| 020 | KK 08 3924-2784+18•1 | KK 08 3924-2804+05•3 | 397 | 3422 | 0.0 |
| 021 | KK 08 3924-2610+14•1 | KK 08 3924-2612+17•3 | 44 | 3466 | 0.0 |
| 022 | KK 08 3924-2842+17•2 | KK 08 3924-2848+13•2 | 120 | 3586 | 0.0 |
| 023 | KK 08 3924-1665+06•1 | KK 08 3924-1667+14•3 | 48 | 3634 | 0.0 |
| 024 | KK 08 3924-1684+04•2 | KK 08 3924-1685+14•3 | 30 | 3664 | 0.0 |
| 025 | KK 08 3924-1697+09•3 | KK 08 3924-1729+18•2 | 665 | 4329 | 0.0 |
| 026 | KK 08 3924-1748+08•3 | KK 08 3924-1772+06•3 | 490 | 4819 | 0.0 |
| 027 | KK 08 3924-1787+06•3 | KK 08 3924-1796+06•3 | 185 | 5004 | 0.0 |
| 028 | KK 08 3924-1806+12•1 | KK 08 3924-1812+16•1 | 127 | 5131 | 0.0 |
| 029 | KK 08 3924-1618+10•2 | KK 08 3924-1622+09•3 | 81 | 5212 | 0.0 |
| 030 | KK 08 3924-3320+14•3 | KK 08 3924-3403+16•2 | 1703 | 6915 | 0.0 |
| 031 | LEADER-0000+00•0 | LEADER-0187+19•0 | 3789 | 10704 | 0.0 |
| 032 | KK 08 3924-1633+15•2 | KK 08 3924-1633+15•2 | 0 | 10704 | 0.0 |

## TELECINE TRANSFER AND PULLDOWN

### NTSC—Originating at 24 fps and Transferring to 30 fps Video

#### 24 fps–30 fps

During the film-to-tape transfer, the telecine unit scans each film frame and records the image to videotape. When working in NTSC, the video rate is 29.97 fps. PAL is a video frame rate of 25 fps. While in NTSC, the telecine unit creates an even ratio of film frames to video frames. Since 24 cannot divide evenly into 29.97, the film is referenced to the video signal and a pulldown is introduced. The pulldown is the same ratio as between 30 and 29.97; a pulldown of 0.1%. When the same pulldown is applied to film, the film rate during the transfer is actually 23.976 fps. This is a 0.1% pulldown from the original film rate of 24 fps.

$$30 \times .01\% = 0.003$$

$$30 - 0.03 = 29.97$$

$$\text{and } 24 \times .01\% = 0.024$$

$$24 - 0.024 = 23.976$$

To evenly distribute the 23.76 frames per second across 29.97 fps video, a 2:3 pulldown is created. A 2:3 pulldown refers to a situation where one film frame is recorded to two fields of video while the next film frame is recorded to three fields of video. The calculation is: 12 film frames of 2 fields is a total 24 fields + 12 film frames of 3 fields gives us a total of 36 fields. Then 24 fields + 36 fields = 60 fields of video which is equal to 30 frames.

A standard definition of pulldown identification is: 2:3 pulldown is a repetitive pattern that occurs every four film frames. These four film frames are given the letter identification of A, B, C, and D. This pattern of ABCD occurs six times per second and is continuous for each run of the transfer. Referring to figure 7-11, the definition of these pulldown frames is:

A frame is two fields of the same timecode frame.

B frame is 3 fields with a timecode change between fields 2 and 3.

C frame is two fields with a timecode change between the two fields.

D frame is 3 fields with a timecode change between fields 1 and 2.

Another method of distinguishing among the video fields is to refer to the pulldown frames with their field indicator. For example:

A1, A2, B1, B2, B3, C1, C2, D1, D2, and D3.

In this way, the pulldown relationship can be identified anywhere in the transfer sequence.

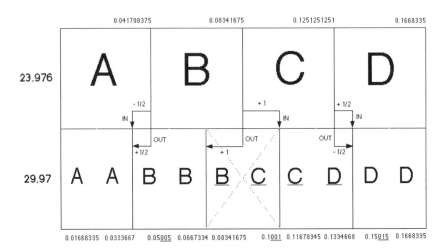

**Figure 7-11** The NTSC 2:3 pulldown relationship between 23.976 fps film and 29.97 fps video. Illustration by Patrick O'Connor.

## 30 fps–30 fps

There are times when film is shot at 30 fps and this is often done when anticipating an NTSC video post-production for special visual effects creation. In this case, the film is transferred at the same rate as video (29.97 fps) so that there is no pulldown created during the telecine process. Instead, the film is merely slowed down by 0.1% to arrive at a running speed of 29.97 fps. Many film cameras can be set to shoot at a 29.97 fps film speed, thereby creating a true 1:1 relationship to the video transfer without performing a 0.1% slowdown.

## PAL

A PAL telecine transfer can occur in two different ways. First, the film is transferred at the same rate as the video rate thus creating a 1:1 relationship to the video. When this happens, there is a 4.1% speedup in relation to the original shooting speed of 24 fps. Transfers done in this manner have no pulldown introduced and, therefore, tracking the timecode-to-keynumber relationship is very easy.

The second method is to keep the film rate at 24 fps while the video rate is 25 fps. This type of transfer does introduce a pulldown relationship. Unfortunately, it is not a standard 2:3 pulldown as found in NTSC, but the pulldown identifiers can still be ABCD (figure 7-12).

In a 24 fps to 25 fps situation, the transfer must make 24 film frames equal 25 video frames for each second. For each second of duration, only one single film frame must be duplicated to create the equal duration in video. As the addition of one entire video frame (two fields) would be jarring to the eye (it could possibly create a visually static moment), the extra frame is instead distributed across two different video fields. Note that it is not one exact film frame that is duplicated across two fields, but two different film frames (frame numbers 12 and 24) that are each extended by one field.

The sequence thus becomes: the first eleven frames of the pulldown sequence are recorded to two fields, while the next single film frame is recorded to three fields. The next eleven film frames are recorded to two fields, while the last film frame is recorded to three fields. The calculation is: (11 film frames × 2 fields) + (1 film frame × 3 fields) + (11 film frames × 2 fields) + (1 film frame × 3 fields) = 50 fields of video = 25 fps. To simplify: 2 (22) + 2 (6) = 50 fields ÷ 2 = 25 frames of video.

The same definition used for NTSC can apply:

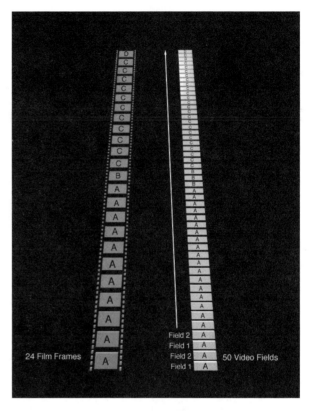

**Figure 7-12** PAL pulldown relationship between 24 fps film and 25 fps video. Illustration by Jeffrey Krebs.

A frame is two fields of the same timecode frame.

B frame is 3 fields with a timecode change between fields 2 and 3.

C frame is two fields with a timecode change between the two fields.

D frame is 3 fields with a timecode change between fields 1 and 2.

These frames can be further identified within the sequence either as A1–A11, B, C1–C11, and D where 1–11 refers to the film frame, or A1–22, B 1–3, C 1–11, D 1–3, where 1–22 refers to the video field.

## Location Timecode for PAL

When using location timecode in the field for film transfers, the timecode rate is 24 fps. This creates a 1:1 relationship between the film frame and its corresponding audio. In the case of the 4.1% speedup during transfer, the timecode is reestablished as a 25 fps timecode. This allows the 1:1 relationship to exist between all elements even after the transfer.

An alternative method while shooting on film is the use of a different timecode. Often, the film negative will be exposed with a 24-frame timecode while the audio recorder will have 25-frame timecode. This relationship can be tracked during the telecine session with an exact sync relationship established at the beginning of every second. Frame A1 will always be the true sync point between picture and sound. The successive frames for only that one second will only be shifted until the beginning of the next second.

## USING LOCATION TIMECODE FOR PICTURE AND SOUND SYNCHRONIZATION

Location timecode is given "frame" boundaries based on the timecode being generated. In-camera timecode is based upon the running speed of the camera. A camera running at a normal film speed of 24 fps will generate a 24-frame timecode on each frame. For audio, the audio recorder will generate a timecode of either 24 or 25 frames when posting in PAL, and a 30-frame timecode (in either drop- or non-drop frame) when posting in NTSC.

There is a specific relationship when using audio timecode for syncing picture and sound based on timecode. Only a 24-frame timecode for the audio will give a true sync point reference for each frame in every second. However, since these audio tapes need to be sync-locked to a video signal during the post-production process, a timecode of 25 frames or 30 frames is commonly used.

NTSC will have true sync references six times for each second whereas PAL will only have one true sync point for each second. The picture-to-sound difference can be calculated based on the following formula: When working with 24-, 25-, and 30-frame timecode, 600 becomes an important number. 600 is the first common number to 24, 25, and 30. We can refer to the numbers 0–600 as units. We will use these units to describe the time discrepancy between the different timecode and shooting rates.

## NTSC 24–30

A relationship exists at any point based on the pull-down ratio between film and Sound TC. This relationship exists as well for video since it counts in 30 frames-per-second timecode. Film frames count between 0 and 23, and SMPTE 30 frames count between 0 and 29. Zero is the absolute sync point reference for all speeds and equals the first frame of film and the first frame of SMPTE 30 timecode.

Figure 7-13 shows the picture and sound sync relationship between film frames and 30-frame audio timecode during a one-second sequence.

With 2:3 pulldown, we can chart the relationship in graphical form. Film frames 1, 5, 9, 13, 17, and 21 are duplicated in order to preserve the pulldown sync relationship. The differing film and video units are tracked by finding the least common multiple of the

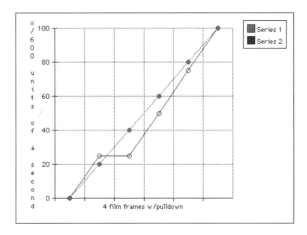

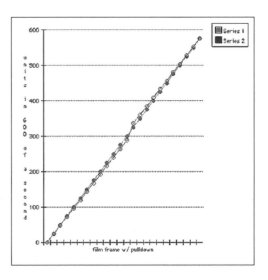

**Figure 7-13** Picture and sound sync relationship between film frames and 30-frame audio timecode during a 1/6 of a second sequence.

different frame rates. Actually, 600 is the least common multiple of 24, 25, and 30. By creating a spreadsheet based on the formulas below, we can track the exact sync relationship between picture and sound and the difference between the two. We can refer to 600 as units of a second. The difference in units divided by 600 will show the relationship in seconds.

| 30 FPS Sound Timecode | Film Frame | Film Unit | Sound Unit | Sync Difference In Seconds |
|---|---|---|---|---|
| 0 | 0 | 0 | 0 | 0 |
| 1 | 1 | 20 | 25 | –0.0083 |
| 2 | 1 | 40 | 25 | 0.025 |
| 3 | 2 | 60 | 50 | 0.0166 |
| 4 | 3 | 80 | 75 | 0.0083 |
| 5 | 4 | 100 | 100 | 0 |
| 6 | 5 | 120 | 125 | –0.0083 |
| 7 | 5 | 140 | 125 | 0.025 |
| 8 | 6 | 160 | 150 | 0.0166 |
| 9 | 7 | 180 | 175 | 0.0083 |
| 10 | 8 | 200 | 200 | 0 |
| 11 | 9 | 220 | 225 | –0.0083 |
| 12 | 9 | 240 | 225 | 0.025 |
| 13 | 10 | 260 | 250 | 0.0166 |
| 14 | 11 | 280 | 275 | 0.0083 |
| 15 | 12 | 300 | 300 | 0 |
| 16 | 13 | 320 | 325 | –0.0083 |
| 17 | 13 | 340 | 325 | 0.025 |
| 18 | 14 | 360 | 350 | 0.0166 |
| 19 | 15 | 380 | 375 | 0.0083 |
| 20 | 16 | 400 | 400 | 0 |
| 21 | 17 | 420 | 425 | –0.0083 |
| 22 | 17 | 440 | 425 | 0.025 |
| 23 | 18 | 460 | 450 | 0.0166 |
| 24 | 19 | 480 | 475 | 0.0083 |
| 25 | 20 | 500 | 500 | 0 |
| 26 | 21 | 520 | 525 | –0.0083 |
| 27 | 21 | 540 | 525 | 0.025 |
| 28 | 22 | 560 | 550 | 0.0166 |
| 29 | 23 | 580 | 575 | 0.0083 |
| 30 | 24 | 600 | 600 | 0 |

The difference in the seconds columns shows the sync relationship between picture and sound. A minus sign indicates when sound is behind picture, and a plus sign indicates when sound is ahead of picture. Figure 7-13 shows the pattern of picture and sound during one second in time. The solid dots indicate the 30-frame time sound timecode, while the hollow dots indicate film frame with pulldown. Note that there is true sync six times per second, indicated by a picture and sound difference of zero. Also shown in Figure

7-13 is a closer view of the relationship over a one-sixth of a second sequence.

The error that exists can be calculated using the following formula:

$$\text{Error} = (S \times 20) - (f \times 25) \div 600$$

where S is the sound timecode.

Let's use as an example film frame 18. In order to obtain the value of V, we divide 18 by 4 and get an absolute of 4. Adding this to 18 equals 22. We then substitute these values into the formula:

$$(22 \times 20) - (18 \times 25) \div 600 = 440 - 450 \div 600$$
$$= -10 \div 600 = -0.0166$$

Our result shows an error where sound trails picture by 0.0166 of a second.

To find the corresponding sync timecode of a film frame, one can use the formula below. We are not concerned with the HOURS: MINUTES: SECONDS of the timecode but just the FRAMES portion of it, since true sync is at the top of every second.

S = sound frame timecode.

$f$ = film frame timecode.

Scan be derived by $S = [f \div 4] + f$.

For example, to find the video TC from film TC 12:30:14:20, we can ignore the 12:30:14 portion of the timecode and just deal with the :20 frames. The formula shows:

$$S = [20 \div 4] + 20$$
$$S = 5 + 20$$
$$S = 25$$

Therefore, film timecode 12:30:14:20 is in sync with sound timecode 12:30:14:25.

## PAL

Just as we can track the sync relationship of film and SMPTE 30 timecode relationships, the same can be done for PAL when the film negative timecode is 24-frame and the sound timecode is 25. There is only true sync at the top of every second, unlike NTSC where there are 6 points of sync every second. In order to create a one-to-one relationship when recording in the field, both negative and sound elements must be coded with a 24-frame timecode.

| 25 FPS Timecode | Film Frame | Video Unit | Film Unit | Difference In Seconds |
|---|---|---|---|---|
| 0 | 0 | 0 | 0 | 0 |
| 1 | 1 | 25 | 24 | 0.0016 |
| 2 | 2 | 50 | 48 | 0.0033 |
| 3 | 3 | 75 | 72 | 0.005 |
| 4 | 4 | 100 | 96 | 0.0066 |
| 5 | 5 | 125 | 120 | 0.0083 |
| 6 | 6 | 150 | 144 | 0.01 |
| 7 | 7 | 175 | 168 | 0.0116 |
| 8 | 8 | 200 | 192 | 0.0133 |
| 9 | 9 | 225 | 216 | 0.015 |
| 10 | 10 | 250 | 240 | 0.0166 |
| 11 | 11 | 275 | 264 | 0.0183 |
| 12 | 12 | 300 | 288 | 0.02 |
| 14 | 13 | 325 | 336 | –0.0183 |
| 15 | 14 | 350 | 360 | –0.0166 |
| 16 | 15 | 375 | 384 | –0.015 |
| 17 | 16 | 400 | 408 | –0.0133 |
| 18 | 17 | 425 | 432 | –0.0116 |
| 19 | 18 | 450 | 456 | –0.01 |
| 20 | 19 | 475 | 480 | –0.0083 |
| 21 | 20 | 500 | 504 | –0.0066 |
| 22 | 21 | 525 | 528 | –0.005 |
| 23 | 22 | 550 | 552 | –0.0033 |
| 24 | 23 | 575 | 576 | –0.0016 |

Again, the sync difference between picture and sound is demonstrated in the last column. A plus sign indicates when sound is ahead of the picture and a minus sign indicates where sound trails the picture.

The sync relationship between 24 and 25 can be described as:

Error = $f \div 600$ when $f < 12$ or $f - 24 \div 600$ when $f > 12$.

$f$ is the film frame.

Therefore, let's use this formula to calculate how far out of sync we are on film timecode :08.

$$8 \div 600 = 0.0133.$$

As 0.0133 is a positive number, sound is ahead of picture by 0.0133 of a second in relation to the film frame.

Here is another example for a film timecode which is greater than :12. Let's find the sync difference between film TC :20.

Error = $20 - 24 \div 600$

Error = $(-4) \div 600$

Error = $-0.0083$

Therefore, sound at this point is 0.0083 of a second behind picture.

## DIGITAL POSTPRODUCTION TRANSFER SESSION

With digital filmmaking film transfers, there are many differences from the traditional film-to-tape process. Electronic camera reports are sent via modem from the location, and these files contain the total aggregate database of merged field reports. The full database contains camera report, sound report, continuity report, as well as location date and timecode. The date and timecode separate each take and make each entry unique. This allows different views of the same take to be accessed. For example, let's say that the director needs to see information about scene 3, take 2. That take could be accessed by the command: Find 3/2. Once accessed, this take now has a unique shoot date and timecode associated with it.

As other information is added, it is merged into the original database. This master log book can now reside on a disk connected to a computer server. A server is typically a computer that contains information that can be accessed by many users. Reports can be generated and printed for use by all the different departments and disciplines.

The file containing all the data compiled thus far would then be imported into the telecine operating system. The operator would load camera roll "X" onto the telecine unit and the reader heads would then read the date, timecode, and keynumber from the edge of the negative or print. The database would retrieve all information concerning roll "X" it finds in its database including the corresponding sound roll number.

The appropriate sound roll or rolls would be loaded to match the camera roll mounted on telecine and these takes would be transferred. All the data compiled from the location reports would then be merged into the telecine data logs that will then add VTR and keynumber information to the database. At this time, the telecine operator could add extra data, such as timing lite information. This single database is then available to all for the retrieval of any information from the pre- to postproduction stages.

The telecine transfer could then be automated due to the information gathered in the databases. Each of the takes on camera roll "X" would have fields determining whether or not the take is to be printed. Printed takes are known as circled takes, are identified in the system, and only these takes are transferred. For each selected take flagged in the database, the negative would be cued up based on the timecode reference on the negative. This reduces the amount of time and money spent in telecine.

With the audio referenced by timecode, a visual reference to this timecode can be seen in the picture if an electronic clapper such as a Smartslate is used during production. A Smartslate looks like an ordinary clapboard but there are LED displays of the timecode on the front of the clapboard. The timecode being displayed is the same timecode that is being recorded by the sound recorder. When the clapper is closed, the timecode at the clap is frozen and displayed for a few short seconds, and the user bits, showing date and sound roll ID, are displayed. Thus, each take's sync reference is identified at the start of every take and this aids in the syncing process. The telecine operator can stop at the clap, enter the timecode (seen in the picture) and the reel-to-reel audio tape player will chase to the entered timecode and lock up for the transfer of the take. There will no longer be a rocking back and forth of the sound reel in the process of finding the correct sync point.

## In-camera Timecode and Timecoded Audio for Syncing

The most powerful way of locking picture and sound for syncing is by using a combination of in-camera timecode and timecode on the audio recording. As a result, both elements will receive the same timecode and the operator will not have to enter a timecode for the sync chase during telecine. While the film is being transferred, the timecode is read from the film negative as the audio deck chases and locks automatically to the matching timecode on the negative.

## PAL Postproduction

When using in-camera timecode for PAL postproduction, a 24-frame timecode is applied to both the negative and the audio. As both will be sped up during the transfer, this allows the one-to-one relationship to al-ways exist. Shooting at 25 fps would work the same way except the timecode would be a 25 fps timecode applied to both picture and sound.

## Sound Transfers and Audio Pulldown

Sound can either be transferred directly from the mag when there is a workprint involved, or the original 1/4" reels can be used. Each reel is loaded onto reel-to-reel players and is referenced to the video signal in order to lock the machines together in sync. The same pulldown process we encountered with the picture (2:3 pulldown) applies to the sound. When 0.1% pulldown is applied to audio, the original 60 KHz signal is now referenced at 59.94 KHz. In so doing, the film and sound elements will be in sync on the video dailies.

## Audio Pullup

When returning to the film finish, the reverse is done and the sound elements are sped up to compensate for the pulldown. This is known as a pullup. One way of doing this is referencing the mag machine to 59.94 Hz (in sync with the pulldown film of 23.976 fps). Once the transfer is complete, the mag will no longer be referenced to video and will play back in sync with film running at 24 fps. This type of re-referencing of the signal always happens in an analog state. Some DAT machines will allow pullups and pulldowns when using digital transfers via the AES/EBU protocols.

Recently there has been a proposal to shoot film at a rate of 23.976 fps in the camera, to allow digital audio to occur throughout the postproduction process. Since the transfer is always done at 23.976 fps, there is no pulldown involved. In time, it will be interesting to see where this idea will lead because the normal shooting rate of film, at 24 fps, has remained unchanged for decades. In the past, there was a proposal to shoot film at 30 fps in order to be compatible with video, but the idea was quickly rejected. Such an increase in the frames per second would have caused a significant increase in negative costs.

## Barcode Readers and Bench Logging Procedures

RIM, Research in Motion, is a company that manufactures barcode readers for telecine units or for logging benches. Logging benches are used for a continuous transfer of film material when there are many breaks in keynumbers. This typically occurs when the individual takes are assembled together in order to create a transfer reel or flat. Recall that KeyKode readers can only detect breaks when the keynumber changes, and a new keynumber can be as far as eight frames away in 35mm and ten frames away in 16mm.

Telecine transfers are more efficient by reducing the amount of times that the transfer process is started and stopped. This can be accomplished by making a continuous transfer and disregarding the breaks in keynumbers. The negative can be logged on a bench, either before or after the transfer, and by using a common sync point that has been established before the transfer (such as making a physical punch mark on the negative) an exact log can be created. This log is based on footage and keynumber. Bench logging systems are also available by Evertz Microsystems and Excalibur. Shown in figure 7-14 is a bench logging reader.

Here is how the bench logging procedure can be implemented: Establish a sync point reference on the negative. This can be a punch or a clap reference. This sync point is then "zeroed" on the footage counter. The electronic reader sends this information to a computer; the data consist of footage counts and the keynumber that is being read.

When the system detects a keynumber break, it electronically beeps. The operator then stops, rewinds to the splice point and re-establishes a new reference sync point. The operator then continues rolling down the negative. When the next new keynumber appears,

the logging program counts the offset from the new sync point and enters the keynumber of the frame at the splice point (figure 7-15). This continues until the end of the transfer roll is reached.

When the negative is then placed on the telecine unit, the only information required is the timecode and the pulldown of the sync point reference established earlier (i.e. the punch frame).

Later, when the telecine file and the bench log file are merged, a new file indicating all the breaks, keynumbers, timecode, and pulldown information is available. Some programs do not require merging, and instead simply add timecode and pulldown phase to their own database. These files are then loaded into the DNLE system in order to create lists after editing is complete.

## Post Telecine Synchronization

Another procedure that can be utilized to offset the cost of telecine is to transfer the picture without sync audio and to synchronize audio to picture at a later time, usually in an offline edit room. This is particularly true when there is no common timecode between the negative and the 1/4″ sound rolls. The MOS source videotape becomes the master tape in this situation. Either the 1/4″ audio playback machine or DAT is then used as the source.

It is important to remember that the audio must be referenced to 59.94 Hz in order to be in sync with the film that is now playing back at 23.976 fps. The master tape for picture is played back and paused on each slate clap of each take, and the audio is also

**Figure 7-14** The Evertz bench logging reader for 35mm film. Courtesy of Evertz Microsystems, Ltd.

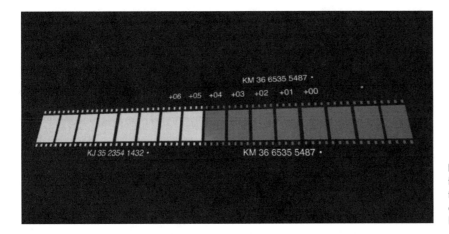

**Figure 7-15** A splice between two different keynumbers. This indicates how there can be a different keynumber after a splice break. Illustration by Jeffrey Krebs.

played back and paused on the clap. A normal audio-only insert is made for the length of the take, and this procedure continues until all the takes have been synced. The EDL that is created is an EDL that only contains timecode. Later, this EDL can be merged with the telecine file in order to obtain the full database that is needed for list creation. A sample EDL would be:

001 SR19 AA C 17:01:10:01 17:01:51:01
01:00:00:00 01:00:41:00

where

| | |
|---|---|
| 001 | = the event |
| SR19 | = the sound roll ID |
| 17:01:10:01 | = sound timecode IN point |
| 17:01:51:01 | = sound timecode OUT point |
| 01:00:00:00 | = VTR timecode IN point |
| 01:00:41:00 | = VTR timecode OUT point |

This EDL can be translated into a database that will show the video and timecode sync point relationship. The name of the EDL will be the name of the tape or video reel ID.

| Tape | VTR TC Start | VTR TC End | Sound TC | Sound Roll |
|---|---|---|---|---|
| 001 | 01:00:00:00 | 01:00:41:00 | 17:01:10:01 | SR19 |

When this file is merged with a bench-logged file, all additional information, such as keynumber, pulldown, comments, and descriptions can also be added.

## OUTPUT OF CUTLIST AND OPTICAL FILM EFFECTS INFORMATION

When the editing process is complete, the cutlist that is generated from the DNLE system must be able to communicate with traditional film postproduction processes. The traditional types of effects that can be created with an optical printer can now be previewed on a DNLE system and it is critical to know how they are created and how they relate to what must be re-done at the optical printing stage.

### Creating Traditional Film Opticals

Optical effects for films are created during the printing stage. The original negative elements are aligned in an optical printer, and based on a frame count relationship, a new negative is created that is the combination of the two or more original negative elements. Some common effects include freeze frame, which is created by repeating a single film frame while the new negative is exposed for as many frames as are necessary to arrive at the required duration for the freeze.

Skip frames are used when motion needs to be accelerated by skipping frames during the printing. This will create a sped up effect when the new element is played back at sound speed.

Stretching frames creates the appearance of an action being slowed down and is accomplished by repeating a frame for a specific amount of time. For example, each frame could be repeated two or three times depending upon the amount of slow motion required.

Reverse action is created by printing the last frame first and working backwards until the first frame of action is reached. If the film were just played in reverse then exposed onto a new negative, the picture would be upside-down when projected, as well as being in reverse. Therefore, a true optical effect must be created.

Blowup is the ability to enlarge a section of the picture based on ten different fields in the final print. Shown in figure 7-16 is a blowup chart that is used to define that portion of an image that is to be enlarged.

Repositions are accomplished by moving the picture north, south, east, and west on predefined fields.

A flop over is done to reverse the line of action so that left and right are switched. This has the same effect as looking at a picture in a mirror and is often used to correct screen direction errors when actors cross the line of action.

Matte and chroma keys are accomplished by running the negative through multiple passes and exposing the areas needed to create the effect. Mattes are used and wherever there are black areas of the matte, these areas will not be exposed. The unexposed portion of the negative is ready for exposure of a new element during the next pass.

The DNLE system must output optical count sheets to instruct the lab operator as to how to recreate the optical effects. Some systems will also al-low previsualization of several picture layers, such as foreground and background elements and their relationships, when they are combined as either superimpositions or keys.

## NEW PROCESSES THAT UTILIZE MACHINE-READABLE KEYNUMBERS

Since the keynumber is machine-readable, this data can now be read and referenced automatically in databases at playback speeds on the telecine. By having a direct link to the frame, timing lite information can now be referenced exactly to the frame and not just on a running footage count of the camera roll. Other information can now be tagged in the database, and the exact frame can be retrieved automatically by machine controlled negative transport systems.

Optical printers, if properly outfitted, can now be controlled by keynumber to recreate the optical effects created on the DNLE system. There are several systems on the market that provide automatic printing of the answer print without cutting the film negative. One company, Kodika, does so by importing a cut list into the controller's computer. The unexposed negative is loaded in the printer, and each master camera roll is loaded on the source side of the printer as dictated by the cumulative footage counter of the master cut list. If the system is given an "A" mode list, meaning that all the events are in show order as edited for screening, then the system will sort the list into "C" mode where all events are sorted based on source camera roll. When this happens, the master footage is out-of-order based on the order of the source reels.

The source events from the original camera negative are printed onto the new negative in a checkerboard fashion until all the source camera rolls have been loaded and printed. This type of system will also handle standard length dissolves, or those lengths permitted by the specific type of printer being used.

The technology of the traditional film laboratory has undergone very little change in the 100-plus years of filmmaking. With digital filmmaking methods, the processes that must be carried out in the laboratory, and the data that must flow between the DNLE system and the laboratory are areas of rapid change and improvement for film laboratories.

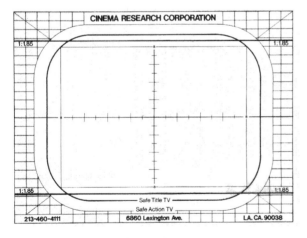

**Figure 7-16** A blowup chart used to define the portion of an image which is to be enlarged. Courtesy of Cinema Research Corporation.

# 8

# The Digital, Nonlinear Postproduction Process

## MAINTAINING A VISION FOR THE FILM

Filmmakers around the world yearn for control over the process of making their films. Some filmmakers live for the preproduction and previsualization stage. The famous director Alfred Hitchcock often remarked that for him a film was finished as soon as the preproduction stage was over and that there was nothing more creative in the process. At least for Hitchcock, all aspects of creativity were exercised during this precious first phase of filmmaking.

In actuality, however, we know that this is false. Hitchcock was very stringent in the marketing techniques used for his films. This is true in the now-famous marketing ploy which accompanied *Psycho* where theatergoers were not to be admitted once the film had begun! What Hitchcock was doing, clearly, was stating his preference: he wanted control over preproduction, was reportedly bored during the production and postproduction stages, and became reinvolved during the marketing and distribution stage.

Maintaining control over one's artistic vision in the filmmaking process is, for many, a Herculean achievement. The reason? As with any film, there must be a presence which rallies and organizes. Absolutely no amount of technology will fix the problem of a truly bad performance. Filmmaking can be a collaboration of a few people or hundreds of people, and a crew of 400 is not unusual on a big budget film that is straining to make a specific release date. Other films are the penultimate definition of the cliché shoestring budget. And, clearly, films made on tiny budgets can do extremely well with audiences and film critics, while films made for millions of dollars can evaporate from the public eye with amazing speed.

With digital filmmaking, filmmakers have the technology and the communication methods to con-

tinue to shape a project long after sets have been struck and cast and crew have departed. Even if the filmmaker is thousands of miles away from the center of postproduction, it is possible to contribute to the decision making process as if the filmmaker were in the same room as the editorial staff. This is all possible while the filmmaker is busy at work on a new film.

## PARALLEL FILMMAKING REPLACES SERIAL POSTPRODUCTION

In this chapter, we describe the digital, nonlinear postproduction process. In the past, postproduction of a film was largely serial in nature. Picture editing was undertaken and finished. Each reel of the film was locked, and work began on the sound portion of the film. There was very little parallel work taking place. The significance of this is that filmmakers had to be very sure, very early on in the postproduction stage that they were taking the correct approach at putting the film together. If not, often the film would be taken out of their control and finished according to the desires of the investors.

There are advantages to working in parallel. First, for both the director and the editor, knowing that they can work on a particularly troublesome scene up to the last possible minute is of great importance. How do they afford this luxury? By having the confidence of knowing that, around them, sound work has already begun and is progressing nicely. The reason? Because the editor has already posted an earlier reel of the film for the sound design team.

Or, consider a title sequence for a film. Depending upon the film's budget, the sequence may be left to a dedicated design company or the filmmakers may implement the title sequence. Working in parallel, director and editor can create the montage of images that will play behind the title sequence and send these images, via phone lines, to a design company. The design company can see the images, their cadence and tempo, and can begin working on an appropriate title approach.

## INDUSTRY VIEWPOINTS

### Martha Coolidge—Director

*Angie* (1994), *Lost In Yonkers* (1993), *Crazy In Love* (1992), *Rambling Rose* (1991).

For film director Martha Coolidge, the term digital filmmaking describes a growing movement towards an ever increasing use of digital tools and techniques that will continue to assist filmmakers in realizing their visions. Says Coolidge,

> In the last several years I have been using digital, nonlinear editing systems on my films, but I am very aware of the fact that there are many aspects of computer technology for making films. Even if you start from the basic idea of budgeting a film—this used to take weeks to do, and it has now been computerized and now takes very little time. Even on the most basic word processing level, we now have software

**Figure 8-1** Photo of Martha Coolidge. Courtesy of Martha Coolidge/Guttman Associates.

which will instantly format a screenplay. The result of all these digital technologies is that you save time working on planning the movie and you realize these savings for creative time.

On the subject of previsualization techniques for filmmakers, Coolidge continues,

> I have many director friends who have made good use of electronic storyboarding for action sequences and I think it is an incredible tool to visualize how the movement will appear on set. We used to rely on illustrators but now you can input the set and the characters and experiment with movement in 3-D for certain pictures and it is a worthwhile expenditure of time. I feel that electronic previsualization is going to be very useful to me. I can take location shots and modify exactly what I want so that I know what the film will look like. In terms of visual effects, the digital, nonlinear editing system is great at pre-visualizing many of the effects you have in a film.

Digital, nonlinear editing also offers many benefits for Coolidge, who adds,

> It turns editing time into thinking time. It doesn't really make the first cut faster, but it is more thorough. Recuts and changes are substantially faster. You can do more cutting and make sure you have the best performances. All sound is going to be digital and that will be a significant change and we won't have any mag. We now do mostly our temp mixes from the digital editing system. . . .
>
> On *Angie* (1994), we had this fantasy ballet sequence and we got to a point in the movie where this sequence was very long and had to be shortened. We had very little time because we were faced with having to finish the movie. So my editor, Steve Cohen, and I experimented with different versions using multi-layered dissolves that would have taken weeks to get back from the lab. But on the digital, nonlinear editing system, we tried different things and did mixes and shortened the sequence in no time. On the laserdisc version of the film you can even see several different versions we tried as we worked up to the final version. This is something we just couldn't have done on film—it would have been completely prohibitive and we just would have chosen a path and lived with it. . . .
>
> The most exciting results of digital in filmmaking is that there are no limits to your imagination. There may be cost factors, but I think that *Jurassic Park* is just the tip of the iceberg. We can create the past, the present, and the future. There is no limit.

## THE DIGITAL PICTURE EDITORIAL PROCESS

Digital picture editing is relatively new to the film-making process, and the history of electronic, nonlinear editing is short. Introduced primarily in 1984, there have been three stages of electronic editing: videotape-based, laserdisc-based, and the digital, nonlinear editing stage.

## How Electronic Editing Systems Work

The concept behind electronic editing is simple. By transferring film to a new medium, the footage can be accessed more rapidly than by winding through various film rolls. There are two important characteristics of an electronic editing system. First, it must be nonlinear, and the system must allow the order of shots to be easily changed without consequence to already edited material. Second, the system must be random access, meaning it must be possible to get to any frame of the footage without having to proceed sequentially through the footage.

## Videotape-based Systems

In 1984, the first system to appear was the Montage Picture Processor. Following the Montage was the Ediflex system in 1985 (figure 8-2) and TouchVision

in late 1986. Each system offered a different user environment and work method, but all shared the same basic method of bringing nonlinearity to the editing task.

The underlying concept of the tape-based systems is achieving nonlinear editing by using multiple videotape machines. A sequence is created by cueing each machine to a different shot and then playing back the shots in their intended order (figure 8-3). In this way, editing can proceed in a nonsequential manner. Nothing has to be committed to a final order until the editor is content (figure 8-4).

These systems were nonlinear, but they were not random access. Because videotape was involved, access to the material was still sequential. The editor still had to cue the point on the videotape and wait for this to occur. By having identical footage on all the tape machines, the editor has a nonlinear editing system. Instead of editing on film, where the splices would first have to be removed and the order of the film pieces changed and then respliced, here just the directions to the tape machines are altered.

For example, let's assume that a system is configured with 12 VHS machines. The editor is creating a sequence with ten shots. Since the same source material is on the duplicate cassettes, the system can easily find the first shot in machine 1, the second shot in machine 2, and so on. After the editor chooses appropriate in points for each of the shots, ten machines will work in tandem, cueing to their in points. Each

**Figure 8-2** The Ediflex nonlinear editing system. Photo courtesy Ediflex Systems.

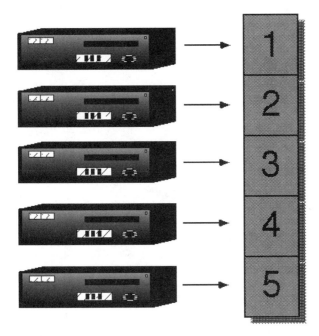

**Figure 8-3** Multiple machines are used to seek out sections on videotapes. After reaching their cue points, the machines playback the sequence in its intended order, shots 1,2,3,4,5. Illustration by Jeffrey Krebs.

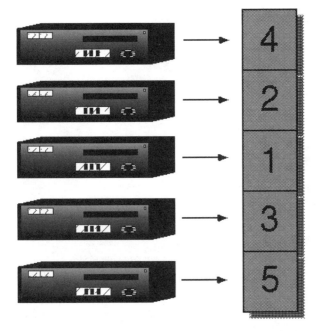

**Figure 8-4** By directing the machines to cue to different sections of videotape, the sequence being edited appears reordered. Here, the original sequence order of 1,2,3,4,5 is changed by merely directing the source machines to playback material in the new order of 4,2,1,3,5. Illustration by Jeffrey Krebs.

shot is then played back at the correct time, and the sequence can be viewed in its entirety.

## VIRTUAL RECORDING AND THE PLAYLIST

Each wave of nonlinear editing systems adheres to the concept of virtual recording. Here, no video and audio signals are being recorded from one tape to another. Instead, a list, a playlist, is created. The playlist simply keeps track of how the different shots were ordered and this list is used to cut and conform the original film negative. A playlist determines which shots were used and their order. If we want to create a sequence where we see a gun, then a man walking, and finally a finger on the trigger of the gun, the playlist, represented by timecode numbers, looks like this:

| Segment | Play | From | To |
|---|---|---|---|
| 1 | Gun | 05:00:02:01 | 05:00:05:12 |
| 2 | Man Walking | 05:05:08:09 | 05:05:18:09 |
| 3 | Trigger Finger | 05:02:04:01 | 05:02:09:01 |

By re-ordering the playlist, the images are automatically rearranged and played in a new order.

## Multiple Versions

By manipulating the playlist, we can create multiple versions of a sequence. This lets the editor experiment with alternative versions for a scene. After a scene is cut, we can duplicate the playlist. By duplicating the playlist, the scene is duplicated. Then, the new copy of the scene can be altered. There are now two versions of the scene. Even if only one frame is altered in the second version, it is different from the first version. This flexibility and power to change just one thing must be available in all nonlinear editing systems.

## Laserdisc-based Systems

The second wave of nonlinear editing systems began in 1984 with the introduction of the EditDroid. It offered what videotape-based systems did not: random access. Because a laser mechanism can skip from one section of a disc to another very quickly, from 900 milliseconds (ms) to two seconds (1 ms = 1/1000 second), the editor could jump to any shot almost instantly. Nonlinear editing is simulated through the use of multiple laserdisc players. Shown in figure 8-5 is the CMX 6000 laserdisc-based editing system.

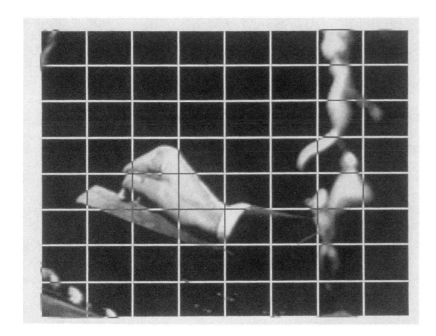

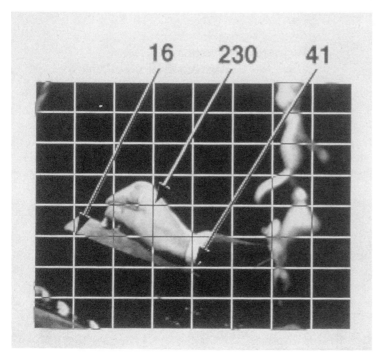

**Figures 8-5a–b** The flash convertor is used to divide a picture into its precise elements (the pixels of the image) and assigns its brightness value into a number. Illustration by Rob Gonsalves.

## Digital-based Systems

Digital, nonlinear editing systems appeared in 1988. They were first used in the postproduction industry of television and enjoyed enormous growth from 1989 to 1993. From 1988 to 1995, over 45 different digital systems were introduced. However, only a fraction were able to address the needs of the digital filmmaking process. Digital systems operate by converting analog signals into digital signals and storing these signals on computer disks. The process of analog-to-digital conversion is called digitization. The process of reducing the amount of data that represents the original information is called compression.

A digital system has three attributes: it is nonlinear, random access, and digital. Perhaps the easiest way to think of a digital editing system is as a word processor for pictures and sounds. Once the film footage and sound recordings are in digital form, they can be easily be arranged and rearranged.

## THE DIGITIZATION PROCESS

Digital editing requires that the video and audio signals be transferred to computer disks. Normally, this is a real-time procedure; a ten minute camera roll that was transferred to videotape takes ten minutes to be digitized.

### Within the Computer

Within a digital, nonlinear editing system are various computer boards, one of which is a picture digitizing board, capable of taking a video input and transforming the analog (or possibly digital) video into binary form. These digital data become the pictures and sounds that the film editor manipulates as easily as words in a word processor.

### Pixels and Flash Convertors

A pixel is the smallest element that makes up a picture, and pixels are the patterns of dots that make up an image on a viewing screen. Pixel matrices are calculated by multiplying the number of pixels that are contained both vertically and horizontally over the span of the viewing screen. When a picture is played from videotape and the digital, nonlinear editing system is about to digitize the incoming video signals, a series of very complex time-critical operations must occur.

On the digitizing board are computer chips which function as flash convertors. These convertors take each pixel and convert its brightness value into a number. The convertors take these numbers and place them into computer memory; at that point, the image has now become a set of numbers. There will typically be convertors that are assigned to each major component of the picture, one convertor each for the red, green, and blue. Shown in figures 8-5a–b are examples of how a flash convertor operates.

While the picture files are being digitized, the audio signals will also be digitally sampled, usually by a second computer board, and the data that now represent sound will be stored to disk (figure 8-6).

### Digitize and Store to Disk or Digitize-Compress Store to Disk?

The next stage in the digitization process could be to store the data to computer disk. As each frame of video is digitized, it would be passed from computer memory, to and through the computer bus, and stored in various forms, such as in RGB or YUV color space to computer disk magnetic (figure 8-7). These

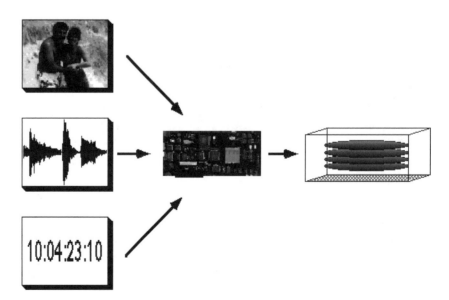

**Figure 8-6** Video, stereo audio, and timecode are digitized in real time from the source videotape. The video is compressed, and all signals are stored to either magnetic or optical disc. Illustration by Jeffrey Krebs.

10:04:23:10

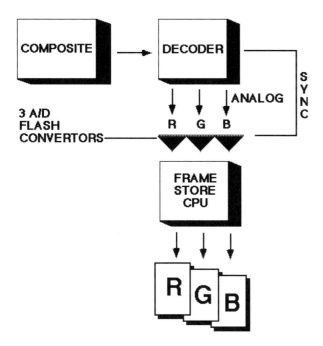

**Figure 8-7** The digitizing process begins as composite analog video is decoded into its analog components and flash converted. Adding a chip based CPU to the RGB framestore provides the ability to operate on incoming pixels before the main CPU must process them. With this decreased workload, the main CPU can now perform compression schemes. Illustration by Jeffrey Krebs.

disks represent the storage mechanisms and determine how much footage the editor can access.

## Storage Requirements of Video

One frame of video represents many pixels. As a result, large amounts of computer memory are required to store several seconds of video. The number of pixels are affected by the different pixel matrices that there are in video RGB, NTSC, PAL, etc. Let's say that we have just digitized NTSC video that represents the film that we are going to edit digitally.

The RGB data that results from an NTSC picture sub-sampled to 640 × 480 can be calculated as follows (note: an RGB picture has no inherent resolution with regard to pixel dimensions):

640 × 480 = 307,200 pixels × 3 (RGB) = 921,600 bytes (921.6 kB)

Thus, it takes slightly under 1 MB to store one video frame at this pixel matrix. Each second of video requires 27.648 MB of storage (921.6 kB per frame × 30 frames per second).

## Storage Requirements of Film

While the storage requirements of video may appear large, one film frame requires much more space. For Academy format 35mm four perf film, a pixel matrix of 3,656 × 2664 at 10 bits per pixel is required. This equals approximately 40 MB of information for just one frame of film! While each second of video requires 27 megabytes, each second of film requires 960 megabytes of storage. Further, a 1 gigabyte (GB) disk (1 GB = 1,000 MB) would provide approximately 36 seconds of full resolution video and slightly more than one second of full resolution Academy format film. Clearly, the storage requirements are staggering. After all, even if a two hour film had a shooting ratio of only 5:1, this would represent 10 hours of material, or 864,000 frames of film which would have to be stored.

## Applying Compression for Specific Tasks

For editing, we do not require that film frames be stored at their full resolution and we can compromise picture quality for increases in storage. These compromises take the form of digital video compression.

## DIGITAL VIDEO COMPRESSION

To store a practical amount of footage there are two possibilities: add a huge amount of computer disk capacity, or decrease the storage requirements for each frame thereby consuming less space per frame. This is the goal of digital video compression—a reduction in size for each frame that is stored to disk.

The third item of interest is the video compression board. This board receives the data from the digitizing card. Recall that at this point the pixels have been flash converted and converted to binary data. Now, however, instead of the data being stored to disk, at full resolution and uncompressed, the data are sent to the compression card. From the compression card, the data are sent to and stored on computer disk.

## Reducing the Data: Single Field or Double Field?

The first step in reducing space is to determine whether one or two fields per frame will be stored. In film, each frame equals one picture. However, in video, to draw the full video frame requires that the signal be alternately scanned: first the odd lines are drawn, and then the even lines. These odd and even lines are called fields. When two fields are put together, the result is one video frame. NTSC video plays back at 60 fields per second while PAL video plays back at 50 fields per second.

We can decide if two fields will represent each video frame (which ultimately is going to represent one film frame), or if we are going to represent one film frame by one video field. By storing only either the first field or the second field, we can instantly reduce the storage requirements by 50%. This is one of the first steps that digital, nonlinear editing systems take. For other processes in the digital filmmaking methodology, this would not be acceptable.

## Lossless Compression

At this point, we have digitized one-half of the effective resolution of the frame. Although we are still digitizing losslessly, we are not storing the image at its full resolution. Next, data leaves the digitizing card and enters the compression card. Compression operates on the basis that there are analyses that can be performed that will determine redundancies. When the analysis is complete, redundancies are coded and stored. For example, if we have the sentence, "only the lonely," we calculate that there are two each of the letters o, l, n, and y, and one each of the letters t, h, and e. By assigning small values to the letters that appear frequently (and therefore have to be counted more often) and higher values to the letters that appear less frequently (and therefore have to be counted less often), we can decrease the amount of data it takes to store the original file.

This is a lossless compression technique: the original file is momentarily replaced by a table of data that is a compressed form of the original file, one that requires less space. This table of data is then uncompressed, returning the file to its original state and nothing in the original file has been lost.

## Lossy Compression

Lossy compression, on the other hand, takes a file and reduces its size by discarding information that cannot be reconstituted. In a digital, nonlinear editing system, here is one method of applying lossy compression: data leaving the digitizing card enter the compression card. Here, lossy compression techniques are applied to further reduce the amount of data for each frame. There are software-only and hardware-assisted compression techniques.

## Software-Only Methods: Subsampling

The amount of data for each frame can be reduced by subsampling. We can reduce the combined number of horizontal and vertical pixels and the amount of color information. Recall that normally the frame-store units would have to pass 921,600 bytes to the computer bus:

$$640 \times 480 \times 3 = 921,600 \text{ bytes/frame} \times 30$$
$$\text{frames} = 27.648 \text{ MB/sec}$$

If instead of displaying the image in $640 \times 480$ we displayed it in $128 \times 96$ and reduced the bits per pixel to one byte (e.g., three bits for red, three bits for blue, and two bits for green equaling eight bits or one byte), what would we save in storage requirements? Our calculations show:

$$128 \times 96 \times 1 = 12,288 \text{ bytes/frame} \times 30 \text{ frames}$$
$$= 368.6 \text{ kB/sec}$$

Clearly, we save a lot, for only 370 kilobytes versus 27 megabytes are required for each second of footage. On a 1 GB disk, our 27.648 MB/sec sample provided us with only about 36 seconds of storage. However, now, at 370 kB/sec, the 1 GB disk provides 45 minutes of storage!

## Hardware Assisted Compression

Whereas software methods achieve their smaller file sizes by discarding information, hardware provides more time to examine each frame, determine redundancies, and assign numeric values. Software provides algorithms to determine which sections of the image can be compromised.

## Types of Digital Video Compression

There are several methods of compressing digital video such as DVI, JPEG, MPEG, and Wavelets. Each

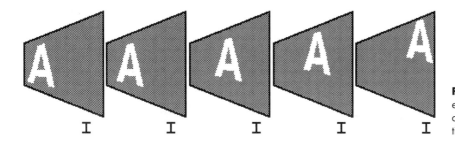

**Figure 8-8** Intraframe coding allows each frame to carry its own information and to be drawn independently. Illustration by Jeffrey Krebs.

of these methods accomplishes its tasks differently, but the goal is equal: to reduce file size requirements while preserving as much image detail as possible.

## Asymmetric or Symmetric Processing

Compression methods may be either asymmetric or symmetric. Asymmetric means it takes more time to compress the image than to play back the image. Symmetric means it takes the same amount of time to compress and play back the image. Asymmetric compression methods are not acceptable for digital video editing because it would take longer than real time to digitize.

**DVI—Digital Video Interactive.** DVI supports both still images and motion video and can be both asymmetric and symmetric in nature. There are two types of DVI: presentation-level video, asymmetric (PLV); and real-time video, symmetric (RTV). It is the RTV form of DVI that is used in digital, nonlinear editing systems.

**JPEG—Joint Photographic Experts Group.** Symmetric JPEG is based on still images. It is based on intraframe coding, where each frame contains all the information that the frame requires in order to be displayed (figure 8-8). An intraframe-coded frame is not dependent upon data in a previous frame. For editing, it requires a compression method that treats every frame distinctly; otherwise the editing system would constantly spend its resources finding reference frames.

For digital video editing, DVI and JPEG are the most popular methods of compression.

**MPEG—Moving Picture Experts Group,** asymmetric and symmetric. Unlike JPEG, MPEG is based on motion. MPEG is actually a combination of intraframe and interframe coding. Interframe coding offers a major benefit over JPEG compression: a significant savings of storage and a ratio of 3:1 is a usual estimate. This seems as if it would be an overwhelming advantage. After all, if we could normally only store one hour of footage under JPEG, we could now store three hours under MPEG.

However, the method by which MPEG stores its information is based on predictive coding methods. There are a series of frames referred to as I, P, and B frames. I is an intraframe-coded frame and is independent of other frames. It is also referred to as an intrapicture. P is a predicted frame. Data are predicted from a previous intraframe frame or from a previous P frame. B is a bidirectional frame. Data are interpolated from the closest I and P frames (figure 8-9). It is through this method of determining where a frame will be based on surrounding frames that MPEG is able to achieve more economical storage.

Unfortunately, editing requires access to every frame. If an editor wants to edit from one frame to a different frame, and one frame is an I frame and the

**Figure 8-9** The interframe coding methods of MPEG compression. Each frame is not drawn independently. Instead, certain frames are predicted, resulting in a decrease in the amount of storage required. Illustration by Jeffrey Krebs.

other frame is a B frame, the editing system needs time to locate the surrounding frames that the B frame references.

## Applications for MPEG

While MPEG is not currently optimized for editorial challenges, MPEG 1 and MPEG 2 can offer benefits for storage and transmission. For example, a CD-ROM (compact disc read only memory) has a bandwidth limitation of approximately 180 kB/sec. MPEG 1, with a bandwidth limitation of about 150 kB/sec, provides just the range for a CD-ROM application. A comparable image under JPEG, however, would not function given the bandwidth constraints of the CD-ROM. Another aspect of MPEG that makes it quite exciting is the promise that it holds for reducing transmission time for sending data from one location to another. If a JPEG file took one hour to send, an MPEG version of the same file may take only twenty minutes to send.

## From Editing System and into the Home

Using compression to deliver programming into the home is undergoing massive investigation, research, and design. MPEG 2, at a possible 1.5 MBits/sec data rate, could be transmitted over multiplexed ISDN lines and enter the home via the telephone pole. This makes it possible to deliver films into the home on a "video on demand" basis. Imagine that you want to watch Orson Welles's *Citizen Kane* at 3 A.M. or John Sturges's *The Great Escape* at 4:30 in the afternoon, downloading it from a file server and onto your television set at will!

**Wavelets**—Wavelet compression is divided into two processes: a scaling function and a convolving function. The scaling function takes the original picture and squeezes it down to reduce it on the x and y axes (figure 8-10). Once the image has been scaled, the convolving process, which seeks to encode error, is run. The information in the original picture is compared to the differences in the scaled version, and the

**Figure 8-10** The first step in Wavelet compression is the scaling function. The original picture is reduced on the x and y axes. Courtesy Aware, Inc.

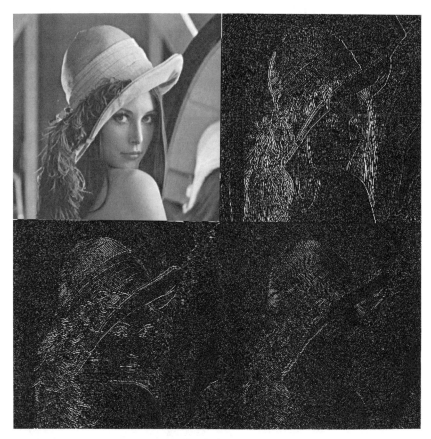

**Figure 8-11** This is the result of the first level of a wavelet transform. The three portions of the picture shown in outline are represented as quantized information. This procedure continues for each cycle of transformation. Courtesy Aware, Inc.

**Figure 8-12** A variation of a Mandlebrot fractal set; the original pattern is magnified to reveal sections which resemble the original pattern. Illustration by Rob Gonsalves.

differences represent error. The goal is to store one of four portions of the picture and then to quantize the other three portions of the picture (figure 8-11). This quantizing reduces the amount of data that must be stored to represent the picture.

**Fractals**—Instead of breaking a picture into frequencies, fractals utilize fractal patterns to represent every possible pattern that can exist. By dividing a picture into a fraction of its whole, these smaller sections can be searched and analyzed fairly quickly. On a smaller level, instead of trying to find the pattern for the entire picture, the search is for smaller patterns of pixels (figure 8-12).

In this way, pixels do not have to be transmitted for each section of the original picture. Instead, the process continues until the entire picture has been broken down into subsections and analyzed. The result of this is a string of coordinates. To play back an image, these coordinates from the data stream are processed, and then, returning to the fractal set, data are copied based on the coordinate locations needed. The data represented by each of these x, y, and z coordinates are then copied and merged. The result is a recreation of the original picture. Fractal compression is an asymmetrical process.

## HOW HARDWARE ASSISTED DIGITAL VIDEO COMPRESSION WORKS: JPEG EXAMINED

Under JPEG, mathematical procedures called discrete cosine transforms (DCTs), lossy compression algorithms, are used to analyze frames. JPEG decodes and encodes gray scale and color images and varies the amount of compression that is applied. The greater the ratio, the smaller the resulting file; the smaller the ratio, the larger the resulting file. For editing, the average ratio ranges from 20–50:1.

### Chroma Subsampling

As the RGB signals leave the digitizing card's framestores, the signals are usually converted into YUV: luminance and color difference components. With 8 bits each, we have a 24-bit sample. Some JPEG compression algorithms decimate color samples (figure 8-13). It is here that lossy compression begins. One possible way to proceed is to alternate discarding a chroma sample. For example, the compression algorithm would not touch luminance but would process a sample of U, discard V, process V, discard U, and so forth.

Through one cycle, a 24-bit per pixel sample could be reduced to a 16-bit per pixel sample. This would result in an image display that still retained a reasonable amount of color and detail. For example, with 16 bits per pixel, 256 levels of color (quantization levels) can be represented. The 16 bits per pixel are similar to the 4:2:2 color handling of professional videotape recording methods.

### The Discrete Cosine Transform

Next, the decimated U and V samples, along with Y, luminance, are analyzed by the DCT. The purpose is to represent a picture by frequencies and not by pixels. The DCT of JPEG divides a picture into 8 × 8 squares. By comparing brightness values from square to square, data are generated which represent how the pixels are arrayed. Each 8 × 8 square is analyzed.

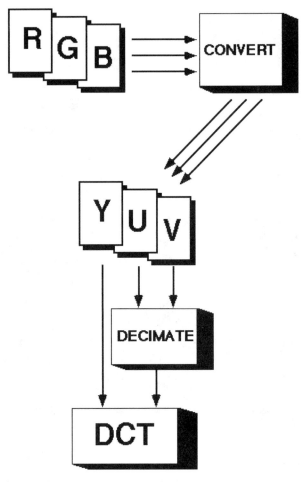

**Figure 8-13** The RGB signals are converted to YUV and the color portion undergoes decimation. Next, the signals enter the discrete cosine transform stage. Illustration by Jeffrey Krebs.

### Quantization

The quantization stage introduces the ratio of JPEG compression. It is entirely lossy, and discarded information cannot be replaced. A quantization table (Q table) operates based upon human visual system (HVS) studies. Determining which frequencies the eye does and does not detect well and how much luminance and chrominance information can be removed are issues that are critical in using Q tables correctly. Studies have shown luminance is the most important element to be maintained when compressing an image. Further, up to 90% of the color information can be removed.

## Applying the Q Factor

The Q factor is a number that determines how mildly or how strongly the frequencies will be changed. As the Q factor becomes higher, the file size decreases. As the Q factor becomes smaller, the file size increases.

$$\text{Frequencies} = \frac{\text{Quantized frequency array}}{\text{Q factor}}$$

This results in numbers that represent each $8 \times 8$ array. These 64 frequencies are now represented by smaller numbers. Next, the numbers are run length encoded (RLE) which helps to transmit less data to be stored on disk. When the editor wants to view a take,

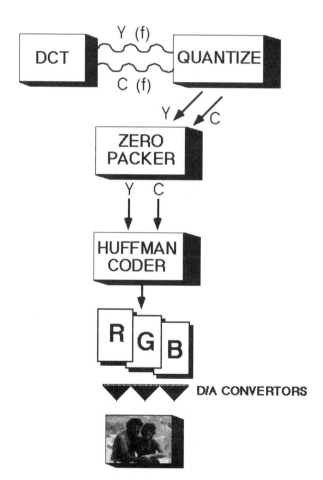

**Figure 8-14** Inside the Discrete Cosine Transform. YUV signals are now represented as frequencies and enter the Quantize section. These frequencies undergo compression, are zero-packed and further coded. The RGB information undergoes a D/A conversion, resulting in a viewable signal. Illustration by Jeffrey Krebs.

the data is accessed from disk, decompressed into YUV, reprocessed by three D/A convertors on the framestores, sync is reapplied, and a picture is viewable (figure 8-14).

## STORAGE SYSTEMS

Computer disks provide the storage mechanisms where our images and sounds are stored. There are a variety of disk types and reasons for using each. The three disk characteristics that are important are: capacity, data transfer rate, and access time.

> *Capacity* Capacity is measured in kilobytes (kB), megabytes (MB), gigabytes (GB), and terabytes (TB).
>
> *Data transfer rate* Data transfer rate can also be termed read/write speed, or transfer speed. Data transfer rate is measured in kB/sec and MB/sec. The disk's data transfer rate represents the bandwidth limitation of the disk drive.
>
> *Access Time* Access Time is measured in milliseconds (ms). A millisecond is 1/1000 of a second. How quickly material can be retrieved from a disk after it has been requested is the access time of the disk. The access time is frequently different depending upon the disk type.

### Disk Types

Computer disks for digital, nonlinear editing systems come in two forms: magnetic and optical. Each type differs with regard to the three basic disk characteristics.

#### Magnetic Disks

Magnetic disks offer a data transfer rate of between 0.5 to 6 MB/sec (1.5 to 1.8 MB/sec for SCSI 1 type; 3.0 to 4.0 MB/sec for SCSI type 2 and higher, between 5–6 MB/sec with SCSI type 2 accelerator boards), a capacity of up to 21 GB, and an access time of 8 to 16 ms.

Magnetic disks will sustain data transfer rates which allow very high quality pictures to be digitized and stored to disk. Also important is the rate at which cost is dropping. In 1989, a 600 MB magnetic disk cost approximately $6,000. In 1991, the disk had doubled in capacity to 1.2 GB and the cost was $5,000. By 1994, a 9 GB disk cost $2,000. Magnetic disks can be linked together, and it is possible to have more than 250 hours online and accessible to the editor.

### Optical Discs

Optical discs offer smaller data transfer rates, smaller capacities, and slower access times. There are two forms of optical disc: magneto-optical discs and phase-change optical discs. It is important to note that the data transfer rate is not equal over the surface of the disc. The outer ring of optical discs is considered the "fast" portion, while the inner ring is considered the "slow" portion.

If we are interested in working with a certain picture quality and a certain audio sampling rate, we must be sure that the disk type can sustain the rates. If we have chosen a picture resolution which requires 18 kB/frame and a mono audio sampling rate of 44.05 KHz, our calculations are:

18 kB/frame × 24 fps = 432 kB/sec + 44.05 KHz × 2 bytes (16 bit samples) = 432 kB/sec + 88.1 kB = 520.1 kB/sec

For a SCSI type 2 magnetic disk, this sustained data transfer rate is easily achieved. However, depending upon the optical disc, it may not be possible to digitize this material. If the optical disc we are using has a data transfer rate of 500 kB/sec on the outer portion and slows down to 360 kB/sec on the inner portion, we are not going to be able to reliably write the data as we fill up the disc.

## MANAGING STORAGE BASED ON PROJECT TYPE

Managing storage requirements is one of the most challenging issues when using a digital, nonlinear system. There are several methods of balancing storage costs versus amount of footage required. Determining how to configure an editing system will require some testing and effort.

*Scenario 1:* Access needed to all footage at all times, and storage unlimited.

When this is the case, the guidelines are very simple. Take the total amount of footage you will have and digitize a representative sample of the footage. This will provide an average kByte per frame indication. With this information perform the following calculation:

Avg. kB per frame × 24 fps/sec + number of audio channels × audio sampling rate = number of kB/sec × 60 sec/min = number of kB/min × number of minutes of footage = number of kB required

Last, divide the number of kB needed by the storage mechanism in kB to arrive at the number of disks required.

For instance, let's say that we have digitized some sample 35mm film shot in Academy format and find that the average kB per frame is 18 kBytes. We want to use one audio channel at 44.05 KHz. For 100,000 feet of film, we would require approximately 3.6 nine gigabyte drives, each of which would hold approximately 306 minutes of material (see figure 8-15).

Planning accordingly, we would configure our system to hold four 9 GB disks. This would provide us exactly with the functionality we desire—all footage accessible at all times.

*Scenario 2:* Access to all footage not needed, and storage limited.

When presented with a situation where we have limited storage, but access to all footage is not needed, we determine if it is possible to work in stages. We could break the film into sections, and load footage just for that section. For example, let's say that 100,000 feet has been shot. Our budget only allows us to purchase two 9 GB drives, and we want to work in a resolution that consumes at the rate of 18 kB/frame. We know from scenario #1 above that we really should have two additional 9 GB drives.

Next, what type of film is being edited? If it is a documentary, is it in sections? For example, perhaps it is a documentary about six different musicians and each musician will be showcased in a separate segment. If this is true, we could segment the footage and start editing by working on a segment at a time. The 100,000 feet gives us 18 hours divided equally among six musicians for an average of three hours per segment.

*Scenario 3:* Access to all footage needed, and storage limited.

Let's again take our 100,000 feet of footage and we have one 9 GB disk. At first, we plan to use a picture resolution that consumes 18 kB/frame and requires 3.6 nine GB drives. We cannot segment the work, as we need access to all the footage.

*Solution #1:* Can we work in a lower resolution? If instead of 18 kB/frame we use a resolution that averages out to 9 kB/frame, we would still require 2.1

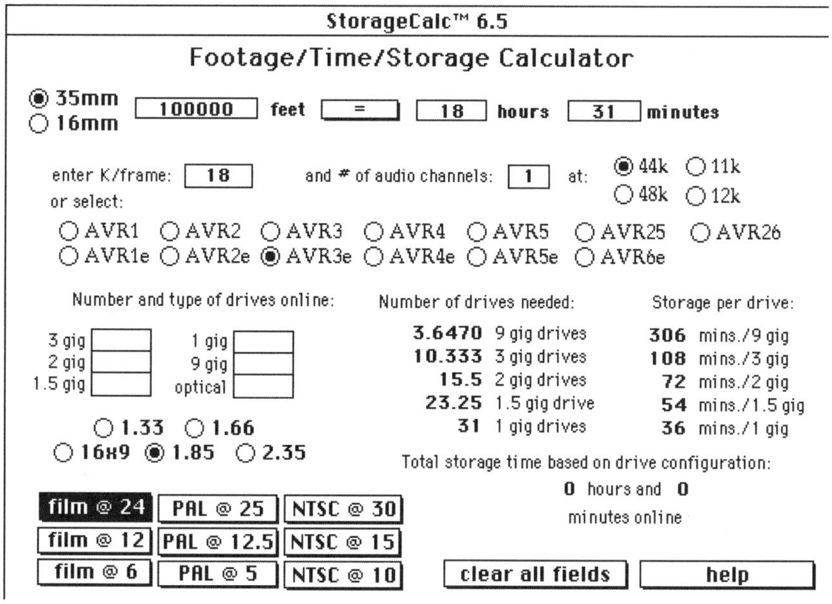

**Figure 8-15** 100,000 feet of 35mm film shot in Academy format at an average of 18 kB/frame and one audio channel at 44.05 KHz requires approximately 3.6 nine gigabyte drives, each of which would hold approximately 306 minutes of material. Courtesy of Hand-crank'd Productions.

nine GB drives (figure 8-19). We choose even a lower resolution, at 4 kB per frame. Our calculations show that we need 1.2 nine GB drives to get all the footage on line. At 4 kB/frame, the images will be quite compressed, and we may not be happy working at this resolution, but we will most likely be able to fit all the material online without requiring additional disk drives.

*Solution #2:* If we determine that 9 kB/frame represents a resolution we can work with, we still require 2.1 nine GB drives. What would happen if we worked at 12 fps instead of 24 fps? This would present itself to us as if one frame is held for two frames in order to make up 24 images per second. This is, obviously, not a pleasant alternative, but it is an alternative. At 12 fps played at 24 fps, we would require 1.4 nine GB drives.

## HOW ASPECT RATIO AFFECTS STORAGE

If the film was shot in a different aspect ratio, such as Cinemascope (2.35:1) there would be fewer kBytes consumed per frame. For example, our 100,00 feet at 9 kB/frame in Academy format would require 2.1 nine GB drives. If shot in Cinemascope format, the footage would require 1.8 nine GB drives (figure

8-16). For films that have a great deal of footage, the benefits are quickly realized.

## INDUSTRY VIEWPOINTS

### Joe Hutshing—Film Editor

*The River Wild* (1994), *Indecent Proposal* (1993), *JFK* (1991) Academy Award for Best Editing, *The Doors* (1991), *Born on the Fourth of July* (1989) Academy Award for Best Editing, *Talk Radio* (1988).

An Academy Award winner for best editing, Joe Hutshing has never specified that a film be edited on film or electronically and, instead, often selects the best tool that fits the story being told. Hutshing, who has consistently worked on films for which large amounts of footage have been shot, is energetic when discussing the possibilities of editing electronically. Says Hushing,

I always use the typewriter to word processor comparison when thinking of nonlinear editing. Because when you are working on film it's the same as if you only had one piece of paper—you make a mistake, it gets battered and beaten up—well that's your workprint. With nonlinear, you make everything perfect before you print it out. On *The Doors* one concert

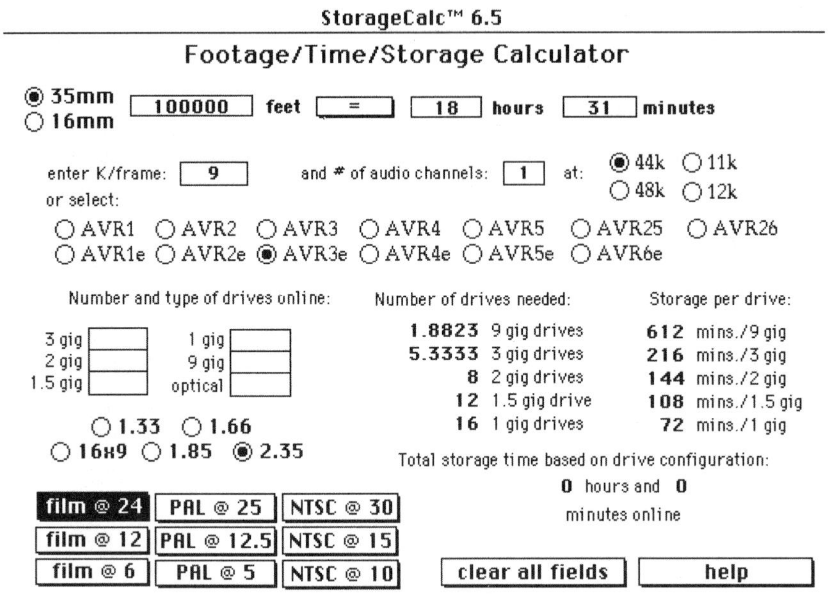

StorageCalc™ 6.5

## Footage/Time/Storage Calculator

◉ 35mm   ○ 16mm    [ 100000 ] feet [ = ] [ 18 ] hours [ 31 ] minutes

enter K/frame: [ 9 ]    and # of audio channels: [ 1 ]   at:  ◉ 44k  ○ 11k
or select:                                                     ○ 48k  ○ 12k

○ AVR1  ○ AVR2  ○ AVR3  ○ AVR4  ○ AVR5  ○ AVR25  ○ AVR26
○ AVR1e  ○ AVR2e  ◉ AVR3e  ○ AVR4e  ○ AVR5e  ○ AVR6e

Number and type of drives online:    Number of drives needed:    Storage per drive:

3 gig [    ]    1 gig [    ]        1.8823  9 gig drives      612  mins./9 gig
2 gig [    ]    9 gig [    ]        5.3333  3 gig drives      216  mins./3 gig
1.5 gig [    ]  optical [    ]         8  2 gig drives      144  mins./2 gig
                                      12  1.5 gig drive     108  mins./1.5 gig
  ○ 1.33   ○ 1.66                     16  1 gig drives       72  mins./1 gig
  ○ 16н9  ○ 1.85  ◉ 2.35          Total storage time based on drive configuration:

                                            **0** hours and **0**
[ film @ 24 ]  [ PAL @ 25 ]  [ NTSC @ 30 ]      minutes online
[ film @ 12 ]  [ PAL @ 12.5 ]  [ NTSC @ 15 ]
[ film @ 6 ]   [ PAL @ 5 ]   [ NTSC @ 10 ]   [ clear all fields ]   [ help ]

**Figure 8-16** Changing the aspect ratio from 1.85:1 to 2.35:1 for the same 100,000 feet of 35mm film reduces the storage requirement from 2.1 to 1.8 nine gigabyte drives. Courtesy of Handcrank'd Productions.

scene had eleven cameras and there were about 60 KEM rolls for that one scene. We were working in nonlinear and it was wonderful because it's faster and I don't have to spend time loading up rolls and finding trims.

Hutshing is also quick to point out that the database and optical effects that can be previsualized on electronic, nonlinear systems are particularly helpful. Continues Hutshing,

The organization and database features of nonlinear systems is wonderful and one of the strongest points. I access so many takes that it's important to know where everything is. On *The Doors* we did a lot of dissolves that looked great. Some movies call for opticals more than others. It's just so quick that you can access takes and can see the shot step printed or skip printed. . . .

Nonlinear makes you a better editor because you can be far bolder with your cutting techniques because you don't have to worry about battering your workprint, and since you can make unlimited versions, no one gets upset about attempting experiments. I give cuts of scenes or strings of sequences to my director on VHS who takes them home and then we go over it via phone, both simultaneously watching the scene. While you can debate whether or not you save time using nonlinear, the fact is that I do go

home earlier and I can keep up with camera. Working on digital, nonlinear editing systems is such an elegant way to cut. I can't express strongly enough how much I love editing this way.

**Figure 8-17** Photo of Joe Hutshing. Courtesy of Joe Hutshing.

## INDUSTRY VIEWPOINTS

### David Brenner—Film Editor

*Born on the Fourth of July* (1989) Academy Award for Best Editing, *The Doors* (1991), *Heaven and Earth* (1993), *The River Wild* (1994), *No Fear* (1994).

Winner of the 1989 Academy Award for best editing, David Brenner is a classically trained film editor who has used electronic, nonlinear editing systems to edit his most recent films. Says Brenner,

> One of the big losses I've felt in nonlinear editing is interaction and collaboration with assistants. This is simply due to the fact that "assistant stations" are only affordable on huge budget shows. So, if you want someone to work on your cuts for you—try alternates, make trims, smooth out sound—they have to work when you're not on the machine—late at night or early in the morning. And after a while that takes its toll. In film cutting rooms, on the other hand, you could hand someone a reel and a list of fixes, and they could take it onto a KEM of their own. I think this is one of the big reasons, combined with the buggy edit lists and telecine nightmares, that

**Figure 8-18** Photo of David Brenner. Courtesy of David Brenner.

> few assistants love the digital revolution as much as editors.
>
> And yes, there is a lot to love. Digital editing has enabled me to spend more energy being creative and less with physically doing things to achieve that: threading reels, winding them down, marking film, pulling them out, splicing them into a cut. Now the time it takes to make a cut is exponentially faster. It's like the distance between an idea and its fruition has been shortened: you imagine a cut, or a series of cuts, and the physical and mental steps necessary to seeing those cuts are drastically reduced. So you feel freer to try more ideas, different ideas, alternative ways of doing something.
>
> In fact, the existence of these alternative ways—the accessibility of different versions of a cut—has changed the way I edit. When I finish a first pass, I'll leave the editing room for awhile, then come back, look at it and take notes, as if I were the director judging it fresh. Then I'll address those notes on a copy. I have become my own critic, my own foil in the editing dialectic. Because the whole process is so much faster, I'll often have time to do this two or three times before the director ever sees it.
>
> In this way, I think, digital editing has made me braver. I'm much more likely to experiment, to take a weird idea and run all the way with it, when I know I can go back to what I had with the flick of a mouse.
>
> Because there is so much at your fingertips on a digital system, there is a great temptation for the chaotic. This can be a great thing—you can be very wild, create real kinetic moments, complex collages. But on the other hand, we have to be careful not to let technology take over certain fundamentals of storytelling. Rapid cuts and chaotic rhythms don't always work. A well-cut traditional dialogue scene looks nothing like MTV.
>
> On *The River Wild*, Joe Hutshing and I returned to working on film. At first it was actually kind of great, doing things the physical way. There is a great security in knowing that what you've just cut exists in the real world—a hard copy, not some kind of edit list that can be corrupted or lost. Boom, you take it into a screening room right then. However, when I was working on the "Gauntlet"—a climactic river sequence shot over three months, two states, and fifteen hours of dailies—I was dying for a digital editing system. Since we kept it all in daily rolls—we never liked things cut into selects—I had to take copious notes and make an elaborate map of what was what. On a digital system, I could make a pictorial reference system and keep everything in dailies. I would have been able to spend more time with my family!

## EDITING A FEATURE FILM ON A DIGITAL, NONLINEAR EDITING SYSTEM

Shown in figure 8-19 is an example of the flow of information in digital editing. What is it like to edit a feature film digitally? There are specific directions that can be taken for a digital filmmaking postproduction process.

1. Make a flow chart of the entire postproduction procedure before filming has begun. This flow chart should take into account exactly what will happen from the first day of filming until the prints are made for distribution. Many of the issues that you will encounter will have been discussed elsewhere in this book.
2. The chart should take into account the detailed path that picture and sound will take. Determine exactly what will happen to the original sound elements from the moment that the shoot is over each day. Will the sound be recorded on open-reel tape with pilot tone? Will sound be recorded on DAT? Will it have timecode? Is all the sound going to be redone, or will the sound be used for final delivery?
3. Within one chart, all of the parallel processes you expect to put into place should be shown. This is the only way to see the interdependencies that exist from path to path.

### Editing *Patriots*

What follows is a representative example, taken from an actual feature film whose picture and sound were edited exclusively on digital, nonlinear systems.

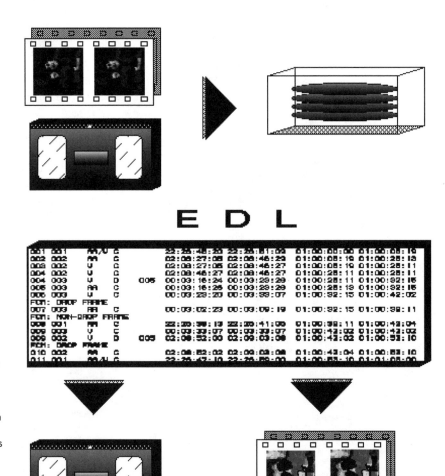

**Figure 8-19** This diagram indicates the flow of information that is possible when using a digital, nonlinear editing system. First, negative or positive film or videotape is transferred to computer disk. Editing proceeds in a nonlinear fashion, resulting in the creation of an edit decision list. The EDL serves as both a video edit decision list and a film cut list. For a video release, the video EDL is used to conform the original source tapes to create a finished master tape. For a film release, the film cut list is used to create a finished cut negative. Illustration by Jeffrey Krebs.

Film Description: *Patriots* (Boston Pictures, 1994). Shot on location in the United States and Ireland. 35mm feature film release with international distribution. Running time: 83 min. Written and directed by Frank Kerr.

This feature film was shot with edge coded film while sound was recorded on 1/4″ audio tape with center track timecode. The approximate shooting ratio was 13:1. The filmmakers decided to avoid creating workprint and to carry forth sound elements from the digital editing systems to the final mixing process. This decision was responsible for saving thousands of dollars. If a lower budget feature film shoots at a 9:1 ratio (18 hours of shot film to two hours of finished film), approximately 100,000 feet of film will be exposed. Depending upon the telecine facility, perhaps as much as 25¢ per foot of film can be saved by not making a film workprint. Multiplied by 100,000 feet, a savings of $25,000 can be realized.

## Transferring the Film

After developing the film negative, a one-lite transfer was done to 3/4″ videotape. This was an MOS transfer, and a burn-in video display of the film's edgenumbers was included. A floppy disk containing information about the relationship of film edgenumbers and videotape timecode facilitated digitization. Five ten-minute camera rolls were transferred to one videocassette. A film rate of 23.976 fps was used to transfer to video running at 29.97 fps. The film, shot in Super 16mm, would eventually be blown up to 35mm for release. After a check of the film's negative to ensure that it was in proper condition, the negative was stored and was only returned to for negative cutting.

## Transferring the Audio

Original audio from 1/4″ audio was transferred to DAT. This DAT recording was jam-synced to the timecode of the original recording. Since recording audio with timecode in the field is characterized by a series of starts and stops, there are timecode breaks, referred to as discontinuities in timecode. Due to the longer running time of DAT tapes than the 1/4″ reel, an average of three 1/4″ sound rolls were transferred to one DAT tape.

## The Digital, Nonlinear Editor

In general, these systems have three common layouts: a footage display area, an editing area, and a graphi-

cal view of the sequence. The footage display area is often referred to as a bin, serving as an analogy to the film editor's canvas bin. While the terminology may differ, there are three common concepts to be found in DNLE systems. They are: the clip, the transition, and the timeline.

A clip refers to any portion of picture or sound that has been digitized. These items are digitized and given labels: names, such as Scene and Take: Sc. 5, Tk. 1. The film editor should think of a clip as being nothing more than a representation of a piece of film or a piece of mag track.

A transition refers to the relationship of two adjoining clips. The shots can transition, or proceed, from one to the other in many different forms. If the scene shows clip A changing quickly to clip B, the transition has been a cut. If clip A slowly fades away while clip B fades in, the transition has been a dissolve. DNLE systems usually have specific modes of operation that allow the editor to concentrate on manipulation of the transition.

A timeline is a graphical representation of the scene being edited and represents the various picture and sound tracks that make up the scene. Whereas a film synchronizer can only show a small section of a scene, and has a limited number of tracks, the DNLE timeline can be very sophisticated.

## Displaying the Footage

There will be an area where footage is contained. These computer windows are sometimes called bins, for they are representations of the film editor's canvas bin (figure 8-20).

Bins form the backbone of a powerful database. In figure 8-21, statistical information that shows the digitized clips, their corresponding edgenumbers, duration in feet and frames, and timecode numbers is readily accessible to the editor.

For *Patriots,* in-depth logs were kept. Now working in the digital, nonlinear editing system, new bins were created. The appropriate material was placed in each of these bins. The categories were:

1. Sound Roll Bins (audio only)
2. Dailies Day # Bins (picture only)
3. Syncing Bin
4. Scene Bins (synced clips)
5. Edited Scenes Bin (editor's cut)
6. Director's Cut Bin
7. Sequence Bin (finished projection reels)

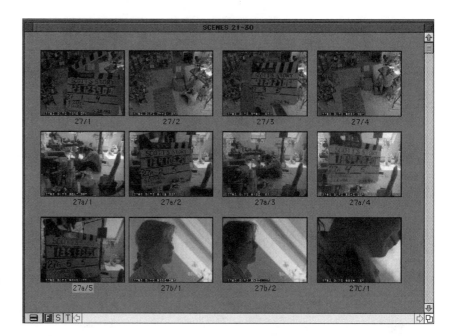

**Figure 8-20** Displaying footage on the DNLE system. Bins contain digitized footage, and when the editor needs a shot, it is called up from the bin and the actual computer file is played. Footage courtesy of Stephanie Cornell.

| | Name | KN Start | KN End | KN Duration | Start | Auxiliary TC1 | Camroll |
|---|---|---|---|---|---|---|---|
| | 21/1 | KJ 72 0284-8398&17 | 8447&09 | 24+13 | 15:00:02:11 | 20:59:18:20 | CR33 |
| | 21/2 | KJ 72 0284-8448&01 | 8506&05 | 29+05 | 15:00:43:11 | 21:04:56:00 | CR33 |
| | 21/3 | KJ 72 0284-8506&17 | 8564&07 | 28+31 | 15:01:32:11 | 21:07:01:00 | CR33 |
| | 21/4 | KJ 72 0284-8565&00 | 8613&09 | 24+10 | 15:02:20:25 | 21:09:43:00 | CR33 |
| | 21a/1 | KJ 72 0284-8614&05 | 8680&09 | 33+05 | 15:03:01:26 | 21:32:00:00 | CR33 |
| | 21a/2 | KJ 72 0284-8681&17 | 8740&14 | 29+18 | 15:03:58:06 | 21:34:23:20 | CR33 |
| | 21a/3 | KJ 72 0284-8741&01 | 8796&04 | 27+24 | 15:04:47:16 | 21:36:17:11 | CR33 |
| | 21a/4 | KJ 72 0284-8796&18 | 8829&13 | 16+16 | 15:05:34:02 | 21:38:49:00 | CR33 |
| | 21a/5 | KJ 72 0284-8830&02 | 8897&12 | 33+31 | 15:06:01:22 | 21:40:32:00 | CR33 |
| | 21b/1 | KJ 72 0284-8897&18 | 8923&01 | 12+24 | 15:06:58:07 | | CR33 |
| | 21c/1 | KJ 72 0284-8923&04 | 8946&09 | 11+26 | 15:07:19:10 | | CR33 |
| | 21c/2 | KJ 72 0284-8946&10 | 8966&13 | 10+04 | 15:07:38:22 | | CR33 |
| | 22/1 | KJ 75 0539-9738&13 | 9802&12 | 32+00 | 16:07:20:16 | 09:58:37:15 | CR36 |
| | 22/2 | KJ 75 0539-9803&02 | 9871&11 | 34+10 | 16:08:14:07 | 10:09:02:06 | CR36 |
| | 22/3 | KJ 75 0539-9872&00 | 9934&03 | 31+04 | 16:09:11:20 | 10:11:08:25 | CR36 |
| | 22/4 | KJ 75 0539-9934&08 | 9993&00 | 29+13 | 16:10:03:20 | 10:13:27:20 | CR36 |
| | 22/5 | KJ 75 0539-8392&08 | 8455&16 | 31+29 | 16:10:54:06 | 10:17:37:00 | CR37 |
| | 22/6 | KJ 75 0539-8456&06 | 8518&19 | 31+14 | 16:11:47:14 | 10:19:24:20 | CR37 |
| | 22/7 | KJ 75 0539-8520&17 | 8566&11 | 22+35 | 16:12:41:07 | 10:24:00:00 | CR37 |
| | 22/8 | KJ 75 0539-8661&01 | 8726&12 | 32+32 | 16:14:38:02 | 10:35:04:22 | CR37 |
| | 22/9 | KJ 75 0539-8726&19 | 8800&15 | 36+37 | 16:15:33:00 | 10:37:00:10 | CR37 |
| | 22a/ser | KJ 75 0539-8566&12 | 8660&07 | 46+36 | 16:13:19:11 | | CR37 |
| | 23/1 | KJ 60 0633-6555&14 | 6766&04 | 105+11 | 17:19:13:22 | | CR40 |
| | 24/1 | KJ 60 0633-6413&13 | 6458&16 | 22+24 | 17:17:15:11 | | CR40 |
| | 24/2 | KJ 60 0633-6458&19 | 6509&13 | 25+15 | 17:17:53:03 | | CR40 |
| | 24/3 | KJ 60 0633-6510&00 | 6554&19 | 22+20 | 17:18:35:20 | | CR40 |
| | 25/2 | KJ 80 0184-6927&03 | 7003&09 | 38+07 | 12:23:30:25 | 23:57:54:10 | CR26 |
| | 25/3 | KJ 80 0184-7004&13 | 7073&09 | 34+17 | 12:24:35:12 | 00:01:00:21 | CR26 |
| | 25/4 | KJ 80 0184-7073&18 | 7100&03 | 13+06 | 12:25:33:03 | 00:03:42:10 | CR26 |
| | 25/5 | KJ 80 0184-7100&15 | 7169&15 | 34+21 | 12:25:55:15 | 00:04:46:10 | CR26 |
| | 25/6 | KJ 80 0184-7170&04 | 7242&19 | 36+16 | 12:26:53:11 | 00:13:20:10 | CR26 |

**Figure 8-21** DNLE systems can provide intricate databases. Here, statistical information that shows the digitized clips, their corresponding edgenumbers, duration in feet and frames, and timecode numbers forms a database that is readily accessible to the editor.

Sound Roll Bins (audio only)—The next stage was to digitize both picture and sound. First, each DAT tape was transferred to computer disk. Audio was sampled at 48 KHz, and the transfer was an AES/EBU digital transfer, rather than an analog transfer. As each timecode discontinuity was encountered, a new audio-only (no picture attached) clip was created and deposited into the bin.

Dailies Day # Bins (picture only)—Next a videotape was loaded into the DNLE system. Because entire camera rolls had been transferred, all that was necessary was for five clips, one for each of the five camera rolls on that videotape, to be digitized. This resulted in five entries made in the bin. The bin was given a name that corresponded to the day number; for example, "Dailies Day 001 bin," "Dailies Day 002 bin," and so on.

## Syncing the Dailies

Syncing Bin—A syncing bin, really a temporary location, was used to facilitate syncing sound to picture. For example, let's say that all of the audio clips had been digitized for all the takes in Scene 2. These audio clips would be taken from their sound roll bins and placed in the syncing bin. Next, the individual picture takes for Scene 2 were taken from their camera rolls and also placed in the syncing bin.

By correlating the burn-in information in the MOS picture clips with the timecode of the audio only clips, syncing dailies became an automated procedure. This routine helped to save many hours and is a model for digital filmmaking—syncing dailies within the DNLE system offers great advantages.

## Screening the Dailies

After assurance from the laboratory that the negative for a day's dailies was without problems, the actual screening of synced dailies for *Patriots* was done digitally. With the director viewing the now synced clips, the editor could enter director comments directly into the appropriate column in the bin. The time spent at this stage can be critical to a first assembly. For *Patriots*, a first assembly was done a mere five days after shooting ceased.

Scene Bins (synced clips)—The next step was to remove the newly synced clips from the syncing bin. The clips were then moved into their appropriate scene bins. For *Patriots*, the 119-scene film was broken down into twelve scene bins. Bins were labeled Sc.1–10, Sc. 11–20, Sc. 21–30, and so forth. Into each of these bins were placed the appropriate clips.

## Database Capabilities

DNLE systems offer extensive database capabilities. A common editing function is to sort and sift through a bin to display only shots for a specific scene. For example, the editor could make a query of the computer to only display footage relating to scene 5 even if that bin contained footage from scenes one through ten.

## Editing

Once all the footage for a specific scene had been shot and synced, editing began. During editing, the process of digitizing, syncing, etc., continued, with the assistant editor providing the necessary support, leaving the editor to work on the main editing tasks.

## The User Interface

DNLE systems seek to preserve the essential components of film editing, a feed reel and a takeup reel, and a synchronizer block. Successfully recreating these tools in a software and hardware based computer system requires inventive software engineering and constant input from the editorial community. What follows is a brief, but representative editing session on a DNLE system.

## Splicing and Extracting

Shown in figure 8-22 is an example of a DNLE system interface. The screen to the left can be thought of as the feed reel on a film flatbed, while the screen on the right represents the take-up reel. The area below is the timeline representation. The footage in the left window represents a raw take while the footage in the right window represents the scene being edited. Note that in the timeline, there is a graphical representation of the shot that has been edited into the sequence.

By using various tools, some which perform tasks similar to the film editor's basic tools—such as splicing and extractions—a sequence is built. Of course, on a DNLE system it is possible to make splices and extractions anywhere within the scene. If a shot must be removed and the shot exists at the beginning of the scene, it can be excised and the remaining shots simply shuffle up accordingly.

## Trimming Edits

Now that the two shots are cut next to one another, it may be necessary to trim the actual edit points. Making the transition between two shots flow smoothly is a task that the editor must continually perform. DNLE systems usually offer a dedicated way of trimming transitional points whereby the editor can see exactly how the shots transition and can quickly add or delete frames from either, or from both sides.

## Optical Effects

There are a variety of optical effects that can be seen on DNLE systems. Heretofore, the film editor would have to wait to see the actual optical effect after it was delivered from the optical house. Instead of transitioning as a cut, shots can transition as a dissolve. Depending upon the DNLE system, optical effects can be viewed in real time, or will involve pre-

**Figure 8-22** An example of a DNLE system interface. The footage in the left window represents a raw take while the footage in the right window represents the scene being edited. Note that in the timeline, there is a graphical representation of the shot that has been edited into the sequence. Footage courtesy of Stephanie Cornell.

compute time where the system must enter the effect to computer disk before it can be viewed at sound speed.

Shown in figure 8-23 is a more complicated optical effect. Here, note that there is not just one picture track, but that there are two tracks. These are known as virtual picture tracks. There are virtual audio tracks as well. Note how there is a shot on picture (labeled V1) track 1 and a shot of smaller length on picture track 2 (labeled V2). A superimposition effect is

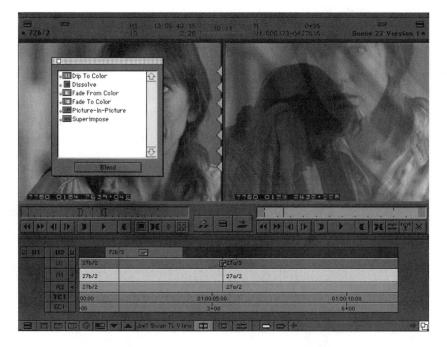

**Figure 8-23** Achieving a more complicated optical effect. By adding virtual picture track 2, a superimposition effect is placed on the shot, and it becomes superimposed over the shot on track 1. Such optical effects creation that is simultaneous with the choosing of the takes and the trimming of the takes represents great power for the editor. Footage courtesy of Stephanie Cornell.

placed on the shot on track 2, and the shot becomes superimposed over the shot on track 1. This sophisticated optical effect can be viewed and trimmed accordingly until the editor is satisfied with the result. Such optical effects creation that is simultaneous with the choosing of the takes and the trimming of the takes represents great power for the editor.

For *Patriots,* optical effects such as dissolves, fades, slow-motion effects, blow-ups, re-sizes, and masks were utilized. These effects were all visualized during the editing process, accepted or rejected, and eventually translated into an optical count sheet for creation on film.

## Virtual Audio Tracks

DNLE systems offer a major benefit in the form of high quality audio capabilities. Virtual audio tracks allow the editor to create a sequence that can have very extensive sound support. Shown in figure 8-24 is the sequence, except now it has six tracks of sound that have been added. Note how the various segments on the different audio tracks represent music, sound effects, sync dialogue, and so forth. The diagonal slashes found on some of these segments represent audio crossfades. With this level of sophistication and audio quality, the audio work done during the editorial stage can be brought to the sound department.

## Timeline Views

A representation of the sequence being edited is of great assistance. It allows you to quickly see the pacing of a scene, which shots are longer than others, and serves as a common reference for both editor and director.

## The Director's Cut

When the editor has completed cutting, each scene is put together to form a reel. This reel represents the actual projection reels that would be used in a theater. They are about ten minutes each. Thus a 120-minute movie would consist of twelve ten-minute reels. For *Patriots,* the editor's cut was assembled into reels and screened for the director. This process leads to the director's cut and can be a painstaking process, or a very straightforward process, depending upon how close the first assembly is.

For *Patriots,* a new series of bins was created. Into these "Director's Cut Bins" were placed duplicates of the first assembly reels. These duplicates allowed the director to make any necessary changes, while simultaneously providing him the ability to go back and use the original assembly. Finally, after revisions were complete, each projection reel was then placed into a "Sequence Bin." This bin contained the entire completed film, broken down into twelve ten-minute reels.

## Cutting the Negative

A negative cut list is generated that instructs the negative cutter as to how to assemble the original camera negative. This is usually accompanied by a videotape. This tape contains both picture and sound and serves as a guide to the negative cutter; however, the list takes precedence. For *Patriots,* a videotape copy of the entire film, along with various lists, provided to the negative cutter. The negative was then conformed and blown-up to 35mm. This 35mm negative then produced the 35mm print.

One note is necessary regarding the change list procedure. If a workprint is being conformed (not the

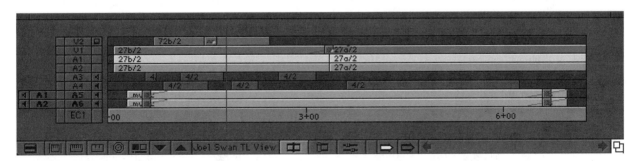

**Figure 8-24** The virtual audio tracks of a DNLE system. The sequence now has six tracks of sound, and the various segments on the different audio tracks represent music, sound effects, sync dialogue, and so forth. The diagonal slashes found on some of these segments represent audio crossfades.

case with *Patriots*), changes may be required. In the DNLE system, the sequence is changed accordingly, and a change list is generated. This change list instructs the assistant editor as to how the workprint must be re-conformed.

## Audio Elements

For *Patriots*, it was determined that any audio work done during the picture editing stage would be brought forward to the sound editing stage. By using a digital audio workstation (DAW), the audio elements, multiple audio tracks, and all scene information translated into the DAW. This saved a great deal of time for the filmmakers. To complete both picture editing and audio track digitally allowed far less duplication of work.

## WHETHER TO PROJECT FILM OR VIDEO FOR SCREENINGS

When a workflow chart is created, one decision concerns the manner in which film dailies will be viewed. Will dailies be viewed on film, or will no workprint be made and, instead, will dailies be viewed on a best-lite video transfer or from the compressed digital playback from the DNLE system? Another critical decision is how the edited sequences will be viewed. There are four possibilities:

1. The filmmakers decide the entire film will be viewed on film. In this case, the DNLE system creates a negative cut list, and a selected workprint is created, conformed, and screened. The filmmakers are able to see the actual film images. However, if opticals were created during digital editorial process, they would either have to be created and cut into the conformed workprint, or they would be missing from the screening.
2. The filmmakers decide that only a few specific scenes will be workprinted and projected. In this case, the goal is to minimize expenditure on creating and conforming workprint for the entire film, while still being able to judge how certain scenes play on the large theater screen.
3. The filmmakers decide to screen video. This is a newly emerging method where the filmmakers do not project a film screening, but instead use

the DNLE system to directly output its sequences to videotape. A mixed, temporary soundtrack would also be a by-product of this method. The savings are quite significant and there are some interesting possibilities that arise. For example, consider that a preview is held at 11 A.M. The audience response cards are filled out and reviewed. The overwhelming response is that the audience feels that a fighting sequence between two characters is too prolonged and is far too brutal.

Armed with this information, it becomes possible to re-edit the reel so that the fight scene still carries the impact, but takes into account what the audience identified as a problem area. These changes can be made, output from the DNLE system, and all in time for a 2 P.M. screening! Even very complex and numerous changes can be made, and several different versions can be screened in one day. This is a capability that has always eluded filmmakers who must preview their films.

## *INDUSTRY VIEWPOINTS*

### *Edward Salier, A.C.E.—Editor*

Film: *Lunch Wagon*; *Silent Scream*; *Alice, Sweet Alice*, TV Series: "Max Headroom," "Quantum Leap," "Lois & Clark: The New Adventures of Superman."

Edward Salier, A.C.E., started his film editing career in New York City editing documentaries and feature films. After moving to Los Angeles to pursue career opportunities, and at a time when most editors had not even heard of an Apple computer, he wrote a computer database program for film logging, and designed an interface to log dailies. He is currently editing drama series for network television, using a variety of digital, nonlinear editing systems. Says Salier,

> The most dramatic change has been the digital realm of postproduction. Having the digital media available is like editing on film but on a word processor. The power that provides is incredible—you have access to all the film and if a director comes in and wants to see a specific take you are not fishing for trims—it's practically instantaneous and that opens up the creative process.

**Figure 8-25** Photo of Edward Salier, A.C.E. Courtesy of Edward Salier.

For Salier, the digital, nonlinear editing system also provides a great degree of previsualization capabilities which he is quick to exploit. He continues,

I can now do the types of previsualization for special effects that have never been available. That has opened up a tremendous creative potential and this has been the most exciting facet for me—to be able to sit down and composite shots and to be able to manipulate images using programs like PHOTOSHOP.

There is an example of a shot that I did in "Lois and Clark" where Superman has to fly down to rescue a child, and he thinks he sees this child but it's a holographic projection, so he flies right through this image. Normally, you'd have difficulty in trying to visualize these elements and time them. I had a green screen of Superman in a flying position and on my digital editing system I can resize him, reposition him, move him around the frame, and time my moves within the shot to where he reaches out and grabs this child. We had a back plate with the boy and I literally cut him out of the shot using PHOTOSHOP and I composited Superman and the boy and at the right moment I faded in and out of the proper elements.

So, being able to present that to the visual effects supervisor, director, and producer is just incredible. I can add sound effects and music, and the result is

that everyone knows exactly what we are trying to achieve. Before I had this capability, I would have had to describe the shot to the visual effects people, they would have to make it in a very expensive online suite, and then it may not turn out the way I wanted it. So, what I created in three to four hours saved untold thousands of dollars. And most importantly, everyone was able to see what I was trying to accomplish. I'm no longer limited to a splice and splicing tape.

Learning all of these new techniques has really kept me busy, and I am working constantly. Improvements I would like to see include being able to transmit this information. I would like to see the input from a digital telecine into the digital, nonlinear editing system and then be able to access that information directly, stored at high resolution, and each person could work on the material at whatever resolution they required.

Still, with all the new tools available to Salier, he is quick to assert that there is still a strong requirement for creative ideas and that one should be sure to allow for the proper amount of time to let an idea mature. Continues Salier,

Even though access is immediate, you need time to think about the creative aspects. You need to think and contemplate. There is no need to fear a miscut negative during the matching back process. As soon as producers and directors can see these composited shots they accept the idea of digital postproduction very quickly. Having edited for 20 years, it's a real challenge and it's given me a whole new aspect on the craft and for me that's really exciting—I'm starting over again—doing the same type of things but broadening it considerably and it's very exciting.

## DIGITAL AUDIO POSTPRODUCTION

### Traditional Film Track Laying and Mixing

During the editing stage, the film editor is usually limited to a small number of tracks, usually one to two. Working with more tracks of sound is accomplished by interlocking more than one editing table. Working in this manner has limited many film editors who are intent on accomplishing more sound work to better illustrate how a scene is intended to play. Digital, nonlinear picture editing systems allow the editor to work with dialogue, music, and to place sound effects.

Traditionally, once a film editor had completed the picture portion, only one or two tracks of mag sound, usually dialogue, would accompany the workprint. These two mag soundtracks would then become two rolls in a series of magnetic rolls that represented all the tracks in the film. Depending upon the number of tracks that the film required, there may be many rolls of mag stock.

Since there are a fixed number of mag stock playback machines involved in the traditional mix, many of these rolls would first be mixed-down during pre-mix sessions. Then, all the elements that make up the finished soundtrack for the film would be rolled together as the film is mixed.

## DIGITAL AUDIO WORKSTATIONS, DIGITAL AUDIO EDITING, AND MIXING

By digitizing sounds to computer disk, sound design and sound editing can proceed entirely in the digital domain. In general, DAWs have the picture that the editor is working against available on videotape, while all the audio exists in digital form. However, DAWs, which replace the videotape playback of the picture portion of the film with digital images, are becoming the standard. Shown in figure 8-26 is an example of a DAW that uses a digital picture. The

images have been stored on computer disk, and the editor no longer has to wait for the videotape machine to cue.

Since their introduction in the 1980s, the design of DAWs has been centered around providing on-screen versions of tools that the sound editor requires every day. Shown in figure 8-27 are examples of the waveform representation of a sound take and some of the sound editor's tools replicated in software.

## Sound Design

Designing sounds can be made easier through the use of computer manipulation. For example, let's say we have a comedy scene where a character is pulling off a fake nose from another character's face. The director wants the sound that is heard when the nose is pulled off to "sound funny." It is left to a sound designer, and to a sound editor, to provide the right sound. Using a DAW, the sound of a cork being taken out of a bottle could be digitized into the computer, and a series of digital signal processing (DSP) tools could be used to radically change the sound. It could be time compressed, causing it to be accelerated. It could be offset slightly from a copy of itself to give a slight doubling effect.

As important, the sound designer can work in this way to create many different versions of the sound. All of these alternatives can be placed in position and shown to the director.

**Figure 8-26** An example of a digital audio workstation which provides a digital picture. "Audiovision" photo courtesy of Avid Technology, Inc.

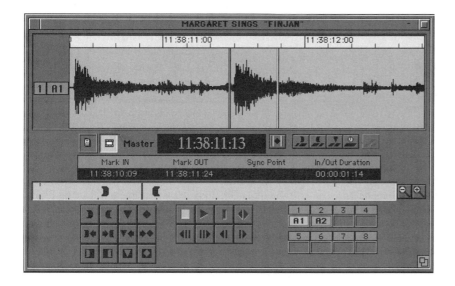

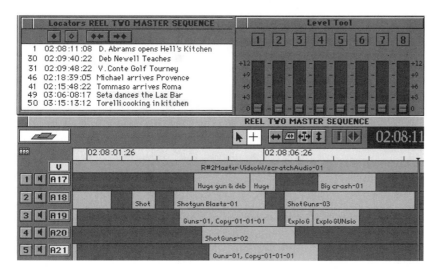

**Figure 8-27** (Top) This waveform representation of a sound take on the digital audio workstation allows the editor to quickly locate and isolate sections with sophisticated tools. (Bottom) Additional tools found in the digital audio workstation that allow the editor to quickly locate material, create levels, and view the sequence being built as a graphical representation.

## INDUSTRY VIEWPOINTS

### Gary Rydstrom—Sound Designer/ Re-recording Mixer, Skywalker Sound

For Gary Rydstrom, an Academy Award winner for his work in sound effect editing, the digital filmmaking process holds great promise. Says Rydstrom, who has worked on such films as *Jurassic Park* and *Terminator 2: Judgment Day*,

> My job is to be in charge of sound effects for films from the very first stages of original recording to the

final mix. If you record literally what you see in a particular scene, it's often not what you think the item should sound like. What we do in sound design is to get a mood across, and often we end up playing with sounds that aren't literal and making them strike you in a certain emotional way. What's great about digital and what it's done for me was to make it quicker to experiment. I could very quickly call up sounds and create new sounds and I could repeat what I tried until I got something that I was happy with. This degree of speed and precision was missing in analog.

During *Jurassic Park*, we could see animatics and it allowed us to get an idea of what would eventually be on the screen. The first step is to go out and record sounds. We usually use DAT machines as they give us an advantage in portability and increased recording capacities. During this stage, we don't exactly know what we are going to get. It's amazing how rich the real world is for creating sounds. It's like hunting to find as much stuff as we can. What I do then is to sift through this material. I sample sounds into my workstation and then start to combine and re-combine them into new sounds.

Next, you start to fit the movie with these sounds and you begin to see how it is working. We occasionally show these to the director, but I like the fact that for a good part I am alone on a project. At any given time a dinosaur in *Jurassic* may be made of three or four animals; using a DAW to blend the sounds was indispensable, and it allowed me to make many voices sound like one voice. So much of sound editing is rhythm and there's nothing better than having a keyboard interface where you can perform things to the picture. You can't really anticipate every mouth movement or every dinosaur roar, but you can quickly change how long a sound is playing, and it makes it much easier to fit a sound to the picture you are seeing.

Once the raw elements are edited digitally, our premixes and mixes are done on mag. In many cases, Dolby encoded, SR six-track mag sounds better than digital because there's more head room. After the mix is completed, we go back to a digital format for playback in the theater. While we are in the mixing stage, my digital workstation is right there on the stage, because when you are mixing, you find that some things don't work in combination and throw off the overall rhythm of the scene. So, you need to punctuate things in the scene, and it requires changing things quickly.

One of the most promising developments is in theater sound. Big films come out in 70mm and six track sound, and now there are thousands of theaters that are capable of playing six-track digital sound, whether it's Dolby SR, DTS, SDDS, and so on. So, it's a much better experience for the person who goes to see films. But at the same time, one of the issues with six-track digital is that it's almost limitless in terms of its dynamic range. The filmmaker may want to make things really loud, but it's not the volume that's important, it's having the right sounds. With digital editing techniques, doing it faster isn't the answer, it's trying new things that's important.

Rydstrom also points out that digital networks that allow filmmakers to work from afar have grown in importance. He continues,

On *Terminator 2* I took a day and played some elements back for James Cameron over a T1 line where he was 400 miles away. It has been a big advantage for us, because the director and I can continue working from our separate locations. The trend will be for more and more people to have these systems in their homes while tying into our mixing rooms.

There is a magical thing that occurs when picture and sound work together. Sound sometimes tends to be painted on top of the film as opposed to working within the picture. We tend not to have a lot of time to change it. So, if you could work alongside the picture editor and the special effects editor, you would have time to experiment and interrelate things. When digital editing systems, both for picture and for sound, begin talking to each other and sharing files that are compatible, that will be very exciting. You'll do the basic sound editing and begin to swap sounds and pictures back and forth. It will allow us to create better films.

## Editing on a Digital Audio Workstation

Shown in figure 8-28 is an example of a scene that is being track-layed in a DAW. The scene is a shootout and consists of dialogue, music, sound effects, foley, and ambient sound. Shown are some of the twenty-four tracks of sound that make up this scene. Note how the timeline representation shows the various pieces of sound that have been cut into position, their relative length, and how they have been layered on top of one another in order to create the constant sound that the scene demands. Also note that some of the clips of sound are straight-edged while others are diagonal-edged. The diagonal lines represent fades or crossfades.

Figure 8-29 shows a zoomed-in view of one section of the scene that is being track-layed. In order to work on a section of sound, the editor may choose to edit the sound via the audio's waveform pattern. Below, the one audio waveform in the bottom-most clip has been replicated digitally and now fills in the entire duration of the audio clip. Techniques such as cutting, copying, and pasting audio from one section into another are extremely useful and efficient. In this example, an ambient track has been created out of one usable section of audio.

## Digital Mixing

The process of mixing a film has been affected by digital technology. For lower budget films, the entire film can be mixed digitally, without ever having to utilize mag stock and players. This can represent

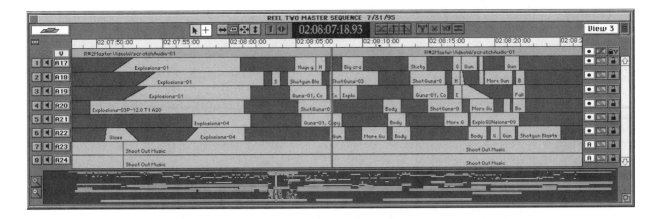

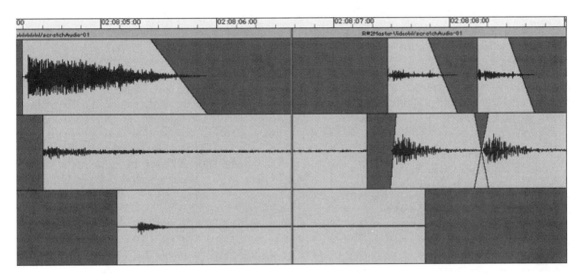

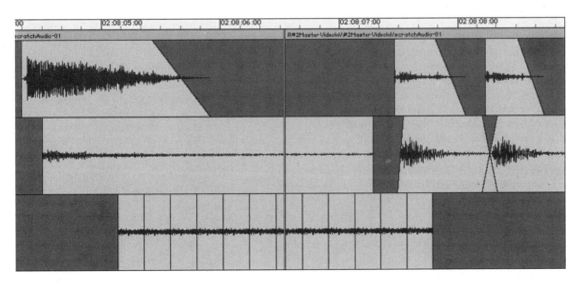

**Figures 8-28 and 8-29** A scene that consists of dialogue, music, sound effects, foley, and ambient sound that is being track-layed in a digital audio workstation. Note the timeline representation of various sounds, their position, relative length, and their layered relationship that creates the constant sound that the scene demands. The diagonal lines represent fades or crossfades. Courtesy of Darren Abrams.

quite a cost savings. There are also simple but practical considerations as well; the amount of mag stock used in a multi-track, big-budget feature film can weigh as much as 30,000 pounds and has to be stored and, eventually, discarded. Today, many films have been created through the use of DAWs for track laying. The tracks are then usually output to multi-track digital or analog magnetic tape players and then soundtrack is premixed and mixed. Even at the sound stage, it is routine for a DAW to be used to call up different sound effects.

## INDUSTRY VIEWPOINTS

### Larry Blake—Sound Editor, Re-recording Mixer

For sound editor and re-recording mixer Larry Blake, there is no hard and fast rule regarding digital vs. analog recordings.

> People make too much of the quality issue when comparing digital and analog technologies. If you are using Dolby SR in conjunction with a well-tweaked analog machine—1/4″ in production, or mag fullcoat and multitrack in post—the end result will be, all things equal, the same as if you had recorded digitally.
>
> The big advantages of digital, on a pure sonic basis, are that you don't have to work as hard to achieve a given level of quality. Plus, making safety copies is a pain in analog—not even factoring in the generation loss—where cloning is pretty straightforward in digital. And since I find myself spending too much time on technical matters as it is, the "creative" side of me likes that very much indeed.
>
> Where digital has it all over analog is in editing flexibility and access. No doubt about it, many great sound jobs have been cut on mag, and I don't think you can really hear the difference. However, there are things that you couldn't do on mag that you can do easily on a digital audio workstation, such as minute edits and cross-fades in dialog. Also, on a workstation you are making changes and decisions off-line. As a result, you do things that you maybe could do, but simply wouldn't do because of the time and trouble. For example, you wouldn't audition something for the director if you had to lace up 15 dubbers to hear everything at one time, as is the case with mag.

Blake has some strong opinions on the subject of sound design.

I think it's a pretentious term if only because it has existed since the beginning of sound films. There are certain high-tech jocks who would have you believe that fancy digital equipment is a sine qua non of sound design. The classic early sound design job is *King Kong,* for which Murray Spivack did some amazing work with only a varispeed rheostat at his disposal. Even as late as 1977 you had film sound being revolutionized by one insanely creative guy (Ben Burtt) and a four-track Tascam. Personal skill will always be the X-factor.

Regarding the process of supervising the sound on a feature film, Blake says,

> From the first time you read the script and start recording sounds, to the day that you start editing, you must anticipate what's coming up next. On the film that I just finished, *The Underneath,* we have a few "live" music sequences in a bar and the director, Steven Soderbergh, was adamant that you have to feel as if you were there. The second part of my challenge was to make it all feel as if it was happening live, although the scenes would be shot to playback.

During the shooting of films that he will supervise in post, Blake tries to see the unedited dailies and to discuss the track with the production mixer.

> Too often these days dialog takes a back seat to music and sound effects. For Steven Soderbergh, Paul Ledford, who does the production sound on his films, and myself, the production dialog track rules. We do very little looping and keep the audibility and sonority of dialog much more up-front than is considered normal.

Blake, who has worked on films with long postproduction cycles as well as films that had very short delivery times, is quick to point out that digital workstations are not always the best answer.

> We often think that digital always has the leg up over analog in matters of speed, flexibility, and quality. More often than not that is true, although not when you have to throw a movie to two dozen sound editors and finish it in three weeks. There isn't one workstation that can do changes to dubbing units, premixes, and final mixes the way it can be done on a bench.
>
> But if schedules permit, I still believe that workstations are without a doubt the only way to go. And indeed, I take strange pleasure there is not one frame of *King of the Hill* or *The Underneath* on a sprocketed medium prior to the optical track negative.

Blake says that the key to using new technologies is being sure that one does not give up anything vis-à-vis standard techniques.

> On every new film that I work I try to guess how far I can push technology before it breaks and embarrasses me. From initial forays with 1/4"-to-multitrack sound editing to editing on a workstation, and from cutting the picture 3/4" control track off-line to 24-frame EditDroid laserdiscs to 24-frame Avid Film Composer, we haven't fallen on our faces yet. And once the software and storage allows you to not only edit on workstations, but also to pre-mix and final mix to them, we'll finally be free of having to weld sound onto a linear piece of analog or digital tape. Logistically, feature film postproduction will be a whole new ball game then, and we can only hope that the creative side will reap its share of benefits.

Blake, who was the supervising sound editor, re-recording mixer, and postproduction supervisor on such films as *Sex, Lies, and Videotape, King of the Hill,* and *The Underneath,* also writes on film sound in a monthly column for *Mix* magazine. He lives in New Orleans.

## ACCEPTANCE OF DIGITAL, NONLINEAR EDITING BY THE FILMMAKING COMMUNITY

"What are they doing in Hollywood?" is a question often asked by filmmakers who do not have access to new technology. For the filmmaker struggling to make a release date and who must finish cutting picture so that the sound people can have the locked reels, knowing that, in another part of the world, a director is using every last possible moment up to the release date to work on a difficult scene can make one envious.

In mid-1993, filmmakers rapidly adopted digital, nonlinear editing methods. One fascinating statistic is that by April, 1994, there were 70 feature films in various phases of postproduction in Hollywood. Of these 70 films, 30 were being edited on film. An astounding 40 films, or 57%, were being edited digitally! These films ran the gamut from low budget films to budgets over $100 million. In just a few years, the acceptance of digital editing in the world center of filmmaking has seen an amazing progression.

## INDUSTRY VIEWPOINTS

### Neil Travis, A.C.E.—Film Editor

*Clear and Present Danger* (1994), *Patriot Games* (1992), *Dances With Wolves* (1990) Academy Award for Best Editing.

Winner of the 1990 Academy Award for best editing, Neil Travis has pursued electronic nonlinear editing since 1992 and has become a staunch supporter of digital, nonlinear editing systems. For Travis, the technology that is now available to the editor to enhance personal creativity without the drudgery of the physical labor associated with traditional film editing has become a significant development in his career. Says Travis,

> In terms of digital filmmaking technology, electronic editing has made the biggest change for me. When I finished *Dances With Wolves* I determined that I did not want to work on film again. I had been a first editor for twenty-five years but I had just about had it. We had over a million feet of film that I was working with and we were constantly winding it, stepping on it—I was just getting grumpy. So, one of my assistants introduced me to the Montage II nonlinear system and that represented a giant leap for me. Now I've moved on to the digital editing systems. It has been a whole new rebirth for me and a great gener-

**Figure 8-30** Photo of Neil Travis, A.C.E. Courtesy of Neil Travis.

ator of energy. Most of the physicality of film editing would be a big barrier when the director asked for a change but as a result of using the digital systems my job has become purely editing and focusing on the creative problems of the film.

Previsualization has also grown in use, and Travis notes that his participation on a film may include the review of sequences that have been electronically previsualized. He says,

> We had an electronic storyboard on *Clear and Present Danger* for a sequence we called "The Kill Zone." And the director asked me to come out to the set so that I could judge if we had gotten everything we needed to put the scene together. And it would have been just impossible, if I hadn't gotten an idea of what was in the director's head. But since I had watched the storyboard on video, I had developed an insight into what (director) Philip Noyce wanted. So when he called me onto the set, I could visualize everything. It took about two to three days of sitting there viewing the 8mm video assist tapes.

Another advantage of digital postproduction techniques for filmmakers is that the postproduction schedule is being significantly reduced. Notes Travis,

> Increased pressure as to postproduction schedules is a fact of life. As the budgets get bigger, you want to release the picture as quickly as possible. I have a rule of thumb—if you want one editor to complete a picture, you should allow twice the time to get an answer print as it took to shoot the film. The big problem I find in terms of postproduction scheduling is that the studios do not allow for any time for ideas to germinate—just for the amount of time to put the film together. Editing is in a sense rewriting the movie that may end up looking entirely different than on the script, and that re-creation can take a lot of thought. The idea of electronic editing helping in terms of time—well it certainly does—but it helps immensely in terms of changes and your attitude towards making changes. I can probably make five changes electronically in the time that it would take me to make one change on film.

Using electronic editing has proven to Travis that there are ideas that he will try which he may have heretofore left untried, or may have taken many attempts on film to achieve the same result. Travis says,

> On *Patriot Games* we had a sequence called "The War Room" scene and Jack Ryan is watching TV im-ages of a commando strike somewhere in the Middle East broadcast from a satellite and which Ryan indicated should take place. He is watching this in horror and in that process, to illustrate the tension and horror, I made the cut and then went through to each cut and started taking two frames off the cut, and I kept doing this until some shots were only four frames long. And the audience was right with us, and they felt that tension. Now that is something that I don't think I would have attacked in the same way if I was working on film. The thought that I would have very little pieces of film—I would have needed reprints and picture dupes—but electronically I went for it and there were hundreds of little cuts in the sequence.

In speaking of traditional film editing versus the digital systems, Travis is quick to point out that while film editing is a craft, it can be enhanced through a different set of tools. He notes,

> You can cut film if you have a pair of scissors and a flashlight. Editing is not about equipment—it's about emotion, beats, timing, where the actor's eyes are. Electronic editing has liberated me from being bogged down by technique. I find the optical effects great to work with and the sound capabilities are helpful to me. I enjoy the concept of putting music and sound effects in my cut, even though I usually don't have a lot of time to accomplish this. I just think that it increases the quality of the film in every way and it is incredibly liberating for me.

## Why Such Rapid Growth?

For the digital filmmaker, these are the some of the major issues that have led to the adoption of digital, nonlinear editing systems.

1. Digital preservation of data.
2. Access to all footage.
3. New picture manipulation tools.
4. New audio manipulation tools.
5. Parallel work activities and avoiding duplication of work.
6. Networking capabilities.

## Digital Preservation of Data

As film exits the telecine stage, it comes to the editor in the form of videotape, or has already been transferred to computer disk. Regardless of how pictures and sounds come to the editor, information that originated from the very early stages—script, previsualization, and on-location logging—must be available to the editor. This preservation of information is possible in a digital postproduction environment.

## FROM FILM TO DIGITAL, NONLINEAR EDITING SYSTEM

### From Videotape

If picture and sound have been transferred to videotape, a log is available which dictates what sections of the videotape should be input into the digital, nonlinear system. This log was created during the time of telecine, but is a product that has made use of merged notes made by the script supervisor who had been logging on-set. In this way, the film transfer can proceed as efficiently as possible—only required sections will be transferred.

### From Computer Disk

If picture and sound have been transferred directly from film to computer disk, the log that was created on-set is merged with the telecine log. The editor receives the computer disks and editing begins. As the editor adds information, such as additional comments from the director, or notes to the sound designer or composer, the log grows and is available to the other postproduction areas that are working in parallel with editorial.

### Access to All Footage

One of the requirements that many filmmakers have is that access to all the footage, at all times, be made feasible. The great benefit that digital systems have had is that the filmmaker can have all footage online. If the director wants to work on material for scene 1 and the editor must steal a character's reaction shot from scene 82, filmed in the same surroundings as scene 1, having access to all the material is necessary. Today, hundreds of hours of storage are available to the filmmaker.

### New Picture Manipulation Tools

A dizzying array of tools are available to the filmmaker using digital, nonlinear systems. Particularly important are the optical effects capabilities that are at the editor's fingertips. With digital editing, the time delays for conceiving and finally visualizing a desired effect are no longer necessary. Optical effects such as slow motion, skip motion, blue and green screen matting, and even text generation for the creation of titles are available.

## Digital vs. Optical Effects

One important aspect of editing film on a digital system is that the optical effects that are shown on the screen may not be created with the same characteristics as film. Sometimes, there is a bit of confusion surrounding this point. Take, for example, a dissolve. A dissolve in occurs between two images when one image fades away while another image fades in. The duration that it takes to make the transition completely from one image to the next image is the length of the dissolve.

But it is important that the digital editing system takes into account how a piece of film interacts with another piece of film. There are simple ways to digitally show a film style dissolve versus a video style dissolve. A video dissolve occurs in a linear, or straight line. A 72-frame dissolve in video will have the first image beginning its fade out at frame zero, and at frame 72 will be completely off screen. This would be graphed as a straight line. A piece of film, however, will react differently. A 72-frame dissolve for two film elements will be graphed as a bell curve, where the first image does not begin its fade out at frame zero. Instead, a ramp is realized, and for this reason, film dissolves appear quite smooth due to the nature by which they hold their highlights as the image fades away and the incoming image begins to dominate.

For the film editor who is attempting to create a very special dissolve to make a certain filmic point, knowing that what is happening on the screen is actually how it will look when the laboratory delivers the completed optical is critical.

Very complex imagery, where multiple layers of film are fading in and out, and are superimposed over other film layers, can be visualized by the editor and director. The control over every aspect of the optical effect, such as a superimposition that is of a certain transparency at one moment and at another point becomes less transparent, and therefore more dominant in the shot, is left with the filmmakers. The overwhelming result is that the director and editor know that a visual effect not only is going to work, but that they have chosen the best take, and have given the effect the best treatment that the scene deserves. This is one of the most important benefits of this new set of picture manipulation tools—security. In the words of one filmmaker, "Using this technology has made me the least anxious of any film I've done."

The benefits of this visualization during the editorial stage translate to all the other departments. Consider the film's music composer who gets a phone call and is told—"Okay, we just finished editing scene 47. This is the point where the battle begins. It's the scene where our hero, Aram of Yerevan, begins the battle to win the Lady Nazen. There's a section where we had to cut in black leader because we haven't received the optical that shows him dreaming of returning to his homeland. It's 23 seconds of a lot of superimpositions, images of people from his past. When can you have it done?"

This conversation may appear fanciful, but it often is the case that composers are working under such conditions. Most composers are able to proceed regardless. However, could they have done a better job had the images been present? This is the nagging question that digital filmmaking methods seek to answer. By providing more tools to the editor, those twenty-three seconds of imagery may be available to the composer. The end result is that the composer is not working against a blank screen and is sharing the same visual sense as the director and editor.

This cross-pollination and cross-collaboration that results are undeniable. In a clichéd sense, everyone is finally marching to the same drummer, because the signals are not verbal descriptions left up to the visual interpretation of the listener. Instead, they are visual signals processed visually by the next person who will touch the project. This different form of communicating what has to be done is why digital filmmaking holds so much promise.

## INDUSTRY VIEWPOINTS

### Anne Goursaud, A.C.E.—Film Director and Film Editor

Director: *Embrace of the Vampire* (1994), Editor: *Bram Stoker's Dracula* (1992), *The Two Jakes* (1990), *Ironweed* (1987), *Crimes of the Heart* (1986), *The Outsiders* (1983), *One from the Heart* (1982).

For director and film editor Anne Goursaud, the use of a digital, nonlinear editing system has been an extremely rewarding experience not only as an editor but also as a film director. Goursaud, director of *Embrace of the Vampire* (1994), feels that digital, nonlinear editing has provided her with the speed and

**Figure 8-31** Photo of Anne Goursaud (right), A.C.E. Courtesy of Anne Goursaud.

features that allow her to explore untold options. Says Goursaud,

> I became interested in electronic editing when I saw video editing, but I was very dubious because it was so primitive compared to the flexibility of film editing. My opinion has changed drastically by using a digital, nonlinear editing system. It has the same flexibility as film editing, and more. It also fits my personality better—every time I have an idea I cannot resist the compulsion of trying it. And I used to do it when I was film editing—I would labor endless hours trying my ideas to discover in the end that they did not work, and often, it was impossible to retrieve the original cut. Digital editing allows me to satiate my curiosity.
>
> It also makes me more daring. I feel less internal pressure when I am going through the chaotic phase of editing (out of which come the best ideas) knowing every cut, every idea has been saved.

Equally important to Goursaud is the ability to previsualize effects that would normally either be done on film or on video. She says,

> We do as many optical effects as required and on *Embrace* . . . we did supers, dissolves, fades, flops—and it was fabulous. You can get so spoiled. You can also put all your temp music on and get a great idea of

what you are going to have when it's all done. When I was cutting in film, I used to say if only I could have film editing, but with the electronic access to the data and information.

Having quick access to all of the footage that is relevant to a scene is the advantage that director Goursaud feels is the single most important benefit of digital editing systems. She notes,

Performance selection is facilitated by the fact that you can review takes quickly and that you can build selects from different takes in a matter of seconds. Digital editing speeds up the tedious process of performance cutting.

On a lighter note, Goursaud concludes,

Part of an editor's pride is not to have a million splices passing by when you screen the film (it is like showing your dirty laundry!). But with digital, no one is ever going to know how hard you tried, what you had to do to get there. With digital editing you can be more daring and have more freedom.

## INDUSTRY VIEWPOINTS

### Steven J. Cohen, A.C.E.—Editor

*Three Wishes* (1995), *Angie* (1994), *Lost In Yonkers* (1993), *Teamster Boss* (1992), *Rambling Rose* (1991), *Crazy in Love* (1991), *The Image* (1989), *No Man's Land* (1988), *LBJ: The Early Years* (1987).

Emmy—"LBJ: The Early Years," Best Editing for a Miniseries or Special; CableACE Nomination, *The Image*, Best Editing for a Theatrical Special.

Member, Motion Picture Academy, American Cinema Editors, Advisory Board, AFI—Apple Computer Center. Faculty member, American Film Institute Center for Advanced Film & Television Studies.

Steve Cohen has been editing motion pictures for over fifteen years. He has cut features and movies for television, documentaries, commercials, and trailers. He has worked in film, tape, nonlinear tape, and digital. He has been on the forefront of electronic nonlinear editing applications for feature film postproduction, is integrally involved in the development of digital, nonlinear editing, and has been a direct contributor to the success that DNLE systems have enjoyed in recent years. Says Cohen,

**Figure 8-32** Photo of Steve Cohen, A.C.E. Courtesy of Steve Cohen.

Just as desktop publishing "virtualized" ink and paper, and samplers and synthesizers virtualized sound and rhythm, so the Media Composer and systems like it have virtualized film and video. In all cases, they've brought about a revolution in the lives of the people involved. The transition to digital motion pictures has just begun, but I can make some general observations about what's been happening for editors.

First, the new editing systems are only tools in exactly the same way that a hammer, or a paintbrush or a Moviola is a tool. The tasks we're doing with these devices are much the same as those we did without them, telling compelling, articulate stories with pictures and sound, meaning and rhythm shaping all the ineffable elements that make a motion picture exciting. Have the new machines changed our style of editing? Probably. We see faster rhythms everywhere which is at least partially due to the fact that we now have the tools to make that kind of editing easy. And the new tools have made our work more polished because it's now so easy to rework the film until everything in it has been realized. But have they changed the essence of our craft? Not at all. The editor still edits. And it's in the editor's eyes, ears and heart that the picture comes together.

Some of us have chosen digital tools because they're fast and flexible. Others use them because they offer the ability to do new creative tasks: temporary sound work or preliminary opticals and titles. And some of us use them because they are just plain fun. I personally love the challenge of making tools that serve the needs of artists helping creative people express themselves easily and powerfully. Whatever the attraction, we editors are participating in the first stages of a revolution that will soon effect the whole world as digital video becomes available in every home and on the screen of every television set and computer.

That revolution is almost here. If it's half as wrenching, and half as exciting as the one we've been experiencing, it will be quite a ride.

## New Audio Manipulation Tools

Sound is a critical element, but during the editorial process, tools to manipulate sound are often lacking. Usually relegated to only two tracks of sound, the editor will most often create basic dialog tracks with little else. One of the things that excites filmmakers most about digital editing is that it provides precise and very detailed sound work. These include:

## More than Two Audio Channels

For example, at the very minimum, four channels of sound are available, allowing the editor to simultaneously hear four different tracks of sound.

## Virtual Audio Tracks

In analog work, when a film editor wants to cut with more tracks of sound, a new set of audio plates is added to the flatbed. If the editor wants to cut with eight tracks of sound, it quickly becomes quite unmanageable. As a result, editors don't usually attempt intricate sound editing. With digital systems, many virtual audio tracks are available. The editor can cut the basic dialog tracks, add music, sound effects, etc. Scenes can be presented without the usual rough edges that simple audio editing provides. Let's say we have a dialog scene between two characters and the editor is using takes that were shot at different times and on different days. Presenting such scenes can be difficult—often there will be different background ambience and extraneous noises.

Normal operating procedure is that these defects will be cleaned up later. With digital techniques, there are alternatives. By using multiple audio tracks, the editor can add an entire track of nothing but looped background ambience at a constant volume. The editor can add some temporary music and even some

sound effects. Suddenly, the presentation of the scene becomes quite a different experience. Was the director expecting to see and hear a more realized version of the scene? Most likely not.

## Professional Audio Quality

Digital, nonlinear editing systems will typically offer different audio sampling rates. These range from the use of scratch quality audio in a range of 22 KHz, 44.1 KHz (compact disc), and 48 KHz (digital audio tape). In addition, inputs into the system can be either analog or digital. If digital sound was captured on set or on location, a digital transfer from the original recordings to the editing system can be made—no loss of quality, no digital to analog to digital conversion, and sound as good as the original recordings.

## Significant Audio Editing Tools

In analog work, film editing for sound can get as accurate as the space occupied by one film perforation. If a particular word must be trimmed, it can be trimmed to a maximum length of 1/24 of a second. However, if a particularly difficult syllable must be trimmed, and it requires that the sound be snipped at, say, 1/72 of a frame, the editor cannot physically make the cut that is required. By sampling the audio into a digital system, the audio can be cut at a sample level. If the audio has been sampled at 48 KHz, there are 48,000 samples for each second of audio. It is possible to cut out a mere 5 samples from somewhere within the 48,000 samples of the file.

## Parallel Work Activities and Avoiding Duplication of Work

Our earlier example of the multilayered images, which can now be visualized, applies well to the topic of parallel work activities. Consider what must happen for a film to be released to a theater. In the case of a special visual effect, if this capability was not available to the filmmakers during the editorial stage, the effect would have to be described and previsualized, and it must eventually be created either optically and photographed to film, or created digitally and recorded to film.

Either way, there is time involved in accomplishing this task. If the special visual effects staff can be given an exact blueprint to follow, parallel work can begin while the editor and director have moved on to edit different scenes.

Avoiding duplication of work is critical. But in many cases, work done in one stage of the process is not easily translatable to the next stage. Recall our audio editing stage. If the filmmakers know that the audio will be done on a DAW, it would be a timesaver if the audio files from the picture editing system could be read directly into the DAW. There would be no duplication of work and no lost time. But this is only possible if the picture editing is working on a digital editing system and if the actual audio files are compatible between the two systems.

If there is such compatibility, as the editor finishes cutting a scene, the scene and its audio files can be sent to the DAW, and the required sound work can begin for the scene. This can be very seamless, if there is a common file format or some type of interchange format.

Popular audio file formats are Audio Interchange File Format (AIFF) and Sound Designer II (SDII). Many DAWs utilize proprietary file structures but may both import and export these two file types. If files are not compatible and cannot load into the DAW, the audio must be re-sampled. This is usually an automated process.

## TRANSMISSION NETWORKS: SENDING AND RECEIVING THE DATA

### Networking Capabilities

In digital filmmaking, parallel processes give rise to a requirement to not only share information, but to also share actual picture and sound files. Further, digital filmmaking methods can operate without regard to the physical distances that may separate the various individuals and departments. There are several types of computer networks that facilitate this type of communication.

Networking, whether only a link between two computers or a link between five computers in different parts of a country, represents one of the most exciting developments in digital filmmaking. This aspect will become so popular and ingrained in filmmaking, that it will be difficult to remember a time when it was not the norm.

## Networks Linking Production, Postproduction, and the Review Process

Here is a situation that involves state of the art networking requirements.

The production crew of a feature film is shooting a scene in a city in the United States of America. The output of the video tap from the camera is being converted to digital data that is sent down phone lines to the postproduction center, 1500 miles away. The signal arrives and is digitized to the computer disks of the digital, nonlinear edit system. A scene is quickly cut together and is sent to the sound department, which is 30 miles away. The scene is also sent to the special visual effects department and work is begun on creating an effect that is integral to the scene's success.

Production ends for the day, and the next day the production team members are seated in front of an interactive, two-way screen which allows the director to see the cut scene, some of the visual effects treatments, and even a rough sound mix of the scene. Let's say that the visual effect has a defect that the director does not like. The director can use an electronic pointer which can be positioned on-screen to outline the trouble area. Through the use of small cameras mounted on the screens, each party involved in the conversation can see the other and can be superimposed over the background images.

The routines outlined above are not fantasy. These networking capabilities are available now to filmmakers. Feature films such as *Backdraft*, *Bugsy*, *Jurassic Park*, and *Terminator 2: Judgment Day* have utilized various pieces of the networking capabilities described above.

Another example is for situations that require remote automatic dialogue replacement (ADR). The use of such networks allows an actor to replace his lines while staying in his location. Simultaneously, and thousands of miles away, the director can watch the picture in synchronization with the new lines.

## User Requirements

There are a variety of networking methods. It is important to understand the requirements between two users, or among multiple users. The nature of what the user is trying to send, receive, or accomplish will dictate what type of network is required.

A. *File information.* Basic information that is usually not data intensive. For example, a log that is useful sent between two computer users.
B. *Video files.* Usually data intensive; they will most likely exist in different resolutions.
C. *Audio files.* Not as intensive as video files; typically stereo.
D. *Video and audio.*
E. *Control commands.* Allows a remote user to control machine(s) at another user's site.
F. *Full interactivity.* Expands the capabilities to include real time conferencing.

## Network Terminology

To better understand various types of networks and how they are used in certain situations, there are some basic terms which are present in any discussion of networks.

bit—digital unit, represented by 0 or 1

byte—8 bits

bps—bits per second

kB—kilobyte (1,000 bytes)

Kbps—Kilobits per second (1,000 bits per second)

Mbits—Megabits per second (1,000,000 bits per second)

Bandwidth—refers to the theoretical rate at which information can be sent. This does not take into account any system related constraints.

Throughput—refers to the actual rates achieved when system constraints are applied (such as multiple users and hardware/software interdependencies).

BBS—bulletin board service, a location where computers can link together through a common server.

Server—a dedicated computing system which serves as a central store of information and one which multiple users can access.

## Overview of Basic File Transfer Times

Information networks are growing rapidly, and they are critical to the evolution of digital filmmaking.

There are now a variety of different ways for the filmmaker to send and receive data. However, before we discuss advanced transmission techniques, here is an overview of a basic transfer mechanism, a modem, and common transfer categories.

## Modem

A modem is used to transmit and to receive digital data. The channel that the data can travel through, however, is small, at 1.2 kB/sec. The throughput capability of an ordinary phone line is approximately 1 kB/sec, leaving some room for overhead and control codes that must be sent with the message.

Modems are used to turn digital information into analog information. The analog signals are in turn represented as sounds, which can travel over a phone line. The receiving modem turns these analog signals back into their original digital form. Modems are available in baud rates of 300, 1200, 2400, 4800, 9600, 14400 bits per second (bps) and higher.

A 9600 baud modem can transmit approximately 9.6 kbits/sec. We then divide 9.6 kbits by 10 (9600 kbps ÷ 10 bits = approximately 1 kB/sec) to get 1 kB that the modem can pass each second.

### Example 1: Small File Transfers

Let's say an editor wants to receive a log from a sound effects facility. The sound effects company has created a data log that allows the computer to find a specific sound effect and a bulletin board service (BBS) that the sound effects company offers. The editor connects to the BBS and sees the file. There is a size associated with the file—10 kB, ten kilobytes. The editor begins to download the file, meaning that the file begins its copying process from the company's BBS to the editor's computer.

How long will the process take?

The editor is using a 9600 baud modem. We know that this modem will transfer approximately 1 kB/sec. If we have a 10 kB file and can transmit 1 kB/sec, the process to get the file will be approximately 10 seconds. However, recall that there may be restrictions placed on this throughput. The quality of the phone connection, and the integrity of the host computer, can slow down the process. If everything goes well, the editor could have the file in ten seconds.

### Example 2: Audio File Transfers

Now let's say that the editor wants to receive a temporary piece of music from the film's composer, and the only equipment that they share between them are computers and modems. The music piece is very short, only a music sting really, and it consists of stereo 44.1 KHz sound and is 2 seconds long. To calculate how much data this is, we use this formula:

Audio sample rate × number of audio channels × sec ÷ kB /sec

44.1 kB/sec × 2 audio channels = 176.4 kB/sec × 2 sec = 352.8 kB that must be transferred.

The modem that the editor is using is still capable of passing only 1 kB /sec. Next, 352.8 kB ÷ 1 kB = 352.8 seconds ÷ 60 sec./min. = 5.88 min.

One can easily see how larger files can add significantly to the amount of transfer time required. This is even more severe when we begin to add video to the file being transferred.

### Example 3: Video and Audio File Transfers

Now let's say that the editor wants to send a short section of video and audio to the composer. The sequence consists of video at low resolution—5 kB/frame. Audio is one channel of 44.1 KHz sound. The scene is 15 seconds long.

Our calculations show the following:

5 kB/frame × 24 fps = 120 kB/sec + 44.1 kB/sec × 2 byte (the audio samples are 16 bit) = 120 + 88.2 kB/sec = 208.2 kB/sec × 15 sec = 3,120 kB (3.120 megabytes).

We must transmit 3.120 megabytes of information. Using the 9600 baud modem, we calculate as follows:

3,120 kB ÷ 1 kB/sec = 3,120 seconds ÷ 60 seconds/minute = 52 minutes

Clearly, adding pictures to our files adds significantly to the time required for the transfer. Notice, however, that there are variables that we can alter.

1. The size of the file can be altered through the use of compression.
2. The time of the transfer can be altered through the use of different transmission methods.

These two variables are combined to allow digital filmmaking to proceed without the egregious use of time as described in example three above. Even so,

it is an improvement over a possible alternative: waiting for an overnight package!

## TYPES OF OPERATION, NETWORKS, AND TRANSMISSION TYPES

As the amount of data that filmmakers want to share back and forth increases, as does the level of interactivity, huge demands are placed on the capacity of the network. There are several different goals for networking in a digital filmmaking model. A general description of some of these goals includes:

1. *Sending and receiving files from point-to-point.* Using one computer each, two users send and receive files from one another (e.g., assistant editor to editor).
2. *Shared access to files; could be simultaneous access to single files.* Using several computers, one computer for each person, individuals have access to a common server. The server may have a file which multiple users need simultaneously (e.g., four editors who are working off a set of common disk drives and who may need to use footage that another editor is using).
3. *Sending and receiving files from local and wide area networks.* For example, files that are generated in one location and that are required in another location.
4. *Interconnecting multiple systems over wide areas.* Let's say we are doing very involved computer animations for a film. The designer is in Milan, Italy, and once the design is finished for one segment, the user ties into a network which allows the files that require a great deal of rendering to be sent to a computer that is in Rome. Distribution of work can be accomplished: the designer and the director collaborate over the network in a discussion of what needs to be accomplished in a different sequence, while each participant sees and interacts with shared images over the network.

Further, this type of networking capability facilitates the specialist to stay in the environment that is best suited to the work that must be done. If the best choice for the film is a music composer who lives in Paris who does not want the disruption of traveling far distances, work can proceed regardless of distance by connecting the composer with others involved in the digital filmmaking process.

## Computer Networks

Networking two or more computers together is not difficult to accomplish. There are point-to-point connections and central, shared connections. Point-to-point, at its simplest, connects two computers to one another. The central and shared computers may contain databases or information that many users can tap into, query, and obtain materials from. These central stores of information are often referred to as servers because they serve the demands placed upon them by those requiring data stored on the server.

## Local Talk Networks

Computer networks can be very sophisticated and have different bandwidth and throughput capacities. For example, the network protocol for the Macintosh computer is AppleTalk, and it has a bandwidth capacity rated at 230 kbits/sec. Its throughput, however, could be far less.

## Sharing Files between Assistant Editor and Editor

Now let's say that we have an assistant editor and an editor who are working digitally. They are in the same office, separated only by a wall, and their computers are connected. No modem is necessary for this transfer, as a point-to-point network is in place. The assistant editor has a file that the editor needs. By using file sharing software, the editor is able to access information from the assistant editor's system. Whether the file is a word processing document, or a sound effect, or a data intensive picture file, the transfer can proceed, at approximately 230 kbits/sec.

## Shared and Simultaneous Access to Files: Linking Computers during Digital Editing

There are situations when it is much more cost-effective to utilize shared volumes of storage. Take, for example, a film that has a large amount of footage and three editors using three separate systems. Normally, each editor would have a local set of storage disks. Editor 1 would not be connected to the disks of either Editor 2 or Editor 3. There could be an instance where Editor 1 needs a shot that comes from a scene that Editor 2 is working on. The only way that Editor 1 could get this shot is to bring a disk drive to Editor 2's system, connect it, and have Editor 2 make a copy of the shot (a data copy) to Editor 1's disk.

One alternative to this is to have all three editors share common storage from which they can access any footage. This capability exists today and is developing steady use.

## DECREASING THE TRANSFER TIME, INCREASING THE OPERATIONAL POSSIBILITIES

### Ethernet

Ethernet is a form of local area network (LAN). It consists of a coaxial cable that can extend to approximately 1.25 miles and can offer up to 1,000 nodes (computers and peripheral devices). Ethernet operates on a principle known as carrier sense multiple access (CSMA). While all LANs require computers to "wait their turn" before sending information, CSMA allows a computer to send information, and when the cable is not in use, another computer can begin sending its information.

Communicating via Ethernet requires that an Ethernet card be placed in the computer and Ethernet cabling be used to connect the various nodes on the LAN. The cabling used, however, is not inexpensive. There are also variants of Ethernet that are much cheaper because they run on "twisted pair" telephone wire instead of coaxial cable. This network type is also referred to as a token ring network, given the name because as each new participant enters the network, the overall throughput decreases.

Ethernet is rated at a bandwidth capability of 10 Mbit/sec. However, the more practical throughput is only about 2 Mbit/sec (about 200 kB/sec) to any given computer. Still, Ethernet will allow editor and assistant editor to share files faster than a local talk connection.

### Integrated Services Digital Network

Integrated services digital network (ISDN) is a transmission standard that is designed to combine different information types: voice, fax, and low resolution video. ISDN requires that a communications link be placed at the transmitting and receiving sites. These installations require a use fee and are offered by telephone companies.

At 64 kbits/sec, the bandwidth is not that much greater than dial-up service. However, up to 24 channels of ISDN can be combined, a process known as multiplexing. Multiplexing can greatly increase the bandwidth capacity, in this case, to 1.5 Mbit/sec.

Recall our example of the editor who needs to upload picture and sound to the film's composer. We calculated that this would take about 41 minutes. If, however, the editor and music composer have ISDN installed at each site, the files can be sent much faster. We must transmit 3,120 kB of information. Our calculations are:

1.5 Mbit/sec × 10 bits = .15 Mbit/sec = 150 kB/sec

3,120 kB ÷ 150 kB/sec = 21 seconds.

Clearly, the comparison is astounding—what used to take 41 minutes can now be accomplished in 21 seconds!

## Fiber Digital Data Interconnect

Fiber digital data interconnect (FDDI) is a transmission method that uses fiber optics to transmit and receive signals. These fibers are transparent and are usually constructed of either glass or plastic. Fiber optics transmit energy by directing light instead of electrical signals. Electrical signals are encoded into light waves, transmitted, and received and decoded back into electrical signals.

It may not always be economical to create a network based on copper conductive wire when fiber optics can be used. FDDI is expected to be offered in two configurations: bandwidths of 100 Mbit/sec and 200 Mbit/sec. Due to throughput constraints, a 100 Mbit/sec FDDI network will most likely deliver about 2 MB/sec. Still, the progression is impressive, for now, the file that the editor needs to send the composer, at 2.46 megabytes, can proceed in almost, but not quite, real-time!

## Applying Compression Techniques Prior to Transmission

The first method of decreasing our transmission is to increase the throughput of the network communication. The second method is to decrease the size of the files that we need to send. There are compression techniques that can be applied to picture and sound files.

For example, if we have stereo 44.1 KHz audio files that we need to send, a 3:1 compression algorithm can be applied to the data. Now, instead of 176.4 kB/sec of information, the audio files can be encoded and compressed to 58.8 kB/sec and transmitted in one-third the time. The receiver will decode and decompress the files. While the compression algorithms are not lossless in the exact sense of the word, they are able to withstand several generational passes.

There are a variety of compression algorithms. Some, such as AC-2 from Dolby Laboratories, are optimized for audio. Others are optimized for video. Lossless algorithms can be used for compacting information databases. By applying compression to the files, less powerful networks become more capable. For example, through this technique, stereo audio files can be sent over ISDN in real time. This would otherwise not be possible.

## Additional Transmission Methods

DS-0—DS-0 is the basic unit used to measure fiber optic capacity. At 64 kbps, one DS-0 channel is required to send a single voice call.

DS-1—DS-1, also known as digital service-one, has a capacity of 1.5 Mbps.

DS-2—DS-2 has a capacity of approximately 6 Mbps.

DS-3—DS-3 has a capacity of approximately 45 Mbps. At 45 Mbps/sec, a DS-3 line can be used to transmit compressed video.

T1—T1 is equivalent to a DS-1 channel. T1 and T3 are common carriers of signal that require dedicated systems installed at two or more sites that will be in communication with one another. Often misinterpreted as terrestrial, T1 and T3 links are not solely terrestrial in nature; they can involve communication using satellites as well as over land.

T1 links have a bandwidth of approximately 1.5 Mbps/sec (about 150 kB/sec), which is about one-half greater than a network using Ethernet, but equal to 24 channels of ISDN.

T3—T3 links are equivalent to 28 T-1s. This provides a significant bandwidth of approximately 45 Mbps/sec.

## Playing Motion Video over the Network

When both compression is applied to and throughput is increased for the network, it becomes possible to play real time video. There are a wide variety of applications. Real time remote casting sessions and even digital dailies are possible. Just consider the time savings for the film transfer-to-digital editing link. If the film is being transferred in Los Angeles and editing is in San Francisco, the output of the telecine can be digitized, compressed, encoded, and even data encrypted for security purposes and sent. The migration of postproduction work has clearly already begun.

## Transmission Methods Designed for Video Playback

### ABVS

Phone companies are now offering specific services designed for the transmission of video. These services consist of the transmission, codecs (coder/ decoder), and software. Advanced Broadcast Video Services (ABVS) is the Pacific Bell (California, USA) system that uses 45 Mbit/sec capability to send full-screen, full-motion NTSC video with four channels of 3:1 compressed audio.

Different codecs can be used with the basic transmission service. One company, Alcatel, offers a codec based on MPEG technology (but not MPEG), that, when combined with DS3 lines can provide full-motion and full-screen video at 45 Mbit/sec. This technology backbone was used to provide the real time interactivity which was used on the motion picture, *Jurassic Park*.

### ATM

Asynchronous Transfer Mode (ATM) is not in and of itself a network, but, rather a packaging scheme for data. It is a packetized method that takes data in small 53 byte sections and sends it in random fashion down a network. The packets are then reconstructed at the receiving end and any missing packets are requested and sent. The advantage that ATM represents over, say, DS3 is that the bandwidth is unlimited and compression becomes unnecessary. ATM, sending forth its packets to any portion of the network that is not in use, will result in significant throughput. ATM can be run on DS3 or T1, but the technology is optimized for use with optical network delivery systems.

### Synchronous Optical Network

Synchronous Optical Network (SONET) is an optical fiber delivery method that operates at higher rates than DS3 or T3 technology. Using synchronous transport signal, or STS 1, a bandwidth of 51 Mbits/sec can be achieved. Most impressively, STS3 operates at 155 Mbps.

These STS signals use optical channels that can be combined to provide greater bandwidth. The optical channels (OCs) come in the following versions:

OC-1. A 51 Mbit/sec channel.

OC-3. A 155 Mbps channel. This could be used to send and receive uncompressed composite digital NTSC Video.

OC-12. This is a 622 Mbits/sec channel that can carry uncompressed component digital NTSC Video.

OC-48. This channel can carry multiple 45 Mbps optical channels for a total of 2.4 gigabits.

Combining ATM with STS 3 over SONET will result in delivery loads in excess of 100 Mbps/sec. By adding multiple optical channels and running ATM over STS 3, a gigabit (one billion bits) per second transfer is achievable. This would allow us to deliver in real time multiple channels of sound, uncompressed video, and full interactivity.

## The Role of Digital Video Compression for Networking

Digital video compression, in the form of MPEG, will allow the transmission of images on the order of S-VHS resolution into the home. Video-on-demand, the notion that Viewer X in a city can use a television top set to browse a large video library and order a specific title that will then be downloaded into the viewer's home, is just one of the industries that will make use of compressed digital video.

For the filmmaker, receiving digital video in the home, in real time and without expensive phone service and specialized equipment, will allow, say, a director to monitor the results of visual effects creation while working on different projects from the home. On a mass consumer scale, new industries will develop around such technology.

## INDUSTRY VIEWPOINTS

### Tom Scott—EDnet, Entertainment Digital Network

For Tom Scott, telecommunications networks lie at the heart of digital filmmaking. Scott, with co-founder Tom Kobayashi, both formerly of Skywalker Sound, spearheaded the use of T1-based digital communications in order to deliver digital audio for feature film applications. There are a multitude of applications for this technology within the digital filmmaking process. Using fiber-optic lines, EDnet is able to transmit and exchange high quality digital audio, compressed video, and multimedia data. Says Scott,

> There are quite a few applications such as the remote approval of music and audio mixes, recording of remote voice overs, and dialogue replacement. For example, an extraordinary percentage of our "digital patch" service is for recording voice overs. Using two switched 56 kbps lines or one ISDN line we can provide high quality monochannel service in each direction, which is quite sufficient for a production to be able to record voice overs using talent in another part of the country. Commercials are big users of this service. . . .
>
> Another significant use is for remote dialogue replacement, or ADR. There are a variety of lines that

**Figure 8-33** Photo of Tom Scott. Courtesy of Tom Scott.

can be used depending upon what needs to be achieved. Whether we use multiplexed ISDN lines, fractional T1 lines, or ABVS at 45 Mbits per second is simply a choice that is made when we determine what it is that the client is trying to do.

For the 1993 film *Searching for Bobby Fischer,* EDnet provided links between Skywalker Sound in Santa Monica, California and London, England in order for director Steve Zailian, working in California, to direct actors Ben Kingsley and Robert Stephens in their dialogue replacement sessions. According to EDnet, the producer had indicated that it would cost from $8,000 to $10,000 for each actor to fly to California for a one day ADR session. The actual cost utilizing EDnet was $2,500 to record both actors in one afternoon, minus studio costs. Continues Scott,

> Another application is the approval of pre-mixes. For *Forrest Gump* we set up a system in director Robert Zemeckis's home. While he was involved with picture editing in Santa Barbara, in Nicasio at Skywalker Sound, they were working on film copies of cut scenes. In the month of preparation for the final mix, they were able to play him pre-mixes over the network. He could hear total pre-mixes and could make his comments, while the crew in Nicasio took notes. Anytime that you have to say, "We'll take the morning off to re-cut the bicycle sounds" you can save a lot of time by knowing that the changes are going to be requested and you can plan for them. So, using this technology, the filmmakers were able to save tremendous amounts of time.

Scott continually tracks the developments of transmission technology such as ISDN, T1, DS3, and so forth. He says,

> ATM is a packetizing and transmission protocol which sends its information in 53 byte packets. The ATM technology knows how to re-ask for packets that have not been received properly and then to reassemble the packets it has received. The technology is really optimized for SONET, an optical fiber delivery system which is sometimes referred to as STS3, with a payload of approximately 100 Mbits/sec. It will be widely available in just a few years.

Scott also sees huge opportunities in sending video along with audio over network lines. He notes,

> Pacific Bell's ABVS (Advanced Broadcast Video Service) uses the next step DS3 lines, at 45 Mbits/sec, and

can be used to transmit broadcast quality NTSC video with Dolby AC-2 audio. At the SMPTE convention in November 1993, we demonstrated sending broadcast quality video along with two channels of AC-2 encoded audio over DS3 lines into a digital, nonlinear editing system.

Scott also sees uses for MPEG digital video compression technology. He continues,

I can imagine using MPEG 2 as a way to send approval copies directly into the filmmaker's home. Even sending MPEG 2 over a T1 line would be easy to accomplish, as soon as the MPEG encoders become more affordable. Imagine if you were on location in Arizona—you could send the negative right out of the camera, Fed Ex'd to the lab, and get high quality video of your dailies back to the location via digital telephone lines as soon as the negative comes out of the "soup." Three years from now there will be inexpensive technology for approvals and it will be fueled by the desires for video on demand.

## WILL FILM EDITING BECOME OBSOLETE?

This same question was asked about the use of film in local television stations to gather news. For years, 16mm black-and-white, and then color film was used to capture the stories that were shown nightly. As new electronic alternatives in the form of portable video cameras and recorders became prevalent, the use of film became virtually nonexistent. Today, it would be very difficult to find any television stations shooting film for news. Technology that offered more options and flexibility became available and gradually obviated the need for using film.

Over time, the same evolution will happen to the craft of film editing. There will be so many overriding advantages of working digitally, that the film editorial process will become affected greatly. To that extent, there will be more inefficiency associated with the film editorial process. And, when inefficiency is a concern that is examined, digital filmmaking methods can greatly reduce the duplicative work to which the filmmaker is subjected.

## Audio Advantages

By taking the sound tracks from the digital editing system, the time and effort saved can be applied to other aspects of the film. If there is one thing that will enlighten one as to the inefficiencies of film editing, it will be a discovery of the wonderful capabilities of working with multiple channels and tracks of professional quality audio. There will, however, be some hybrid situations where actual film workprint and digital methods will co-exist.

## Workprint to Digital Disk: Digitizing from the Flatbed

When a film is being workprinted, it will be conformed using the cutlists from the digital editing system. However, since there is workprint in the cutting room, it can be used to remove an expensive step in the digital editing process. This involves going directly from film flatbed to computer disk, removing the telecine transfer stage and videotape from the entire film to digital process.

Let's say that we have 100,000 feet of 35mm 4 perf film shot at 24 fps. This represents 18 hours and 31 minutes of material. Instead of transferring the material to videotape, it is possible to use flatbeds modified to include a CCD (charged couple device) video camera. This allows the film to be played and transformed into electrical signals that can then be digitized directly to computer disk. This capability, in effect, turns the film flatbed into a "cheap telecine."

## Faster than Real Time Digitizing

There is an additional benefit to this process and that is the potential for faster than real time digitizing. For example, for 1:1 digitizing, the film would be played at 24 fps and digitized in real time at 24 fps. For faster digitizing, in countries that utilize the NTSC video standard of 30 fps (actually 29.97 fps), the film could be played at 30 fps, captured by the CCD camera at 29.97 fps, stored to disk, and played back at the film's normal speed of 24 fps. This would speed up the digitizing process by 25%. If we have 18 hours of material that must be digitized, we can accomplish the task in 13.5 hours, 4.5 hours faster.

Both methods are based on locking the bi-phase signal of the KEM or Steenbeck flatbed to a black-burst signal. In doing so, the digitizing station will understand and share a relationship to the speed of the flatbed's playback. Because the speed is locked, it does not waver or fluctuate. Once the relationship is established, the bi-phase is now slowed by 0.1%. Thus, the playback is now 23.976 fps. There are also boxes to speed the bi-phase to 29.97 fps. This would then create a 1:1 relationship between film and video.

In one fell swoop, the entire telecine and videotape stages are removed from the process. It is clearly an option that must be taken seriously for those filmmakers who will continue to use film and digital in the cutting room.

## INDUSTRY VIEWPOINTS

### Van Ling—Filmmaker, Digital Consultant

*The Abyss* (1989), *Terminator 2: Judgment Day* (1991), *True Lies* (1994), *Congo* (1995).

A summa cum laude graduate of the University of Southern California Cinema School, Van Ling spearheaded the use of Macintosh systems for storyboard processing and visual effects design on writer/director James Cameron's feature film *The Abyss*. In addition to serving as Cameron's technical researcher and creative liaison for all aspects of production on the film, he played a significant role in the design and creation of the visual effects, and subsequently served as Vis-

ual Effects Coordinator and Creative Supervisor on *Terminator 2: Judgment Day*.

He produced both *The Abyss* Special Edition and the *Terminator 2* Special Edition, and was the writer/director of the laserdisc supplements for those films. An active voice in the call for integrating digital technology into all areas of filmmaking, Ling served as Head of Production for Cameron's production company Lightstorm Entertainment for many years before forming his own production company, Banned from the Ranch Entertainment, with partner Casey Cannon. In addition to doing freelance consulting on visual effects, digital graphics, and laserdiscs, Ling has most recently created digital graphics and displays for the Kennedy/Marshall film *Congo*.

What do you see as the defining trends in making films?

> I think that the movie industry is moving towards the two ends of the spectrum in that as the stakes get higher and the technology improves, both the big-budget studio films and the smaller independent films are going to benefit. On the one hand, the big studio films are going to get bigger and try to outdo each other in terms of spectacle; this is what BIG films are about: big sets, big stars, big action, big budgets, big successes, or big failures. There's a lot at stake, so the major studios and filmmakers are going to use whatever cutting-edge technology they can to make their movies worth the seven or eight bucks it cost for a ticket.
>
> On the other hand, there's been a resurgence of the smaller, independent or relatively small-budget film; part of it is a backlash against all of the big stuff, but a lot of it is due to the fact that more people are able to get their films made, their stories told. This may seem weird, especially given the attitude that people think the studios are only interested in the big stakes now, but there's a growing niche of films and filmmakers who do not have the access or the interest in the technological whiz-bang and stuff.
>
> Ironically, these people are also able to benefit from the technology that is being used by the big guys in that many of the new tools, especially the digital ones, are now available to everybody. This certainly has been true in the music video area, where as the big guys are moving into major paintbox or high-end digital manipulation, the older analog effects mixers and basic digital effects are becoming more affordable and accessible to the smaller guys. I think there will always be room for both ends of the spectrum, because no matter what your level of technology or complexity, it's still all about storytelling and engaging the viewers' interest.

**Figure 8-34** Photo of Van Ling. Courtesy of Van Ling. Photograph by Alan Weissman.

How has knowing that certain technologies are available to the filmmaker affected how productions proceed?

On the one hand, it's allowed better planning and allocation of resources in order to save money and time for the production; on the other hand, it's allowed people to get sloppy, which in the end results in excessive spending and missed deadlines. Again, there are two sides to it, and it all comes back to technology being either a tool or a crutch. I've seen productions that have really benefited from the previsualization process using the computer, saving time and money by determining what they need before they even start preproduction; I've also seen shows where they've gotten lax on the set and said "oh, we can fix it in digital; we can have them paint out that wire or track that matte," and then have it bite them in postproduction when they find out that fixing it in digital is going to cost way more than if they had just taken a moment on the set to make a few tweaks. Sure, it's possible to fix it using these new technologies, but sometimes it's more expensive. At the most basic level, these new tools shouldn't affect how productions proceed at all, other than by expanding the range of possibilities a filmmaker has. It doesn't change the fact that he or she must still have a clear vision and a clear concept of how to get that vision onto the screen.

What are the benefits to the filmmaker who uses the technology that companies such as Digital Domain and ILM are offering?

Freedom is probably the major benefit. These tools and technology should give the filmmaker more narrative breathing room, because he or she no longer has to restrain a vision just because there is no way of getting that image out of your head and onto the screen. A lot of filmmaking, the technical end especially, has always been a challenge of cleverness and ingenuity. How can you get across the image or story point in the most efficient, elegant, succinct and cost-effective way? What companies like DD and ILM are offering is not so much a technology, but ideally what I call a "visioning service." They are offering not only a bunch of computers but a group of artists who work in the medium of digital imaging. They are at best people who are there to support your vision as a filmmaker and participate in the collaborative process. They know the tools and they know the aesthetics and can cogently discuss with you what you are trying to get across, giving suggestions and running with ideas. At the very least, they can be a bunch of computer guys who might not have a strong artistic

sense but can hack their way through anything if they just knew literally what you wanted to see, and not have to understand why you want the shot a certain way. These places can be useful if you simply need a high-tech service bureau, where you are willing to carry the burden of the work. It's the difference between going to a graphic design house and going to a self-service Kinko's Copies on the corner. Both have their place, depending on your style of filmmaking.

Additionally, digital technology has expanded the scope of narrative and communication by allowing creative assets to be continuous across several different media. It has allowed the smooth crossover of films with ancillaries like video games, interactive CD-ROMs, television, laserdisc, and other new markets and creative opportunities. Digital assets can be shared between these different platforms, and a single vision can be maintained across them all. Filmmakers and storytellers who never thought about these other media are now giving them a serious look, because they can now be part of the developing creative process rather than an artificial addition after the film has come out.

What should the filmmaker be wary of with regard to the pervasiveness of technology in modern filmmaking?

Most importantly, be wary of losing touch with what all of the technology is for in the first place: communication through storytelling. The same creative freedom this technology affords you is that same one that requires more creative discipline to maintain your focus. Like in many other fields, it can be very easy to fall into the temptation of the technological imperative in that if the technology is out there, you should be using it or you'll be behind the times. It's more like we need to remain behind the timeless, which is the nature of weaving a good yarn. People think technology is cool, quite rightly in some cases, because it is a tangible look at the future. Movies are part of that forward-looking tradition as well, in the sense that it can give you a glimpse of what might be or what you may never experience directly. There's often a comparison between movies and dreaming, because it's image-based and totally malleable. Digital Domain actually used a line about that in one of their trade ads: "Dream with your eyes open." That really sums up what you can do. But you can just as easily make it into a nightmare if you're not careful. Just because you can do something a certain way does not mean you should. The scariest thing to me after we did *T2* was that I had many reports from colleagues in the industry who said that their directors came in and said "I've just seen *T2* and we've got to find a way to put some computer shots into our movie to keep up to date and relevant." That's purely a case of letting the trends in technology guide your actions, rather than the other way around.

The problem is still the same, though, regardless of the technology; you still have to have an idea, a story, an image, in your head as a filmmaker and you still have to get it out of your head and onto the screen in a way that connects with other people. The technology is just a broader tool for you to do that. If it's the right tool, great; if it's not the right tool or there's a simpler, more efficient or more cost-effective way to do it, then don't use it.

What do you feel are some of the breakthroughs that have been accomplished and what remains to be accomplished technologically in the area of film-making?

The development of digital filmmaking tools in the mainstream is probably the most significant advance in the industry, but I think the biggest breakthrough has simply been the acceptance of digital technology as a tool that can be effectively used in ALL genres, not just the science fiction or fantasy areas. Many of the digital tools were first developed for this arena, but have managed to establish a foothold in the basic palette of the filmmaker. This is really not so much a technological breakthrough as it is an attitudinal breakthrough.

What I think remains to be accomplished technologically is really being able to hone those tools so that they become more storyteller-friendly. Companies like Digital Domain, ILM, and others are trying to get the technology out from under the stigma of being technology . . . a camera is a piece of technology, but filmmakers today aren't afraid or wary of them any more, if they ever were. To a lot of filmmakers, the technology is some kind of scary black box that can do neat things, but by being some kind of arcane and mysterious process it seems to be out of the film-makers' control. Some people are threatened by that, and they feel that they have to learn all of the technology and computer jargon if they're going to use the technology at all. Some digital service facilities actually promote this idea, if only to keep themselves looking important and their prices high. Others are realizing that you need to take your technologies to the filmmaker, not make them come to you. These companies are trying to take the mystery and techno-babble out of the process and show the filmmaker that they still have complete control over their im-agery. Entertainment-driven technology, not technology-driven entertainment, is what it's all about.

Some people think that digital methods are a radical shift from analog methods and that the whole filmmaking paradigm is shifting, displacing traditions and narrowing views. It's not that radical a shift if you look at it as the creation of new and more power-ful tools to do the same thing we've always been trying to do. Analog and digital do not have to be mutually exclusive; they can be symbiotic. Each can support and inform the other. Music on CD is essentially the same as music on cassette . . . when all is said and done, it's still about the music. In a way, the term "digital filmmaking" is kind of a misnomer—no matter what the adjective tag is, it's still filmmaking, storytelling, communicating.

(And incidentally, I'm writing this on a Power-book while sitting on an apple box at the foot of an active volcano out in the middle of the Costa Rican jungle. That's the magic of the movies.)

## DIGITAL, NONLINEAR EDITING SYSTEMS FOR FILM EDITING

When evaluating digital editing systems, there will usually be two categories: first, systems that both capture and play back material at its native 24 fps, and those that capture material at either 25 fps or 29.97 fps and use a match-back process to create a negative cut list from a 25 fps or a 29.97 fps edit decision list. This is an important distinction. What follows is a list of digital, nonlinear editing systems that have been used to edit film-originated and film-delivered pro-gramming; some of these systems play material at 24 fps and some play back at either 25 or 30 fps.

### Avid Film Composer

The Avid Film Composer, the companion system to Avid's Media Composer, was recognized with a 1993 Emmy award for Outstanding Technical Achievement in Digital Editing System. The Avid Film Composer was awarded a 1994 Academy Award for Scientific and Engineering Achievement.

The Avid Film Composer consists of an Apple Macintosh CPU and a choice of magnetic hard drives or magneto-optical discs. Operating under the Macintosh operating system, it offers timeline-based editing, database and pictorial shot displays, and multiple-camera support.

Various levels of single-field picture quality are available with four tracks of audio sampled at 44.1 and 48 KHz, and the system is 24/25/30 frame capa-ble. Additional logging, digitizing, and assistant sta-tions are supported.

EDLs and film cut lists in 16, 35, and 70 mm are supported, including assemble, scene pull, and change lists. Import of 16mm, 35mm, and 70mm edge lists is supported along with import of telecine logs including Aaton, Evertz, and flexFile.

Credits include: *A Bronx Tale, The Fugitive, Needful Things, Strange Days, True Lies, Two Bits, Wolf,* and others.

## D/Vision Pro

The DVision/Pro digital, nonlinear editing system is from TouchVision Systems, the designers of the original, tape-based, TouchVision system.

Utilizing an Intel 80386 or 80486 CPU, and either optical or magnetic disks, the system provides a variety of single-field picture resolutions.

With multiple tracks of audio sampled at 44.1 KHz, the system is 25/30 frame capable. Featuring D/Vision's Source Catalog, a visual database, still frame samples from captured footage can be searched and displayed on-screen.

EDLs and negative cut lists are available.

Credits include: Use of portable-based system on *Forrest Gump* and others.

## Ediflex Digital

The Ediflex Digital editing system is the latest offering from Ediflex Digital Systems. Ediflex, maker of the Ediflex 1 and 2 first developed in 1984, introduced in 1985 a nonlinear editing system which used multiple VHS machines to offer random access to material.

The Ediflex Digital system consists of an Intel 80486 CPU, high resolution graphics display monitor, and a choice of 1.3 GB magneto-optical or magnetic hard drives. Operating under a DOS operating system running Microsoft Windows, the system features a variety of film-style tools.

Four levels of single-field picture quality are available with two tracks of audio sampled at 44.1 KHz, and the system is 24/25/30 frame capable. Featuring timeline and image-based editing, the system also includes a script on the screen, referenced to source material. EDLs, negative cut lists, optical count sheets, pull lists, and change lists are available.

Credits include: *All's Fair, Children of the Corn II, Freeway, Hellraiser III, House Party, Shaking the Tree, Tango War,* and others.

## EMC Primetime

The EMC Primetime is the successor to the EMC2, recognized with a 1993 Emmy award for Outstanding Technical Achievement in Digital Editing. The system was introduced at the 1988 SMPTE show in New York City as the first digital, nonlinear offline editing system.

The EMC Primetime system consists of an Intel 80486 CPU and a choice of magneto-optical or magnetic hard drives. Operating under a DOS operating system, the system features storyboard editing, visual timeline of display edits, and fast access to multiple-camera scenes.

Various levels of single-field picture quality are available with two to four tracks of audio sampled at 11, 22, and 44.1 KHz, and the system is 24/25/30 frame capable.

EDLs and 16mm, 35mm, and 70mm edge lists are supported along with import of telecine logs created by Aaton, Evertz, and flexFile based systems.

Credits include: *Army of Darkness, Hard Target, High Strung,* and others.

## Lightworks

The Lightworks editor was introduced in 1991 and is based on an enhanced 80486 computer and consists of primary storage on magnetic disks with backup to phase-change or magneto-optical discs, or Exabyte tape. The Lightworks was awarded a 1994 Academy Award for Scientific and Engineering Achievement.

The system offers various levels of single-field picture quality with two tracks of audio sampled at 32, 44.1, or 48 KHz. Import of shot logs and telecine logs are supported, such as flexFile, Keylog, and other database files tracking 24 fps codes with 2:3 pulldown references. The system features timeline-based editing, and file cards can be used to find shots by ID, location, or scene numbers. Output consists of EDLs, negative cut lists, pull, and change lists.

Credits include: *Clear and Present Danger, Mrs. Doubtfire, Eight Seconds, Intersection, The Pelican Brief,* and others.

## Montage III

The Montage III digital editing system is the latest offering from Montage Group, Ltd. Montage, maker of the Montage 1 and 2, first developed in 1984; it was the first videotape-based nonlinear system and utilized up to seventeen Super Beta Hi-Fi VCRs to offer random access to material.

The Montage III, a 1993 Emmy award winner for Outstanding Technical Achievement in Digital Editing, consists of an Intel 80386 or 80486 CPU, and utilizes Intel's RTV digital video compression. Storage can be 1 GB removable optical discs or magnetic hard drives. Operating under a DOS operating system running Microsoft Windows, the system features a variety of film-style tools.

It offers four levels of single-field picture quality with two tracks of audio sampled at either 44.1 or 48 KHz, and is 24/25/30 frame capable. The system features an electronic grease pencil which allows the user to make notes directly onto clips. EDLs, negative cut lists, and change lists are among the numerous lists that are available.

Credits include: *The Making of a Legend: Gone With The Wind, The Parent Trap III, Sworn to Silence, Kids Like These, Home Sweet Homeless,* and others.

# 9

# The Film-Digital-Film Connection

## DIGITAL MANIPULATION OF THE FILM IMAGE

The use of computers to change, augment, and reshape original film images has been a practice that has steadily been on the rise. Further, the use of computers has created characters and scenes which were integral to the stories that the filmmakers sought to tell. Without computers and software, filmmakers would not have been able to realize some of the fantastic scenes and creatures that films in the 1990s have brought. Such examples as the realistic dinosaurs of *Jurassic Park* (1993), the liquid metal T1000 of *Terminator 2: Judgment Day* (1991), and the mask with magical properties of *The Mask* (1994), are all examples of the film-digital-film connection.

In this chapter, we discuss the use of computers to digitally alter and enhance film images. This is one of the most intriguing and promising aspects of filmmaking as it brings with it the possibility of not only fixing problems that originated during the production stage, but also of creating fantastic images that will provide memorable cinematic moments.

The term film-digital-film refers to the method of originating images on film, storing and manipulating them as digital information, and returning the digital information back to film form. There are many uses for a film scanning, digital manipulation, and film recording process. Among them:

Digital "backlots" from stock footage

Digital color correction, filter effects, and painting

Digital compositing

Digital creature creation

Digital film restoration

Digital wire removal

Digital image enhancement

Digital artifact removal

Integration of computer generated material with original film elements

While it is often thought that the film-digital-film methodology largely supports only films that have intricate special visual effects sequences, this is a mistaken notion. Many of the capabilities above are used extensively in films that cannot be considered special effects films. Yet, without these digital tools, such films as: *Bill Bailey Won't You Come Home* (1994) [digital backlot from stock footage], *Fearless* (1993) [digital color correction], *In The Line of Fire* (1993) [digital blue screen compositing], *Cliffhanger* (1993) [digital wire removal], *Coneheads* (1993) [digital artifact removal], and *True Lies* (1994) [integration of computer generated material] would have required seeking out other means of creating their various images.

Shown in figures 9-1a–b is an example of how the film-digital-film process was used in *Cliffhanger* to put an actress in a setting that would have otherwise been too dangerous to attempt. The background shot of the mountain has been combined with the foreground shot of the actress who is against a blue screen and falling away from the camera. The shots are scanned from film into the digital film workstation, the wires are digitally removed, and the shots are composited together to create a believable shot.

## DIGITAL RECREATION OF THE HUMAN FORM

Using computers to take the human form and to change it has been one of the areas where digital film

**Figure 9-1a–b** Blue screen shooting and wire removal from *Cliffhanger*. The background of the mountain for helicopter crash sequences was built in the parking lot of Boss Film Studios. "Sara's Fall" was accomplished through the use of blue screen and digital wire removal. Shown is the blue screen live action and the finished composite. Courtesy of Boss Film Studios. Photo of "Sara's Fall" by Virgil Mirano.

workstations have yielded stunning results. Figure 9-2a shows how the human form and the way it moves can be translated into data that a computer can then manipulate. These witness points are then correlated to analogous points on a computer-generated skeleton (figure 9-2b).

Shown in figure 9-3 are several frames that show the progression of the computer-generated T1000 to live action. Note how the action that the filmmaker can now include in films is no longer dependent upon a static shot, or on a locked-down camera. Instead, the action can be free-flowing, with intricate camera moves which can be duplicated either through computer tracking of the movement or by motion control camera software.

Further remarkable effects can be achieved through the use of realistic texture-mapping where environmental or human shadings are placed onto the computer-generated object. Figure 9-4 is an example where the animated computer model of a splitting head was texture-mapped with an image of the actor's face and then composited onto the film image of his body to create a seamless shot.

## INDUSTRY VIEWPOINTS

### Ed Jones—President, Cinesite, Hollywood, CA

Academy Award Winner, *Who Framed Roger Rabbit?* (1988)

For Ed Jones, recipient of the Academy Award for his contribution in revolutionizing the animation

**Figure 9-2a** The motion of witness points placed on Robert Patrick's body were tracked and captured from different angles as the actor walked to form the basis for replicating natural movement in the computer generated T1000. From *Terminator 2: Judgment Day* (1991). Courtesy of Carolco Pictures and Twentieth-Century Fox, Ltd. All rights reserved.

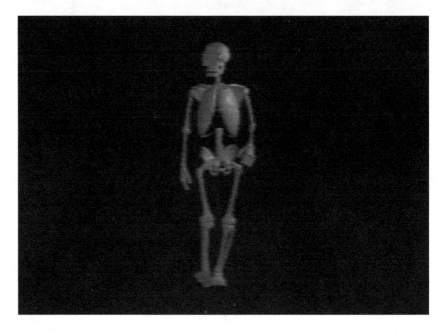

**Figure 9-2b** One of a series of steps to create the T1000. The witness points captured as motion data are correlated to analogous points on a computer-generated skeleton. From *Terminator 2: Judgment Day* (1991). Courtesy of Carolco Pictures and Twentieth-Century Fox, Ltd. All rights reserved.

techniques used in producing *Who Framed Roger Rabbit?*, the integration of digital technology in creating visual effects and digital imaging services has been a lifelong goal. Jones, who spent thirteen years at LucasArts' Industrial Light & Magic and contributed to over 90 films, including *Raiders of the Lost Ark, ET: The Extraterrestrial, Return of the Jedi,* and *Terminator 2: Judgment Day,* comments on the various technologies available to today's filmmaker. Says Jones,

I see a lot of powerful opportunities to create stories and the ability to use open architecture systems and computer platforms to merge film, video, and multimedia—a cross-pollination if you like—will form a new technology for filmmakers. There are also great creative benefits to the filmmaker from a postproduction sense.

I see a lot of scripts that previously couldn't be told. But now, using previsualization and computers, we sit down and say "Let's just try to see what char-

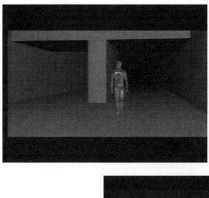

**Figure 9-3** Several frames which show the progression of the computer generated T1000 to live action. Figure 9-3a shows the 3-D figure's placement in a 3-D computer environment to match the camera angle in the live action; figure 9-3b shows the 3-D CG figure composited into the live action background; figures 9-3c–e show the mattes used to isolate and transform the CG figure into the live film image of the actor. From *Terminator 2: Judgment Day* (1991). Courtesy of Carolco Pictures and Twentieth-Century Fox, Ltd. All rights reserved.

acters and images we can create and manipulate." And we might create four or five minutes of effects which show the filmmaker how to utilize the effects properly and to use the effects as exclamation points not as the nouns and the verbs. Digital previsualization really has great benefits in that way and filmmakers get an instinctual and creative grasp of what they can and cannot create. They know why shots have to be done in certain ways and, hopefully, they come away with, "Wait, this set of stories and characters is within my realm and budget."

Digital techniques, and the digital imaging technologies of scanning, manipulation, and recording back to film, as practiced by Cinesite, have great benefits when understood correctly by the production team. Jones continues,

Studios are concerned with reducing production schedules. Usually there is some precedent that is set. Studios make seventeen to thirty films per year and they do so for the same amount of money each year. They therefore have to find ways to cut costs. The only real way to do this is in the postproduction schedule by introducing new tools that allow you to create, edit, and finalize in reduced time.

What you can do in digital postproduction can affect production schedules. When you are shooting green screens, you don't have to spend as much time to get the production elements exact. We can shoot things against black, blue, or green and be sure that we can remove the unwanted elements to combine them into seamless composites. So, you are not waiting undue amounts of time for a crew to set up a specific background and you can use this time to remain on schedule during principal photography.

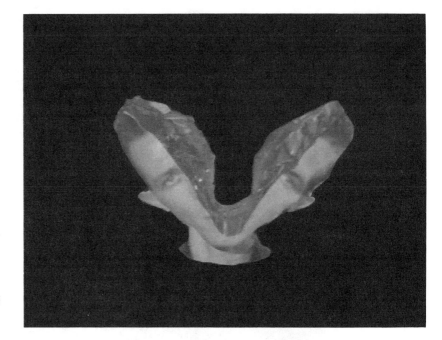

**Figure 9-4** A computer manipulation of a 3-D model of actor Robert Patrick's head was used to create this startling split-head effect. This animated computer model was texture-mapped with an image of the actor's face and then composited onto the film image of his body to create a seamless shot. From *Terminator 2: Judgment Day* (1991). Courtesy of Carolco Pictures and Twentieth-Century Fox, Ltd. All rights reserved.

Jones also feels that it is important to educate members of the filmmaking community for whom digital technology may appear to be very foreign territory. He says,

> We've brought in Directors of Photography who really have great eyes and great control in knowing how to light something and this technology can really expand their toolbox. DPs look at the technology that we offer at Cinesite as an extension of their talents—if they need a little bit more of something—they know now that they can still continue the creative process long after the sets have been struck and this is the thing that has really excited them. As they get more engrossed in the technicalities, they suddenly get so excited because the results are in the right direction and seeing them instantly on the computer screen gives them immediate feedback. If they can find new tools to help them tell the story, they want to be part of that technology.

For Jones, the quest for refining digital methodologies for the filmmaker is a personal goal. He concludes,

> Digital imaging allows people to combine and create images that they have never created before. You can get all the way down to the pixel level and grain structure and put these elements together in a better way. If you can tell a great story everyone will listen,

**Figure 9-5** Photo of Ed Jones. Courtesy of Cinesite Digital Film Center.

and if you can put great images on the screen—that's the real satisfying part for me—to develop and to make this technology available as fast as possible.

## THE BASICS OF THE FILM-DIGITAL-FILM PROCESS

The method of digitally manipulating film requires scanning the film, digitally storing the images, and recording the images back to film. There are three distinct pieces of hardware/software that form this structure: the film scanner, the digital manipulation software, and the film recorder. While the film scanner and recorder form the backbone of this process, it is the hardware and software that are used to digitally manipulate the images that are undergoing rapid change; we can refer to this portion as the digital film workstation (DFW).

## CREATING OPTICAL EFFECTS— THE OPTICAL PRINTER

Prior to the use of DFWs, optical effects for films were created by optical printers. An optical printer takes one or more film elements, aligns them, and rephotographs the elements onto a new piece of film. It is very important to be aware of generational loss as each successive film pass brings with it the potential for a degrading of the image quality. Also, because the result of the optical printing is not known until the new piece of film is developed and printed, there exists the potential for redoing complicated opticals.

## Optical Cloning

Optical printers have been used to replicate items in a frame and to create crowd scenes for at least sixty years. However, the successive generations required to perform this feat have demanded close attention to quality control. With digital film workstations, computers make these demanding tasks easier and faster to accomplish.

The film-digital-film process begins with the scanning of the original film elements into the DFW. The first component in this process is the film scanner.

## THE FILM SCANNER

To manipulate film in the DFW, the original film elements must be scanned from the film negative and stored in digital form. Scanners have been available for this purpose and have used technologies such as cathode ray tube (CRT), laser, and charge coupled devices (CCD). There are several components to a film scanner, and these include the manner in which the film is illuminated and the film transport mechanism. In general, CRT-based systems are the most common, but laser technology can provide very focused beam sizes and avoid the inherent flare characteristics of CRT technology.

The Cineon system (figure 9-6) from the Eastman

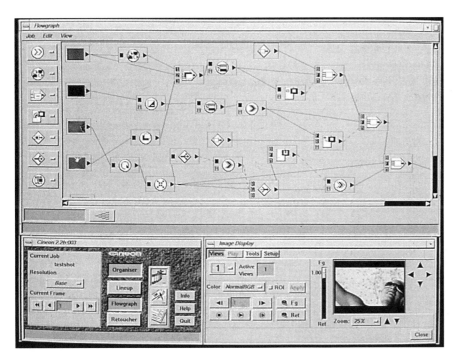

**Figure 9-6** The Cineon system from the Eastman Kodak Corporation.

Kodak Corporation employs lasers which are designed to expose the red, blue, and green components of Eastman EXR Color Intermediate Film 5244. It accomplishes this through the use of 458 nanometer (nm) blue argon, 453 nm green argon, and 633 nm red helium-neon lasers.

The transport mechanisms of film scanners can be of two types: shuttle systems that have been used in most conventional optical printers, or in the case of the Cineon, a custom transport which combines the pin registration of standard motion picture shuttles with the curved surface found in drum scanners. According to the Eastman Kodak Corporation, when film is wrapped around a curved drum, "the flatness of the film is maintained to a higher tolerance than possible with conventional flat film gates." A mechanical tolerance of +/– 0.0001 inch is maintained and on a 35mm scanner, with 4K resolution, this corresponds to =/– 0.5 pixels.

## Image Format and Samples

Various film formats and samplings can be made depending upon the capabilities of the chosen specific film scanner. For purposes of comparison, an NTSC picture digitally captured in RGB at a pixel matrix of $640 \times 480 = 307{,}200$ sampling points. However, 35mm film, digitally captured at a pixel matrix of $2{,}000 \times 2{,}000 = 4{,}000{,}000$ sampling points or approximately 13 times larger than the video image. The amount of data that must be captured is staggering.

In general, a film scanner that operates at 4K resolution will provide excellent results in achieving a seamless integration of the DFW elements with the rest of the film. Shown below are the scanned width and number of samples of 35mm film for Cineon operates.

| Format | Width (mm) | Samples |
|---|---|---|
| Academy | 21.94 | 3656 |
| Cinemascope | 21.94 | 3656 |
| Full Aperture | 24.57 | 4096 |
| VistaVision | 24.57 | 4096 |

Film frames are not scanned in real time. Instead, the process is a time intensive task that may take many seconds for each frame. As improvements are made, the amount of time required for scanning each frame will decrease. Generally, a scanning and recording time of approximately ten seconds per frame is considered quite good.

## Storing Images

As each frame of film is scanned, it becomes digital data. Often, the data is stored in an interleaved RGB pixel format. The amount of storage that is required for one frame of 35mm film (depending upon the format) can be 40 MB/frame. A 1 GB (~1000 MB) disk would yield only slightly over one second of storage for the scanned and digitized film images.

Once the images have been digitized, they must be stored onto some form of digital storage. Most often, some form of digital data tape is used as the cost of storing the images on computer disk would be quite great. In general, the faster the data transfer rate, the more expensive the device. To compare, an 8mm tape backup system is capable of backing up 1.5 MB/sec at a cost of $4,000 while the Ampex DST system backs up 15 MB/sec at a cost of $195,000. When the time arrives for manipulating the images, the digital data is transferred from tape and stored onto computer disk where they will then be accessed by software on the DFW.

## DIGITAL FILM WORKSTATION SOFTWARE

There are many different software applications that can be used to affect the digitized frame. The common effects that are done on DFWs are: wire removal, blue screening, compositing of digital and mechanical elements with live action footage, electronic matte painting, and pixel manipulation.

## Wire Removal

As stunt work has become more dangerous, stunt persons have been asked to take on more risks than ever before. In the past, it has been difficult to conceal the wires that are used to suspend stunt persons when dangerous heights are encountered. Using DFWs, it is possible to utilize the computer's ability to isolate specific colors to remove any safety wires that are visible in the frame. As a result of digital wire removal, it is possible to now put the actual actors into situations which heretofore would have been too dangerous to attempt.

Removing objects from the film frame is also a common request. There are many instances where it simply would have taken too long to remove something from the frame which does not belong in the finished shot. For example, if a car is moving by a sign that identifies a location different from where the story takes place, the sign can be electronically painted out of the frame, while a background is put in place of the sign.

For the motorcycle jump in the Los Angeles canals, in *Terminator 2: Judgment Day* (1991), a large support crane and clearly obvious steel cables were used to safely support the stunt rider. Later, after digitizing the shot into a digital workstation, the suspension mechanisms were entirely painted out of the required frames. Such examples of computer-aided wire

and harness removal were performed by PDI, Pacific Data Images.

Shown in figure 9-7, for purposes of illustration, is a recreation of how wire removal may be accomplished. By using the pixels from a clean background and substituting them for the pixel areas that define the wires, the wires are essentially removed from view. Additional techniques are used to paint and blur certain sections in order to reconstruct the tracking of the camera lens. The original live action footage shows the rigging from which the motorcycle and driver have been suspended. Next is a magnified view that shows the wires of the rig as black against the sky background. We progressively zoom in on the areas of the wires by using the digital film workstation software, and we see that the pixels that make up the dark areas of the frame can actually be painted out and blurred to accomplish realistic and totally believable wire removal.

**Figure 9-7** A recreation of how wire removal can be accomplished. The surrounding pixels of the clear sky are used to replace the pixels occluded by the suspended wires and rigging. From *Terminator 2: Judgment Day.* Courtesy of Carolco Pictures and Twentieth-Century Fox, Ltd. All rights reserved.

## INDUSTRY VIEWPOINTS

### Richard Edlund, ASC—Visual Effects Supervisor and Founder of Boss Film Studios, Marina del Rey, CA

*Star Wars, Raiders of the Lost Ark, The Empire Strikes Back, Return of the Jedi.*

For Richard Edlund, a four-time recipient of the Academy Award for Best Visual Effects, the entire range of filmmaking is undergoing a change and a movement from analog technology and methods to digital processes. Says Edlund,

> Visual effects are now coming out of the analog age and into a digital age. To me it's a breath of fresh air. The means to an end in the past has been the optical printer and techniques that have incorporated everything from miniatures to matte paintings to shooting in water tanks—in short, any means that we could come up with in an analog world and that could then be composited together in the optical printer. So, we've been wrestling with that technology and it's hard work—if you have a matte that doesn't fit you overexpose the inter-matte to shrink it so it will fit, and now maybe the matte has to be repositioned—all of these tricks and techniques have been borne out of necessity.
>
> My job is to trick an audience that is very astute—they have seen millions of feet of film and when you try to achieve an effect that is the least bit

**Figure 9-8** Photo of Richard Edlund, ASC. Courtesy of Boss Film Studios.

funny, you lose the audience and you've failed as a visual effects artist.

Edlund, who has a career that spans more than 25 years, now views digital technologies as being revolutionary in redefining how visual effects are accomplished. He continues,

The digital means have been there for a while, and I have used them, but the cost has been the chief problem, as well as resolution and control. With the arrival of the relatively low cost workstations and the scanning and recording techniques that we now have, we are now able to address each frame separately and each pixel separately. So it has opened up another renaissance—the last being *Star Wars* which utilized robotic photography and optical printer technology. Now that we have the digital means at our disposal, the industry is opening up to a giant palette that is available and we really have a blank canvas to work upon.

The use of digital technology to create new and fantastic images that heretofore would have been economically prohibitive translates to new freedom for the filmmaker. Says Edlund,

The filmmaker is going to be able to experience a total freedom from the standpoint of the storyteller so that he or she can fantasize and not even think about what can or cannot be done. The wall of visual effects is going to come tumbling down. Because we can work right there with the filmmaker, the process becomes director-friendly and the technology is not limited to the effects-type movie. The effects will become more transparent and we'll be able to create a lot more shots for less money.

Take a look at *Cliffhanger*, a film in which we produced the visual effects. This is a good example of wire-removal. The entire film could not have been done without this technique. All the actors had wires to protect them. The old way of shooting wires was very hit and miss—you had to shoot it a specific way. Now we just shoot and remove the wires digitally. There were also some very sophisticated shots that had to be done—snow was created and there was one scene where the camera comes up and you see Sylvester Stallone. But when it was shot, a rock was not built into the set and, instead, you saw two-by-fours! So we added rocks, mimicked the tracking shot and accomplished this in 3-D, with three-dimensional rocks that we created in the computer.

The obvious idea of being able to show the director a significant previsualization of the movie will be standard operating procedure as time goes on. We still use old fashioned techniques—matte painting is an old technique. Now our artists are painting in the computer, creating mattes—which has become so straightforward and malleable. You can try things without the fear of trying things—our artists love it. That's a very important point because we still need artists—we are a talent-driven business regardless of the digital technology that surrounds us.

## INDUSTRY VIEWPOINTS

### Hoyt Yeatman—Director/Visual Effects Supervisor/Cofounder, Dream Quest Images

For Hoyt Yeatman, cofounder of Dream Quest Images and Dream Quest Digital, each day brings forth new challenges in his desire to provide the feature filmmaker with a variety of "never before experienced" special visual effects. Yeatman has overseen the special visual effects of some of the most innovative films in recent history, among them *Total Recall* and *The Abyss*. For Yeatman, whose background is firmly routed in the entire range of film-based special effects, and who is the recipient of an Academy Award for the 1989 film *The Abyss* in the category of Best Achievement in Visual Effects, each film Dream Quest Images is asked to work on is approached with

**Figure 9-9** Photo of Hoyt Yeatman. Courtesy of Dream Quest Images.

a complete investigation of what must be accomplished while taking into account the budget and timetable that the filmmaker requires. Says Yeatman,

> I think one of the things that really separates us is that we come from a film background and we are firmly routed in miniatures, optical printing, animation, motion control, blue screen, and matte paintings. But we've been able to apply new technologies along with the original film-based tools. As a result, we've been able to combine in unique ways things like the traditional film blue screen and adapt it back to digital techniques. The result is that we really use a variety of techniques—some are traditional film methods while others are digital techniques which are being created each day.

The film-digital-film methodology that forms the basis of creating special visual effects relies on a chain of film scanning, digital manipulation, and film recording. Yeatman continues,

> When we decided to enter this area, we began by building our own input device and we found technology in different areas such as the medical and military industries that we could use to create a film scanner of high quality. But what's really important is that one of the key things we do here every day is to talk in film language—when it comes to things like

scanning a film negative, you can describe what you're doing as if you were in a film lab, and we try to maintain a faithful job in maintaining the conventions of film in a digital world.

After scanning the selected film negative into the digital system, a variety of software tools is used to manipulate the material in some fashion. Digitally adding to or deleting items from the frame are common occurrences. Combining computer-generated imagery with live-action footage is an area of major attention, such as visual effects in films like *The Abyss*. Throughout this period of combining digital and film elements, the user interface and the interactivity between artist and filmmaker are most important. Although working in a digital environment is often thought of as facilitating faster working methods, it is important to allow ideas to mature. Says Yeatman,

> It's interesting to see the difference when a client sits down and helps you put together different shots, and even transitions from shot to shot. But feature films differ from commercials because due to their nature they usually take longer to do and you actually have to be aware of the fact that many times the machinery works faster than the human brain works. There is really something to be said about having the time to sit back and think about what it is that the filmmaker is trying to do; in many ways there is a gestation period for a film when you are designing and executing effects for feature films. Many times, artists just can't make judgments that quickly. If you look at where video was ten years ago, when commercials were done, we actually finished on film and then you had your opticals. We then progressed to where you would have twelve videotape machines locked together to create multi-layered opticals. Now you have the digital revolution, but rather than having two to three weeks to composite shots together, you are lucky to get two to three days. And there's no getting around one fact—art does take time!

Among the first uses of film-digital-film methodology was often to remove items in a frame that the filmmakers could not take the time to fix during the production process. However, Yeatman describes many artistic advantages that become possible by using digital technology. He notes,

> The idea of having a digital paint system to be able to paint out things in a frame can allow the filmmaker to be more innovative and creative. You can do rod puppetry where you don't have to worry about un-

wanted things appearing in the frame. You can do bigger stunts but have more safety for the people involved. These things were the early things that we were doing. As a result, creative filmmakers can be more intriguing in the way that they use the frame. Blue screen work is particularly easy now. Originally, in the optical printer, it's the performance of the person doing the printing. There is no way of knowing whether the operator has gotten the first layer right—99% of the time it's right—but in the old days we would spend 70% of our energy in opticals trying to figure out what is wrong with an effect. But now, with digital technology, it's really about making things work and seeing the results quickly.

When digital hit, the initial reaction was, "Can we fix this problem in digital?" But you don't get the best results if you don't shoot it correctly to begin with. In film there is a saying when a shot has to be fixed. It goes, "Flop it, crop it, or drop it," meaning that's all that you can do and if it doesn't work, then you should lose the shot. However, now that digital is available, the reaction is often, "Just fix it." The exciting thing is when a filmmaker uses this technology to tell a story and to show new things and not just to fix things.

It is precisely this hope of bringing new images to the filmgoing audience that inspires Yeatman, who feels that the digital environment can open up great areas of creativity for the inspired filmmaker. He continues,

Once you are in digital, new doors can be opened for design that are not possible in film and on an optical printer, such as floor contact with blue screen which in digital is easy to deal with but extremely difficult in film. For compositing, digital is the only way of doing it. You don't have any lines, scratches, and mattes. A lot of the physical problems that the optical printer has to deal with just vanish. The normal way you can composite a shot in digital has greatly opened up the possibilities for the film director. It's extremely exciting what you can do with the elements and you can have more elements than ever before. But you need someone who has the vision.

A lot of the magic that is developing in digital and film is in mixing 2-D and 3-D. Digital, front projection, and a large bag of tricks that we have here are all being combined. I do feel that the best approach will be a hybrid of methods when we try to find what the best technique is to solve the problem. I think that many of the scripts that were previously impossible to do, will become possible. Very soon you'll start to see actors who are off-screen actually acting out the characterizations of little animated figures on the screen.

Everyone is starting to make a seamless transition of film to digital and back to film. Most of this will be worked out in the next few years as we get more universally available film scanners and recorders, and look-up tables that take into account how film reacts to the world. Within ten to fifteen years, there will be mastering systems that are filmless. Images will become just that—images—and I do see CD-ROM as an important medium of the future. Today, the technology is fairly crude, but there is a race for better and better technology.

The competition for entertainment is really high for theaters showing films, and they will be hard-pressed to keep their audiences. I do feel that transmission of images from facility to artist is really very near. And I do think in the near future you'll see a fragmentation of the work force—you'll ship the data models of something that you are creating to a very clever and talented artist that you want to use who will work at home.

Each day is something new. How often do you get the opportunity to see the technology change in one's lifetime? So, it's very, very exciting—it's a whole new world.

## Electronic Matte Creation

The creation of backgrounds that are not part of live action has traditionally fallen to the art of the matte painter. The application is very common: let's say we have a character who walks into a home beyond which is a castle. The actor is filmed on location walking to and through the door, and this piece of film is then combined with a matte which contains the background of the castle. This matte has been painstakingly painted by hand. Both the film and the painting are combined, rephotographed, and a new piece of film is created that now shows the composite effect.

There are actually a variety of ways to create this effect. For example, the area that will later contain the background of the castle may be matted out, or blackened out, when the actor is filmed, and this black section is then replaced with the matte painting. Early techniques of matte photography actually used the paintings, which were painted onto glass, and photographed the scene through the glass in order to create in-camera completed mattes.

Matte artists are turning to computers to create electronic matte paintings. The benefits of using digital painting systems are considerable: the artist can try new ideas and if they do not turn out satisfactorily, they can easily be discarded. Even beyond this liberating capability is the ability to create different paint shades from an electronic palette of 16.7 million colors, and to re-use these mixes. Imagine the painter who has mixed a new color and wants to re-use it. Using digital painting systems, this can be easily accomplished.

## INDUSTRY VIEWPOINTS

### Scott Billups—Cinematographer, Digital Previsualization, Production, Special Effects

For a long-time advocate of digital technology, the premise of digital filmmaking is somewhat old news. Scott Billups, who has been a crusader of the methodologies of incorporating digital techniques into all phases of traditional filmmaking, is a renowned expert in the field of digital previsualization and production. Notes Billups,

> Previsualization has always been part of filmmaking from the first minute that a filmmaker takes a napkin and starts to draw stick figures, but this is work that has to be done over and over again in another medium. One of the major benefits that I see with digital technology is that you can create something and you won't end up throwing it away—if you've created a wireframe environment and you really like the motion that you've made through the environment, you can incrementally add texture, camera moves, and so forth until you have a really polished and finished piece.

In the area of visual effects, Billups is quick to point out that the technology available to the filmmaker is becoming very good, but that it must be complemented by strong, traditional technique. He continues,

> The digital composite is so clean, but you need good directing and good cinematography skills. The technology only enhances good methodology. We are in a transitional period—if you remember when desktop publishing began, everything that you saw at the beginning looked like the type styles in a ransom note until people remembered, "Oh, yes, we have to remember good taste!"—and the same thing repeated with desktop video.
> Already, we are seeing great postproduction tools such as Parallax, Flame, Cinefusion—it's very conceivable and very feasible to do a picture like *When Harry Met Sally* in an entirely digital environment, with digital backgrounds and so forth. When

you want to see some really superb digital technology, take a look at films such as *The Abyss, Terminator 2: Judgment Day,* and *Adams Family Values* and you'll see some really hard-core previsualization at work.

For art direction and location management, Billups points out that digital technologies can offer many benefits. He says,

> There are great things you can do such as 3-D set construction where you can create environments and sets. You can check the sun's position through a day's cycle in order to see where shadows will be at certain times of the day. You can ascertain the feasibility of shooting in a specific location. Maybe when you were thinking about laying a dolly track in a particular position you didn't take into account that an oak would cast a shadow in your shot after a few hours—and making changes once you are out on location can be very time consuming.

Three-dimensional environments created in the computer can be seamlessly melded with action filmed by motion control camera rigs for a believable marriage of computer and live action material. Billups explains,

> Essentially you have a camera hooked up to a rig which tells you exactly where the camera is every 1/10th of a second over about twelve different axes. So as the camera is moved, these moves are time-coded and frame coded to disk as a simple ASCII file. When you go back to the studio, the computer plays back the ASCII file, you can then integrate any additional material, and you can create a real time composite on video. You can then take the composite to a film recorder in order to create the piece of film which you'll eventually project.

Billups, who has been a pioneer in many of the technologies that comprise digital filmmaking, has even designed an option for a video camera that records images not on video but on a magnetic hard disk. He prides himself on being able to work with directors as a collaborative member of the filmmaking crew. Says Billups,

> We did some work on a Philippe Mora film, *Pterodactyl Woman from Beverly Hills.* (Actress) Beverly D'Angelo undergoes a transformation where she emerges through stages as a dinosaur. So, we scanned her in Cyberware and we did some transpositions and the director was able to see the process through

all the stages. Then we took aerial shots from West Los Angeles and had another element of a pilot shot against a blue screen. We pasted this real move within a model and we zoom out and see the pilot in this model and we keep zooming out and we see the plane against the background of West LA. Then we bring in the digital pterodactyl—and you just have a real hard time telling what is real and what's been created (see figure 9-10). It would have been so cost prohibitive to do this, with a real plane, and air clearance, and so forth—and we can create all of this on the Macintosh and SGI on the desktop.

It is also in the creation of old environments that no longer exist that digital technology holds great promise. Billups concludes,

> Phillipe Mora has a film in progress called *Götterdämmerung* and he was faced with, essentially, rebuilding the German Chancellory, which, if he really had to do it would have cost about $40 million. So, within the computer, I built it and instead of trying to build this enormous building, we were able to build it all within the computer. We carried this over to extras duplication where we had night rally scenes with about 100 extras and we used digital technology to multiply and replicate the soldiers to give the impression of a huge rally. . . .
>
> There really isn't much left that we cannot do. But, you have to know the basics of filmmaking because there isn't any substitute to good filmmaking technique.

## Computer-generated Environments and Animation

Computer software is also used to create cities and landscapes which are entirely computer generated. Worlds that are conceived in the minds of the screenwriter can be created through the use of sophisticated computer software that can show the viewer three-dimensional views of the landscape. Animation, and the traditional view of animation are also being greatly affected by computers. For decades, animation has been defined as consisting of individual hand drawings that were then painted and photographed sequentially to provide the illusion of movement. Much of this has changed with the use of computers. Whether it is the computer animation of a character that does not exist in real life, such as a dinosaur in *The Flintstones* (1994), or the pseudopod of *The Abyss* (1989), the use of sophisticated computer modeling and animation programs to create and animate characters will redefine the classic concepts of animation.

Computer-generated animation can often be combined with either live action elements or hand-drawn paintings to create startling visuals. Figure 9-12 shows frames which formed the basis for the nuclear blast which devastates Los Angeles in the 1991 film, *Terminator 2: Judgment Day,* as created by 4-Ward Productions. The animation portion, created using ElectricImage software on an Apple Macintosh,

**Figure 9-10** A scene from the film *Pterodactyl Woman from Beverly Hills* includes aerial shots from West Los Angeles, a pilot shot against a blue screen, and a digitally created pterodactyl—all seamlessly interwoven as a digital composite. Courtesy of Scott Billups.

**Figure 9-11** A computer-generated environment. Courtesy of Gribouille.

was combined with "before and after" paintings of downtown Los Angeles to provide an animated transition of the two elements yielding an immensely realistic feeling of destruction in motion.

## Art Direction

Shown in figure 9-13 is an example from the 1994 film *Crooklyn* where highway signs were completely computer-generated and recorded to film. To provide a specific tone, note how the sign for "Welcome to Maryland" has been constructed. Some of the light bulbs have been electronically painted out and streaks through the sign, signifying age, have been added. Such techniques lend to the visual believability of the computer-generated graphic.

Computer-generated images are also being used for what has traditionally been the bailiwick of the optical printer—opening titles. Traditionally, opening titles were created optically by combining graphics with backgrounds, or, often, through the use of film animation. Working in extremely high resolution, each frame requires approximately six megabytes to store within the computer's memory.

## Pixel Manipulation

As images are stored to computer disk, they exist as digital files that consist of a specific matrix of pixels.

There can be thousands or millions of pixels that make up one digitized film frame depending upon the resolution size. By applying certain pixel manipulation techniques to a digitized frame, the look of the image can be significantly changed.

Imagine the director who wants an ethereal dream sequence for a specific scene. Normally, the director would consult with the DP to agree upon the methods that would be used to accomplish the visual feeling that the director requires. The DP may elect to use certain camera filters and lighting gels and may combine these techniques with certain methods used in the later processing of the film.

Now consider the filmmaker who films a scene where an actor is having a hallucination. The director wants to show the character's face change in various ways. By applying picture filters to the series of digitized frames, it becomes possible to perform pixel manipulations on the frames. There are various companies and software packages, including CoSA After Effects, Discrete Logic's Flame, KAI's Power Tools, and Parallax's Advance that can be used to create some of the most ingenious picture manipulations that would not otherwise be possible using the optical printer.

The user interface to create such effects and illustrate the layering of images that combine to create an effect often is represented by a timeline which shows the various elements and their relation to one another.

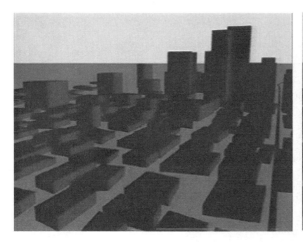

**Figure 9-12** Several frames from a low-resolution test which formed the basis for the nuclear blast that devastates Los Angeles, as created by 4-Ward Productions. The animation portion, created using ElectricImage software on an Apple Macintosh, was combined with "before and after" paintings of downtown Los Angeles to provide an animated transition of the two elements yielding an immensely realistic feeling of destruction in motion. From *Terminator 2: Judgment Day.* Courtesy of Carolco Pictures and Twentieth-Century Fox, Ltd. All rights reserved.

**Figure 9-13** A computer-generated image which assists in creating believable art direction. This example from the 1994 film *Crooklyn* shows a highway sign which was completely computer-generated and recorded to film. Created by Michael Arias and courtesy of Balsmeyer & Everett/Syzygy Digital Cinema.

## INDUSTRY VIEWPOINTS

### *Steven Poster, A.S.C.—Director of Photography*

*Someone To Watch Over Me, Rocky V, The Cemetery Club, The Boy Who Could Fly, Testament.*

For director of photography, Steven Poster, the digital filmmaking revolution is here today, providing the cinematographer with a new set of tools that must be understood and mastered. Poster has been able to perfect his traditional cinematography skills with new digital techniques. Says Poster,

I feel there will be a major change in the next few years and that will be a movement away from printing film dailies. In a sense it's a great loss in that DPs won't get the opportunity to see print until the movie is finished.

We are all learning to deal with a new vocabulary to prepare film on set for use in special effects that will be accomplished later in digital. Even after the film has been shot, I am sometimes called in to consult on how to light computer-generated images that will be used in context with film that I've already shot—as a result, there is more work in the postproduction area and more work for cinematographers.

Poster has found that digital postproduction methods often can assist to correct items that were not exactly correct during the time of production. He notes,

I had an experience with Cineon which helped us tremendously. On *Cemetery Club* we had a car shot and there was a piece of steel rigging in the shot and we were not in position to rephotograph the shot. So I was able to scan the frames digitally and remove the

steel. When I showed the director the fix he was totally blown away. But beyond fixing things like this, digital compositing allows a tremendous ability to design and to create. *Jurassic Park* is just one example, but you can create looks that never existed by colorizing and working with specific palettes.

The use of digital technology for Poster holds great promise in promoting the art and craft of cinematography. He says,

The vast majority of cinematographers are curious to work in this new digital medium. I see a tremendous

**Figure 9-14** Photo of Steven Poster, A.S.C. Courtesy of Steven Poster.

interest from my colleagues who want to explore the developments. There are so many areas where digital can affect filmmaking. I can see rapid prototyping devices, where props can be made instantly. The computer can take us from planning to shooting stage to editorial, all digitally. Someday I'll be in my hotel room and I'll receive digital samples of the dailies. I can make suggestions and send my ideas and digital samples of my ideas for color timing back to the laboratory. It will make communication clearer and faster among everyone involved in making the film.

## THE FILM RECORDER

Next, the digital files must be recorded back to film. When a recording is made to film, it is done so in non-real time and careful attention is paid to the type of film stock that is used so that the "digital negative" will match the color and density specifications of the original negative. In this way, the new piece of film that has been recorded can be printed to match the surrounding film elements.

## AVOIDING THE GENERATIONAL LOSS OF MULTIPLE FILM PASSES

One of the most important aspects of using DFWs is that it is common to combine multiple layers of images to create the optical effect that the filmmaker wants to achieve. By working digitally, the completed composite effect is then recorded to film without suffering the normal effects of generational loss that would otherwise be experienced through the use of the optical printer.

### The Process of Creating a Multi-layered Digital Film Composite

An example of a multi-layered digital film composite can be found during a thrilling scene in 1994's *True Lies*. In this composite, critical elements have been added that lend to the overall believability of the shot. The vapor trails which one expects to see emanating from a missile and which would normally not be shot during production, have been computer-generated and added to the shot. The result is a much more realistic effect.

Figures 9-15a–f show the elements that make up the composite. Figure 9-15a is a green screen element, where the camera tracks through a miniature. Note the window sections in the rear where the color green will eventually be replaced with a skyline of buildings. Figure 9-15b is another green screen element of actor and missile. Figure 9-15c is a pyrotechnic element which will serve as the missile exhaust, while figure 9-15d is a computer-generated element of a vapor trail. These first four elements are combined to create the pre-composite of the background that is shown in figure 9-15e. The final composite, with the actor and missile added, is shown in figure 9-15f.

## RECREATING A CLASSIC LOGO USING COMPUTER ANIMATION TECHNIQUES

Traditionally, logos of film studios were created through the use of film animation and multiple passes through the optical printer. With advances in digital technology, the classic Columbia Pictures logo was redesigned and created using computer animation. Shown in figure 9-16 is an example of the resulting 15 second animation, which utilized Wavefront Technologies Composer software. It is a combination of 66 layers of clouds, 7 layers of lighting effects, and a 3-D model created from a clay statue, and was designed and directed by Joel Hynek, First Light, Inc., with animation provided by the Kleiser/Walczak Construction Company.

## IMAGE MONITORING

Some systems provide for the calibration of the computer monitors to achieve the same look that the projected print will have. Filmmakers can be more assured that what they are seeing on the computer screen will be accurately represented when the digital work is transferred back to film. In the case of Cineon, a color temperature of 5400 degrees Kelvin with a maximum contrast range of 1000:1 is established and matches the standard for motion picture projection.

## INTERACTION BETWEEN THE DNLE SYSTEM AND THE DIGITAL FILM WORKSTATION

In designing and discussing special visual effects or sequences that will utilize digital image manipulation, effects will often include an actor's performance. Often these scenes are edited for performance and pace and then the film elements are "pulled" and

a

b

**Figure 9-15a–f** Elements which form a multi-layered digital film composite from *True Lies* (1994). Figure 9–15a is a green screen element, where the camera tracks through a miniature while figure 9–15b is a green screen element of actor and missile. Figure 9–15c is a pyrotechnic element for the missile's exhaust, while figure 9–15d is a computer-generated element of a vapor trail. These first four elements are combined to create the pre-composite of the background (figure 9–15e). The final composite, with actor and missile added, is shown in figure 9–15f. Material from *True Lies* ©1994 Twentieth Century Fox Film Corporation. All rights reserved.

c

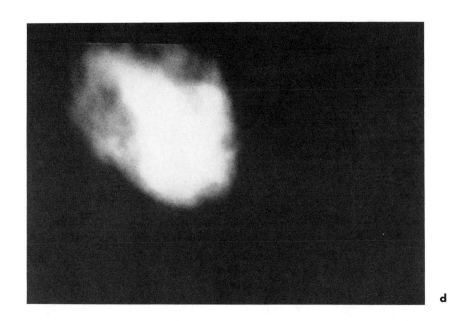

d

e

f

**Figure 9-16** The new Columbia Pictures logo animation created with Wavefront Technologies COMPOSER. 66 layers of clouds, 7 layers of lighting effects, and a 3-D model created from a clay statue were composited together. Designer/Director: Joel Hynek, First Light, Inc.; Animation: Kleiser/Walczak Construction Company. Copyright 1993 Columbia Pictures.

scanned into the DFW for manipulation and final output to negative. There are many different types of software used for film work. Among them are Eastman Kodak Corporation's Cineon and Quantel's Domino. These systems utilize software and hardware to provide the tools necessary for facilitating the digital work necessary for film compositing.

## File and Flowchart Compatibility

It is important to know how the work done on the DNLE system will track, or move forward, to the next stage of postproduction. When one is considering what systems to use, it is critical to determine how information is shared between the DNLE system and the digital film workstation. Let's explore how this interaction would work with the Cineon system.

During editing, the more difficult and involved effects are reserved and flagged so that they may be scanned into a digital film workstation. During the DNLE stage, the editing system should provide all of the edited relationships of the film elements involved in the effect. Next, some form of file compatibility is necessary in order to share information between the DNLE system and the digital film workstation. One file format that may be used is the Open Media Framework (OMF). An OMF composition contains all of the effects and their associated parameters to fully describe all relationships between source material and effects. The chronology would be:

1. The editor creates an effect on the DNLE system, such as a wipe with a duration of 48 fps between two shots. The editor reviews the effect, decides that it is appropriate, and an OMF composition is sent to the digital film workstation.
2. The digital film workstation imports the OMF file containing the composition that describes the effect. Because the composition includes all of the database information that relates to the film's edgenumbers, the original film elements are easily located and scanned into the digital film workstation.
3. The digital film workstation is then used to recreate the effect done on the DNLE system manner. The result is a full resolution version of the effect that was previsualized on the DNLE system. If approved, this effect will later be recorded back to film for use in the projected print.
4. If the editor desires, the newly created effect can be exported from the DFW and imported into the DNLE system. Thus, if the editor wants to see the finished effect cut into the correct position in the sequence, it can easily be accomplished.

## Time and Economic Savings

By reimporting the rendered effects into the DNLE system, there is a potential for a great savings in time.

Often, time delays are introduced because the director must see and approve the visual. By working digitally, there is no longer a need to record the effect to film, transfer to video, and digitize the effect into the DNLE system. Instead, digital file compatibility allows the direct importation of the rendered element, along with its own unique file name and numbering scheme, which allows it to be tracked along with the other film elements when it becomes time to create the cut lists.

## DIGITAL AUDIO FOR THEATER PRESENTATION

There are several different methods that can be used to deliver sound to the filmgoer. Before discussing the various possibilities, it is helpful to understand a brief history of sound for film exhibition.

### Sound for Film Presentations

During the 1930s and 1940s, film sound was based on optical soundtracks and by the 1950s, in quest for a better audio experience, magnetic sound was introduced. This was used in conjunction with some of the 70mm film extravaganzas such as *The Robe* (1953), *How The West Was Won* (1962), *Lawrence of Arabia* (1962), *It's A Mad Mad Mad Mad World* (1963), and *The Alamo* (1960) and was characterized by the use of five speakers arrayed across the front of the screen providing full stereo and surround sound. The film format utilized was known as Cinerama, a widescreen process invented by Fred Waller, where three film cameras were electronically synchronized.

The recording techniques to create the sound for this type of presentation often utilized six discrete microphones, which also required that an intricate and sometimes frustrating panning of the dialogue had to be accomplished. For example, if there were four people on-screen, each person would be heard as if talking from a specific place on the screen. When reverse angles were encountered, the audio mixers would have to ensure that the voices were panned back and forth; all in all, a very laborious affair.

For music, recordings were wide with at least five microphones, and the result was a very natural orchestral sound and the feeling was as if being in the actual presence of an orchestra.

As sound for films has changed and has largely become digital, the manner in which recordings are accomplished has also changed. Still, there is something to be said about the manner in which films from the 1950s and 1960s were recorded; many film historians feel that the recording techniques of today are inferior in terms of providing the natural sound of earlier recording methods.

Cinerama had four stripes of magnetic stock on 35mm film but even this method became very expensive in delivering encompassing sound to filmgoers. Faced with these various ways of delivering film sound, Dolby Laboratories delivered Dolby stereo optical sound for *Star Wars* (1977) which encoded four tracks of sound on optical. A chronology of film sound would thus appear: mono optical, six channel discrete audio on 70mm film, four channel discrete audio on Cinemascope, four channel matrixed optical sound with Dolby stereo, and Dolby 70mm with subwoofer information. Eventually, Dolby SR with more dynamic range became available and was still optical.

### Digital Sound Systems

As digital audio systems grew in popularity, filmmakers experienced various options regarding the use of digital audio in presenting their films. CDS was the first digital system and consisted of encoded digital audio on 70mm magnetic stripe film and was used in such films as *Days of Thunder* (1990).

The use of external digital playback devices which serve as the primary sound system is based upon the ability of the film print to generate timecode and to slave an external disk to the film via a shaft encoder. There are various ways of incorporating digital sound into a film presentation. Among them are methods of slaving an external audio compact disc which has the film's soundtrack, encoding digital sound between the film sprockets, or encoding digital audio on the outside edges of the film in order to have both a digital track and a backup analog track in case the digital mechanism fails.

Imagine an actor walking towards the camera, and that you are hearing his footsteps directly in front of you and coming towards you. Next, the actor walks completely "around you," that is, walks to the right, behind you, to your left, and then returns in front of you. During this time, you have heard his footsteps pass from one speaker to the next, and you have been provided with the aural feedback necessary to complete the effect that the filmmaker intended. Such complete delivery of sound is something that filmmakers can now design into a shot before it is even filmed.

While there are several different manufacturers and methods of delivering digital film sound to the filmgoer, the essential aspect is to do either by encoding digital audio somewhere on the actual film print, or by using an external device which plays in synchronization with the film images. Each system has its advantages and disadvantages, but the important aspect is that film audiences today have available to them a film experience unlike any before in terms of multi-channel digital audio. Here are some of the various methods of delivering digital audio to the filmgoer.

## Dolby Stereo Digital®

Dolby Laboratories, long a leader in excellent sound delivery for films, utilizes an optical soundtrack that is comprised of blocks of data that are located between the sprocket holes on one edge of 35mm Dolby Stereo SR-D prints. These prints carry both the digital and analog soundtracks, and therefore can be used in any theater. Should an area become damaged around several sprocket holes, the digital sound processor will automatically switch playback to the analog SR (spectral recording) track until the damaged areas is bypassed, and will then return to digital. Playback requires a digital soundtrack reader (sound head) which can mount atop the film projector (figure 9-17), or

**Figure 9-17** The Dolby Stereo Digital Soundhead which can mount atop the film projector or is built into one of the combined analog or digital sound heads directly on the 35mm projector. Courtesy of Dolby Laboratories Licensing Corporation.

can be built into one of the combined analog or digital sound heads directly on the 35mm projector. The Dolby Digital Film Sound Processor can be rack mounted and it incorporates easily into the film projection room. The Dolby Stereo Digital soundtrack provides left, center, right, separate left and right surrounds, and a subwoofer channel.

## Digital Theater Systems (DTS®)

DTS is a sound delivery system for films designed for six track theaters. It is a dual system where the digital audio is played back from CD-ROM discs. Timecode is printed on the film print, along with a conventional stereo optical track, and the code is used to synchronize digital sound to picture. The timecode lies between the picture and optical soundtrack and is printed onto the release print from the soundtrack negative (figure 9-18).

This system provides left, center, right, split surrounds (or mono surround) and subwoofer channels. Up to three-and-one-third hours of play time is available with digital audio sampled at 44.1 KHz. Film breaks and changeovers are automatically tracked. Digital audio data compression at a ratio of 4:1 is used to store the six channels of audio for the long play rate capacities.

## Sony Dynamic Digital Sound (SDDS®)

The SDDS system provides eight discrete audio channels on film. Figure 9-19 shows the matrix of digital information on the left side of the film print, adjacent to the picture, while on the right side the stereo optical track is present. The system supports five screen speakers for 70mm sound on 35mm film with directional surrounds and subwoofer. Real time audio compression encoding is utilized. Shown in figure 9-20 is the process for creating the actual film print. Both 35mm picture inter-negative and 35mm sound negative with eight digital optical channels, as well as the conventional analog optical track, are combined at the 35mm film printing stage. This creates an exposed theatrical print that has picture, eight digital optical channels, and the backup analog optical tracks.

During playback the SDDS digital playback processor reads the eight channels of optical information and sends the information to the various speakers. The optical playback processor simultaneously reads

**Figure 9-18** Timecode lies between the picture and optical soundtrack and is printed onto the release print from the soundtrack negative in a DTS system. Courtesy of Digital Theater Systems.

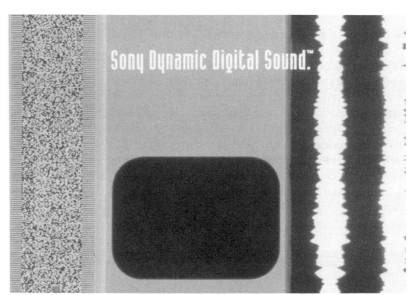

**Figure 9-19** The SDDS, Sony Dynamic Digital Sound system, showing the matrix of digital information on the left side of the film print, adjacent to the picture, while on the right side the stereo optical track is present. Courtesy of Sony Digital Picture Editorial and Sony Dynamic Digital Sound, Inc.

the two stereo optical channels, and in case there is any need to return quickly to the analog optical tracks, crossover is automatic.

A common question is whether there are different procedures required for dubbing a feature film when it will be shown in a theater equipped with digital sound playback systems. In the case of SDDS, the procedure is the same for dubbing a stereo optical release—pre-dub, stem record, and printmaster. The main difference is that recording is done to an eight track instead of to a four track format. Monitoring is done in the SDDS eight track format: Left, Left Center, Center, Right Center, Right, Subwoofer, Left Surround, and Right Surround. SDDS is mastered in eight track and all subsequent mixes (six or four track) are created from the SDDS stems.

## ON-LOCATION DIGITAL FILMMAKING: CAPTURE, EDITING, AND TRANSMISSION

### Digital Transmission and Distribution

There are many applications for the use of digital networks in digital filmmaking. For production and postproduction, high-speed digital networks allow filmmakers to observe location filming in real time. For example, on the feature film, *Radioland Murders* (1994), the 35mm film was being shot on location in Wilmington, North Carolina, while editing was simultaneously being done in Northern California. By using multiplexed 56 kbit transmission lines (24 to-

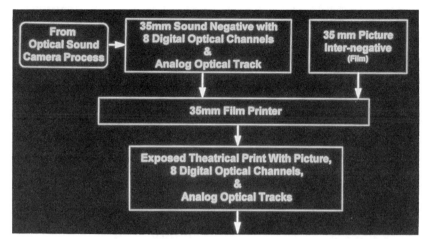

**Figure 9-20** Both 35mm picture inter-negative and 35mm sound negative with eight digital optical channels, as well as the conventional analog optical track, are combined at the 35mm film printing stage. This creates an exposed theatrical print that has picture, eight digital optical channels, and the backup analog optical tracks. Courtesy of Sony Digital Picture Editorial and Sony Dynamic Digital Sound, Inc.

tal), a throughput rate of approximately 1.5 Mbps/sec was achieved. After one channel of picture and one channel of audio were compressed, the signal was scrambled for security purposes, and yielded a picture quality akin to full-screen VHS at 30 fps. This capability allowed the postproduction team to view direct feeds from the production and allowed for teleconferencing as edited sequences were shown to the production crew.

The digital transmission of picture, sound, and data files holds promise in two major areas of digital filmmaking: postproduction and viewing.

## Postproduction Use of Digital Transmission

For editing, digital transmission holds much promise. For example, let's say that the location for editing is 500 miles from the telecine facility that is creating the dailies for digital editing. It is possible to remain in an all-digital environment in order to facilitate this work. By creating digital files for picture and sound directly in telecine, and transmitting them over network lines to the editing site, many benefits are realized. First, editing can begin immediately after the transmission has been received. Second, travel time and expense is eliminated, and third, convenience is dramatically improved. The manner in which filmmakers put together the show, from the on-location production stage, through the postproduction stage, and on to the delivery stage will forever dramatically change as the digital video compression and network technologies become more powerful.

Editing on-location, directly from the film cam-

era's video tape, will become popular. The postproduction team will access takes which require digital matte painting as they occur on location. More directors will supervise the final audio mixes for their films while remaining at home, working on preproduction for their next projects. Perhaps the most telling image that describes the digital filmmaking enterprise is a group of individuals who communicate with one another and are linked by the ability to share files with one another, even though they may be many thousands of miles apart.

## Basic Methods of Operation

In the past, recording, broadcasting, and transmission were relegated to the use of satellites. Typically, satellite use is expensive, scarce, and prone to weather disruption. In addition, audio quality tends to be highly distorted with a limit of 12 KHz. With advances in digital video and audio compression, and increased capability of telephone lines, filmmakers can take advantage of these methods of transmitting data.

While there are many companies who are offering services that allow filmmakers to work from great distances, the requirements are: digital video and audio compression, some form of digital storage, and network capabilities. Several companies have pooled their resources in creating demonstrations of "editing by wire." Among them are Alcatel Network Systems, Dolby Laboratories, Entertainment Digital Network (EDNet), and Pacific Bell.

Through the use of digital video codecs, component and composite color video signals compressed to 45 megabits/sec (equivalent to 650 phone calls) as well as HDTV signals can be delivered over DS3 lines (DS-3 has a capacity of approximately 45 Mbps/sec). Multiple channels of audio between 20–48 KHz quality and optional data control channel can also be delivered.

At the National Association of Broadcasters convention in March, 1994, a demonstration of editing via wire was made and is indicative of the new digital filmmaking communication links. Each day, audio and video from an EDNet origination point in San Francisco was transmitted via DS3 to Las Vegas, a distance of nearly 400 miles. Through an Alcatel/Pacific Bell-designed network, the signals were then routed to different partner booths. In so doing, program creators in Las Vegas were able to actually edit and add special effects to the video and audio materials that were actually on hardware located in San Francisco!

Another example that shows the collaboration between artists and facilities that is possible was presented at the Society of Motion Picture Television Engineers in October, 1993. It involved linking two postproduction facilities—one in San Francisco and one in Los Angeles. Work done on two television commercials in D1 picture quality was shared between the creative staffs of the two facilities. While one facility edited picture, the other facility was able to add audio tracks and music. This occurred while advertising agency representatives took active part in the creation of the two finished commercials.

## Digital Distribution

Transmission of digital and audio files from one location to another during the digital filmmaking process is well on its way to implementation and common practice for filmmakers. However, the actual distribution of films has remained a process requiring creating additional release prints of films and shipping them to movie theaters.

The intent to deliver motion picture programming digitally and to display the program electronically is highly controversial. There are two main reasons: quality of the electronic signal versus the projected film image, and the required cost of changing theaters over to video displays. With film providing image resolutions in excess of anything that is currently achievable by electronic methods, the image clarity of the original filmed image will not be preserved. Clearly, if image quality were the only concern, the current state of technology would not be able to measure up to the filmed image.

However, there are also reasons for digitally distributing programming, as there are theater and home-use applications for this technology. Motion picture studios, live event promoters, and home viewers can benefit by receiving programming digitally. Consider the film studio that must preview a film several times. If the studio could transmit electronically a version of the preview to several preview sites, collect audience response cards, and edit a new version of the film to be redistributed the same day at a later screening, think of the reduced time it would take to get a film into the marketplace.

## Special Event Filmmaking

It is also important to continually remind ourselves to break free of the notion of what constitutes the stereotypical filmgoing experience. There are entertainment experiences that are being developed every day, from the special venue experiences of tourist attractions, such as films shown in 360 degrees, to "ride" films, which allow the audience to interact with the films being shown. It is clear enough that the methods by which specially created programming will be delivered will most likely be in an electronic form.

What, indeed, would the reaction be if two world famous film directors announced that they were going to make a feature film with world renowned actors and state-of-the-art special visual effects and that the film would be transmitted and viewed electronically in specially designed theaters charging, say, three times the price of a normal film ticket, and that this would be the only way the film would be viewed? Would the project be given the financial support required? Would people go based upon the facts and their curiosity? Would it matter that they were seeing projected video and not projected film? The answers to these questions are elusive but the questions must be asked.

## Operations, Archives, and Exhibition

There can be several methods of digitally distributing programming. One company, Alcatel Network Systems, outlines its plan for a "cinema of the future" method by using codecs to compress films into digital form, transmit via ATM, and decompress the signals at the theater site for projection in HDTV. These ATM switches are capable of directing the signals to multiple destinations. Instead of the theatergoer, perhaps it is the home owner who is receiving programming on a pay-per-view or video-on-demand basis.

Figure 9-21 is an example of how a film studio operation could utilize digital technology in the storage and distribution of film and live programming. By converting film or live/taped HDTV signals to digital video, the files can be sent via 45 Mbps/sec network-capable lines to those who need to access the programming.

Figure 9-22 shows a file (programming) that has

been stored in a network archive for distribution to two cities via OC-48 (multiplexed 45 Mbps optical channels for a total of 2.4 gigabits/sec). The day before a film is to be premiered at a theater, the files would be transmitted into the theater and stored on the local digital storage disks in preparation for the opening of the film.

Figure 9-23 shows a premise for a multiple screen exhibition theater where a distribution network has been put into place, and which provides for the scheduled showings of films from the central server.

**Figure 9-21** How a film studio operation could utilize digital technology in the storage and distribution of film and live programming. By converting film or live/taped HDTV signals to digital video, the files can be sent via 45 Mbps/sec network-capable lines to those who need to access the programming. Courtesy of Alcatel Network Systems.

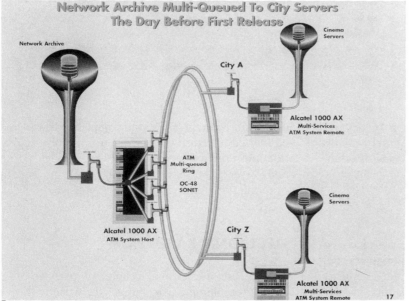

**Figure 9-22** A program that has been stored in a network archive for distribution to two cities via OC-48 (multiplexed 45 Mbps optical channels for a total of 2.4 gigabits/sec). The day before a film is to be premiered at a theater, the files would be transmitted into the theater and stored on the local digital storage disks in preparation for the opening of the film. Courtesy of Alcatel Network Systems.

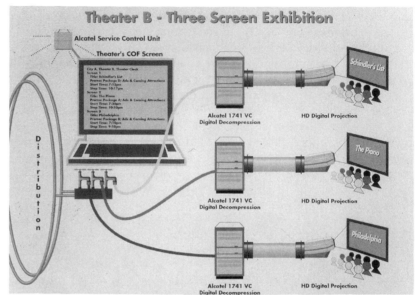

**Figure 9-23** A premise for a multiple screen exhibition theater where a distribution network has been put into place, and which provides for the scheduled showings of films from the central server. Courtesy of Alcatel Network Systems.

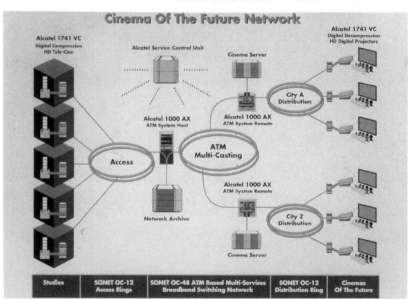

**Figure 9-24** A premise for a "Cinema of the Future Network," utilizing ATM with OC-12 access rings. Courtesy of Alcatel Network Systems.

Figure 9-24 shows a premise for a "Cinema of the Future Network," as offered by Alcatel Network Systems, utilizing ATM with OC-12 access rings.

## FILM RESTORATION

Another use of digitally storing film images is for attempts in restoring the film back to its original condition. For films that suffer from color fading, scratches, and other artifacts of aging, the original film negative can be stored in the DFW, and computer software can be utilized to return the negative to the color saturation and tinting of its original form. Though potentially a very laborious process, the results of digitally restoring film negative are quite impressive.

## ELECTRONIC BASED FILM

Another use of electronic technology for video originated programming is to "treat" the video with special processes designed to emulate the qualities of film. For programs that are recorded on videotape, after editing is completed, the show master videotape is run through a proprietary system to give the video a film-like appearance. There are several companies that offer such services, including Filmlook, based in California.

## INDUSTRY VIEWPOINTS

### Robert Faber—Filmlook, Inc.

While filmmakers have turned to the use of film to achieve a certain look, a number of productions have utilized electronic technology that imparts the film look to video originated material. One such method is Filmlook, an Emmy award winning and patented, broadcast quality, real time process. This videotape-to-videotape digital process provides a choice of 24 or 30 simulated frames per second while rendering film texture, film grayscale, and film color. Says electronics engineer, Robert Faber,

> Filmlook was developed and first demonstrated in the spring of 1989 and has had a US patent since June of 1990. It is a real time process whereby several items are addressed—the gray scales are altered to mimic the density curve of film, and both 3:2 film pulldown and film grain is simulated and in fact, we can exaggerate the graininess depending on the look required. The result is that video originated material takes on the appearance of film. . . .
>
> Filmlook has been used on two-hour television movies, television series, and regional commercials and producers and studio executives have reported a $35,000 to $50,000 difference in cost-per-episode for a multicamera sitcom shot on video versus film. It's been used for shows such as "The Five Mrs. Buchanans," "Blossom," "Twin Peaks," "Baywatch," "Beakman's World," "I'll Fly Away," and "The John Larroquette Show." . . .
>
> We are also going to be Filmlooking the home video version of the critically acclaimed film documentary *Hoop Dreams* (1994), produced by Fineline Pictures and originally shot on videotape. The producers felt it was better to use the original video and Filmlook than using the film and telecine for the video release.

## METHODS OF PROGRAM INTRODUCTION AND PROMOTION

### Previews and Marketing of Motion Pictures

One of the most intriguing developments is the use of computer networks and computer bulletin board services to present information on new motion pictures. In certain areas of the world, there are vast computer connections that allow computer users to access information posted by others.

Motion picture studios in the United States have already begun to utilize the capabilities of computer network and CD-ROM technologies to bring to the public information about films about to be released. By using compressed video, generally in the form of a QuickTime movie (figure 9-25), a filmmaker can post onto a computer network a version of the film's trailer (preview), which any consumer of the network can view.

By using these new routes of information dissemination, and by taking advantage of what is essentially a free network, filmmakers and distribution companies have found that they are able to promote

**Figure 9-25** There are all types of applications for compressed video, such as this QuickTime movie. A filmmaker can post onto a computer network a version of the film's trailer or a behind-the-scenes look at the film in order to generate interest prior to the film's release.

and generate interest for a film simply by making visual and print information available to the consumer.

Filmmakers and film studios can also benefit from the use of CD-ROM technology. Often, there will be special issues of film and cinema magazines that will contain a CD-ROM, which is dedicated to the making of a particular film. The disc will show the making of the film, the behind-the-scenes work done in previsualization, makeup, and so forth, and can be a very cost-effective method for promoting the film.

## INDUSTRY VIEWPOINTS

### Peter Moyer—President, Digital FilmWorks

Digital imaging, previsualization, and compositing are accomplished regularly under the guidance of Peter Moyer, who outlines how digital technology is providing filmmakers with the means of increased creativity. Having completed many of the visual effects in *The Shadow* (1994), Moyer outlines some of the experiences of working on such a complex film:

> We did twenty-eight shots for *The Shadow* and some were incredibly complex. One shot had twenty-six

**Figure 9-26** Photo of Peter Moyer. Courtesy of Peter Moyer.

different color correctors and seventeen different DVE repositions. One shot involved a blue-screen foreground being composited with a mirror crack and it proved to be a very difficult shot. When you break a mirror, the light shifts in many different ways, so you have to be able to recreate that in the computer for the effect to be believable. When you take this type of effect into a digital environment, you have control over all the variables. To accomplish this shot photochemically would just not have been practical.

Moyer is quick to point out that while digital technology is often thought of as simply being used to fix production problems, there are specific areas where digital imagery excels. Continues Moyer,

> If you are using this technology to make up for sloppiness in the production stage, you are not using this technology correctly or at its fullest extent. It's really best used for scene restoration, optical compositing, and matte painting. One thing that you'll be sure to achieve with a digital composite is a clean negative, and you cannot achieve that photochemically. One of the things that I've found is that if we have accomplished a really complicated composite we feel very confident that it is the best that it can be and that if we tried to create the same effect optically, we would probably be down at the lab every three days and we would not have the same control that we have grown accustomed to.

The technical requirements for creating some of the fantastic shots that make up *The Shadow* placed high demands on the storage systems used. In addition, the combination of computer hardware and software was carefully chosen to take into consideration the rapidly changing digital imaging environment. Continues Moyer,

> The particular images that we had were complex. We did them at 2K resolution Academy format which required 13 megabytes per frame. We had a 96 gigabyte disk array that was completely filled and an additional 30 gigabyte disk which was filled. We scanned the film and then started to move the files into different workstations running software such as Cineon, Cinefusion, and Matador. We use SGI computers which basically double in speed every two years and halves the price. We utilize general purpose computers so that when we are not doing painting we can, for example, be doing 3-D work. We are seeing software being written by people who understand what we do in our business.

Moyer takes pride in being able to educate first time users of digital imaging technology and feels that it is important to guide filmmakers through the process so that each is assured that his or her vision will be maintained despite the reliance on technology. Says Moyer,

> No matter how involved the composite is, it's all changeable. We've found that people can be a bit reluctant at the beginning. When we began to work on *The Shadow* the filmmakers knew what they wanted and we started to show them very detailed previsualization of how things would be put together and this was instant visual gratification for them. Now, the director can show up at the compositing sessions and make sure his or her voice is heard—before, this would be unheard of—you'd do the work and wait to hear if it was accepted or not. Due to the way that we structured the work being done on the show, we were sometimes asked to create difficult shots and in some cases we were able to turn shots around in one day which is quite remarkable.

Moyer, who has been instrumental in building a state-of-the-art digital imaging facility, has great hopes for networking facilities and artists across vast distances. He concludes,

> I really look forward to the development of high speed data links so that we gain the ability to share material and to view material across long distances and without a lot of delay. It won't matter where an artist is—if you have found somebody who is a really talented compositor and lives in Australia, you can send your work there and monitor the progress remotely.

## INDUSTRY VIEWPOINTS

### Mark Galvin—Executive Producer for Feature Film and Television, Dream Quest Images

As Dream Quest Images' Executive Producer, it is Mark Galvin's role to ensure that Dream Quest is at the fore of new and challenging roles in the areas of special visual effects for feature films and television programming. The previsualization and postproduction solutions that Galvin's team has devised for a variety of films, including *The Crow* and *The Three Musketeers,* have combined to provide audiences with images that are both striking and seemingly un-

**Figure 9-27** Photo of Mark Galvin. Courtesy of Dream Quest Images.

apparent to even the most discriminating filmgoer. Says Galvin,

> We think of the services we provide as tools that offer more control for a director. The scariest words that a director used to hear when setting up a special effects shot used to be, "Don't move the camera." But digital allows the filmmaker to be free of these restrictions. When you are talking to a director, you are often asked, "Is this possible—can it be done?" The biggest thing we've done to date is previsualization. Digital technology has brought more previsualization to the filmmaker than ever before, as in *Grand Canyon,* where we actually built a mock-up of buildings and streets in filmcore and we brought in Director Lawrence Kasdan. With a video camera, we showed him the different focal lengths and what shots would look like, and it was very successful in answering a lot of questions that the director had. . . .
>
> Here digital is a more efficient way of allowing a director to tell a story. One thing about having a shot digitally stored is that you don't have to wait that extra day to see how the performance of the film optical camera operator was. A lot of things can affect the optical printer's performance—which is really lining up cross-hairs down a bore scope! But in digital you have a precision that is easy to get and you can give a director a lower resolution video image which can be viewed. The result is that you get this interaction among computer, artist, and director. Digital af-

**Figure 9-28** An example of an entirely computer-generated moving matte painting from *The Three Musketeers*, created by Dream Quest Images. *Courtesy of Dream Quest Images.*

fords the seamless work that you cannot see—there is an awful lot of very subtle work that is done right now, but there are also a lot of things that we can do better.

Two of the films that I am proud of are *The Crow* and *The Three Musketeers*. If we've done our job right, the audience never knows we were there. For director Stephen Herek, we did matte shots on *Three Musketeers*. I know people who say, "You worked on that show? What did you do?"—and that's the best compliment one can hear!

Shown in figure 9-28 is an example of an entirely computer-generated moving matte painting from *The Three Musketeers*, which was created by Dream Quest Images. Continues Galvin,

On *The Crow*, we were asked to provide certain visuals after the accident that took Brandon Lee's life. The reality of the work that we performed on this show was that we were trying to accomplish something that had not been done before. We were asked to create scenes which had not been completed or had never been shot. To do this, we had to digitally lift Brandon's face from one scene and actually place him into another different background. A good example of this is where Brandon enters his apartment for the first time. This shot was created by lifting Brandon out of an alleyway and placing him behind a door in the new scene. All that the audience sees or knows is that Eric Dravin, Brandon's character, opens

a door and enters his old apartment. And that is all that matters.

Shown in figure 9-29 are the various stages as well as the completed process shot from *The Crow*.

**Figure 9-29** The various stages and the completed process shot from *The Crow*. *Courtesy of Dream Quest Images.*

The components of original footage and an empty plate were judged against a reference shot with a stand-in. Next, the footage of actor Brandon Lee was isolated from the original footage and steadied. Using a displacement map, the composite was seamlessly created to provide the shot that was required. Galvin continues,

> Digitally, we worked on fifty-two shots for *The Crow.* Maybe twenty shots can be discerned by someone with a very good eye as being miniatures—but that is fine because that is the style or look that the director, Alex Proyas, was going for. But no one can tell that it wasn't Brandon walking through that door—and that we had created the shot. That's a really good example and it's really high praise.

On *The Crow,* the working relationship with director Alex Proyas and assistant director Andrew Mason was wonderful because they both have strong effects backgrounds from working on commercials. But while we were creating the shots using our digital methods, Alex was marvelous because he knew exactly what the shots should be. The mood and style had been set. We were able to enhance and realize that mood that Alex wanted.

# 10 Digital Filmmaking for Television and Film Presentations

## DIGITAL FILMMAKING FOR TELEVISION PRESENTATIONS

For television shows that shoot on film, the editing process and flow remain the same as for a video originated show, but there are considerations when editing television for film-based, dual finish shows. Dual finish refers to generating both a video rate EDL and a film negative cut list. Television shows that shoot film do so for various reasons: to ensure that the production has the look of film and to allow easy transfer of original material to other video standards such as PAL or HDTV.

Generally, the concept of dual finish is more of an issue in NTSC, as shows destined for the PAL video market will most likely be shot at 25 fps which is PAL's native rate. There is, therefore, a 1:1 ratio of the video EDL to a negative cut list for a PAL production when shot in this manner.

### Shooting Film at 24 fps for NTSC Television

Television shows shot on film are shot at 24 fps and the 2:3 will exist for the EDL and negative conform. Since 24 fps does not equal 30 fps, one of the lists will always be in a match-backed state. The choice is clear: either the editor edits on 1/30th of a second boundaries to create a 30 frame EDL, which is frame-for-frame accurate, or the editor edits on 1/24th of a frame boundary and creates a negative cut list that is not frame-for-frame accurate.

When the opposite list needs to be created, a match-back situation ensues. Since it is impossible to create 1:1 lists for both EDL and the film cut list, either list will be in a match-back state. We can refer to these lists as primary and secondary target lists. If the viewing audience first in the queue sees a video version, the primary concern is a video conform during online editing. The primary list is a timecode EDL that reflects the frame boundaries of the source video tapes. What the editor saw during the editing stage is what will be seen after the online. For films, where the primary list is the negative conform, editing at 24 fps allows the editor to see every film frame, and where the editor cuts is how the resulting conform will appear.

## MATCHING BACK

When a sequence is edited at 30 fps, the match-back process happens in order to translate the relationship between the timecode and the key numbers. The direction is from a 30 frame timecode EDL to a 24 frame key number cut list. There are several software applications available on the market that provide this functionality. Typically, there exists a database that contains all the sync-point relationships between the timecode and key number. All data is referenced to the timecode and to the reel ID of the timecode. The database can be logged in entire camera rolls or by separate takes.

The minimum information required to create a match-back cut list is:

Timecode =     Key number =     Pulldown phase

For example:

01:00:00:00    KJ 35 1234-6578+00                A

Shown in figure 10-1 are examples of the database that will be used to create match-back lists.

The database will most often contain extra information to better facilitate conform. Additional information such as camera roll, lab roll, scene/take can be integrated into the database. Some programs will also track an extra field of timecode so that an audio conform of the original sound elements can be made. These extra fields of information allow the negative cutter to find camera rolls much faster and pull the required film elements. Some programs will also create pull lists that show how to pull the film in the order of lab or camera roll, or heads out or tails out depending on the wind of the camera roll.

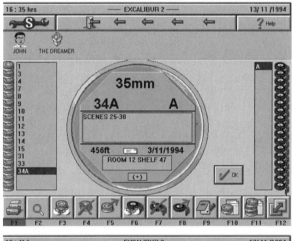

**Figure 10-1** The next step is to identify individual camera rolls as well as the scene and takes found on each roll. Courtesy of Excalibur Filmlab Systems, Intl. The identification of sync point relationships between keynumbers and timecode. Courtesy of Excalibur Filmlab Systems, Intl.

When we have a situation where every video frame matches back to a film frame, we can call this a "natural relationship" between video and film, where one video frame matches back to one film frame. It is also a very naive way to think, that for each frame of video you will get a frame of film. The match-back program uses very simple calculations to find a key number. This can be done via a 4/5ths equation. For example, suppose our sync points are:

$$01:00:00:00 = AA\text{-}0000\text{+}00 = A$$

Let's say that we are looking for the corresponding key number for timecode number 01:01:10:00. The offset from the sync point would be calculated: 01:01:10:00 minus 01:00:00:00 = 01:10:00. We then take 01:10:00 and turn it into a total frame count: 1800 frames (30 fps/sec – 60 sec/min) + 300 frames + 0 frames = 2100 video frames.

Since 5 video frames equal 4 film frames, we divide 2100 by 5 and multiply by 4 = 1680 film frames.

If we are working in 35mm film, there are 16 frames per foot. We divide 1680 by 16 to get the footage offset: 1680/16 = 105 feet. Since there is no remainder, it matches exactly to AA-0000+00 + 105 giving a key number of AA-0105+00.

## Frame Calculations

The match-back becomes a bit more complicated when frames are added to the equation. Let's take the same video duration and add three frames to it. Instead of 01:10:00, let's use 01:10:03.

01:10:03 = 1800 + 300 + 3 = 2103 video frames divided by 5 = 420.6 video frames multiplied by 4 = 1682.4 film frames divided by 16 frames (per foot) = 105.15 feet.

We next multiply the remainder .15 by 16 to provide us with a frame count which equals 2.4 film frames. During the match-back equation, the pull-down phase must also be considered. In this case, the sync point was an A frame at timecode frame :00. This means that for this range of transfer, all time-codes ending in :00 and :05 will be A frames. The 2.4 frames left over will match to the C frame of the pull-down phase. Timecodes :01 and :02 would match-back to the same film frame thus adding only one frame to the key number offset. There still remains 0.4 of a frame. This 0.4 needs to be carried over to the next edit event and entered into the equation at the end of the next cut. We cannot simply discard the 0.4 of a frame, and it must be factored into the next edit event; it must be accounted for or a cumulative error will occur. Over time, all of the remaining 0.4 frames will accumulate over the course of an entire show. A drift of sync will be about one frame for every 30 seconds.

Since we matched-back to the C frame, we are now 1/2 frame ahead in duration. These cumulative "roundings" are added and adjusted on a per-cut basis. If the end of the next cut left a 1/2 frame addition to the duration, then the total frame cum. at this point would be +1 frame. When the error margin reaches +/−1 frame, an adjustment can be made. Depending on the error, the adjustment will be made to make the cumulative error return to zero.

Shown below is a sample cut list that shows how compensation adjustments have been made to return the cumulative error to zero.

## Worst Case Examples for Duration Adjustment

Now let's look at some worst case examples where we can better illustrate the reason for duration adjustment. There are two cases that may exist: one, when the duration has gone longer and the adjustment is made by removing frames, and, two, when the duration is short and frames are added to make the adjustment.

## Going Long

Shown in figure 10-2 is an example of how a duration has gone longer and a frame removal adjustment must be made. As we know:

Video = 30 frames = 1 second

Film = 30 frames = 1.25 seconds

Here, the editor has put together a sequence of single-frame edits. All the video frames happen to match back to A film frames. Remember that the A frame is the only frame where one frame is equal to two video fields without a timecode change.

The editor's sequence is 30 frames long. The editor expects the resulting sequence to play for one second, which it should since 30 frames in NTSC video is equal to one second. These 30 video frames match back exactly to 30 unique film frames. Since all frames used were "A" frames, there is no compensation involved and these 30 video frames are now conformed back to 30 individual film frames.

However, there is now a discrepancy in durations. If we played these two sequences, one video and one film, at their native play rates, the video would be one second long, and the film would be 1.25 seconds long (24 frames + 6 frames). This is a case where the film has gone long. We say gone long when the playback of the conformed sequence is

Avid MediaMatch™ version 4.3 Fri Jun 30 14:43:16 1995
Project: civil wars
Assemble List for edl file master:

| Seq | First Edge Number | Last | Length | Total | Conform |
|-----|-------------------|------|--------|-------|---------|
| 001 | 83011599-9640+13 | −9651+04 | 10+08 | 10+08 | 0.0 |
| | Source: 04;00;03;06 04;00;10;06 | | | | |
| | Record: 01:00:00:00 01:00:07:00 | | | | |
| 002 | 83011598-8034+09 | −8043+10 | 9+02 | 19+10 | −1.0 |
| | Source: 04;02;31;22 04;02;37;25 | | | | |
| | Record: 01:00:07:00 01:00:13:03 | | | | |
| 003 | 83011598-8224+06 | −8240+08 | 16+03 | 35+13 | 0.5 |
| | Source: 04;04;04;18 04;04;15;11 | | | | |
| | Record: 01:00:13:03 01:00:23:26 | | | | |
| 004 | 83011598-8538+03 | −8553+07 | 15+05 | 51+02 | 1.0 |
| | Source: 04;04;58;04 04;05;08;12 | | | | |
| | Record: 01:00:23:26 01:00:34:02 | | | | |

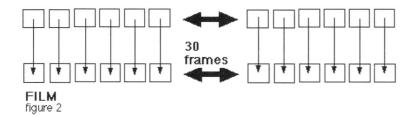

FILM
figure 2

YIDEO - 30 FRAMES = 1 SECOND
FILM - 30 FRAMES = 1.25 SECONDS

Going Short

YIDEO

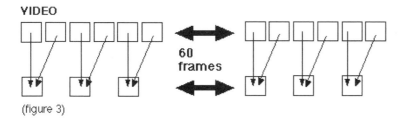

(figure 3)

YIDEO - 60 FRAMES = 2 SECONDS

**Figure 10-2** An example of how a duration has "gone long" and the resulting frame adjustments that must be made. An example of how a duration has "gone long" and the resulting frame adjustments that must be made.

longer than the expected duration as determined by the duration of the video sequence. To solve this discrepancy, the software application would have to remove six frames from the tail of the sequence to provide a one second duration for the film medium.

## Going Short

Also shown in figure 10-2 is an example of how a duration has gone shorter and a frame addition adjustment must be made. As we know:

Video = 60 frames = 2 seconds

Film = 30 frames = 1.25 seconds

This is a case where the duration of the film is shorter than the expected video duration. Here, the editor has put together a two second video sequence, consisting of 60 video frames. The editor created this sequence by editing together short, two-frame edits. To show how difficult the match-back process can become, we have chosen an example where the editor

has used only B frames, meaning that both video frames match-back to the same film frame.

Therefore, what will happen is that the original sequence of 60 video frames will not match-back to 60 film frames but will, instead, match-back to only 30 film frames. However, the result is that what is a two second video duration is only 1.25 seconds long in film duration. The film has come up short. Here, a total of 18 frames would have to be added in order to create a film duration of 48 frames, or two seconds.

Obviously, these are worst case examples, but what should be clear is how the importance of pull-down identification and tracking is essential to a frame accurate negative cut list. In most cases, events will compensate in overall duration, requiring only the single frame adjustment to remain in sync between the two mediums.

## GENERAL MATCH-BACK

When a "normal" production sequence is run through match-back software, tracking of video duration and film duration uses this method of natural mapping. By also keeping track of the pulldown frames, certain events will have a frame added to or subtracted from the tail of the cut. It is most often preferred to add or remove frames from the tail rather than at the head of a cut. By doing this, any point in the EDL will have equal duration to its cut negative counterpoint, and knowing this pulldown relationship allows the match-back systems to find the correct key number. This is why match-back can never be "frame accurate" but only exact to +/– 1 frame at any single point in the sequence. This type of match-back only occurs in NTSC where there is a 2:3 pulldown relationship between film and video.

## PAL DUAL FINISH SHOWS

In PAL, dual finish shows have the telecine transfer done at 25 fps with a 4.1% speed-up. This creates a 1:1 relationship. Since there is no pulldown involved, the match-back program is only doing a simple offset count to find the key number. Durations are more of an issue since 4.1% represents quite a bit of difference over time. To create two versions of the same duration, the sequence needs to be edited to match that duration. Most editing systems will run two master timecodes to keep track of video versus film durations. A track of SMPTE 24 frame timecode and a SMPTE track of 25 frame timecode are used. At any one point in the sequence, the editor can check its point in the terms of the different time bases. Usually a version is created first, either for video or for film. Once the primary sequence is finished, the alternate version is created.

## EDITING AT 24 FPS FOR A DUAL FINISH

When a 24 fps editing system is used, most often the primary list is a negative cut list and each key number is exact with no match-back occurring. It is only when an EDL is desired for the online conform that a match-back situation occurs. Since all editing decisions were made on 1/24th second boundaries, a list based on 1/30th second boundaries is needed. The same algorithm is used for determining the cumulative total duration: the EDL duration must match the duration of the cut film. Just as in the negative cut list, all adjustments are made at the tail of each cut.

If video-only EDL's are made, the match-back process used for negative conform can be used. Where problems may occur is when an EDL for both video and audio are needed for the online. Adjustments need to made across all channels so that a straight cut for a video/audio event remains a straight cut after the adjustments are made. If this does not happen, then all straight cuts where picture and sound should occur at the same record master timecode will be adjusted by +/–1 frame. This type of adjustment can add hours to the online and will require spending more money.

## USING DIGITAL TECHNOLOGY FOR A DUAL FINISH SHOW

It would be helpful to analyze the postproduction flow of a television program that must deliver both NTSC and PAL master videotapes along with the potential requirement of delivering a cut negative. The program is "The Young Indiana Jones Chronicles." There are many special visual effects and blue screen composites in the show. The manner of postproducing this show is unique and represents many of the new techniques that are being applied to digital filmmaking for television.

The show is shot on standard 16mm film at a rate of 24 fps. The transfer is done with a 2:3 pulldown to Betacam videotape, and during this time ASCII files of the telecine transfer are created and are subsequently imported into the digital, nonlinear editing system. The footage is digitized and editing begins at 24 fps for accurate film frame editing as well as the benefits of saving disk space. The process of digitizing film that has been transferred to video saves a total of six of the pulldown frames that have been added to every one second of video.

Once editing is complete, a scene pull list is generated from the edited sequence. A scene pull list is a list of every take used, listed only once for the first time the take is encountered. Once all the takes have been identified, the camera rolls are then reloaded in telecine and transferred to D1 videotape at a rate of 30 fps. This creates a 1:1 relationship between film frame and D1 digital frame. The audio will come from the conformed audio sources later during online, so this transfer is concerned only with picture. However, what is noteworthy is that the D1 master tape will now take the place of the negative throughout the rest of the postproduction process.

## FILM TO TAPE TO FILM TO TAPE (FTFT)

Some applications have a feature that allows a one-lite EDL to be translated to a color-corrected EDL. Let's examine this workflow. All dailies are first transferred to video as a one-lite transfer. This means that the only variable that is corrected for during the transfer is exposure, and as a result, very little color correction is done at this stage.

Next, the show is completely edited and then a pull list is generated. A pull list is a list in lab or camera roll order of the entire take that has been used. This take pull is sometimes referred to as flash-to-flash pull, which refers to the overexposed or flash frames that exist when a camera is coming up to and out of speed. The selected takes are then carefully retransferred to the master tapes for online editing with the proper scene-to-scene color correction. Should additional color correction be necessary, fine tuning can be done online in a tape-to-tape situation. During the second transfer pass, the key numbers are entered into another database with the newly generated timecode reference and pulldown phase sync point. Once these relationships have been established, the FTFT applications have the ability to translate the old timecode reference from the one-lite transfer to the color corrected timecode reference. This is done by using the key number as the common denominator. The EDL remains unchanged except for the source reels and source timecodes. Record master timecode and effects remain untouched.

Shown in figure 10-3 is a log file that shows the relationships between keynumbers and timecode.

From the one-lite transfer database, we have:

07;00;10;06 = AF 01 4401 – 5977 + 00 A

Next, shown in figure 10-4 is the relationship between the keynumber and the new timecode.

01:00:00:00 = AF 01 4401 – 5977 + 00 A

Therefore, the translation process would consider that:

07;00;10;06 = AF 01 4401 – 5977 + 00 =
01:00:00:00

and a new list is then created using the hour one timecode prefix, instead of the hour seven prefix.

Shown in figure 10-5 is the original one-lite EDL, while shown below it is the color corrected version of the same EDL.

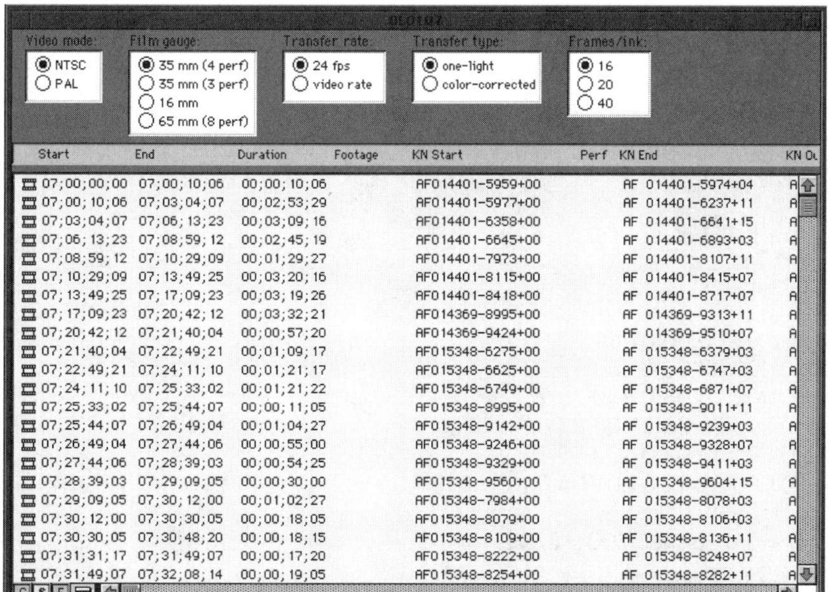


| Start | End | Duration | Footage | KN Start | Perf | KN End | KN Ou |
|---|---|---|---|---|---|---|---|
| 07;00;00;00 | 07;00;10;06 | 00;00;10;06 | | AF014401-5959+00 | | AF 014401-5974+04 | A |
| 07;00;10;06 | 07;03;04;07 | 00;02;53;29 | | AF014401-5977+00 | | AF 014401-6237+11 | A |
| 07;03;04;07 | 07;06;13;23 | 00;03;09;16 | | AF014401-6358+00 | | AF 014401-6641+15 | A |
| 07;06;13;23 | 07;08;59;12 | 00;02;45;19 | | AF014401-6645+00 | | AF 014401-6893+03 | A |
| 07;08;59;12 | 07;10;29;09 | 00;01;29;27 | | AF014401-7973+00 | | AF 014401-8107+11 | A |
| 07;10;29;09 | 07;13;49;25 | 00;03;20;16 | | AF014401-8115+00 | | AF 014401-8415+07 | A |
| 07;13;49;25 | 07;17;09;23 | 00;03;19;26 | | AF014401-8418+00 | | AF 014401-8717+07 | A |
| 07;17;09;23 | 07;20;42;12 | 00;03;32;21 | | AF014369-8995+00 | | AF 014369-9313+11 | A |
| 07;20;42;12 | 07;21;40;04 | 00;00;57;20 | | AF014369-9424+00 | | AF 014369-9510+07 | A |
| 07;21;40;04 | 07;22;49;21 | 00;01;09;17 | | AF015348-6275+00 | | AF 015348-6379+03 | A |
| 07;22;49;21 | 07;24;11;10 | 00;01;21;17 | | AF015348-6625+00 | | AF 015348-6747+03 | A |
| 07;24;11;10 | 07;25;33;02 | 00;01;21;22 | | AF015348-6749+00 | | AF 015348-6871+07 | A |
| 07;25;33;02 | 07;25;44;07 | 00;00;11;05 | | AF015348-8995+00 | | AF 015348-9011+11 | A |
| 07;25;44;07 | 07;26;49;04 | 00;01;04;27 | | AF015348-9142+00 | | AF 015348-9239+03 | A |
| 07;26;49;04 | 07;27;44;06 | 00;00;55;00 | | AF015348-9246+00 | | AF 015348-9328+07 | A |
| 07;27;44;06 | 07;28;39;03 | 00;00;54;25 | | AF015348-9329+00 | | AF 015348-9411+03 | A |
| 07;28;39;03 | 07;29;09;05 | 00;00;30;00 | | AF015348-9560+00 | | AF 015348-9604+15 | A |
| 07;29;09;05 | 07;30;12;00 | 00;01;02;27 | | AF015348-7984+00 | | AF 015348-8078+03 | A |
| 07;30;12;00 | 07;30;30;05 | 00;00;18;05 | | AF015348-8079+00 | | AF 015348-8106+03 | A |
| 07;30;30;05 | 07;30;48;20 | 00;00;18;15 | | AF015348-8109+00 | | AF 015348-8136+11 | A |
| 07;31;31;17 | 07;31;49;07 | 00;00;17;20 | | AF015348-8222+00 | | AF 015348-8248+07 | A |
| 07;31;49;07 | 07;32;08;14 | 00;00;19;05 | | AF015348-8254+00 | | AF 015348-8282+11 | A |

**Figure 10-3** A log file that shows the relationship between keynumbers and timecode using MediaMatch software.

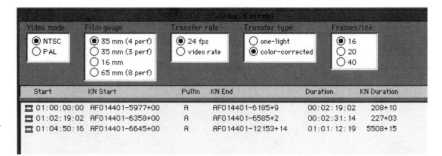

**Figure 10-4** A log which reflects the retransferred takes showing the new time-code to keynumber relationship using MediaMatch software.

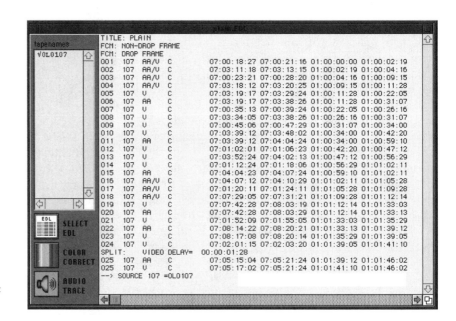

**Figure 10-5** The original one-lite EDL as displayed in the EDL window of MediaMatch software.

Color Corrected Version:
* Avid MediaMatch™ version 4.3 Fri Jun 30 14:47:15 1995
TITLE: MASTER
FCM: NON-DROP FRAME

001 998 V C 09:59:27:06 09:59:34:06 01:00:00:00 01:00:07:00
002 998 V C 10:01:55:18 10:02:01:21 01:00:07:00 01:00:13:03
003 998 V C 10:03:28:10 10:03:39:03 01:00:13:03 01:00:23:26
004 998 V C 10:04:21:26 10:04:32:02 01:00:23:26 01:00:34:02
005 998 V C 10:06:57:08 10:07:15:18 01:00:34:02 01:00:52:12
006 998 V C 10:02:06:00 10:02:18:21 01:00:52:12 01:01:05:03

- - > SOURCE 004 = 0L04 AVID IMPORT ID = 0AB8B148B 0001F82DC
*= >Color-Corrected Reel Names follow:
>>> SOURCE 998 0L04_CC

## Retransferring the Film Using Different Frame Rates

Using the color-correct feature of match-back applications (FTFT) as discussed in chapter seven, the next process is similar except for the difference in frame rates. Where most color-corrected transfers are done at the same rate as the original, this transfer was done at 30 fps (actually 29.97 fps). The reason this is done is because the pulled scenes are transferred in their entirety to D1 videotape in order to create a new "digital negative."

The goal is to allow many versions of the show to be created without destroying the negative. Since the best takes were used for the final sequence, once the negative is cut, that cut negative is the final version. However, by creating a D1 master of all the selected takes, versions can be created whenever necessary and the negative need never be touched.

Another reason is to create a 1:1 relationship between the film frame and the video frame. In this way, visual effects can be created very easily in the digital world without having to keep track of the pulldown. For example, if we are creating a visual effect that requires that a special effect must align with an object in the film frame as it travels from right to left, the new effect must be in synchronization with the pulldown frames of the original element. If not, the new effect will be noticeable as it blurs against the object in the frame; it would continue to move as the pulldown frame of the original remained still. By reducing the film frame and video sequence to the most common denominator, the single frame, this facilitates the postproduction of special visual effects, animation, and composition layers when combining film and video.

The application that translates the original EDL based on pulldown transfer must reflect the new durations when creating the new EDL that has no pulldown. For the same EDL as shown in figure 10-5:

Original EDL Line:

001 107 AA/V C 07:00:18:27 07:00:21:16
01:00:00:00 01:00:02:15

The source timecode reflects a duration of 2 seconds and 15 frames, and this would match-back to the original 63 film frames that were edited into this sequence. When the retransfer was done at 29.97 fps, there was a 1:1 relationship between video and film. The new tape would only have 63 video frames for the same event. The new EDL therefore displays the sources with the 63 video frames, but would need to ripple the record master timecode by the new duration in order to adjust for the speed-up in telecine.

Shown in figure 10-6 is the new database based on a 29.97 fps transfer, rather than the original 23.976 fps transfer.

Shown below is the newly created EDL based on a 29.97 fps transfer, rather than the original 23.976 fps transfer.

The conform can now be automated in a digital format automatically by the online controller. All effects are done digitally. Once the original master has been created, it will be 20% shorter than the original sequence at 23.976 fps with 2:3 pulldown. Using cine-expansion, the D1 master is dubbed to a sub-

```
* Avid MediaMatch™ version 4.3 Fri Jun 30 14:49:01 1995
TITLE: MASTER
FCM: NON-DROP FRAME

001 998 V C 09:59:26:17 09:59:32:05 01:00:00:00 01:00:05:18
002 998 V C 10:01:54:18 10:01:59:14 01:00:05:18 01:00:10:14
003 998 V C 10:03:27:10 10:03:35:29 01:00:10:14 01:00:19:03
004 998 V C 10:04:19:01 10:04:27:06 01:00:19:03 01:00:27:08
005 998 V C 10:06:54:24 10:07:09:14 01:00:27:08 01:00:41:28
- - > SOURCE 004 = 0L04 AVID IMPORT ID = 0AB8B148B 0001F82DC
*=> Color-Corrected Reel Names follow:
>>> SOURCE 998 0L04_CC
* NOTE: Transfer rate of Color Corrected tape is 30 fps.

New Color-Corrected EDL:
001 998 AA/V C 01:00:06:29 01:00:09:02 01:00:00:00 01:00:02:03
```

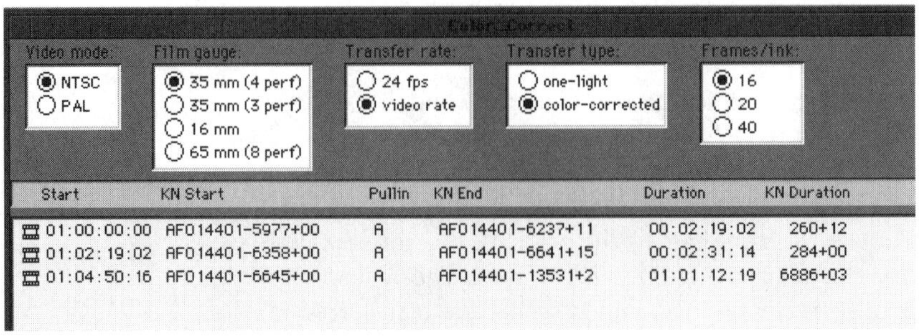

**Figure 10-6** The new database based on a retransfer of the selected takes at 29.97 fps, rather than the original 23.976 fps transfer as shown in figure 10-5.

master. Cine-expansion recreates the 2:3 pulldown of the telecine in a digital format. Once dubbed, the submaster will match frame-per-frame to the same sequence, as if a negative conform had been done and then retransferred to video.

### Audio

The audio is now laid back in sync with the final videotape master that is to be used for broadcast.

## PAL Release

For the PAL release, the D1 videotape is slowed down to 25 fps for the PAL broadcast market. This simulates the negative being cut and then retransferred to PAL with a 4.1% speed-up that would create a 1:1 relationship between the film frame and the PAL video frame. The original audio will also be sped up to stay in sync with the new picture transfer. For music considerations, the sequence may be sped up, but will most likely be harmonized in order to keep the same pitch as the original sound elements. Failure to do this will produce noticeable and, usually, unacceptable pitch changes in the music score. In this way, the negative remains uncut and alternate versions can be recreated for any viewing market.

## ALTERNATIVE METHODS: USING THE NEGATIVE AS SOURCE MATERIAL

A possible alternative method, one that is in the beginning stages of development by several manufacturers of telecine controllers, is to use the negative as source during the online stage. By translating a cut list into a film style EDL, an online controller can control the telecine as though it were a videotape player. The film EDL would contain key number

source, record master timecode, camera roll source, and pulldown phase. A sample film EDL would look like this:

    001 CR21 C KJ123456-1000+00 A1 1090+01
    B2 01:00:00:00 01:01:00:02

where 001= the event number, CR21 = the camera roll, C = cut, KJ123456-1000+00 = the key number in point, A1 = the pulldown phase, 1090+01 = the key number out point, B2 = the out point pulldown phase, and the last two numbers being, respectively, the record time In and Out points.

Telecine controllers such as the TLC (Time Logic Controller) can control up to four devices, a telecine, a 1/4″ audio player/recorder, and VTRs. Most importantly, it is able to create an edit on any combination of film frame and video field. This method also leaves the original camera negative (OCN) intact for different versions of a television show.

On page 230 are examples of an edited sequence that has been translated from the editing system into file formats that could then be re-imported into the telecine control unit.

## INDUSTRY VIEWPOINTS

### Edgar Burcksen—Film Editor

"The Young Indiana Jones Chronicles" (1992 National Academy of Television Arts and Sciences Emmy for Best Editing), *The Dream* (1985).

On the subject of video projection of film dailies and of edited sequence, film editor Edgar Burcksen has considerable experience. Having worked as an editor on "The Young Indiana Jones Chronicles," Burcksen has been involved with digital, nonlinear editing systems for many years. Says Burcksen,

Heading
FIELD_DELIM          TABS
AUDIO_FORMAT         44kHz
TAPE                 501
FPS                  24
VIDEO_FORMAT         NTSC
FILM_FORMAT          35mm

Column

| Start | End | Duration | KN Start | KN End | Pullin | |
|-------|-----|----------|----------|--------|--------|--|
| Scene | Take | Soundroll | Camroll | Sound TC | DESCRIPT | COMMENTS |

Data

| | | | | | | |
|---|---|---|---|---|---|---|
| 05:09:57:10 | 05:10:27:00 | 00:29:20 | KJ391147-4960+13 | KJ391147-5005+05 | A | |
| 14H | 1 | 40 | A68 | 15:41:31:29 | | |
| 05:10:27:00 | 05:11:01:00 | 00:34:00 | KJ391147-5011+03 | KJ391147-5062+03 | A | |
| 14H | 2 | 40 | A68 | 15:43:03:15 | | |
| 05:11:01:00 | 05:12:15:15 | 01:14:15 | KJ391147-5067+03 | KJ391147-5178+15 | A | |
| 14H | 3 | 40 | A68 | 15:44:08:12 | | |
| 05:12:15:15 | 05:12:34:10 | 00:18:25 | KJ391147-5210+11 | KJ391147-5238+15 | A | |
| 8 | 2 | 40 | A68 | 17:21:37:29 | | |
| 05:12:34:10 | 05:13:03:10 | 00:29:00 | ??000000-0000+00 | ??000000-0043+08 | A | |
| 8A | 2 | MOS | A68 | | | |

#GLOBAL
TRANSFER FACILITY Avid Log Exchange-Tewksbury, MA-USA
AATON_KEYLINK Eq#069 Version 5.17
FILM_TITLE 501
TELECINE_SPEED 23.98
VIDEO_REEL 501 (24 ndf NTSC)
FILM_GAUGE 35mm 4perf 24fps
AUDIO FPS 30
AUX_TC_FPS 30

#EVENTS
video tc audio tc aux tc keycode date/tag cam/lr
001 05:09:57:10 15:41:31:29 KJ391147 4960+13
05:10:27:00 15:42:01:19
Scen 14H Take 1 CmR A68 SnR 40

002 05:10:27:00 15:43:03:15 KJ391147 5011+03
05:11:01:00 15:43:37:15
Scen 14H Take 2 CmR A68 SnR 40

003 05:11:01:00 15:44:08:12 KJ391147 5067+03
05:12:15:15 15:45:22:27
Scen 14H Take 3 CmR A68 SnR 40

000 Manufacturer Avid Tech. No. 013 Equip ALE Version 00100501 FLEx 1001
100 Edit to Field A1 NTSC
110 Scene 14H Take 1 Cam Roll 40 Sound 15:41:31:29
200 35 24 Key KJ391147 4960+13
300 501 At 05:09:57:10 For 00:29:20
100 Edit to Field A1 NTSC
110 Scene 14H Take 2 Cam Roll 40 Sound 15:43:03:15
200 35 24 Key KJ391147 5011+03
300 501 At 05:10:27:00 For 00:34:00
100 Edit to Field A1 NTSC
110 Scene 14H Take 3 Cam Roll 40 Sound 15:44:08:12
200 35 24 Key KJ391147 5067+03
300 501 At 05:11:01:00 For 01:14:15
100 Edit to Field A1 NTSC
110 Scene 8 Take 2 Cam Roll 40 Sound 17:21:37:29
200 35 24 Key KJ391147 5210+11
300 501 At 05:12:15:15 For 00:18:25

**Figure 10-7** Photo of Edgar Burcksen. Courtesy of Edgar Burcksen.

We are still dealing with masking the 4:3 video picture to the wide screen aspect ratio of 1:1.85, and it leaves a lot of the frame unused—space you would like to use to improve the picture quality. One year at the National Association of Broadcasters convention, I saw a presentation by Sony they call ATV (advanced television) a transitional system compatible with NTSC and HDTV. It consists of the normal NTSC signal in a different aspect ratio: 16 × 9. This aspect ratio, the same as HDTV, translates to approximately 1:1.77. It is not the usual standard of 1:1.85, but it is far better than the 4:3 aspect ratio of video.

While this presentation was for the benefit of television broadcasters, there are many issues that remain open before the television public is presented with an alternative to a 4:3 aspect ratio; there also are other potential uses for 16 × 9. Notes Burcksen,

Where there exists the real need for this new format is in the film industry. The electronic revolution in postproduction is hampered by the lack of an adequate projection format. Even if a film is edited electronically, an assistant still may cut a workprint for screening purposes, thus keeping much of the old process of the cutting room with trim bins, tape splices, walls of boxes with rolls of film, and an archaic filing system in place. With the introduction of electronic editing in film, we have enhanced the creativity and flexibility of the editor, but we have not sped up the process of film editing. . . .

The 16 × 9 ATV format would be a perfect solution for finally ridding the editing room of film. By eliminating repetitious and redundant work, the editorial staff could be reduced, and the post process could be shortened without giving up, and actually increasing, quality and flexibility. The conforming of a video daily is automatic, from an EDL through two VTRs and edit controlling software. Projection of the conformed ATV tape though a video projector with light valve technology and line doublers would produce a picture on the screen without scratches, grease pencil marks, splices, repaired rips, and so forth. Fades, dissolves and simple visual effects would be in place as well, in a resolution better than the 525 lines we are accustomed to in NTSC. ATV provides 600 lines of horizontal resolution on a digital component signal, more than good enough to judge picture, drama, and pacing. . . .

It should be clear by now that a change over to ATV in the film industry would be driven by an economic need to streamline and shorten the postproduction process. On film budgets ranging from ten to 70 million dollars, it makes a big difference to get your investment paying back weeks or months earlier. It would make film an even more attractive investment vehicle, because if packaged and managed correctly, there is not an industry which pays investments back sooner than film. I am sure that when ATV is introduced to the film industry, it will be adopted rapidly and massively. In their slipstream, the film industry will be followed by films for television, episodics, and other productions.

## INDUSTRY VIEWPOINTS

### Richard Marks, A.C.E.—Editor

*Apocalypse Now* (1979), *Terms of Endearment* (1983), *Broadcast News* (1987), *Say Anything* (1988), *Dick Tracy* (1990), *Father of the Bride* (1991), *I'll Do Anything* (1994), *Assassins* (1995)

For Richard Marks, A.C.E., the use of a digital, nonlinear editing system has encouraged him to experiment with ways of cutting a scene while keeping within the stringent time schedule of delivering a big budget Hollywood feature film. Says Marks,

The basic reason I moved to electronic nonlinear editing is that the capability of the equipment began to be geared toward the work that I do in theatrical motion pictures. Originally, the electronic systems were for commercials and did not allow me to work in the fashion that I had been used to—in the early systems the pictures were not very good and the storage was very limited. Now, all that has changed, and it became a better mousetrap—and it's impossible to ignore a better mousetrap.

Editors can approach this new technology with a great deal of trepidation. I made the plunge—the time was right and it's been just a great experience. When I cut on film, I would do my first cut on two Moviolas and then move to the KEM to make small changes and to screen the cut material. When I started to work on *I'll Do Anything*, it was initially conceived as a musical, and I cut the musical sequences using the Edit-Droid. It was a strange interim initiation process—it wasn't exactly nonlinear and you didn't have enough storage to have all your footage available, but for the work I had to do, it was a fantastic system. At the same time, the Avids were coming up strong and we got an Avid to play with for a couple of months and it was as if a door opened up to me.

The funny thing with editors my age is that when you start editing on a digital system you never want to go back. I think the great thing about electronic editing is the ease of use and the instantaneous availability of your footage. This encourages you to experiment. You make a cut, you want to fool around with it a little, and if you do it too much, pretty soon, all you're looking at are tape splices! But digital is the great encourager. You simply do another version, and if you don't like what you're doing, you just go back to the previous version.

I haven't worked with a Director or Producer who hasn't fallen in love with this technology. When I showed this to James L. Brooks, he fell in love with it—it's great for a Writer/Director. On this film, *Assassins*, the director is Richard Donner and he is blown away with the accessibility of the material and the speed of the process—he's just knocked out. This is a man who invested a large chunk of the postproduction budget so that we could be working with a digital, nonlinear edit system.

The instant feedback you get for optical effects and the audio capabilities are phenomenal. I was cutting a scene and there was a shot panning right to left, when I needed one panning in the opposite direction. I found that we could easily print in reverse and we saw the results immediately. I have access to everything, and it's quite incredible to work this way. Once the film is in first cut and you need to put scene 12 where scene 80 used to be, the ability to quickly juggle continuity is so easy on a digital system. . . .

It's changed everything about the way we work, but you can't get caught up in the mechanics and fix-

ate on how wonderful the gizmo is. It's just a better tool. It doesn't change the talent that an editor has, you can just do more things in the same time and that amount of experimentation gives you better results.

## DIGITAL FILMMAKING FOR FILM PRESENTATIONS

For feature films, the primary list is the negative cutlist. The cutlist is a list of key numbers or inknumbers (Acmade codes). These lists are used to conform the picture: either the workprint for screening purposes during the postproduction process, or the actual negative.

The telecine process is the same as far as the 2:3 pulldown is concerned. Either the negative is transferred to create video dailies, or the synced workprint and mag are transferred in single, uninterrupted runs which create consistent pulldown and timecode for the length of the roll. When these select rolls are being transferred, the key numbers can only be updated (in the worst case), at least eight frames away from the splice point in 35 mm, and ten frames in 16mm.

When making these types of transfers, caution must be taken when later editing material close to the splice points. Until the next key number is read from the barcode, as many as eight fames may be associated with the previous key number. If these frames are used in an edit, the negative cutter will reference another camera roll to locate that key number.

Each take from each entire camera roll can be broken down individually within a digital, nonlinear editing system much faster than manually possible; organization is much more detailed, and retrieval of material is easier and faster. With digital technology available in all areas of production and postproduction, film will only be used for the acquisition and screening of films.

For film transfer to video, film negative could be transferred to an inexpensive form of digital video, perhaps digital Betacam or D5. This transfer would most likely be done in a $16 \times 9$ format so that the full raster of the video image area can be used to contain the film picture. By doing this, the video can be projected with greater resolution and, therefore, fewer objections. Since the $16 \times 9$ image is contained within a 1:1.33 image area, the picture is "stretched" or "unsqueezed" during the projection. Transfers done in this way require less letterboxing of the image area in order to represent the original aspect ratio of the film.

It is important to note that $16 \times 9$ is also not the choice of all organizations working in filmmaking. For example, the American Cinematographers Society (ASC) has not adopted $16 \times 9$ as their preference and has, instead, selected a ratio of 2:1. The $16 \times 9$ ratio of the transfer is preferred over the 4:3 ratio due to the image area approach of 1:85. There is, therefore, less loss of information and greater video resolution when using the $16 \times 9$ format for film transfer. Note that this is not for composition purposes, but for transmission purposes.

## SCREENING ON VIDEO VERSUS SCREENING ON FILM

Film directors often want to be able to view the film as a work-in-progress on a large theater screen to determine how the film will play in its correct aspect ratio and on the full size screen. If the director requires this, workprint is required. However, more and more filmmakers are foregoing the need to see the actual film projected and will view the film in progress on video. The quality of video for digital filmmaking and advances in video projection systems are allowing filmmakers like George Lucas to screen on video as opposed to on film.

The video dailies can be projected unsqueezed through a video projector using a video line doubler that further enhances the image quality by hiding the video scan lines. Using video projection systems which utilize light valve technology, it is easy to create an image that is bright, sharp, and very steady. Dailies can be viewed uninterrupted for tape loads in excess of 60 minutes, and audio quality can be either CD or DAT quality (44.1 or 48 Khz).

## DIGITIZING FOOTAGE DIRECTLY TO THE COMPUTER DRIVES

As the negative is transferred to videotape, it can also be digitized directly to the computer drives of the DNLE system. The signal is sent through a digitizing station that is slaved to the edit controller much like the VTR, telecine unit, and audio deck. During this process, all timecodes, keynumber information, and reel IDs can be retrieved, either as data encoded into the VITC or by serial transfer. This information is later used for list creation and conform of the original elements. This process of digitizing directly to the computer drives will eventually obviate the step of simultaneously transferring the footage to videotape. Shown in figure 10-8 is the software interface of a system that is used to transfer footage directly from telecine to computer disks.

The digitizing process "undoes" the 2:3 pulldown created by the telecine unit. Once the pulldown

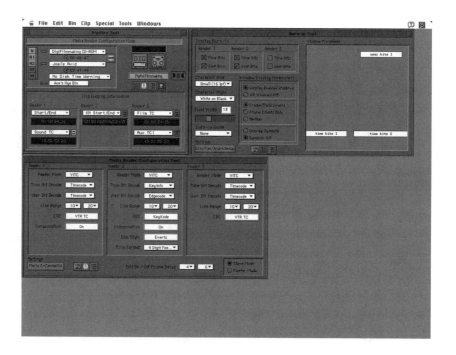

**Figure 10-8** The software interface of a system used to transfer footage directly from telecine to computer disks. (Media Recorder Telecine Courtesy of Avid Technology, Inc.)

pattern is identified, only the original 24 film frames will be captured by the DNLE system. These 24 frames each second are the same 24 frames from the camera negative now represented by the digital files in the digital editing system.

The editor now has access to all the picture and sound elements. Depending on the amount of storage it has online, a typical system can hold anywhere from 20 to 150 hours of dailies. Instantly, the editor can have access to all the dailies down to the single frame. Takes can be retrieved and sorted based on any information contained in the database. This represents a radical change from the traditional film editing process where only nineteen minutes of source reel or edited sequence can be viewed at any one time.

## TOOLS FOUND IN THE DIGITAL, NONLINEAR EDITING SYSTEM

There are tools available to the editor on a DNLE system that just cannot be matched in a traditional film editing environment. Simple fixes such as a reverse angle can be created to cover a take that has broken the line of action. Optical blow-ups can be created to eliminate a microphone that is dipping into the only usable take. These parameters are based on the same ones used by optical printers in a traditional film lab: 10 fields of blow-up with repositions described in directions north, east, west, and south.

### Relating Digital Tools to the Traditional Film Workflow

It is important that the process integrate itself as seamlessly as possible within the traditional workflow. A superimposition can be viewed with levels based on the luminance value of the interpositive. This allows the values of the outgoing and incoming material to match what the optical house will create. Color correction can be expressed in timing lite values on a per-foot and frame basis. This can automate the answer print stage and perhaps create a release print sooner that could save money during the printing stages of release.

If a workprint is being conformed and projected, the digital editor will output a list based on the code applied to the workprint. The editor may decide to use several audio tracks to create a temporary (temp) mix of dialogue, music, and effects. This audio is then output to DAT or Mag and projected double-system

with the print. This saves enormous amounts of time conforming audio. Since the editing system is running at 24 fps and not at 23.976 fps, the audio will be in sync with the projected print.

During the first two years that DNLE systems were used for editing films, when the workprint had been conformed all additional editing was done on film, and not on the digital editing system. This was because DNLE systems did not provide filmmakers with what is known as a change list (figure 10-9). A change list shows what material remains and what needs to be added, trimmed, or removed entirely. This allows an already conformed picture print to be screened very quickly. Any audio changes would just be output in real time to the DAT or mag for interlock projection. Now, the editor can duplicate the digital sequence of the reel, make changes quickly, and view the alternate versions of the cut. Last, the workprint can be reconformed to the new digital version.

### Complicated Film Effects

Complicated effects can be created in high end digital compositing systems for film. In chapter nine, the film to digital to film connection was explored. For the editor who must create a complicated optical effect, using digital systems can be quite satisfying.

## CREATING A FILM TITLE SEQUENCE ON A DIGITAL, NONLINEAR EDITING SYSTEM

One significant drawback of using a 30 fps EDL to create a 24 fps negative cut list is its inability to represent everything that can be created on the more sophisticated DNLE systems. These digital systems have become very powerful in their ability to represent multiple tracks of picture. As an example, take the following sequence.

Shown in figure 10-10 (left to right) are the different elements at various stages of a title sequence. On picture track 1, there are three cuts: A, B, and C. The first requirement is to recompose the background element for better composition by blowing the shot up by 3 optical fields (on a scale of 1–10). We now superimpose a new element onto shot B. However, before we do so, we decide that we need to flop, that is, reverse the angle of the shot, for the superimposed element, so that the actress is facing in the opposite

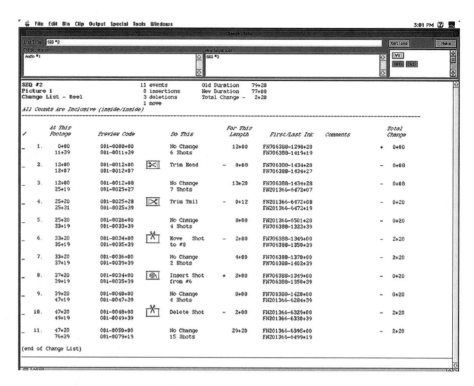

**Figure 10-9** An example of a change list that is used to reconform the workprint.

**Figure 10-10** The different elements and the resulting composite of a title sequence done on a digital, nonlinear editing system. Footage courtesy of Stephanie Cornell.

direction. The resulting superimposition is shown in the fourth image. Finally, in layer three, a title is keyed over the superimposition as well as element B. Below is the resulting graphic display of the composite.

Everything just created cannot be described in a single video style EDL. However, on a DNLE system, the editor is able to create negative cut lists based on individual picture tracks, or a single optical list that describes the entire effect in one list. Shown below are examples of an optical list that describes such a complicated optical effect.

```
Avid Cut Lists    created on Fri Jun 30 14:59:23 1995
   Project: ACTUAL CUTTER Bin: _ smoke
   List Title: long AVR 3
long AVR 3 2 optical units
Optical List

Each shot is described like this:
+———————+ all counts are inclusive
| Starting Key # [event #] | Footage (inside/inside)
| | or
| | Camera all colors are specified
| Ending Key # length of shot | Count as RGB values (0-25)
+———————+

OPTICAL #1 Assemble Event #1 total length: 23+02

Layer 1 of 3
+———————+
| KL 12 3476-0637+00 [1] | 0+00
| |
| Blowup W3 S2 F4 |
| Cam Roll: |
| |
| KL 12 3476-0694+09 23+02 | 23+01
+———————+
Layer 2 of 3
+———————+
| LEADER [1] | 0+00
| |
| Cam Roll: |
| |
| LEADER 4+02 | 4+01
+———————+
+———————+
4+02 | KL 16 2933-1438+07 [2] |
| |
| Superimpose |
| |
| Cam Roll: |
| |
18+21 | KL 16 2933-1474+10 14+20 |
+———————+
+———————+
```

```
| LEADER [3] | 18+22
| |
| Cam Roll: |
| |
| LEADER 4+20 | 23+01
+———————+
Layer 3 of 3
+———————+
| LEADER [1] | 0+00
| |
| Cam Roll: |
| |
| LEADER 6+23 | 6+22
+———————+
+———————+
6+23 | (NO EDGE NUMBERS) [2] |
| |
| Title |
| |
| Cam Roll: |
| |
17+00 | (NO EDGE NUMBERS) 10+18 |
+———————+
+———————+
| LEADER [3] | 17+01
| |
| Cam Roll: |
| |
| LEADER 6+01 | 23+01
+———————+

OPTICAL #2 Assemble Event #2 total length: 0+07
+———————+
| KL 16 3468-5287+10 [1] | 0+00
| |
| Rev. Repeat Frame × -0.3 |
| |
| Cam Roll: |
| |
| KL 16 3468-5287+08 0+07 | 0+06
+———————+
```

## TODAY'S DIGITAL FILMMAKING EDITING PROCESS FOR FILM DELIVERY

Digital filmmaking is characterized by a parallel flow of work throughout all departments. This process, where work can flow from one group to another, is essential. By working in a virtual environment where changes can easily be made up until the moment that the negative is cut, maximum flexibility can be granted to the filmmaker.

## Applying Digital Technology to Feature Filmmaking: The Making of *Radioland Murders*

Filmmaker George Lucas, in 1994, was behind the production of the feature film, *Radioland Murders*, which was shot on location in Wilmington, North Carolina. Postproduction took place at the Skywalker Ranch, which is north of San Francisco. Several important and innovative techniques were used during the creation of this film.

During the shooting process, the output of the video tap was captured on Hi 8 videotape and later conformed as select reels on videotape. At the end of each shooting day, the Hi 8 tapes were then transmitted over a combination of T1 and multiplexed ISDN lines. This allowed the dailies to be transmitted in real time (one hour of dailies required one hour for transmission) into a DNLE system (in this case, an Avid Film Composer) on site at the Skywalker Ranch.

Having received and digitized the video dailies, editors would then proceed. The quality of the video signal through the phone lines was comparable to VHS videotape and was more than adequate for making editorial decisions. Rapid improvements continue to be made to video quality, color, and frame identification.

Heretofore, video taps that dramatically increased the quality did so by sacrificing the ground glass used by the cameraman. By removing the ground glass from the video capture a brighter and cleaner image can be generated, one which removes the different shooting ratio frame guides from the picture. These frame guides can be added digitally to the video image whenever needed.

As editing progressed, rough cuts were generated on a daily basis and then played directly out of the DNLE system and through phone lines to the screening room in Wilmington. Using the DNLE system, the playback could be stopped, replayed, and cued instantly to any point. George Lucas, the film's executive producer, was able to comment verbally to the production team with suggestions and changes while the picture was being viewed.

The film's executive producer and director were separated by almost 2700 miles and yet creativity and collaboration were instantaneous and in real time. Clearly, the trends are undeniable—instead of capturing the image from the film camera first to video, the picture is sent directly from the camera tap and directly to the computer drives of a DNLE system.

Further, the in-camera timecode can be inserted into the picture signal, and the timecode can be decoded at the other end of the phone line and automatically added to the database for EDL creation. The EDLs can then be sent to telecine for the film dailies transfer and then relinked back to an already edited sequence with higher picture quality and key number information reference.

## THE MAKING OF AN ALL-DIGITAL FILM

The film *Rainbow* (1995) is unique because it is an all-digital film, created by Producer Robert Sidaway, directed by Bob Hoskins, with Freddie Francis serving as the Director of Photography, and Bob Lovejoy as editor. The production designer is David Snyder. Vice President and General Manager of the Sony High Definition Center is Dick West, and Steven B. Cohen is the Director of Digital Picture Editorial at Sony Studios.

Shot completely in high-definition television, *Rainbow* is the story of four children who find the end of the rainbow and steal the veritable pot of gold. The high-definition video recordings were then transferred to 525 line NTSC video, digitized into a digital, nonlinear editing system, and then finally imaged back to film.

According to producer Sidaway, the all-digital filmmaking experience had been extremely rewarding. Says Sidaway,

> Our budget is $10 million, which is not very much for a major effects film such as this, so we had to find a way to do the special effects and the magical moments that happen in the movie. Bob Hoskins had worked before on high-def productions and was intrigued by the enormous possibilities that working in high-definition offered. . . .

We decided that we would look at working in high-def and we met with Dick West and John Gault, and everyone was very positive. We were in Montreal deep into preproduction and by the second shooting day, you wouldn't even know that we were shooting anything but 35mm film. The bottom line is that using high-def allowed us to complete this film. Freddie was able to shoot an enormous amount of exteriors and the digital compositing that we had was live, so we could work on the green screens immediately, and in five days we accomplished what would have taken two-and-a-half weeks on film. We saw exactly what we were getting and how the final composites would look. We shot forty-six days total, including underwater green screen shots—to do that work would have taken ten days on the stage, but we did it in two days. It was the key to bringing this film in on budget.

Says production designer Snyder,

I can't think of any surprises that we experienced. The crew was a film crew working as a theatrical film unit. But for me it was a bit different—when we picked colors and fabrics, we wonder how it's going to hold up. Most times you shoot tests on fabrics, you see the dailies, so the idea of being able to see all the elements while they were lighting allowed us to make any changes that we felt were necessary. We can now get a homogeneous look and on the day that we shot, we had no need for dailies.

I see no disadvantage at all to working in high-def. It is especially good for supervising the special effects department. We would see the composited elements on the stage and were able to position things, and this is an enormous advantage. I've done about twenty-five films and we were actually striking the set one hour after filming them!

Continues producer Sidaway,

Because the method of shooting is normal—as far as we were concerned we were shooting film—I think as far as the director is concerned, it gives him enormous confidence. But you have to be disciplined. You can spend a lot of time looking at the monitor and you have to know when you've got what you need.

Adds production designer Snyder,

We got a lot of things in one or two takes because we knew exactly what we were recording and could play it back instantly, even with the composites that we were building live.

Sony High-Def Vice President West says,

The philosophy is to try to make the technology as invisible as possible and to not change anything that the film crews have been doing for years. On this film, they used an Arri matte box, an Arri follow-focus, and this provides them with all the advantages that they are used to. Added to that is being able to see instant replays and compositing live right on the stage. . . .

Once we have a high-def master tape, we write the same frame, three times as RGB information, and at the rate of one frame per second, onto black-and-white positive film and we then take that black-and-white positive and print it onto color negative.

Continues producer Sidaway,

We are editing on a digital, nonlinear editing system, and the first cut is quite a detailed cut. We digitized about 20 hours of material and reached the first cut in two-and-a-half weeks from the end of the shoot. We did the entire cut in four-and-a-half weeks and at times we could have cut 15–20 minutes a day. So we were very happy with the creativity and productivity of editing digitally.

## INDUSTRY VIEWPOINTS

### James Cameron—Filmmaker

*The Terminator* (1984), *Aliens* (1986), *The Abyss* (1989), *Terminator 2: Judgment Day* (1991), *True Lies* (1994).

James Cameron, who has been at the forefront of utilizing digital technology in making films, is a key witness to and participant in the evolution of digital filmmaking. His thoughts are particularly relevant to the scope of how technology is a tool available to the filmmaker and how filmmakers are reacting to emerging digital filmmaking methods.

What do you see as the defining trends in making films?

There's a whole new crop of directors, coming from the world of commercials and music videos, who are accustomed to real time interaction and control at video resolution on the Harry or Paintbox and who are frustrated at film resolution by the clumsiness of the medieval tools of film editing, optical printing and color timing. They're finding these digital tools to be a natural evolution of the image-making process as they know it.

Motion-image processing at high-resolution is already becoming a booming business, but it will really

**Figure 10-11** Photo of James Cameron. Courtesy of Lightstorm Entertainment. Photograph by Richard Foreman.

explode with the arrival of a real, practical, high-quality electronic delivery system. When electronic cinema reaches 100% replacement of mechanical projection, films probably will be finished entirely in the digital domain, in the way that most television production which is shot on film is currently finished. Just as sounds are currently mixed in postproduction in a sophisticated process of refinement, the future of film postproduction will be what I call the image mix. The lines will blur between visual effects, editing, color correction, and conventional image manipulations like flops, dissolves, and fades. It will all become one process, under the director's and the producer's control. Visual effects, composites, live action photography, animation, titles, dissolves, multi-image layouts, color and contrast effects . . . all of these will stream together electronically into a "final" image mix . . . a final, high-resolution online. The speed and flexibility of digital, nonlinear editing has been and will continue to reduce postproduction time substantially. The ability to compile visual effects composites directly into the digital master of the film will obviate the need to shoot effects shots in larger formats such as VistaVision and 65mm. There will be no generation loss between effects shots, titles, dissolves, and the rest of the film.

All of these techniques are available now to the filmmaker while he or she is making a film, but at great cost, both in time and money. Right now, digi-

tized shots are rare in a film, although the number is increasing rapidly. In the future, if the entire film is going to be digitized anyway for exhibition, the filmmaker will be able to fine-tune the image using computers in ways never possible before.

Also, the ancillary markets for films are growing, merging, and mutating at an incredible rate. As we all know, films can create new cultural icons which then have lives of their own beyond the movie theater; characters from movies now live simultaneously in the parallel universes of toys, comic books, video games, computer games, and interactive software. The movie itself is thus an engine which drives an entire ecosystem, a food-chain which permeates many media and markets. Video is clearly the most important of these markets.

Films cost a ferocious amount of money to make. Especially mine. They're financed these days partially, in some cases largely, against video rights. This is so because more people are going to see the film on home video than will ever see it in the theatre, so the home market is where the money is. This is a reality which filmmakers must embrace, and embrace at the earliest stage. I shoot my films in the Super-35 format, because it allows me to put a beautiful anamorphic print in theaters while still allowing me to do an uncompromised pan-and-scan transfer of the film to video later, without the necessity for letterboxing.

At Lightstorm, we take pride in delivering the highest quality video product we can make to the marketplace. It's important to me. I know many directors who are snobbish about video, who see it as a necessary evil, or just an evil, and don't care what their films look like in that medium. They're not interested in the technology that is being used to deliver their pictures. These guys are dinosaurs. I care about anything which increases the size and profitability of video markets, makes my films more profitable, and allows me to continue doing what I love. Any advancement in delivery of my films to more people, more often, is of interest to me.

From this point, the next logical step for me was to create a company which could be an arena for the creation of images digitally, and for the subsequent productization of digital assets in other media, such as games and interactive software. Along the way, I know this process will spawn products and titles for games, interactive media, and other markets, thus vindicating the effort at a business level.

When Scott Ross, Stan Winston, and I were forming our digital production company, Digital Domain, we talked to dozens of the top companies in software, computers, telecommunications, and cable systems. It afforded me a kind of overview of what was on the minds of these movers and shakers. And with all of these new emerging systems and smart set-top boxes and so on, one thing was clear to all of them: it's still about content. What do you put on these great new systems? Obviously, the demand for visual production of every kind is going to increase.

We have all seen in recent years the synergies created by movies, video, music, video games, toys and so on. This will continue as interactive media emerge more fully. You will see more joint-venturing between film studios and interactive media and games companies. More than that, the winners in the coming years are going to be the ones who can successfully capitalize on a given title in many different markets. And the only ones to get really rich in the short run in interactive media are going to be the attorneys.

I don't pretend to have any brilliant answers in these speculative areas, but I know that filmmakers really need to understand and utilize these markets if they are to maximize the effectiveness and communication of their visions.

How has knowing that certain technologies are available to the filmmaker affected how productions proceed? What are the benefits to the filmmaker who uses the technology that companies such as Digital Domain are offering?

The philosophy of Digital Domain—and any good digital production facility—is to make the process highly interactive for the filmmaker, so that they can enjoy the same hands-on control in the area of special visuals that they have in day-to-day production. Visual effects is the perfect arena to initiate artists into the technology that is sweeping into all areas of filmmaking, because it's currently the most visible and understandable interface between creative and technical.

History speaks for itself on the subject of the popular success of films loaded with fantastic visuals. "Effects films" whether they be science fiction, fantasy or adventure, now comprise seven of the top ten grossing films of all time. Only the "fear factor" keeps studios and filmmakers from making more of them. Everyone has experienced the rocky shoals of effects production, where cost and time overruns, shoddy work, and lack of communication have led to frustration, finger pointing, litigation, and a generally bad aura surrounding the whole process.

What we're trying to do at Digital Domain is to provide an exciting, highly interactive environment where creativity is enhanced instead of frustrated, and where filmmakers who previously didn't like or understand the techniques for creating fantastic imagery can feel at home and in control of the process.

This is the true final barrier of the effects business: to demystify the process. To put the tools di-rectly in the hands of the filmmakers. Ultimately, what we're trying to do is usher in the age of "digital directing."

Many practitioners of the black arts of special effects think of themselves, consciously or unconsciously, as wizards. They know things we mortals don't. And they don't like to reveal what they know. Satisfaction for them, in their relatively unglamorous niche of filmmaking, comes from unveiling the magic in finished form. They don't view the director as a partner. They view the director as someone who does not understand what they do, and never will, but who, perversely, they must please and impress in order to get paid. So they enter into a kind of uneasy marriage.

Directors don't love this process either. Directors are meticulous planners who nevertheless have to do their most important work in an environment of rapid decision making and crisis management. They operate in a heightened energy state where creativity is a real time process, where results are immediate, and where shooting becomes a day-by-day battle against time, entropy, and chaos. Directors are willful, impatient creatures whose job is to GET THINGS DONE. Many of them are inarticulate about the visions in their heads, but sure as hell know it when they see it. This applies to design, to photography, to performance . . . all aspects of this technical art of moviemaking.

The director is the captain of the ship, and as captain he or she must be right at all times. Directors naturally tend to avoid situations they can't control, and realms of endeavor in which they may appear ignorant. They don't like processes which are vital to their film to be out of their sight, or beyond their understanding. Directors can look through the camera, and make changes before the shot is made, in order to get what they want. They can see and hear what an actor does, so they can influence and guide and shape a performance, because it is right there in front of them. They like this process.

Effects and animation in particular are not hands-on processes for the director, because they represent an area where a great deal of the creative control of their film is given up to wizards. Most directors don't like animation. It's a field where they give up almost all control to others. Artists draw the character and bring it to life through pencil tests, then cel painting or arduous computer animation. Directors are used to characters played by actors, whom they can talk to. While sometimes it may seem more difficult getting an actor to do something than drawing out 24 separate drawings of a character for every second of film, in general, directors find live-action filmmaking a far more rewarding experience. A renaissance in animation will occur when directors can interact with an animated character as easily as with a live actor, when they can tell it what to do.

We can accomplish this using digital technology. If a director can walk into a suite, resembling a video-post suite, and sit down in front of a monitor displaying a computer graphics character which is moved in real time by a performer in the next room wearing a telemetry suit . . . then the traditional barrier between filmmakers and animation has been shattered. The director can verbally guide the performance of the character through the actor or puppeteers operating the data suit or performance waldoes in the next room, and the director can control the camera's position and movement via the operator next to him or her at the workstation. By assembling a system from various types of motion capture hardware (existing or buildable) and using the resulting data to drive the animated figure in digital 3-D space, we can display a character on a monitor which moves and acts in real time.

Hardware for measuring body movement, hand movement, face and lip movement . . . all of this equipment exists right now and can be refined. Articulated armatures or "performance waldoes" can also be used, to capture movement which does not correspond to the human body. Puppeteers, manually moving a performance waldo of a tail or tentacle, can make that appendage move on a computerized character. Linking software will couple the data to allow a fantasy character to be performed in real time by puppeteers working with the actor in the telemetry suit.

For example, Jack Nicholson could create not just the voice, but the total body performance of a computer-animated demon, while puppeteers nearby cause his tail to lash and his pointed ears to furl and twitch, without fighting unreliable radio controls or tripping over cables. The actor can truly "become" his animated character. I think both directors and actors will be fascinated by the possibilities.

This method can also open up creative possibilities for the camera. By verbal commands the director can ask the workstation operator to move the "virtual camera" relative to the figure of the character, thus coordinating not only the performance, but the cinematic style used to emphasize and underline that performance. The director could say, for example, "I want the camera to swoop down from all the way across the room, arriving just as he turns and coming into a tight close-up on the eyes as he says the first line." By coordinating the camera move with the actor in the telemetry suit, and recording a guide track at the same time, the process begins to resemble conventional filmmaking . . . except that the results are CGI. The data gathered in this type of session can then be used by the computer animators on their own

to create the scene at a higher resolution, cleaning up the motion where necessary and refining the details of the character, adding textures and adjusting the lighting, and so forth. Later, the director can come back into the loop for the compositing of the character into live-action background plates or totally synthetic CG backgrounds.

The digital composite workstation will become one of the director's most powerful tools. There, a director can control, with a great degree of immediacy, the way a composite shot is assembled. He or she may change the line-up, the position of the foreground elements, the color and contrast, and all the myriad values which make the shot look real . . . and more importantly, allow it to tell the story. You can use software to add heat distortion, ripple effects, smoke, and aerial perspective haze, etc. to create a sophisticated palette of subtle techniques. Opticals as we know them are already totally obsolete, replaced by digital composites in the next couple of years.

2-D image processing presents a vast new palette of basic tools, even for non-visual effects scenes. Color and lighting can be adjusted, focus refined, a leading actor's crow's feet can be processed out of the close-ups, negative scratches can be made to vanish, and mistakes like microphones and lamps in frame can be removed. Wires and pylons can be removed from stunt rigs, which means they can be made thicker and stronger on set, making these kinds of gags safer to shoot. I have had direct experience with a number of these pioneering techniques, and they work. We did some of these things in *Terminator 2*, and we're thinking of new things every day. The possibilities are endless.

Again, none of this requires the director or producer to take a graduate course in computer science. The director works through an intermediary who actually enters the commands at the workstation. The director asks for something in plain language, the operator manipulates the images on the screen, and the director can say when it is better, worse . . . or perfect.

This technology, of course, means nothing without the talent to run it. That's where the wizards come in. CG artists must become the guides and partners of the directors who will sit with them and make the magic, not nameless ciphers providing a thankless service. That way they feel more like they're part of the film, and it makes it a more enriching experience. It humanizes the technology for both the CG expert and the filmmaker.

All of this will bring the filmmaker into the creative loop at every stage, and everyone will benefit. Digital people will feel more like artists than mere technicians. Directors and producers will feel a greater authorship in areas of filmmaking which have previously been the realm of specialist wizards. Directors will find effects to be rewarding the more they can participate in the moment of creation, and the more that participation is a real time act. The director can make his or her dreams real on the screen, and enjoy the process. And, most importantly, they can make better films.

What should the filmmaker be wary of with regard to the pervasiveness of technology in modern filmmaking?

Part of the danger is thinking that digital technology will solve everything. It can, but not without a lot of diligence and constant attention from all of us, in both the creative and technical communities. New technologies have spawned whole new areas of doubt and uncertainty, where some feel threatened by the machines, others advocate specific technologies to fit their own agendas, and the filmmaker is left trying to adapt to ever-changing standards while still trying to tell his or her story. The formats and standards war is a perfect example.

And at a consumer level, interactive platforms and software are becoming more and more about dealing with moving images at higher resolution. It's all becoming about ones and zeros. Moving pictures as data. There's actually two factors at work here: quality and quantity. And the way the filmmaking community and the consumer delivery industry are looking at these factors is different.

One of the new digital buzzwords is "bandwidth." It refers to the amount of information that can be communicated at a particular resolution and a particular rate. At a fixed maximum bandwidth of a given technology, you can only raise the resolution by lowering the rate, and vice versa. So your choice becomes more throughput at a lower image quality, or less throughput at a higher image quality. Given this fact, all these new satellite systems, picture-in-picture TVs and "interactive" channels are fighting against the big high-res theater experience because they're shooting for quantity, not quality. HDTV is at odds with all these mega-channel systems and networks as well, for the same reasons.

Looking beyond the plethora of burgeoning video delivery systems for a moment, consider another problem looming on the horizon. The business of exhibiting films has been essentially unchanged technologically for generations. However, probably within the next decade, all first-run theaters will project movies electronically. The motion picture industry worldwide spends a billion dollars a year making release prints, which are used for a month and then thrown away. The economic imperative to go to electronic projection makes the advent of Electronic Cinema a certainty, with time the only variable.

For the filmmaker, this impacts the very medium in which his or her work is done. In a hypothetical Electronic Cinema system, the film would be digitized from a visual image into digital data. The resolution of the image is determined by the number of pixels. Kodak believes that to avoid a loss of quality a film image should be scanned into no less than 12 million pixels per frame (each one carrying 30 bits of color/density data). Others believe that for an exhibition standard one quarter of this is probably enough. No one agrees. No one really knows right now because no one has been able to generate an electronic image on a big screen which is indistinguishable from film . . . yet.

The only thing people agree on is that even at relatively low resolutions, the amount of storage needed to preserve these images is enormous. The biggest problem for the technologists and the buyers of this technology (the major studios) is actually defining the problem . . . What level of visual quality is sufficient to match or exceed the look of a 35mm release print? Using Kodak's Electronic Intermediate standard of 3112 by 4096 pixels (roughly the equivalent of 4000 lines of resolution), with 10-bit channel color, a film image shot originally at 24 frames per second on 35mm negative yields a digital image 40 megabytes in size per frame, or nearly a gigabyte per second. Not only do you need processors fast enough to move these huge volumes of data around, but you need a place to store them, like tape or disk.

Since moving data around costs money, in direct proportion to the amount of data per second, the long-term economic interests of the companies involved in this digital delivery are best served by adopting the LOWEST visual standard necessary to accomplish the goal. Each additional pixel of picture information could cost millions over the years. So we really can't trust the electronics manufacturers, the delivery system companies, or even the major studios, to arrive at the correct standard for electronic film exhibition without being closely monitored by the creative community.

The entertainment industry's track record in adopting technical standards is spotty at best. 35mm has proved adequate, but the 24 frame per second rate is just 6 frames per second shy of the ideal 30 frames per second, which would have reduced flicker almost to zero, given a sharper picture, and been fully compatible with video. A similar compromise was made more recently when the recording industry adopted the 16-bit standard for digital CDs, which is generally acknowledged now to be too low.

So we must collectively adopt a digital film standard, one that is high enough to replicate the film image but low enough to be practical, and can be used for all production and delivery systems; only this way can we really maximize our efforts across all platforms. This standard must be arrived at as a group decision involving everyone concerned: the creative community (filmmakers), the distributors, the exhibitors, the technical groups (SMPTE), the delivery system entities (telcos, RBOCs, and satellite delivery companies), and the chief scientists and engineers working in the fields of input-scanning (Kodak), electronic projection (Hughes, JVC, Matsushita, Sony), digital compression, and digital storage and playback technology.

Opinions differ widely, however. Kodak, which has the most to gain by delaying the demise of the release print, has set its standard very high, but it makes sense as an intermediate standard, designed to preserve the quality of the original negative. However, this makes it impractical as an overall working format given the current storage and processing technology. Even Kodak agrees that to simulate a 35mm release print would probably require less pixels, due to the photochemical generational loss between original negative and release print.

At the other end of the spectrum, Sony has been actively proposing the adoption of their HDTV standard as sufficient to simulate 35mm release print look. They're wrong. I've seen the results, and it just looks like big video. Many people are fooled by the clarity of HDTV on a 30-inch monitor, and say it looks like film, but comparing it side-by-side with a 35mm print on a 30-foot screen would show that it's only about one third of the resolution of film. Fortunately, only Sony seems to actually believe their own hype, and even then there is dissension in the ranks.

Hughes, with their electronic projection system, is currently aiming at a resolving power of 50 line-pairs per millimeter and a contrast ratio no less than 100:1. SMPTE sets their release-print standard at between 60 and 80 line-pairs/mm and the SIGMA Design Group calculates the contrast ratio of film at between 300:1 and 400:1. No one agrees, and most filmmakers are unaware that a major decision affecting the very heart and soul of their work as artists is about to be made without their involvement.

Currently the director supervises the photochemical color correction of the film (which takes weeks), then later supervises the NTSC pan-scan transfer, the NTSC letterbox transfer, the PAL transfers, and so on. With HDTV on the horizon, one or more transfer formats will be added to the list, and directors may have to go back to films done years ago and transfer them yet again! Or risk having some hourly-paid technician screw up the color and framing. And put the original negative at risk yet again.

When Electronic Cinema arrives, for better or worse, at least we should be able to consolidate this madness into one master high-res transfer, then downsample all other formats and needs from that.

The point is that although the filmmaker shouldn't really have to deal with these technological issues, they're still there and will have an impact on an artist's creative vision and creative rights. As we try to make it easier for the filmmaker to achieve a vision without having to know the details behind the process, it also becomes easier to abdicate the responsibility and necessity of understanding the broad strokes and ramifications of the technology. If you know your tools, you can take advantage of the opportunities and cogently address the disadvantages.

What do you feel are some of the breakthroughs that have been accomplished and what remains to be accomplished technologically in the area of filmmaking?

It seems to me that with the relentless forward march of progress in digital/electronic systems in all industries worldwide, technologies will arrive within months or a few years to solve all of the problems related to moving around and storing the huge volumes of image data needed to make an entire film-resolution digital motion picture. When this happens—almost certainly within this decade—and when we define an acceptable digital standard, film will be exhibited using electronic projection rather than the system of projecting from photochemical prints which is in current use and has remained fundamentally unchanged since the turn of the century.

Several major electronics companies are exploring the technology to do this. The plan is to replace release prints entirely by converting all theaters to electronic projection. The movie will be delivered on tape, or can even be down-linked from their satellite network using advanced compression algorithms, or delivered by phone once the fiber infrastructure is in place.

The significance of this to filmmakers and the digital production companies is this: as the time approaches when all films in release are scanned into the digital realm as a matter of course, all digital technologies will benefit by becoming cheaper and more prevalent. Input/output scanners will become the new telecines. Films will be transferred into digital storage in postproduction, and color correcting the movie will become an electronic rather than a photochemical process. This will be a milestone because the control of color and density will be immediate and precise, replacing the byzantine process of guessing and second guessing which takes weeks and puts the negative at risk over and over as each successive trial answer print is struck. This way, the valuable negative is only subjected to one mounting on a laboratory's machine . . . when it is set up on the input scanner for digitization.

Electronic Cinema will help make the digitization of entire films cost-effective. It will incentivize Kodak and others to mass-produce their input-scanners, and will bring down the cost of storage technologies like tape and disk.

Once it is common practice to digitize all films, a true convergence of current trends will take place. The converging trends will be nonlinear editing, electronic intermediate, digital image processing, computer-generated animation and effects, and digital storage/transmission/exhibition of films.

We can visualize a time, soon, when camera negative will be digitized, at some stage early in the postproduction process. It will then be downsampled to a workable resolution and used to edit the film on a nonlinear system. I basically do this now on my films with the Avid Film Composer. All effects work will be composited digitally and supplied as a sort of digital B-roll. The effects will be compiled into the cut of the film at the same generation. Any number of cuts of the film may be viewed at this point, and the viewing can take place at final release quality, which will revolutionize previewing of films.

Color corrections can be made quickly and definitively at a colorimetry workstation, and the control of the image will be vastly improved. Not only the three primary colors can be controlled (as in current photochemical color "timing") but the system will offer control of contrast, black values, secondary hues, and color saturation—at film resolution. In addition, changes in all these values can be made smoothly during shots to address specific moments, as opposed to the photochemical system in which color can only be changed at the cut.

When the completed digital film is then previewed and changes required, they can be made in a few hours. And since no release prints are required, this process can continue up until the day before release, if the film is distributed through a satellite network. The movie can be modified up to the last second before wide release to adjust to market research screening, etc. Trims can be made based on test-audience responses on the day before release. The changes need only be made to the digital master of the movie, which is the source for the uplink feed to the thousands of theaters. For expensive blockbuster movies, this will save in interest charges by creating positive cash flow the instant the film is done.

From the finished high-res master of the film, down-sampled versions can quickly be extracted for PAL and NTSC video, and HDTV or equivalent.

Color, density, and contrast values will remain constant through all versions and formats of the movie, in all media, in all countries. The digital data of the film is stored on some type of tape or disc. It can now be uplinked to satellite and downlinked simultaneously to theaters nationwide. Or it can be delivered over a fiber-optic phone line (if that is in place). For test screenings, premieres and previews, a tape or disc can be hand-carried to the theater.

The uniformity of technology means that you know the film will look and sound the same in all 3000 screens. The color, the brightness, and the sound reproduction will be identical. No quality control issues from the lab making 3000 prints on high-speed printers. Colors mismatching between reels will be a thing of the past. No more scratches, or dirt, or torn-up prints missing whole sections of the movie. The film will look as good in week 12 as it did opening night because it's digital data. It's ultimate quality control in the field. I can envision black-box projectors in the venues that use the phone system to instantly report maintenance problems. They will have on-board self-diagnosing capability, plus the ability to "read" their own screens and adjust, or call for help.

Incidentally, once a satellite or fiber-optic fed electronic projector exists in every local cinema, throwing up a big, bright, clear picture . . . it will be possible to create truly "global" events. As the world moves steadily toward greater culture uniformity, the demand for real time big-screen live events will become enormous. These events can be concerts, special ceremonies, and sporting events like the Olympics or championship fights.

A trickle-down effect of electronic cinema will be the ability to go back and store all currently existing movies in a medium which does not decay the way celluloid film does. Currently all the films we love are chemically aging in their vaults. A negative can be lost or damaged, or simply fade and shrink to the point that it is almost worthless. With a digitized master the film is preserved virtually forever . . . and may be preserved in a number of different places (with clone sub-masters) so it can never be lost to fire, flood or theft. A copy (or clone) of a digital master is identical to the master. Once a film has been digitized at high resolution, it is safe for all time from decay. This has some big ramifications. This will create enormous added value for existing film libraries. Not only does it ensure their lifespan into the indefinite future, but it will give them greater value as higher resolution viewing and delivery systems are made available to the home. Disney has proven that assets decades old have enormous commercial value. *Fantasia* sold over 11 million units in its video release, making a profit of a billion dollars literally 50 years after its release.

We've already begun moving down this path towards convergence. We just need to be diligent and clear-headed—technically, creatively, and financially—about how we bring all of these elements together in the digital domain.

Almost all of these growing trends we've discussed are process-oriented. The fundamental tenets of filmmaking and storytelling, however, will not and should not change, even as the technology is changing and broadening the markets in which films are now operating.

Television, whether cable or broadcast, offers a higher degree of interactivity, but only in the ability to graze among a number of choices in passive linear-narrative entertainments. This multifold increase in choice-making process is still only an evolutionary change, not a revolutionary one. Increasing the number of choices from 40 to 200 channels is a change in degree, not in kind. You can change your mind faster; as a result, programming is getting more and more abbreviated, trying to give you info or sell you something in quick bites before your attention wanders.

Programming on demand, while an obvious improvement, still is only triggering a passive entertainment. True interactivity is different, and perhaps further away. Being able to make real choices, determining the path of characters' lives and actions, changing the outcome of events in a non-predeterminate environment—all of what we can really call interactivity—is in fact the antithesis of one of the basic definitions of storytelling.

Movies and storytelling are the opposite of real interactivity. They create moods, over time. They create characters that we live with, and grow to understand, to hate or love. They create worlds, which we enter, live in, and leave two hours later. They explore ideas in detail, and make powerful dramatic statements by laying groundwork in the first hour which may not pay off until the end of the second. In a movie theater you don't have any choices. The train leaves the station and two hours later it stops, and you get off. Once the initial choice is made about which one to see, they are completely passive entertainments.

That's why in an age of increasing choices, with more cable channels, more networks, more sources for entertainment images at our fingertips, the feature film, this archaic passive form of entertainment, still has vast power.

They are designed to take over sensory control . . . commanding all that we see and hear . . . in an environment in which any action or motion on our part is socially condemned. You don't zap to another channel, take a phone call, go fix a snack, or hold forth wisely for ten minutes on some subject like you can in your living room. All your other senses are down-played. Unless a spring from the seat is digging into your right butt-cheek or a fat guy next to you is hogging the arm-rest, you forget about your body. The "interactivity" level is zero. You get to interact with a box of popcorn. Or maybe with the fat guy if you feel aggressively territorial.

You leave your body behind, and your mind enters the world up there on the screen. You can get up and leave if you don't like the film, and you can go to the bathroom, but the reality is most people don't. We sit, and we watch.

See, I believe this surrender to non-interactivity is part of the power of the experience. It is essential to the transport of the mind and heart, the out-of-body aspect. In the same way that the surrender of choice and will to a higher power is fundamental to most religions and is a deep-seated psychological need of all people, we will still crave the choice-overwhelming experience. The abdication of will. There is no steering wheel on a roller-coaster.

You don't have this at home and you never will, no matter how high-end, high-definition the systems become. Films, in their theatrical presentation, have a power over the senses, the mind and the imagination that a video image in your home can't. Part of it is the picture itself, which is larger and vastly more detailed. But there's something else. What the theatrical movie gives us as an experience is fundamentally different than watching the tube. It is a group experience in a public place, which is why it will always be desirable to offer substantially better image and sound at public venues than one can enjoy at home. And as home system resolution improves, theatrical presentations may have to ratchet up their quality.

The point is that movies cast a spell. They have since their invention, and in some form they always will.

## INDUSTRY VIEWPOINTS

### Francis Coppola—Filmmaker

*Question:* It must be satisfying for you now, many years after you first began the concept of "The Electronic Cinema," to see so many films utilizing digital and electronic filmmaking techniques, such as capturing and editing on set, using digital, nonlinear editing systems and wide area networking to accomplish connecting the distant filmmaker to the postproduction center.

How do you feel about this inevitable adoption of the filmmaking principles you have espoused for so long, and what excites you as we enter this new age of digital filmmaking?

**Figure 10-12** Photo of Francis Coppola. Courtesy of American Zoetrope.

I knew it would happen all along—Francis Coppola

## DIGITAL FILMMAKING

The world of filmmaking and the methods by which films are being made today runs a vast gamut from filmmakers who struggle with antiquated technology that barely works to filmmakers who utilize super computers to create some of the most fantastic film images ever seen. Regardless of the technology, the inevitable growth of the digital filmmaking methods, tools, and processes that have been outlined in this book will define the way that films are made for decades to come. It will not be very long before editing film by hand will pass to the wayside and be looked upon quite nostalgically and romantically.

The growth of cable television, video services via telephone companies, and the insatiable appetite for programming will mean that new filmmakers who could previously not create their visions due to the sheer cost of mounting and maintaining a film production will find ways of using digital methods to reduce their budgets. Simultaneously, they will be able to use digital filmmaking methods to maintain the quality of the presentation without great compromise.

The authors have witnessed an incredible change in the acceptance of digital filmmaking technology through all facets of the filmmaking process. There is nothing more exciting than to see the face of a filmmaker who is new to the many different aspects of previsualization, digital production, and digital postproduction during the moment that the filmmaker puts the pieces together and begins to understand how this inexorable movement of technology will affect his or her creative vision.

## Reader Feedback and Information on CD-ROM Availability for *Digital Filmmaking*

So that we can judge the effectiveness of this book, we are very interested in receiving your feedback. Correspondence can be sent to our Internet address: Tom_Ohanian@avid.com

Also, should you be interested, we would very much like to send you information on the CD-ROM version of *Digital Filmmaking*. The CD-ROM features many of the concepts introduced in the book, along with animations, interviews, and so forth. We look forward to hearing from you over the Internet or you may reach us via the publisher of this book: Focal Press, 313 Washington Street, Newton, Massachusetts 02158-1626 USA. Fax: 617-928-2620. Please address correspondence in care of: *Digital Filmmaking*, Thomas A. Ohanian.

Digital Filmmaking CD-ROM
Name _____
Title _____
Company _____
Address_____
City_____State_____Zip_____
Country_____
Tel.:_____Fax:_____
Internet Address_____

CPU used with CD-ROM
_____ Macintosh
_____ PC
_____ Other

Comments: _____
_____
_____
_____
_____

# 11

# 24p: Twenty-Four Frames, Progressively Scanned

## WHAT IS 24p?

A straightforward definition of 24p is a format that has a frame rate of 24 frames per second and is progressive in nature. 24p has become associated in the television broadcast industry with the HDTV format of 1920 pixels by 1080 rows (1920 × 1080), progressively scanned at 24 fps, with an aspect ratio of 16:9. However, when we refer to "24p", we could easily be describing the oldest motion picture acquisition format—film.

Film by its very nature is progressive; that is, each frame is drawn in its entirety, without the field scanning method used in video recordings. A reel of film with its native play rate of 24 fps can be shown anywhere in the world, because the playback equipment is ubiquitous. Further, thanks to variable frame rates, film is incredibly flexible. Images can be acquired from one frame a year to 12,000 frames a second for, respectively, time lapse and slow motion photography.

Chapter ten describes how film is used as an acquisition format for television programming. Once the film has been transferred to videotape, it is manipulated at either 25 fps or 30 fps during the postproduction-to-broadcast stage. It is very interesting to note the progression of technology as it applies to the broadcasting industry. For example, for television nightly news programs, images were once acquired on film. The positive film was shot, developed, threaded onto film chains, and broadcast to the viewing public. When portable videotape recording equipment came into existence, the use of film gradually decreased until it was completely replaced by the use of videotape. Today it would be difficult, indeed almost impossible, to find a nightly news broadcast still shooting and airing film.

Why then, do television programs—that is, those that typically run in the prime time hours of eight to eleven PM (at least in the United States)—continue to acquire their images on film rather than videotape? What intrinsic value does film have? The following reasons are often cited:

- The show benefits from the look associated with exposing images on film (subjective and objective).
- The show has a delivery requirement in both NTSC and PAL countries, which can best be served by film origination.
- The show has a high production value, which is reflected by the "film look."
- Acquiring on film ensures a long "shelf life."

Figure 11-1 lists various countries and their respective television transmission standards. Phase alternate line (PAL) 625 was developed in Germany and in the United Kingdom and first used in 1967. National Television Standards Committee (NTSC) 525 was developed in the United States and first used in 1954. Finally, Sequential Couleur a Memoire (SECAM) 625 was developed in France and first used in 1967.

In addition to the "look" of film, there exists, naturally, a large talent pool of cameramen and directors of photography who understand the subtleties and range that film acquisition can offer. Often, comparisons are made between a scene shot on film and the same scene shot on video. During the 1999 U.S. television season, only two primetime shows were originated on video; all the rest were originated on film.

| **625 PAL** | **525 NTSC** | **625 SECAM** |
|---|---|---|
| ALGERIA | BAHAMAS | ALBANIA |
| ANDORRA | BARBADOS | BULGARIA |
| ARGENTINA | BERMUDA | CZECH REPUBLIC |
| AUSTRALIA | BOLIVIA | FRANCE |
| AUSTRIA | BRAZIL (PAL-M) | HAITI |
| BAHRAIN | BURMA | HUNGARY |
| BANGLADESH | CANADA | IRAN |
| BELGIUM | CHILE | IRAQ |
| BRUNEI | COSTA RICA | KOREA (NORTH) |
| CANARY ISLANDS | CUBA | LEBANON |
| CHINA | DOMINICAN REPUBLIC | MARTINIQUE |
| DENMARK | ECUADOR | MAURITIUS |
| FINLAND | GREENLAND | MONACO |
| GERMANY | GUAM | MOROCCO |
| GHANA | GUATEMALA | POLAND |
| GIBRALTAR | JAMAICA | ROMANIA |
| HONG KONG | JAPAN | SAUDI ARABIA |
| ICELAND | KOREA (SOUTH) | SENEGAL |
| INDIA | MEXICO | TAHITI |
| INDONESIA | NICARAGUA | TOGO |
| IRAN | PANAMA | TUNISIA |
| IRELAND | PERU | USSR |
| ISRAEL | PHILIPPINES | ZAIRE |
| ITALY | PUERTO RICO | |
| JORDAN | TAIWAN | |
| KENYA | TRINIDAD | |
| KUWAIT | TOBAGO | |
| LIBERIA | UNITED STATES | |
| LIBYA | VENEZUELA | |
| LUXEMBOURG | VIRGIN ISLANDS | |
| MALAYSIA | | |
| NETHERLANDS | | |
| NEW ZEALAND | | |
| NIGERIA | | |
| NORWAY | | |
| OMAN | | |
| PAKISTAN | | |
| PORTUGAL | | |
| QATAR | | |
| SIERRA LEONE | | |
| SINGAPORE | | |
| SOUTH AFRICA | | |
| SUDAN | | |
| SWITZERLAND | | |
| TANZANIA | | |
| THAILAND | | |
| TURKEY | | |
| UGANDA | | |
| UNITED ARAB EMIRATES | | |
| UNITED KINGDOM | | |
| ZAMBIA | | |

**Figure 11-1** A list of various countries and their respective use of different television transmission standards.

## FILM VERSUS HDTV

### Protection of Assets

Fueled by the demand for HDTV programming, program producers are concerned with protecting their assets. It is critical to the worldwide sale of programming that the program be delivered in a form acceptable to the international buyer who, as evidenced by Figure 11-1, may be in a country with a different broadcasting standard. Ultimately, program producers must ask themselves these questions:

Should I shoot my program on film or on video?

Should I shoot on film, the highest resolution acquisition format?

Should I shoot on video, and what type of video should I use?

Will high definition video protect my program as well as film?

### Costs

Prior to requiring a HDTV broadcast master, programs could be shot on film or on video. Ultimately, the viewing public watched a broadcast of an ITU-R 601 video master. Certainly, there were exceptions: we all can attest to viewing fantastic footage of hurricanes and other natural phenomena captured with consumer equipment.

The cost of HDTV delivery, in 2000 dollars, ranges from $20,000 to $30,000 per one-hour episode. Taking into account that a typical season's worth of programming per show is 22 episodes, creating a higher resolution master (higher than 601 video resolution) can add up to $660,000 per year to the cost of a program. Therefore a producer must choose the most economical form of acquisition in order to deliver any resolution that may be required for an international release, whether today or in the years to come.

### 2K and High-Definition Resolutions

In order to augment film acquisition, major manufacturers have created 24p electronic formats, which operate at HD data rates. For both new programming and the transfer of older, film-based programming, the use of 24p high definition videotape is rapidly replacing "conforming" the original film negative to create all the necessary distribution masters.

"2K" resolution is yet another format that has gained great popularity. This resolution is slightly higher than the 1920 × 1080 resolution of high definition. Whether the choice is made to work at 2K resolution (half the vertical resolution of Standard Academy 35mm film), or at the marginally lower 1920 × 1080 resolution, the result is that we can easily decide to distribute the final result on film for theatrical release or down-convert the program for broadcast in any of the formats for either standard or digital television.

### The Death of Film?

Does high-resolution, 2K electronic acquisition mean that originating images on film will cease? For the most part, film acquisition will not disappear. However, it is certainly true that shows that are currently videotape-based will more than likely begin to acquire on HD 24p electronic systems. In addition, lower-budget independent filmmakers may decide to make the switch to electronic HD acquisition. Again, the ability to create multistandard delivery masters or to transfer HD 24p images to film for theatrical exhibition will drive the change to electronic 24p.

Consider the program producer who is currently shooting a show using the 25- or 30-fps interlaced scanning method, recording the images to Betacam or Digital Betacam videotape. Normally, these programs do not have foreign distribution requirements. However, by switching to a tape-based 24-frame video format, producers can "future-proof" their programs for potential worldwide distribution.

### Why 24p?

Out of all the ATSC table formats, 1080/24p has been universally accepted as a production master format. Television productions based in Hollywood, California quickly accepted this format due to its close parallels to film acquisition and film postproduction processes. To provide further support of 1080/24p, at the 1999 Montreux Television Symposium, the International Television Union (ITU) voted that the common interchange format (CIF) for high-definition program content would be

- 1920 × 1080 resolution
- 24 frames per second
- Progressively scanned
- Aspect ratio of 16:9

## THE FOUR COMPONENTS OF FORMAT

Formats can be broken down into four categories:

1. Frame rate
2. Scan format
3. Resolution
4. Aspect ratio

### Frame Rate

Film can be shot at almost any frame rate but is usually exposed at 24 fps for theatrical and NTSC television programming or at 25 fps for PAL television programming. One of the adivantages of film as an acquisition format is that it can shoot at far higher frame rates than video formats. Currently, the highest rate for video is 60 fields per second interlaced for NTSC or 60 frames per second progressive using the 720p HDTV format. Shooting at these higher frame rates helps to create very high quality and smooth slow motion effects. Often this is helpful for analyzing fast motion events. Sporting events and natural phenomena are just some examples that can be viewed in greater detail at slower speeds.

But the main reason that most television programming is shot at 24 fps is because it is the theatrical frame rate standard around the world. 24 fps images can easily be transferred to NTSC (30 frames/60 fields) and PAL (25 frames/50 fields). For NTSC, the film is referenced to video (29.97 frames/59.94 fields), resulting in a frame rate of 23.976. Applying the difference between 30 fps and 29.97 (0.1%) to all elements derives this rate:

$$24 \text{ fps} \times 0.1\% \, (0.001) = 23.976 \text{ fps}$$

$$30 \text{ fps} \times 0.1\% \, (0.001) = 29.97 \text{ fps}$$

$$60 \text{ fps} \times 0.1\% \, (0.001) = 59.94 \text{ fps}$$

Once all the elements have been referenced to the same clock, a 2:3 pulldown is applied. This evenly converts 24 frames into 60 fields. For PAL, the film and audio is sped up 4.1% to create a running speed of 25 fps. Once this speed is created, the film and video have a 1:1 relationship to each other. This process is discussed in detail in Chapter seven. The resulting audio is pitched higher by one half semitone after this process. There are several devices that can be used to maintain correct pitch.

Both the NTSC and PAL methods are well known and professionals around the world are well versed with dealing with either format from the original 24fps material. Thus, any program content, whether a feature film or original television show can easily be converted to any broadcast standard. Of course, this situation remains applicable for HDTV broadcasts as well.

### Scan Format

Film, as we know, is a progressively scanned format. Scan formats are significant to the viewing format of a program. When we watch a standard television broadcast at home, the frames that we see are delivered in an interlaced format. This means that each frame is constructed by displaying the odd lines (1, 3, 5, etc.) first, then the even lines (2, 4, 6, etc.). The odd and even lines, when combined, create the single frame. While we most often refer to NTSC and PAL frame rates as, respectively, 30 fps and 25 fps, they are also measured at 60 fields per second (60 Hertz) and 50 fields per second (50 Hertz).

A major benefit of displaying and broadcasting in an interlaced format is that it acts as a form of compression, reducing the overall bandwidth required for delivering signals. The disadvantage is the associated loss of vertical resolution, known as the *interlace factor*. Some of the artifacts associated with this are loss of detail, caused by flicker. This can be seen along an object's horizontal edges as well as when objects are aligned diagonally. Sometimes these artifacts are referred to as *shimmer* and *glimmer*.

Images on a computer are drawn progressively. Frame one is drawn in its entirety, followed by frame two, and so on. Progressive video formats preserve the progressive nature of film but require more bandwidth for broadcast than interlaced video, assuming that both resolution and frame rate remain equal. A computer monitor displaying a 24-frame progressive image will most often have a refresh rate as a multiple of 24. As a rule, the higher the refresh rate, the better the picture quality. Most computer monitors will easily support a 72 Hz refresh rate—for every frame presented, the monitor refreshes three times $(3 \times 24 = 72)$.

### Resolution

The resolution of an image is usually measured in pixels across the horizontal axis ($x$) multiplied by the number of lines on the vertical axis ($y$). 1920 × 1080 refers to 1920 pixels by 1080 lines. Film resolutions are covered in chapters eight and nine.

With the landscape of terrestrial broadcasting rapidly changing, television is referred to as either standard definition television (SDTV) or high-definition television (HDTV). While definitions vary, it is generally accepted that HDTV offers roughly twice the resolution of SDTV on both the $x$- and $y$-axes.

## Aspect Ratio

The fourth element of format is aspect ratio. *Aspect* is defined as a ratio of horiozntal to vertical units. Thus, the standard television aspect ratio of 1.33:1 (commonly referred to as "one-three-three") or as a $x$-, $y$-axes coordinates 4:3 ("four by three"), refers to four horizontal units for every three vertical units. (When 4 is divided by 3, the result is 1.33.)

The two most common television broadcast standards are 4:3 (1.33:1) and 16:9 (1.78:1). Some European broadcasters have discussed using both 14:9 (1.55:1) and 15:9 (1.66:1) aspect ratios.

Film aspect ratios in use throughout the world include:

1.33—full aperture 35mm and 16mm

1.66—European theatrical projection

1.85—North American theatrical projection

2.35—Widescreen anamorphic / Super 35

## Aspect Rato Conversion

Anyone who has ever watched a theatrical film on a normal (4:3 aspect ratio) television has witnessed the difficulty of aspect ratio conversion. When a film has been shot in the 2.35 aspect ratio and is subsequently shown on a 1.33:1 television, the left and right sides of the widescreen picture are squeezed, thereby stretching the top and bottom of the picture: Actors become tall and skinnier for example, or where originally two actors appeared engaged in conversation, only one actor appears on screen while the other actor has been squeezed off (see figure 11-2).

Feature films being released to television and home video have, for years, had to address aspect ratio conversion. Pan & Scan (P&S) is one method of addressing this issue wherein select portions of the original material are reformatted for the target aspect ratio. Content producers today face a particular challenge as terrestrial broadcasting moves from a delivery ratio of 4:3 to 16:9. Many forward-thinking producers are already mastering in 16:9 and deriving

their 4:3 deliverables from the 16:9 master. Shown in figure 11-3 is a center crop, where the 4:3 image has taken directly from the center of the 16:9 master. Following are some terms common to aspect ratio conversion:

- Pan & Scan—Creates a 4:3 image from a 16:9 source. Source and target share common top and bottom; most cropping is horizontal. (See figure 11-4.)
- Tilt & Scan—Creates a 16:9 image from a 4:3 source. Source and target share common sides; most cropping is vertical. (See figure 11-5.)
- Letterbox—Maintains the original aspect ratio of the image inside the target ratio by adding black bars to the top and bottom of the frame. For displaying aspect ratios wider than 4:3 inside a 4:3 aspect ratio. (See figure 11-6.)
- Side bars—Maintains the aspect ratio of the original image inside the target ratio by adding black bars to the left and right sides of the frame. For displaying aspect ratios narrower than 16:9 inside a 16:9 aspect ratio. (See figure 11-7.)

## The 14:9 Aspect Ratio

The 14:9 aspect ratio is used to limit the amount of letterboxing caused when a 4:3 image is created from a

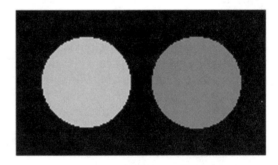

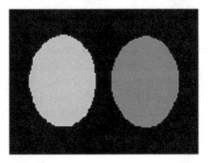

**Figure 11-2** The normal widescreen image and the image in a 1.33:1 aspect ratio. Note how the image has been squeezed, resulting in a loss of information.

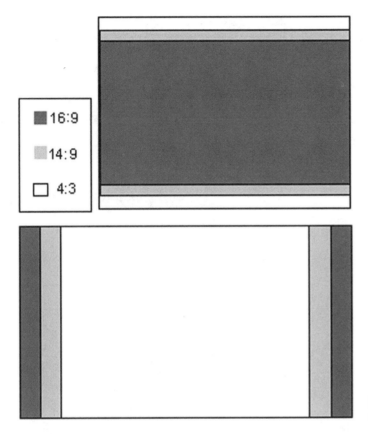

**Figure 11-3** In a center crop, the 4:3 image is taken directly from the center of the 16:9 master.

16:9 master. The 14:9 (1.55:1) aspect ratio provides for marginal top and bottom bands and is somewhat closer to the viewer's normal concept of 1.33:1 (4:3) versus the 16:9 (1.78:1) aspect ratio, with its thicker top and bottom bands. The use of 14:9 is particularly prevalent in the United Kingdom, where terrestrial broadcasters have agreed on these formatting types: the full 16:9 widescreen image, the 14:9 central zone, and the 4:3 central zone.

Since managing 16:9 and 4:3 is difficult, many UK broadcasters consider a 14:9 center cut-out letterbox image as the best compromise. Although the safe action area is 14:9, the safe title area is constrained to the centered 4:3 aspect ratio. UK broadcasters consider this to be a logical option during the transition from a 4:3 to 16:9 broadcast.

During the shooting stage, the camera operator frames the shots for a 16:9 widescreen release while simultaneously protecting action for the 14:9 aspect ratio. This means that anything essential must appear in the 14:9 grid within the 16:9 area. (See figure 11-8.)

During the postproduction process, the 14:9 version is derived from the 16:9 widescreen version and

then letterboxed into a 4:3 display. This provides some cut-off of the sides, which does not contain important information due to the 14:9 protection. The 14:9 (1.55:1) letterbox is not as wide as a full 16:9 (1.78:1) letterbox within the 4:3 (1.33:1) area.

## FILM-BASED AND 1080/24p WORKFLOW

Whether acquisition is done on film or on high-definition videotape, creating a high-resolution virtual electronic master follows this basic workflow. If the program has been acquired on film, the program is trransferred to as similar a format as possible within the electronic realm, the 1080/24p format. The 1080/24p format allows for a one-to-one relationship to the film in a progressive format. Essentially, it reduces the resolution of the original film by one-half, maintaining the native 24 frames-per-second rate and beginning the process of creating the virtual electronic master.

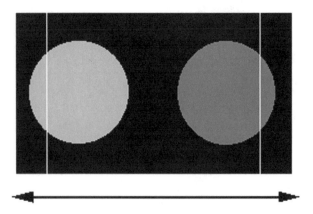

**Figure 11-4** Pan & Scan. Creates a 4:3 image from a 16:9 source. Source and target share common top and bottom; most cropping is horizontal.

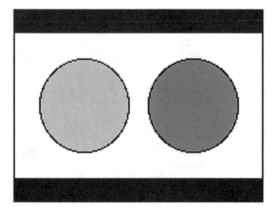

**Figure 11-6** Letterbox. Maintains the original aspect ratio of the image inside the target ratio by adding black bars to the top and bottom of the frame. For displaying aspect ratios wider than 4:3 inside a 4:3 aspect ratio.

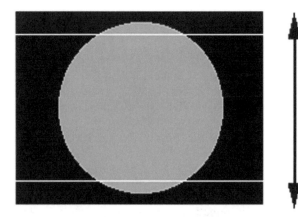

**Figure 11-5** Tilt & Scan. Creates a 16:9 image from a 4:3 source. Source and target share common sides; most cropping is vertical.

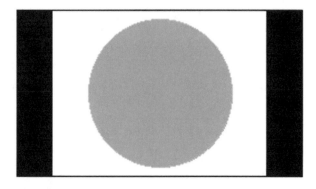

**Figure 11-7** Side bars. Maintains the aspect ratio of the original image inside the target ratio by adding black bars to the left and right sides of he frame. For displaying aspect ratios narrower than 16:9 inside a 16:9 aspect ratio.

There are several approaches in delivering 1080/24p technology to the marketplace. Sony and Panasonic have developed and delivered products that record and play back images at this resolution and frame rate. Digital nonlinear editing systems use hard disk storage to capture, edit, and play back these high-resolution images.

## Segmented Frames

As a footnote, there is an adjunct to 1080/24p which is referred to as 1080p/24sF. The "sF" refers to "segmented frames," whereby one film frame is transferred to two video fields. Over the course of 48 video fields, 24 complete frames are recorded (48 ÷ 2 = 24).

It should be noted that segmented frames has nothing to do with the interlacing of fields. Two separate segments always come from the same original progressive picture frame as transferred from the original film frame. In short, this means that there are no motion artifacts between these segmented frames. At any point in the total system they can be reassembled into a perfect 1080-line progressive frame. (See figure 11-9.)

## CREATING SDTV DOWN-CONVERTS FROM 1080/24p VIDEOTAPE

When the transfer process is complete, we exit with a 1080/24p tape(s), which can then be used to create the

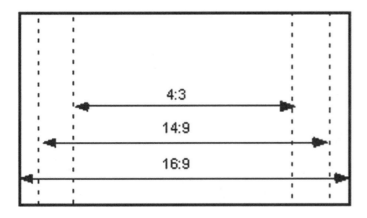

**Figure 11-8** A 14:9 grid within the 16:9 area can be used by the camera operator to frame shots for a 16:9 widescreen release while simultaneously protecting action for the 14:9 aspect ratio.

SDTV versions for delivery to the program buyers (networks, etc.). This down-conversion to SDTV can be accomplished by playing back the HD tape and routing the video signals through a real-time down-converter. Figure 11-10 shows a down-converter, which in real-time is able to simultaneously down-convert 1080/24p material to several different formats.

The actual process of creating an NTSC standard definition videotape from a 1080/24p videotape involves the insertion of 2:3 pulldown, making up the extra six frames required from 24 to 30 frames. To create a standard definition PAL videotape, the 24 fps material is sped up by 4.1%. During either the 2:3 insertion stage (NTSC) or the speed change (PAL), a reduction in image size is done. The 1920 × 1080 signal is scaled on both horizontal and vertical axes in order to deliver the ITU-R 601 image matrices of 720 × 486 (NTSC) and 720 × 576 (PAL).

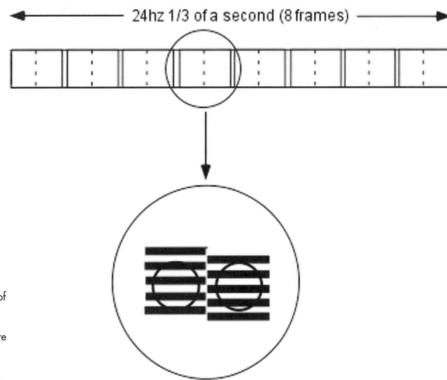

**Figure 11-9** The process of recording segmented frames. Over the course of 48 video fields, 24 complete frames are recorded. These are then reassembled into a perfect 1080-line progressive frame.

**Figure 11-10** A real-time down-converter, which can simultaneously down-convert 1080/24p material to several different formats. Photo supplied by Panasonic Broadcast & Television Systems.

Next, editing can occur using the down converted 601 resolution videotapes (they are really submasters of the original high-definition master). These 601 masters will be edited or augmented even more in order to accommodate the needs of multilanguage versioning and geographic-specific titling. These editorial processes can now be performed at 24, 25, or 30 fps.

## EDITING IN HIGH DEFINITION AND DERIVING THE SDTV SUBMASTERS FROM THE 1080/24p MASTER

Once the 601 masters are created, there are two ways to create the high-definition master. Shown in figure 11-11 is the generation of an edit decision list at a time base of 24 fps along with the translation to both 24-25 fps and 24-30 fps lists. This EDL is used in a traditional online tape-to-tape environment, where an edit controller is used to control two or more 1080/24p tape machines in order to reassemble the show in high definition. The final high-definition master can then be used to derive all the standard definition masters that may be required.

With the different possible combinations which constitute digital television and high-definition broadcast, creating a single postproduction master is very appealing to content creators. The first stage is to work at 24 fps. Whether one chooses to deliver a 24 fps 601 master in NTSC or PAL first or to create a

1080p/24 master and then down-convert to the 601 NTSC and PAL masters is, ultimately, a matter of workflow analysis and program delivery realities.

## INDUSTRY VIEWPOINTS

### Michael Tronick, A.C.E.

*Blue Streak* (1999), *Eraser* (1996), *Scent of A Woman* (1992), *Days of Thunder* (1990), *Midnight Run* (1988), *Beverly Hills Cop 2* (1994).

For Michael Tronick, A.C.E., there are clear advantages to using DNLE systems, culminating in the desire to exercise any creative option that he or his director may wish to entertain. Says, Tronick, an accomplished picture and sound editor,

Pictorially, the advantages of DNLE technology are many. The most obvious advantage is the speed of access to material. I used to live in fear of finding a trim or lift; now that problem is nonexistent. The saving of time is substantial, allowing me the opportunity to try several versions of a scene before finally moving on to the next. Sometimes the sheer physical effort involved in cutting picture and track contributed to a chilling effect of not wanting to pursue other avenues or make changes. Picture changes with the director in the room are more productive since the director can see the changes almost instantaneously. With film, a director would leave after giving me a list of changes and would return upon completion. This can be

**Figure 11-11** The generation of an edit decision list (EDL) at 24 fps along with the translation to both 24-25 fps and 24-30 fps lists.

**EDLs generated from the very same sequence edited at 24 fps. With a common base rate, EDLs can be generated for either PAL or NTSC. EDLs generated via Avid EDL Manager, courtesy Rob Bate.**

**TITLE: 24 FRAME SOURCE / 24 FRAME RECORD**
FCM: NON-DROP FRAME

| | | | | | | | |
|---|---|---|---|---|---|---|---|
| 001 | A001 | V | C | 01:00:51:08 | 01:01:12:05 | 01:00:00:00 | 01:00:20:21 |
| 002 | A001 | V | C | 01:02:11:07 | 01:02:29:00 | 01:00:20:21 | 01:00:38:14 |
| 003 | A001 | V | C | 01:03:23:18 | 01:04:10:19 | 01:00:38:14 | 01:01:25:15 |
| 004 | A001 | V | C | 01:04:57:19 | 01:05:26:08 | 01:01:25:15 | 01:01:54:04 |
| 005 | B001 | V | C | 02:01:30:19 | 02:02:09:04 | 01:01:54:04 | 01:02:32:13 |
| 006 | B001 | V | C | 02:03:07:04 | 02:03:39:01 | 01:02:32:13 | 01:03:04:10 |
| 007 | B001 | V | C | 02:04:44:18 | 02:05:16:11 | 01:03:04:10 | 01:03:36:03 |
| 008 | B001 | V | C | 02:05:59:06 | 02:06:38:15 | 01:03:36:03 | 01:04:15:12 |
| 009 | C001 | V | C | 03:01:21:02 | 03:01:41:19 | 01:04:15:12 | 01:04:36:05 |
| 010 | C001 | V | C | 03:02:24:10 | 03:02:44:07 | 01:04:36:05 | 01:04:56:02 |
| 011 | C001 | V | C | 03:03:36:20 | 03:04:05:09 | 01:04:56:02 | 01:05:24:15 |
| 012 | C001 | V | C | 03:04:50:05 | 03:05:37:06 | 01:05:24:15 | 01:06:11:16 |
| 013 | D001 | V | C | 04:06:57:05 | 04:07:36:14 | 01:06:11:16 | 01:06:51:01 |
| 014 | D001 | V | C | 04:02:24:14 | 04:04:11:23 | 01:06:51:01 | 01:08:38:10 |
| 015 | D001 | V | C | 04:04:58:23 | 04:06:01:08 | 01:08:38:10 | 01:09:40:19 |
| 016 | D001 | V | C | 04:06:55:00 | 04:08:07:06 | 01:09:40:19 | 01:10:53:01 |

**TITLE: 25 FRAME SOURCE / 25 FRAME RECORD**

| | | | | | | | |
|---|---|---|---|---|---|---|---|
| 001 | A001 | V | C | 01:00:49:07 | 01:01:10:04 | 01:00:00:00 | 01:00:20:01 |
| 002 | A001 | V | C | 01:02:06:01 | 01:02:23:19 | 01:00:20:01 | 01:00:37:01 |
| 003 | A001 | V | C | 01:03:15:15 | 01:04:02:16 | 01:00:37:01 | 01:01:22:05 |
| 004 | A001 | V | C | 01:04:45:22 | 01:05:14:11 | 01:01:22:05 | 01:01:49:15 |
| 005 | B001 | V | C | 02:01:27:04 | 02:02:05:13 | 01:01:49:15 | 01:02:26:11 |
| 006 | B001 | V | C | 02:02:59:17 | 02:03:31:14 | 01:02:26:11 | 01:02:57:01 |
| 007 | B001 | V | C | 02:04:33:09 | 02:05:05:02 | 01:02:57:01 | 01:03:27:12 |
| 008 | B001 | V | C | 02:05:44:22 | 02:06:24:06 | 01:03:27:12 | 01:04:05:07 |
| 009 | C001 | V | C | 03:01:17:21 | 03:01:38:14 | 01:04:05:07 | 01:04:25:04 |
| 010 | C001 | V | C | 03:02:18:16 | 03:02:38:13 | 01:04:25:04 | 01:04:44:06 |
| 011 | C001 | V | C | 03:03:28:04 | 03:03:56:18 | 01:04:44:06 | 01:05:11:16 |
| 012 | C001 | V | C | 03:04:38:15 | 03:05:25:16 | 01:05:11:16 | 01:05:56:20 |
| 013 | D001 | V | C | 04:06:40:13 | 04:07:19:22 | 01:05:56:20 | 01:06:34:15 |
| 014 | D001 | V | C | 04:02:18:20 | 04:04:06:04 | 01:06:34:15 | 01:08:17:17 |
| 015 | D001 | V | C | 04:04:47:00 | 04:05:49:09 | 01:08:17:17 | 01:09:17:14 |
| 016 | D001 | V | C | 04:06:38:10 | 04:07:50:16 | 01:09:17:14 | 01:10:26:23 |

**TITLE:30 FRAME SOURCE / 30 FRAME RECORD**
FCM: NON-DROP FRAME

| | | | | | | | |
|---|---|---|---|---|---|---|---|
| 001 | A001 | V | C | 01:00:51:10 | 01:01:12:06 | 01:00:00:00 | 01:00:20:26 |
| 002 | A001 | V | C | 01:02:11:09 | 01:02:29:01 | 01:00:20:26 | 01:00:38:18 |
| 003 | A001 | V | C | 01:03:23:23 | 01:04:10:24 | 01:00:38:18 | 01:01:25:19 |
| 004 | A001 | V | C | 01:04:57:24 | 01:05:26:10 | 01:01:25:19 | 01:01:54:05 |
| 005 | B001 | V | C | 02:01:30:24 | 02:02:09:05 | 01:01:54:05 | 01:02:32:16 |
| 006 | B001 | V | C | 02:03:07:05 | 02:03:39:02 | 01:02:32:16 | 01:03:04:13 |
| 007 | B001 | V | C | 02:04:44:22 | 02:05:16:13 | 01:03:04:13 | 01:03:36:04 |
| 008 | B001 | V | C | 02:05:59:08 | 02:06:38:19 | 01:03:36:04 | 01:04:15:15 |
| 009 | C001 | V | C | 03:01:21:02 | 03:01:41:23 | 01:04:15:15 | 01:04:36:06 |
| 010 | C001 | V | C | 03:02:24:13 | 03:02:44:10 | 01:04:36:06 | 01:04:56:03 |

| 011 | C001 | V | C | 03:03:36:25 | 03:04:05:11 | 01:04:56:03 | 01:05:24:19 |
| 012 | C001 | V | C | 03:04:50:06 | 03:05:37:07 | 01:05:24:19 | 01:06:11:20 |
| 013 | D001 | V | C | 04:06:57:06 | 04:07:36:17 | 01:06:11:20 | 01:06:51:01 |
| 014 | D001 | V | C | 04:02:24:17 | 04:04:11:29 | 01:06:51:01 | 01:08:38:13 |
| 015 | D001 | V | C | 04:04:58:29 | 04:06:01:10 | 01:08:38:13 | 01:09:40:24 |
| 016 | D001 | V | C | 04:06:55:00 | 04:08:07:07 | 01:09:40:24 | 01:10:53:01 |

### TITLE: 24 FRAME SOURCE / 30 FRAME RECORD
FCM: NON-DROP FRAME

| 001 | A001 | V | C | 01:00:51:08 | 01:01:12:05 | 01:00:00:00 | 01:00:20:26 |
| 002 | A001 | V | C | 01:02:11:07 | 01:02:29:01 | 01:00:20:26 | 01:00:38:18 |
| 003 | A001 | V | C | 01:03:23:18 | 01:04:10:19 | 01:00:38:18 | 01:01:25:19 |
| 004 | A001 | V | C | 01:04:57:19 | 01:05:26:08 | 01:01:25:19 | 01:01:54:05 |
| 005 | B001 | V | C | 02:01:30:19 | 02:02:09:04 | 01:01:54:05 | 01:02:32:16 |
| 006 | B001 | V | C | 02:03:07:04 | 02:03:39:02 | 01:02:32:16 | 01:03:04:13 |
| 007 | B001 | V | C | 02:04:44:18 | 02:05:16:11 | 01:03:04:13 | 01:03:36:04 |
| 008 | B001 | V | C | 02:05:59:06 | 02:06:38:15 | 01:03:36:04 | 01:04:15:15 |
| 009 | C001 | V | C | 03:01:21:02 | 03:01:41:19 | 01:04:15:15 | 01:04:36:06 |
| 010 | C001 | V | C | 03:02:24:10 | 03:02:44:08 | 01:04:36:06 | 01:04:56:03 |
| 011 | C001 | V | C | 03:03:36:20 | 03:04:05:09 | 01:04:56:03 | 01:05:24:19 |
| 012 | C001 | V | C | 03:04:50:05 | 03:05:37:06 | 01:05:24:19 | 01:06:11:20 |
| 013 | D001 | V | C | 04:06:57:05 | 04:07:36:14 | 01:06:11:20 | 01:06:51:01 |
| 014 | D001 | V | C | 04:02:24:14 | 04:04:12:00 | 01:06:51:01 | 01:08:38:13 |
| 015 | D001 | V | C | 04:04:58:23 | 04:06:01:08 | 01:08:38:13 | 01:09:40:24 |
| 016 | D001 | V | C | 04:06:55:00 | 04:08:07:06 | 01:09:40:24 | 01:10:53:01 |

### TITLE: 24 FRAME SOURCE / 25 FRAME RECORD

| 001 | A001 | V | C | 01:00:51:08 | 01:01:12:05 | 01:00:00:00 | 01:00:20:01 |
| 002 | A001 | V | C | 01:02:11:07 | 01:02:29:00 | 01:00:20:01 | 01:00:37:01 |
| 003 | A001 | V | C | 01:03:23:18 | 01:04:10:19 | 01:00:37:01 | 01:01:22:05 |
| 004 | A001 | V | C | 01:04:57:19 | 01:05:26:08 | 01:01:22:05 | 01:01:49:15 |
| 005 | B001 | V | C | 02:01:30:19 | 02:02:09:04 | 01:01:49:15 | 01:02:26:11 |
| 006 | B001 | V | C | 02:03:07:04 | 02:03:39:01 | 01:02:26:11 | 01:02:57:01 |
| 007 | B001 | V | C | 02:04:44:18 | 02:05:16:11 | 01:02:57:01 | 01:03:27:12 |
| 008 | B001 | V | C | 02:05:59:06 | 02:06:38:15 | 01:03:27:12 | 01:04:05:07 |
| 009 | C001 | V | C | 03:01:21:02 | 03:01:41:19 | 01:04:05:07 | 01:04:25:04 |
| 010 | C001 | V | C | 03:02:24:10 | 03:02:44:07 | 01:04:25:04 | 01:04:44:06 |
| 011 | C001 | V | C | 03:03:36:20 | 03:04:05:09 | 01:04:44:06 | 01:05:11:16 |
| 012 | C001 | V | C | 03:04:50:05 | 03:05:37:06 | 01:05:11:16 | 01:05:56:20 |
| 013 | D001 | V | C | 04:06:57:05 | 04:07:36:14 | 01:05:56:20 | 01:06:34:15 |
| 014 | D001 | V | C | 04:02:24:14 | 04:04:11:23 | 01:06:34:15 | 01:08:17:17 |
| 015 | D001 | V | C | 04:04:58:23 | 04:06:01:08 | 01:08:17:17 | 01:09:17:14 |
| 016 | D001 | V | C | 04:06:55:00 | 04:08:07:06 | 01:09:17:14 | 01:10:26:23 |

both counterproductive at times as well as costly in terms of time. Although I do enjoy solitude when working, sometimes to really work out a situation, the immediate feedback of the director is extremely valuable, especially on a project with an accelerated postproduction schedule.

Tronick, who in addition to his extensive picture-editing skills has several music and sound effects editing credits, sees distinct advantages to the ability to manipulate sound within the DNLE system. Says Tronick,

Sound-wise, the ability to run several tracks (i.e., dialog, sound effects, and music) makes for a much better presentation of my cut to the director. Film was more limiting; with an eight-plate KEM, I only had room for two tracks. With the Avid, the flexibility is much greater. Just being able to add a simple background track made from existing material to smooth out dialog is very useful. With film, I would have to order reprints from sound transfer. The downside is that sometimes the picture is over-burdened with sound work, and inevitably the Avid tracks have a way of showing up on the dubbing stage. However, there is a tendency by some directors to perfect the audio on the Avid instead of leaving more of the sound work to the sound and music editors.

For Tronick, introducing directors who have never worked with DNLE technology provokes some interesting reactions. Says Tronick,

> The reaction of directors to this technology has been unanimously favorable. Martin Brest was very skeptical on *Meet Joe Black*, because he was accustomed to the subtle nuances he could see on film. Given the amount of film he shot (over a million feet of printed film) and seeing the flexibility of saving different versions of the cut, he became an instant fan of "the robot," as he nicknamed our Avid. For visual effects, the ability to mock up temp composites gives the director an immediate indication of the evolution of a shot. The only drawback, besides resolution, is that on a KEM, you are constantly winding and rewinding takes and it gives the director a chance to review material as you search. With the Avid, you merely point and click and you are there. But that is a minor drawback.

Tronick, who has edited several films that include memorable visual special effects shots, sees clear advantages of DNLE technology in assisting previsualization. Says Tronick,

> The new technology has allowed me to replace the infamous "shot missing" banner with everything from scanned storyboards, to animatronic sequences, to temporary composites. The interface with visual effects supervisors can begin much sooner in the editorial process, as we can import material from visual effects sooner and start shaping a scene. As new versions of a shot come in, we usually import them immediately and are able to give the supervisor feedback to speed the process along and save valuable postproduction time. I can also mock up my own visual effects when necessary and submit them to the visual effects department. On a less technical note, but just as important, shots that I might not use because of some visual flaw can be considered now, due to digital technology (e.g., scratch removal, or painting out an unwanted prop or microphone). The number of feature films without visual effects shots of some type are almost nonexistent.

Tronick, who has worked exclusively with feature films that have acquired their images on film and been exhibited on film, sees specific advantages of an all-digital process:

> I have not had any experience with originating on digital video and delivering on film, but from tests I have seen at Sony Pictures, it is a very promising development. It really depends on the old tradition of screening dailies on film and if you can get the director of photography and director to get on board with the resolution and look of digital video. I'm sure it is only a matter of time before sprocket holes…are obsolete. I think it will streamline the work in the cutting room, causing substantial changes in the methodology of how assistant editors work. The implications on the traditional cutting room are staggering.

Adds Tronick finally,

> Digital nonlinear editing is the greatest achievement in postproduction that I have experienced in over twenty years in the cutting room. I am privileged to be a part of the revolution and to be able to utilize the new technology in my work. There are dangers of too much access to the material and certain abuses of the technology that we should be cautious and aware of. But what few disadvantages exist are far outweighed by the genius in the operation and design of the system.

# 12 Digital Television and Electronic Cinema

## DIGITAL TELEVISION

It is often, and incorrectly, assumed that the words *digital television* mean, by extension, high-definition television (HDTV). This is not the case. Rather, digital television refers to signals transmitted as digital ones and zeroes that are then decoded into pictures and sounds. This dual meaning is encapsulated by the abbreviation H/DTV. Analog television, which most of us have grown up with, is based on sending and receiving analog signals—waves that vary in their amplitude and frequency. Many television and broadcasting industry representatives believe the movement from analog to digital television is as significant as the change from vinyl records to compact discs.

Whereas developing and delivering analog television signals can only be used to watch and receive analog signals, digital television has unique features specifically enabled by the fact that the signals are digital in nature. For example, because digital signals are all encoded as ones and zeroes, additional items can be sent and received. With digital television the viewer can listen to 5.1 discreet channels of CD quality audio, as opposed to the stereo delivery of analog television. Digital signals make it possible for the viewer to receive more varied digital information, say in the form of an electronic delivery of a magazine subscription. This additional programming is often referred to as *ancillary* or *opportunistic data*, or *data packets*. Many of these nontraditional, alternative delivery mechanisms are a result of digital television. First, however, it is helpful to understand a short history of digital television.

## HISTORY

By the mid-1980s, Japanese broadcasters were already delivering high-definition television to consumers. Cameras, recording equipment, and television sets worked together to create stunning imagery. The actual length and width of the picture was larger than standard definition television (SDTV), and the number of vertical lines of resolution was increased. As a result, viewers reported a deeper, almost participatory experience.

The American broadcasting and legislative communities grew increasingly alarmed. It the minds of many, analog television would soon be overtaken by digital television, and it became obvious America needed to develop systems that could compete with the sole Japanese supplier. By 1987, the U.S. Federal Communications Commission (FCC) convened and formed the Advisory Committee on Advanced Television Service (ACATS). By 1990, the idea of advanced television had given way to the notion of a completely digital television pathway. Throughout the early 1990s, systems were created, tested, discarded, and evolved. In December 1996, the ATSC made specific recommendations regarding the broadcasting of digital television in both standard definition and high definition.

### The Schedule

The FCC has mandated a specific schedule regarding when television broadcasters must make the transition to digital television. U.S.-based television broadcasters were granted licenses to broadcast on a digital television channel with the understanding that they would, eventually, return their license to broadcast on an analog channel. Presumably, these analog channels would eventually be granted for other communications, such as telephone and paging services and so forth. The FCC schedule is as follows:

November 1998  Digital television (DTV) commences in the top ten U.S. markets.

May, 1999   All commercial stations in the top ten U.S. markets must transmit a digital picture.

November, 1999   Commercial stations in the top 30 U.S. markets must transmit a digital picture. These markets cover almost 50% of U.S. households.

April, 2003   50% of programming must be carried on a station's DTV channel.

May, 2003   All public television broadcasting must be converted to digital.

April, 2004   At least 75% of programming must be carried on a station's DTV channel.

April, 2005   100% of programming must be carried on a station's DTV channel.

December, 2006   Analog channel must be returned to the FCC.

## DEFINITIONS AND STANDARDS

The difference between analog signals and digital signals is clear. What is the difference between standard definition television signals and high definition signals? The accepted answer to this question is that high definition is defined as being at least twice the definition of standard definition television systems. In NTSC countries, such as the United States, standard definition television consists of 525 lines of resolution made up of interlaced fields at 59.94 Hz. In PAL countries, such as Italy, standard signals consist of 625 lines of resolution, made up of interlaced fields at 50 Hz. In 1999, the Society of Motion Picture and Television Engineers (SMPTE) proposed and adopted ITU-R B.T. 709, establishing that as the common image format (CIF) for high-definition programming. This is set at a resolution of 1920 × 1080, though the issue of frame rates, scan type, and so forth were left open to interpretation.

Thus, a television system consisting of 1080 horizontal lines of interlaced fields would qualify as being a high definition resolution. There are typically four categories to keep in mind when examining digital television: picture resolution, aspect ratio, scan format, and frame rate.

## Picture Resolution

The resolution of a picture is measured in horizontal and vertical pixels. Within one frame of 35mm Academy format film, there are approximately 4000 horizontal pixels and 3000 vertical pixels. Additionally, the amount of bits-per-pixel can be used to calculate the overall resolution of an image.

## Aspect Ratio

The aspect ratio of a viewing system can vary. Analog televisions have an aspect ratio of 4 × 3 (1.33:1), which means that for every four units across, there are three units down. DTV sets, however, have a standard aspect ratio of 16 × 9, resulting in a wider picture. (See figure 12-1.)

## Scan Format

Video signals consist of two fields of alternatingly scanned lines which are then interlaced to create a viewable frame. Thus, each field contains only one-half the total information required by the frame. With progressive scanning, the entire frame is displayed at the same time and in totality. In many cases, depending on the content, a freeze frame from an interlaced scanned image will bear marked aliasing characteristics over its progressively scanned counterpart. Interlaced is abbreviated I/i and progressive is abbreviated P/p.

## Frame Rate

Film runs at a standard 24 frames per second (fps). NTSC video runs at a standard rate of 29.97 fps. PAL video runs at a standard 25 fps. High-definition television systems provide for a variety of frame rates.

Table 12-1 is a recreation of ATSC Table 3, which shows the various combinations that can be used to deliver digital television. Note that 24, 30, and 60 frames per second within the NTSC system translate to, respectively, and additionally, 23.98, 29.97, and 59.94 fps.

Reading across the table, we can see, for example, that the first entry has a resolution of 1920 pixels by 1080 lines, has an aspect ratio of 16:9, provides for different frame rates, utilizes square pixels, and is progressively scanned. The pixel count qualifies this resolution as a high-definition television resolution. Contrast this to the last example, where the 640 pixels by 480 lines do not amount to the required pixels for high-definition television. In the middle of the table, the 704 × 480 resolution qualifies this as standard definition digital television.

**Figure 12-1** A television monitor in 16:9 aspect ratio. Photo supplied by Panasonic Broadcast & Television Systems.

Using this table, a broadcaster can choose a combination that complies in providing digital television to the consumer. However, for our purposes a comparison to film is necessary. Film, as we know, in the 35mm format, consists of

Picture resolution: roughly 4000 pixels by 3000 rows

Aspect ratio: varies, anamorphic versus flat

Frame rate: can be captured up to 12,000 fps; runs at a standard 24 fps.

Scan format: progressive

With this information, we can compare film to one of the HDTV formats:

Picture resolution: 1920 pixels by 1080 rows

Aspect ratio: 16:9

Frame rate: varies
Scan format: progressive

## HDTV DATA RATES

The HDTV signal is enormous compared to its standard definition counterpart:

HDTV = 1920 × 1080 at 30i = 2,073,600 pixels/frame

4:2:2 sampling for Y:Cr:Cb = 2 bytes/pixel = 4,147,200 bytes/frame

0 frames/sec = 125Mbytes/sec or 995,328,000 bits or one Gigabit/sec

HDTV = 1280 × 720 at 60p = 921,600 pixels/frame

4:2:2 sampling for Y:Cr:Cb = 2 bytes/pixel = 1,843,200 bytes/frame

60 frames/sec = 110,592,000 bytes/sec or 884,736,000 bits/sec

SDTV = 720 × 480 at 30i = 345,600 pixels/frame

4:2:2 sampling for Y:Cr:Cb = 2 bytes/pixel = 691,200 bytes/frame

30 frames/sec = 20,736,000 bytes/sec or 165,888,000 bits/sec

Thus the difference between HDTV and SDTV uncompressed images is approximately 6:1. Further, taking into account that HD signals are transmitted in packets of data (packetized), some additional space is

| Horizontal Size | Vertical Size | Aspect Ratio | Pixel Type | Frame Rate | Scan |
|---|---|---|---|---|---|
| 1920 | 1080 | 16:9 | Square | 24 frames | Progressive |
| 1920 | 1080 | 16:9 | Square | 30 frames | Progressive |
| 1920 | 1080 | 16:9 | Square | 60 fields | Interlaced |
| 1280 | 720 | 16:9 | Square | 24 frames | Progressive |
| 1280 | 720 | 16:9 | Square | 30 frames | Progressive |
| 1280 | 720 | 16:9 | Square | 60 frames | Progressive |
| 704 | 480 | 4:3 | Nonsquare | 24 frames | Progressive |
| 704 | 480 | 4:3 | Nonsquare | 30 frames | Progressive |
| 704 | 480 | 4:3 | Nonsquare | 60 frames | Progressive |
| 704 | 480 | 4:3 | Nonsquare | 60 fields | Interlaced |
| 704 | 480 | 16:9 | Nonsquare | 24 frames | Progressive |
| 704 | 480 | 16:9 | Nonsquare | 30 frames | Progressive |
| 704 | 480 | 16:9 | Nonsquare | 60 frames | Progressive |
| 704 | 480 | 16:9 | Nonsquare | 60 fields | Interlaced |
| 640 | 480 | 4:3 | Square | 24 frames | Progressive |
| 640 | 480 | 4:3 | Square | 30 frames | Progressive |
| 640 | 480 | 4:3 | Square | 60 frames | Progressive |
| 640 | 480 | 4:3 | Square | 60 fields | Interlaced |

**Table 12-1** The various possible combinations to deliver digital television.

required. Therefore, an uncompressed HD stream requires approximately 1.2Gbits/second.

## Picture Encoding

The method by which analog signals are converted to digital is the digitization process. Once these signals exist in digital form, they can be manipulated in either an uncompressed or compressed form. With HD signals, the data rate is quite large. A standard NTSC picture at 525 lines at 29.97 fps requires a 3.35 MHz carrier. However, at roughly six times the information, the same image in HD would require an 18 MHz carrier. Because digital channel allocations do not provide for that high rate (they maximize at 6 MHz), compression must be used. This is accomplished through the use of MPEG encoding (see chapter eight). The specific encoding methodology uses MPEG-2 standards, which provides for a variable data rate of between 1.2 and 15 Mbits/sec.

## Audio Encoding

The audio portion of a program is also digitized and encoded. Digital television consists of 5.1 discrete channels of audio: left, center, right, left rear, right rear, and a subwoofer channel, which is considered a subchannel (the .1) due to limited bandwidth. The audio signals of a digital television program are encoded using a compression algorithm from Dolby Laboratories, referred to as Dolby Digital/AC-3, at a compression ratio of roughly 13:1. The AC-3 audio and the compressed picture elements are then sent to the transmitter.

## The Transmitter

An HD signal at approximately 1.2 Gbits/sec is compressed at a ratio of about 66:1 (approximately 18 Mbits) in order to squeeze it into the 19.4-Mbit transmission channel. These signals are then available for decoding by the receiving television. HDTV sets can decode any format and combination. Additionally, special converter units are available that can receive digital transmissions on analog television sets, although the viewer will not receive the benefits of high definition signals.

## Uncompressed and Compressed HDTV

An HD video signal at 1920 × 1080/30i, sampled in 4:2:2 (luminance: chroma difference signals) requires almost 7.5 GBytes/minute.

As with any production and postproduction system, there are different methods of recording and manipulating HDTV. One can choose to work with completely uncompressed frames, at a data rate of 1.2Gbits/sec. However, some manufacturers have chosen to offer both uncompressed as well as compressed HDTV equipment. The compressed versions of HDTV vary, but they typically fall between 143 Mbit/sec. to 270 Mbit/sec systems.

We can compress our original signal, which would require 7.5 Gbytes/minute, using a 4:1 ratio, yielding a data rate of 1.8 GBytes/minute. To calculate the storage requirements for one hour of 4:1compressed HD we calculate:

$$1.8 \text{ GBytes/min} \times 60 \text{ min} = 108 \text{ GBytes/hr}$$

Compressing an HD signal at a ratio of 4:1 usually preserves the high-frequency areas, which hold information on highly detailed portions of the picture, while reducing the overall data rate. Visually, it would be impossible to tell that the image has been compressed. Further, building an infrastructure around marginally compressed HD (4:1) requires less capital investment than constructing the same room to support fully uncompressed HD.

Figure 12-2 shows a videotape recorder (VTR) capable of recording a compressed HD signal. Again, the main advantage in compressing the full-bandwidth HD signal is to save storage space and to decrease networking and transmission requirements. There are varying opinions regarding when uncompressed versus compressed HD should be used. Many industry experts state that compressed HD is perfectly acceptable for broadcast but is most likely inappropriate for postproduction work, especially when the amount of layering or compositing of images is significant.

## DIGITAL NONLINEAR HIGH-DEFINITION EDITING SYSTEMS

In 1989, when the average price for a 600 MB disk was $9000, a digital nonlinear editing system capable of manipulating even compressed HD pictures would have been an extremely difficult product to justify. Within a decade, however, the cost of an 18 GB drive hovered close to $1000. This represents a 30-fold increase in storage along with an almost ten-fold decrease in price! Clearly, the price-versus-minute

**Figure 12-2** The Phillips Voodoo Media Recorder, which supports 24p and 24sF, as well as other ATSC Table 3 formats. Photo courtesy Maskus Ostertag.

relationship of digital disk to videotape seems to be reaching equity. In fact, some videotape manufacturers claim that the cost of one minute of digital disk storage to one minute of videotape storage will equalize somewhere in the 2003–2004 time period.

As a result of this increase in capacity and decrease in cost, digital nonlinear editing systems that operate at both full-bandwidth uncompressed HD as well as at compressed HD levels began to appear in 1999. These systems, depending on which version of uncompressed HD is incorporated, must move a massive amount of data. In contrast to standard definition's 22 Mbytes/sec (ITU-R 601), interlaced HD at 1920 × 1080 at 30i consumes as much as 125 Mbytes/sec, almost six times as much data. Figure 12-3 shows a high-definition digital nonlinear editing system.

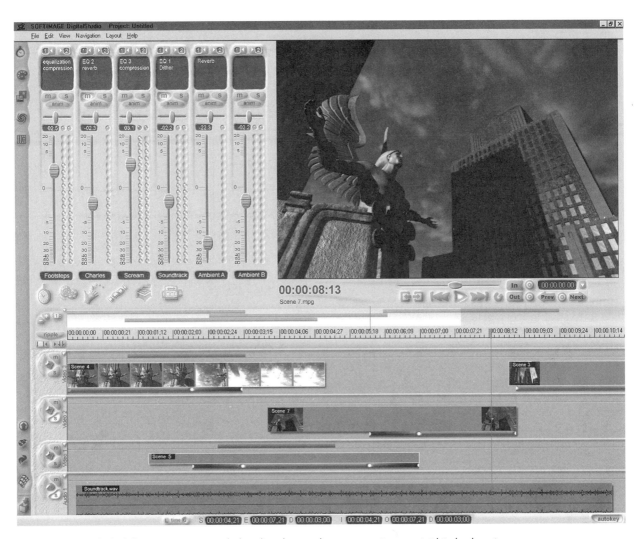

**Figure 12-3** A high-definition, uncompressed, digital nonlinear editing system. Courtesy Avid Technology, Inc.

## EDITING FOR 16:9 AND 4:3

While cameras are switchable between 16:9 and 4:3 aspect ratios, it is especially important to realize that there are decisions to be made when editing programming for 16:9 and 4:3 content. For example, look at figure 12-4: Where should the edit be made—when the figure appears in the 16:9 frame or when the character appears in the 4:3 frame? The character may actually appear several frames or seconds later within the 4:3 frame. While the answer to this question may seem obvious, one can quickly understand the complexity of editing shows in both aspect ratios. This is one of the main reasons why most program creators who are originating on either film or widescreen HD use a center grid to determine the 4:3 safe action area. When it is time to edit, decisions are made when the character is within the confines of the 4:3 area.

## DOWN-CONVERSION

Down-conversion is to the method of extrapolating a smaller image size (raster) from a larger image size. For example, let's say that we are creating a movie-of-the-week for television and instead of originating on film, we are originating on HD. As shown in figure 12-5, by first creating a high-definition master, we can deliver the various standard definition masters,

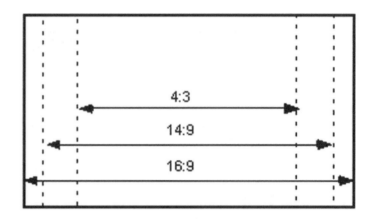

**Figure 12-4** A center 4:3 grid embedded within the 16:9 image can be used to determine where to make critical editing decisions.

taking into account that different aspect ratios may also be required.

In this case, we are originating on a HD system at 1920 × 1080 at 30i (30 fps, interlaced). As we know, it is important to deliver a range of master videotapes at the conclusion of the process: We require the HD version as well as the standard definition version, and we must deliver in both the 16:9 and 4:3 aspect ratios. By reducing the pixel count on the horizontal axis by 2.66:1 and on the vertical access by 2.25:1, we get an image measuring 720 × 480 at 30i, which will fulfill our standard definition television requirements.

The derivation of standard definition images as a result of a down-conversion process from HD images is generally thought to be superior to images originally captured on standard definition equipment.

## UP-CONVERSION

Up-conversion, also known as up-rezing (or increasing the resolution) can also be used to create HD programming from standard definition programming. Why might a program-maker choose to take this approach? One reason is budgetary concerns: It may simply be cheaper and more cost-effective to originate on standard definition equipment and up-rez it to HD. Another important reason is that the program material may only exist in standard definition. For example, a program-maker may be creating a documentary for HD that consists of archival standard definition material; in this instance, the only possibility is to up-convert the material.

Whether down-conversion or up-conversion is used, we can assume that ITU-R 601 SDTV will exist in these forms:

1. As down-converted HDTV: 1920 × 1080 at 30i or 1280 × 720 at 60p
2. As uncompressed SDTV: 720 × 480 at 30i. This would exist on common videotape formats such as D1 or D5.
3. As compressed SDTV. This would exist on common videotape formats such as Digital Betacam, DVCPro 25/50 Mbits/sec, and so forth.

As stated earlier, the creation of SD images from an HD down-convert yields very acceptable if not superior results as compared to original SD acquisition. However, HD images up-converted from SD images will not yield greater definition (sharpness) than the original SD images. If we use our rule of a pixel difference from HD to SD on the order of 6:1, the HD image will be no better than the original SD image used to create the HD version.

Despite these factors, the program-maker may be in a position where up-conversion is necessary. With regard to aspect ratio matching, he or she may have additional decisions to make. Figure 12-6 shows common aspect ratios and the results of attempting to fit traditional 1.33:1 material into a larger matrix. Second from left in the top row is a 1.33:1 image fit into a 1.77:1 aspect ratio. 1.77:1 translates into the 16:9 aspect ratio of HD. In order to fit this image into the screen, black bands (called side panels) are added on the left and right sides of the screen.

An alternative to using side panels is to stretch the 1.33:1 images horizontally to fit them into the 16:9 aspect ratio. The resulting image does, indeed, fit the entire screen, but the distortion may be unacceptable. This situation lends itself to Pan & Scan process.

Conversely, the bottom row in figure 12-6 shows various widescreen aspect ratios and their relationship to the 1.33:1 aspect ratio. Here the top and bottom bands preserve the aspect ratio of the widescreen picture within the 1.33:1 aspect ratio. This situation lends itself to the Pan & Tilt process.

## 14:9 AND 15:9 ASPECT RATIOS

Broadcasters all over the world, through countless surveys and seminars, have essentially come to the conclusion that the majority of their clients—that is

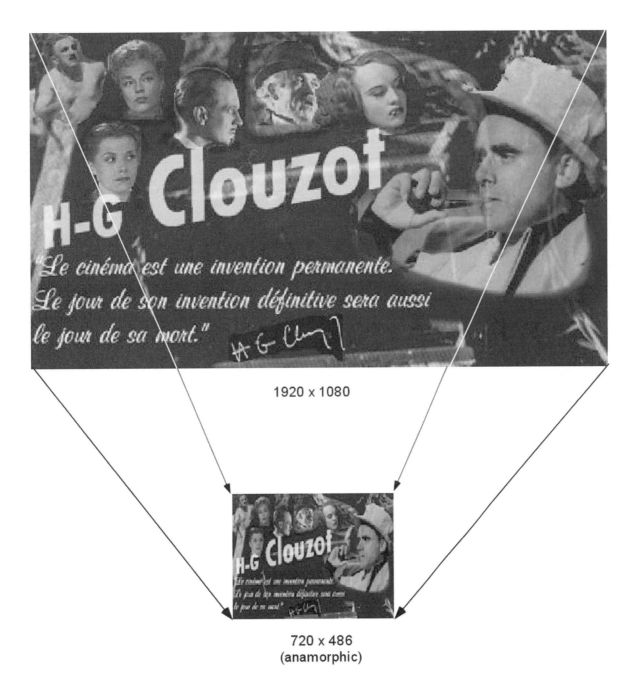

1920 x 1080

720 x 486
(anamorphic)

**Figure 12-5** The process of down-conversion yields smaller images from a larger image.

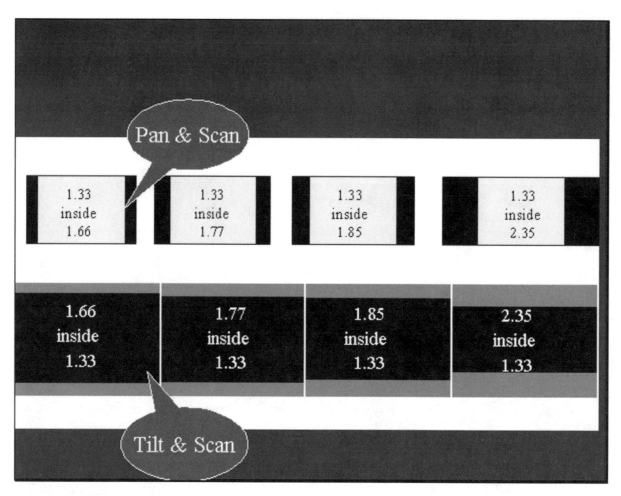

**Figure 12-6** The relationship of the 1.33:1 ratio fitting within widescreen aspect ratios (top row), and the relationship of widescren aspect ratios fitting within the 1.33:1 aspect ratio (bottom row).

their viewers—do not wish to see letterboxed images on their home sets. How, then, can they show 16:9 programming on a 4:3 television set?

One possible answer is to reduce the amount of letterboxing that occurs. With a 14:9 aspect ratio, slight letterboxing results in some loss of the 16:9 sides but yields a result closer to what most viewers are accustomed to seeing. Less loss occurs with the 15:9 aspect ratio. Both of these methodologies are being tried and tested at various sites around the world.

## WIDESCREEN SD TO WIDESCREEN HD

When it is deemed appropriate to shoot SD images for later up-conversion to HD, it is prudent to match the shooting aspect ratio with the display aspect ratio. Shooting a program in SD, but in widescreen, 16:9

avoids the messy alternative of side paneling or horizontal stretching to fit the widescreen television monitor. The combination of stretching and cropping the original SD image would further compound the quality issue when up-rezing to HD.

In shooting widescreen SD, there are four potential delivery possibilities:

1. Delivery as SD widescreen.
2. Delivery as SD 4:3 center cut. A static, center cut is taken of the widescreen SD image in order to deliver a 1.33:1 aspect ratio (figure 12-4). During shooting, the camera operator keeps the important information within the center 4:3 confines of the screen. This is sometimes referred to as *protecting for 4:3*.
3. Delivery as SD 4:3 Pan & Scan. The widescreen image is panned from left to right in order to

maintain focus on critical elements of the image during appropriate times (figure 12-7).

4. Delivery as HD widescreen. The widescreen SD image is up-converted to a widescreen HD image.

## SERIAL DIGITAL TRANSPORT INTERFACE (SDTI)

The method of routing the digital files that make up a HD transport stream can vary. For example, HD videotape machines typically have three methods of output: as an uncompressed full-bandwidth HD signal, as a real-time ITU-R 601 down-convert, and as a digital bit-stream. With the first two, we can see video in real time. With the latter, the digital information is used to transport the data from one location to the next.

Serial digital transport interface (SDTI) supports faster-than-real-time transfers among devices at up to 360 Mbits/sec. Thus, when HD data is moved around, as would be the case in taking HD images and manipulating them in a digital nonlinear editing or graphics system, the method by which one could stay completely digital would be to use the SDTI output/input as the means of interfacing the two pieces of equipment.

## FILM ACQUISITION VERSUS HIGH DEFINITION ACQUISITION

Film versus video is an issue that has been hotly debated for years. Film, with its wide contrast ratio, flickering progressive frame rate, and grain pattern, provides a better viewing experience than video. But as advances are made in high-definition equipment, many filmmakers are looking once again at shooting on high-definition video. The question, "how much resolution is enough," takes on greater importance in any such discussion.

The truth of the matter is that there is no definitive answer. We have all experienced news broadcasts of natural disasters such as earthquakes or hurricanes, in which resolution is hardly important as long as the event was captured and we had the opportunity to see it.

However, high-definition television does have ramifications with regards to how often film will continue to be used; developments in high-definition systems will further impact this issue.

## INTERLACED VERSUS PROGRESSIVE

The major issue in filmmakers adopting video over film in creating motion pictures has not been one of resolution, but scanning method. For example, interlaced standard definition video, running at a frame rate of 29.97 fps, transferred to film, and viewed on a large screen, will in many respects be less than ideal. First, the overall acquisition will be less. Second, the temporal issues of going from an interlaced video acquisition to a progressive film display will most likely yield all sorts of aliasing problems. Last, the frame rate change of 29.97 to 24 fps will have other unintended consequences.

However, many of these problems can be solved through the use of a progressive acquisition format.

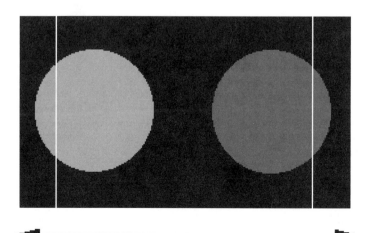

**Figure 12-7** A panned and scanned image. The widescreen image has been panned either left or right in order to facilitate the 4:3 extraction.

Using a high-definition camera and recorder that capture images at 24 fps, and progressively scanning and recording those images are two correct steps to take. The only difference, therefore, between film acquisition and high-definition acquisition is one of resolution. Twenty-four-frame-progressive (24p) high-definition cameras and recorders appeared in late 1999 and early 2000.

## THE 2K PROCESS

A new process is currently in its formation stage for studio-based television production in the United States. The concept is to "scan" all sources at a resolution of 2K pixel frames to a central storage server. The resolution of these frames is higher than all current HDTV proposed standards. Telecine units capable of a full bandwidth of 14-bit digital resolution at 2048 pixels $\times$ 1536 lines ("2K") in each of the three primary colors (red, green, blue) have effectively recreated the maximum color detail available off the film master.

2K creates a "virtual" negative of a quality that meets all tele-production specifications from HDTV to 601. In addition, this frame-based virtual negative allows delivery of both NTSC and PAL outputs.

Transferring film to 2K images helps preserve the original negative because the negative is only handled once—repeated transfers are unnecessary. After the initial transfer, the original film negative can be stored and all postproduction and delivery formats realized using the 2K master.

## DIGITAL FILMS

Given the title of this book, it is important to note that the filmmaking experience and the film viewing experience are, indeed, changing. Several questions come to the fore in the digital filmmaking environment, particularly when HD resolutions are considered. For example:

Does it matter whether it was originated on film or on video?

Does it matter whether we are watching it on film or on video?

These two questions correspond to the two most rapidly moving issues in digital filmmaking: whether to acquire on film or video, and whether to project film

or video for the audience. In chapter nine, we refered to the "Cinema of the Future." That future is upon us. In 1999, *Star Wars Episode One: The Phantom Menace* from director George Lucas showed that digital projection could illuminate a large cinema screen. Several other films followed suit, and soon it became clear that digital projection was by no means decades away. The authors viewed such projections and found them to be clear, crisp, and well within the film-goer's expectations.

As we know, while uncompressed HD still has approximately one-half the resolution of 35mm Academy format film, that resolution may well be good enough for feature film directors and producers to declare that acquiring on HD is viable.

## SHOOTING IN HD FOR FILM PRESENTATION

As stated earlier, the most important aspect of acquiring on HD as opposed to film acquisition has to do with matching frame rates. Shooting at 1920 $\times$ 1080, at 24 fps, and with progressive cameras is the triad of functionality that producers and directors should seek when considering whether or not to shoot HD as opposed to film. Putting aside, for a moment, issues of grain pattern, contrast ratio, and so forth, strictly from the standpoint of frame rate and scan method, it is imperative to choose a common frame rate of 24 fps with progressive scan.

Many films have already been shot on HD and transferred to film. Some have been box office hits; others have quietly disappeared. All that is sure is that more video-originated, HD programs will be shot and shown in the cinema either as moving film or projected digital video.

## OPPORTUNISTIC DATA, SERVICES, AND INTERACTIVE TELEVISION

As viewers we have no control over television except our ability to change channels or opt for a Spanish language track, closed-captioning, or a descriptive dialogue track created for the visually impaired. However, digital television, transmitted to the home as binary signals, can potentially send and receive a whole host of information. In fact a variety of services become possible.

As stated earlier, the 19.4-Mbit transmission channel for a single channel of HDTV can be used in many ways. For example, four standard definition signals can be compressed to fit within the 19.4-Mbit channel. This means that a broadcaster can broadcast four channels within the space of one. Alternatively, a combination of services can be brought to market as a result of the packetized delivery system of digital television.

Recall that the HD signal is sent to the viewer in packets of data. Each packet is reassembled by the decoding television set and presented to the viewer. Simultaneously, it is possible to send packets that have nothing whatsoever to do with a television program. For example, it is possible to send, in digital form, the entire contents of a telephone book of a large metropolitan city while a television commercial is being viewed. Or a viewer watching a commercial for a high-performance sports car could also get ancillary information, such as model, price, accessories, location of nearest dealer, and so forth, to be perused later.

Similarly, a range of interactive services can be made available. For example, during the broadcast of a football game, the user could navigate a series of Web pages. These can range from player statistics to "hot spots" which, when touched on the screen by a cursor, can activate a second Web page informing the viewer as to how a team jersey can be purchased. Regardless of whether the level of interactivity is designed to allow for more information to be acquired or to stimulate a purchase, this level of program "immersion" will take on more importance and predominance as years pass.

All of these types of nonscheduled transmissions fall into the category of opportunistic data services.

## TIME-SHIFTING PROGRAMMING AND DIGITAL DELIVERY

Imagine being able to dictate a series of commands to your television set, specifying exactly which television programs should be recorded and saved for later viewing. In the past, videocassette recorders (VCRs) were used to accomplish this task. Now, however, imagine being able to issue a set of commands to your television such that any program, news clip, and so forth that contains reference to a certain subject would be automatically downloaded and saved for viewing later.

One of the most exciting aspects of digital television is that your set could become a computer with an IP (internet protocol) address. Figure 12-8 is an exam-

ple of an electronic programming guide (EPG), which can be used to navigate programming choices. EPGs will be downloaded and updated at specific intervals so that the latest information is made available to the viewer.

## Replacing the VCR

There are many initiatives underway to replace analog with digital machines. These devices use digital hard disks, onto which are recorded the images and sounds of television broadcasts. Digital information storage has some unique advantages over standard analog storage. Figure 12-9 shows a digital recording unit from Replay Systems.

For example, let's say that you set the device to record a particular program. You arrive home fifteen minutes after the program starts and decide that you would really like to start watching it from the point where the program began recording. With a VCR, you would, of course, have to wait until the show ended and rewind the tape. With a digital unit, you could watch the beginning of the program while the unit continued to record the program in progress. Further, because the information was stored digitally, you could skip over sections, such as commercial breaks. Early versions of these devices appeared in 1999 and offered only limited disk storage. Within three years, manufacturers claim consumers will be able to record almost one thousand hours of material, at a cost of about $500.

Digital recorders could radically alter the concepts of "broadcasting" and "watching TV." It does not take a great a stretch of the imagination to consider being able to instruct our computer/television to scan the Internet for programs that match our personal criteria, and download and record our choices directly to a digital recording unit so we can view and manipulate them when we so desire.

The television as an intelligent device, capable of reaching out into the vast array of information available on the Internet, is upon us. So it is likely that a variety of programming, different from that heretofore available, will be created.

## Interactive Programming and Multiple Story Lines

While the look of television programs has changed from decade to decade, the nature of the programming has remained unchanged—that is to say,

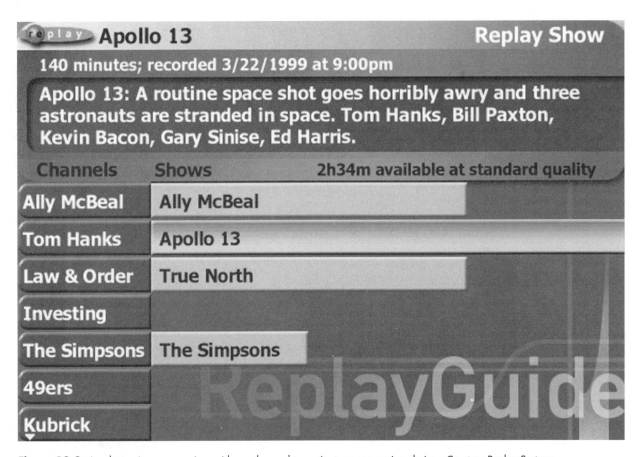

**Figure 12-8** An electronic programming guide can be used to navigate programming choices. Courtesy Replay Systems.

linear—since the inception of television. The length and form of a program are dictated to us. We cannot proceed at our own pace or delve into other areas of interest. This is changing.

Imagine, if you will, a television program on the hazards of cigarette smoking. The program consists of interviews with smokers and nonsmokers. Instead of just watching the show linearly, what if you could click on one of the persons and watch a mini-story just of that person? What if you could then navigate to any number of substories branching off that person's mini-story? The program now takes on some very interesting possibilities. If you were very intrigued by a particular character but essentially bored by all the rest, you would not have to endure the others. You could proceed at your own pace. True, the content would have to be packaged by the program's producers in order for you to access it, but that is all part of the new challenge of making programs for the next wave of interactive, immersive experiences.

Whether we will call it "watching television" or not is, perhaps, the only thing that remains to be seen.

## Internet Broadcasting and the Cinema of One

In 1959 in the United States, a television owner could watch programming on only three channels. By 1997, that average had grown to 45 channels. In years to come, forecasts show that number undergoing rapid growth. In 1959, the cost of reaching one thousand viewers (the cost-per-thousand) was extremely high. As years have passed, and programming alternatives have increased, such as cable, direct satellite broadcast, and so forth, the cost-per-thousand has decreased. While a "broadcast show" once needed to achieve a certain rating in order to be deemed a success and remain on the air, the rating system today is splintered—and targeted.

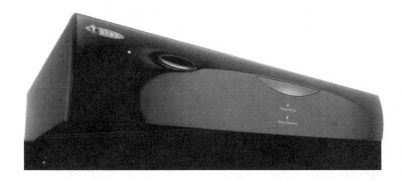

**Figure 12-9** A digital recording unit from Replay Systems. Courtesy Replay Systems.

One reasons for this is the rise of the Internet as a broadcast medium. As technology progresses, the fundamental differences between a television set and a computer that receives digital information will disappear. Similarly, as bandwidth into the home increases, Internet broadcasting will become a viable alternative to traditional broadcasting.

Figure 12-10 shows a logo from an Internet site that streams independent films and videos that can be viewed using a standard Web browser. As a result, films, videos, and events that traditionally would have to be viewed either at the cinema or on television can be viewed by anyone with a computer, at any time of the day, anywhere in the world. The ability to create programming and post it onto a web site for download will beget the "Cinema of One," where the cost-per-thousand concept is radically challenged. Programming that normally would never have been viewed by anyone will be available to a worldwide, international audience. Internet broadcasting and its implications for the program creation is one of the most exciting developments in all of digital filmmaking.

For Nora Barry, creator of the Internet site "The Bit Screen" (www.thebitscreen.com), the Internet represents a unique opportunity to create new types of programming. Rather than simply utilize the extra bandwidth that the Internet provides, Barry finds that the most creative, compelling opportunity lies in the possibility of creating unique programming.

Says Barry,

I worked as a writer for technology companies in the 1980s and early 1990s, and had access to new media as it emerged—interactive videodisc, CD-Rom. I also worked a lot in print and film, and I was very much aware of how my writing changed, depending on the medium in which I was working. So when video on the Internet became a reality, I thought it would be fun to experiment with. I wanted to see what kind of stories could be told in a fluid, interactive environment.

Barry views the Internet as a completely different medium than broadcast or theatrical cinema.

You're sitting with your nose pressed up against a screen, not sitting in an easy chair across the room from a large screen. You've got different expectations when you're watching programs on the Web, so you need a different kind of story. And because the Web is interactive and universal, filmmakers have a lot of very creative options. We have one series—*Scums*—and the first four episodes were shot by two filmmakers in Rome. The next episode in the series was shot by a filmmaker in Ottawa, and the next two episodes by a New York–based filmmaker. Then the two Roman filmmakers will finish up the series. Each of them picks up the storyline and adds to it, and then passes it on. You just can't do that on TV.

Barry also sees clear advantages in the computer's ability to randomize the viewing experience. Says Barry,

We have a filmmaker on the site who's been building a randomly configured film: He creates different video and audio tracks, and then each time the viewer accesses the film, the computer mixes up a different version of the film—you never know what you're going to get when you click on it. We're also building an interactive film that will give the viewer the tools to manipulate scenes and characters. To me, the exciting aspect of what we're trying to do is creating new ways to make films and tell stories, using the technology of the Web. We're not just recycling short videos or films. It's really a different approach.

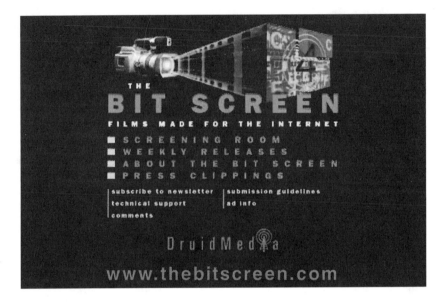

**Figure 12-10** The Bit Screen is an Internet site that streams independent films and videos over the World Wide Web. Courtesy Druid Media.

Barry also sees the explosion in media creation and handling as a driving force in the use of the Internet. Says Barry,

> Access to digital cameras is on the rise, and 95% of what we put on our site is shot and edited digitally. Most of the films on our site wouldn't exist if it weren't for digital technology, in part because it just wouldn't be economically feasible, but also because digital tools give filmmakers more ability.

Concludes Barry,

> The Bit Screen is always going to be a lab for new forms of media. And I think, although we'll eventually see feature-length films released on the Internet, what's exciting is when we see films developed originally with the Internet in mind. It's really an exciting time for filmmakers.

## DIGITAL PROJECTION SYSTEMS

During June and July of 1999, on both the East and West Coasts of the United States, electronic projections of feature films were made over the course of four weeks. Both *Star Wars Episode One: The Phantom Menace* and *An Ideal Husband* were shown to paying audiences. However, while the moviegoer would notice nothing unusual on entering the cinema, no film was being projected. Instead, the entire film had

been digitized, was playing off computer hard disks, and was projected electronically onto the normal-sized film projection screen.

Technological improvements in electronic projection systems have allowed this to occur. However, as with the introduction of any new technology, either

**Figure 12-10a** Nora Barry, www.thebitscreen.com. Courtesy Nora Barry.

creative or financial benefits must be realized before the technology becomes accepted.

First, let us examine the costs associated with the delivery of film into film theaters. The process of delivering film prints to every theater in, for example, the United States in 1998, cost almost $2 billion! Clearly, any technology that could significantly reduce this expenditure would be considered very seriously. It has been estimated that converting a cinema from traditional film projection to digital projection would cost between $100,000 and $150,000. If all screens in the United States were converted, at the cost of approximately $5 billion, it would be three years before the investment was amortized. It should be noted that electronic projection technology can be utilized for a variety of other presentations such as simulcasting live sporting events, videoconferencing, and special-venue programming that requires large meeting areas.

How does the technology of electronic projection work? As we have seen in chapter nine, "The Cinema of the Future" concept requires several key pieces of technology, from the digitization process to the distri-

bution process, to the projection process. Figures 9-23 and 9-24 (chapter nine) and figure 12-11 are diagrams of the digital delivery and exhibition process.

## Projection Systems

Two major forms of projection technology are driving both film distributors and exhibitors to strongly consider digital projection: digital light processing and light amplification.

Digital light processing (DLP) systems are based on breakthroughs made by the Texas Instruments Corporation and its Digital Micromirror Device (DMD) chip (figure 12-12). The DMD chip functions as a reflective surface that is covered with more than one-half million tiny mirrors which, in tandem, vibrate over 5000 times per second. As they vibrate, the micromirrors become reflective and nonreflective, and their positions correspond to binary values.

When a DLP projector is used, a pure white light is optically divided into its red, green, and blue components. The individual color channels are sent to three separate DMD chips. The DMDs reflect the indi-

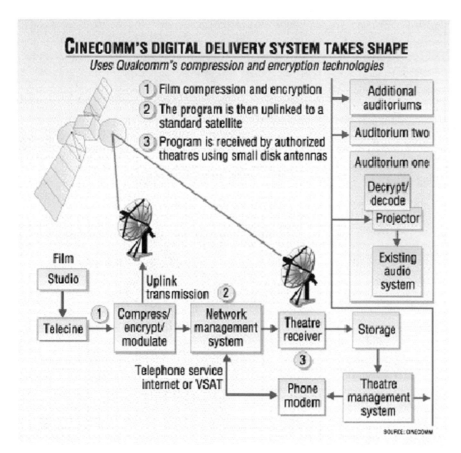

**Figure 12-11** The key processes in a digital delivery system. Courtesy Cinecomm.

01101010100101

1 mirror = 1 pixel

**Figure 12-12** A digital micro-mirror device (DMD) chip used in digital light processing projection systems. Courtesy Texas Instruments Corporation.

vidual red, green, and blue channels, and the resulting images are processed by an optical lens, which projects the image onto a screen (figure 12-13).

Light amplification systems use a liquid crystal light valve that is controlled optically. As shown in figure 12-14, an image source is divided into its individual red, green, and blue components and reproduced on three cathode-ray-tube monitors, which amplify. The red, green, and blue images then combine on a screen. The light valve is reflective: Images projected onto the valve creates patterns that will reflect light sources.

Shown in figure 12-15 is the JVC ILA-12K, an electronic cinema projection system that delivers 12,000 lumens.

## From Film to Disk to Screen

In general, signals destined for electronic cinema projection are transferred from their original film elements (in the case of film-acquired material) or from their high-definition video elements. They are then either digitized to some form of computer hard disk or to videotape. From disk or videotape, the signals are then processed and sent to the electronic projection system.

In the case of a feature film, the completed film may be telecine-transferred to high-definition video-

tape and then played directly from the HD videotape machine via its SDTI output and into the input of the electronic projection system. Or the feature film could be telecine-transferred to HD videotape, then transferred to computer hard disk and played into the electronic projection system. A computer disk subsystem may be chosen to address the usual running time of feature films, which average two hours, which is more than the length of one HD videotape.

A consideration of extreme importance in the transition of film to electronic projection is security. During the digitization stage, encryption schemes can be embedded into the digital signal stream. These schemes could then be decoded by specialized hardware at the electronic projection site.

## DV AND INDEPENDENT FILMMAKING

By the late 1990s, the use of smaller, low-cost digital cameras shooting digital video (DV) began to make an impact on the world of filmmaking. But, truth be told, acquiring on video and transferring to film for the cinema is not simply an affectation of the 1990s or a result of lower-cost, more portable equipment having become available. There are examples of several films which originated on 3/4" Umatic cassette, edited on analog-based tape-to-tape equipment, with the

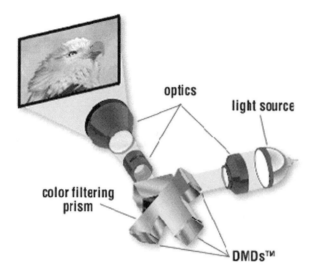

**Figure 12-13** The process of light conversion into red, green, and blue components, which are then reflected by individual digital micromirror devices. The result is an image that can be projected onto a screen. Courtesy Texas Instruments Corporation.

resulting videotape master then being transferred to film. Shown in figures 12-16a and 12-16b is an example of a DV camera, which yields excellent results and is quite portable.

In the late 1990s, two films raised the level of consciousness with regard to the efficacy of using digital cameras to deliver films to cinema halls. Thomas Vinterberg's *The Celebration* (1998), and Daniel Myrick's and Eduardo Sánchez's *The Blair Witch Project* (1999) were acquired on digital cameras or a combination of film and digital cameras. The economic return on an investment that was fairly low in the case of *Blair Witch* was no less than spectacular. The reported budget, in the vicinity of $60,000, produced an in-cinema domestic first-run gross of approximately $135 million! As a result, many independent, and established, filmmakers are now strongly considering using digital technology to acquire their images.

The workflow for acquiring images digitally and transfering them to film for film projection can vary but generally follows this basic pattern.

1. Images are acquired on digital cameras at either 25 or 30 frames per second. Note that eventually, as cost efficiencies bring high-end 24p cameras into the hands of lower budget filmmakers, the use of 25- and 30-fps camera/recorders will begin to diminish.

2. Sound is usually recorded separately. Though in-camera sound recording is certainly possible, overall the quality will benefit from an external ancillary recorder.

3. Images and sound are loaded into the DNLE system and the editing proceeds. DV tapes can be digitized directly into the DNLE system via a single Firewire connection or any number of alternatives: component, S-Video, or composite. If possible, it is best to remain completely digital within the transfer.

There are several factors to consider when a project that has been acquired on DV and will be transferred to film. Chief among these is the notion that DNLE system effects should be used sparingly. For example, using a color effect to enhance a particular hue or using digital video effects should either be avoided entirely or, if necessary, a test portion should be made, transferred to film, and viewed in order to judge results.

While there has been some discussion on the topic, the filmmaker should shoot the material using the full-frame feature of the DV camera, avoiding the on-board 16:9 aspect ratio. Thus, the filmmaker will use the entire frame of the DV

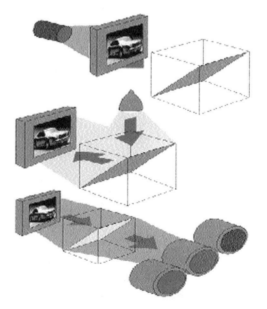

**Figure 12-14** Images projected onto a light valve creates a reflective pattern resulting in an amplification of the original source. The JVC digital cinema projection unit utilizes three such CRTs. Courtesy JVC.

camera, but will shoot as if protecting for a widescreen, cinema delivery.

4. Once picture editing has been completed, a finished video master must be created. The master can be directly output from the DNLE system or a traditional online can be made from the original tapes. It is common practice to work at a lower resolution within the DNLE system through to the fine cut and lock the cut, then proceed to a batch redigitization in order to achieve picture quality at either uncompressed rates or at a marginal, 2:1 compression rate.

The generation of this final master should also be done full-frame, without artificial masks. Masking is done during the transfer to film stage.

5. Video-to-film transfer can be accomplished with various technology. One of the oldest tools is a kinescope, a film camera whose shutter is synchronized electronically to either NTSC or PAL video rates, which shoots the video images off a color monitor. With NTSC video, redundant pulldown fields are eliminated in order to produce 23.976 images and any flash fields or vertical roll bars.

**Figure 12-16a, 12-16b**
The Canon XL1 DV camera-recorder. Courtesy Canon Corporation.

The most common tool for video-to-film transfer when a theatrical, film-projected release is desired is the film recorder (FR). There are two types of film recorders. The first is actually a camera that exposes film by shooting light from a high-resolution monochrome cathode ray tube (CRT) monitor through red, green, and blue filters. The second type of FR uses lasers instead of a CRT. The red, green, and blue lasers scan the film frame in order to reconstruct the image. The CRT- or laser-based FR may not function in real time, depending on the resolution of the image. For example, at 2K resolution, a CRT-based FR may require 10 to 20 seconds for processing one frame. These figures would double for 4K-resolution images.

The electron beam recorder (EBR) is the highest quality FR technology available. An EBR fires electrons at unexposed film, one pass, or exposure, for each of the red, green, and blue elements. The result is much like color separation used in the print media prepress industry, in that the individual red, green, and blue separations are printed in layers to create the color image. EBR systems are not common.

6. Sound for the finished film is most often produced on a system separate from the picture editing system. Once the final tracks of the film are laid out, and the final mix is done, the running speed of the audio is synchronized not with the final video, but with the final film. For example, if we acquired our images on DV and edited in a DNLE system at NTSC rates of 30 fps (actually 29.97), and then recorded our images to film, our final audio track must be done at the rate of the final projection. If there is any doubt as to whether the final audio track should be delivered at the pulldown rate of 23.976 fps or at the non-pulldown rate of 24, the facility creating the video-to-film transfer should be consulted.

**Figure 12-15** The JVC ILA-12K, an electronic cinema projection system that delivers 12,000 lumens. Courtesy JVC.

7. The finished soundtrack is transferred to the optical track and is then married to the film negative in order to create the answer print.

The availability of low-cost, highly portable, digital, video-based camcorders and low-cost, high-performance, digital, nonlinear editing systems has made digital filmmaking a desktop reality. While currently most independent filmmakers must transfer their finished program from video to film, with the advent and eventual adoption of electronic cinema projection, these programs will be able to exit the DNLE system directly or as a finished videotape master, thus bypassing the film transfer stage.

# 13

# A Discussion with the Authors at the Association of Independent Commercial Editors (AICE), New York City.

This chapter summarizes a 24p seminar hosted by the Association of Independent Commercial Editors (AICE) in New York City on June 29, 1999. The seminar was organized by Chris Franklin, Rich Jack, and the staff of Big Sky Editorial in New York. The authors were panelists on a discussion of changes in the film and video industries prompted by 24p methodologies. A full transcript and streaming audio of the actual event can be accessed at www.24p.com, along with examples of many of the elements discussed.

**Chris Franklin (moderator):** What is to be expected in the next five years in terms of production and postproduction?

**Tom Ohanian:** I think the nature of commercials, the nature of advertising is such that they're going to look at a nonlinear presentation. Today, by and large, we tend to use nonlinear tools to create linear programming, which we then watch from beginning to end. The viewer's interaction is fairly passive. One demonstration seen at NAB [National Association of Broadcasters in 1999] included an enhanced television [ETV] track within a nonlinear editing system. There was a sequence, which if you wanted you could play linearly. But then, it was duplicated and we dragged interactive elements to certain places in

the timeline. Then we hit "play" and you were able to see at certain points an overlay of these interactive elements. So you would watch the program, but at certain points these graphics—or text or a link to a Web site—would pop up. And just that demonstration drew some very large interest, especially from the advertising agencies and large corporations who have significant training and sales requirements.

I think the notion of being able not only to have your client come to you and say "you're going to be doing the commercial portion of this" as well as "we want to start looking at some interactive television and some branching of the story" is very close by. There certainly is approaching the time when digital recording devices at the home will allow viewers to zip right past commercials, so what's the compelling reason to have those commercials looked at? Give them something that's a little different. So the ability to take a commercial and suddenly see different versions of it embedded become quite important. The editors will be sitting there, editing and creating the multiple story lines right in the timeline by branching out to a different timeline. I think those things are inevitable.

**Michael Phillips:** This brings you into other forms of distribution such as DVD which already provides nine angles on the disk itself, meaning as you go through the movie you can switch from this angle to that angle and make it like a multi-camera show. The other thing that is interesting about MPEG2 is when you're looking at the movies you buy, they are contained on the disk at 24 frames-per-second—it is the player that does the 2:3 recreation on your monitor. The reason for this is that 24 frames take up less storage on the disk—20% less storage.

**CF:** Why 24P?

**TO:** I think part of the task is education—finding out how people work it. People will say "well why would I want to edit at 24p when I am doing NTSC broadcast?" But there are a lot of good reasons for that, mainly because of different forms of distribution. Ninety-nine percent of prime time shows in the U.S. are film-based at 24 fps. To get to MPEG2 encoding they do a reverse telecine, meaning they take a finished show, run it through an MPEG encoder, and it says, "oh, I know about this 2:3 pulldown." And it wants to remove the 2:3 so it can encode efficiently on the disk, allowing more data, better-looking pictures, and so on. But every time it sees a 2:3 cadence that is broken and every edit point that you edit in the 60-field world, you are not preserving that 2:3 pull anymore, you are just editing this piece to that piece. That's what editors want to do—edit—they don't want to have to keep track of what they should or shouldn't be doing to make it easier for an MPEG2 encoder.

**MP:** You don't want to think, "Are my A:B:C edits correct?" We don't want to have to deal with that. Editing at 24 fps removes all questions because you are editing on original film frames, and every time you hit "play" on a digital non-linear editing system, like the Avid Film Composer or Symphony Universal, the 2:3 cadence is recreated that is perfect from beginning to end. It reinserts pulldown just like a telecine does. You no longer have to cut the negative and retransfer it. Cine-expanding and compressing is all happening on disk with 20% less storage, 20% fewer frames to render, and if you're working in a distributed workflow where you say "I want to send this packet of frames over to my graphics department," it will happen 20% faster. So when you have this data on disk

that exists at 24 fps, you can say "well, let's just take this data now and encode it as MPEG." It is already data—why go through tape to go back to MPEG? All of this is part of what we call this 24p workflow. It's just a matter of thinking, "How can I best use that technology to solve current problems?" Snd it's an easy segue to a 24p environment.

**TO:** This environment, which is being brought about by HD, is basically emulating the film process that we have today. Today, we shoot on film at 24 fps, transfer to video at 30 fps, remove the 2:3, manipulate at 24 fps and then finally reintroduce 2:3 to a 30 fps medium. We are already doing this work. But there is a lot of time involved in that, and the only way to reduce that time is to get to a true frame-based system, of course with all of the other efficiencies Michael was talking about. I think it is something that is more in the limelight now that the other work products people are going to ask about have to do with knowing exactly where the original film frames are for encoding later on.

**CF:** What new formats are to be expected?

**TO:** Today, essentially we get asked for 601 masters in the 4:3 aspect ratio. It's difficult when you are working every day and you just need to get through a job, to look ahead and say, with some degree of predictability, "What are the things that my clients are likely to ask about, ask me for, in the next couple of years?" It is going to be something where it is not only a finished video-tape, but those pieces of gold will show you how to give the client digital data that is ready to be repurposed into many other forms. So 601 versions and 4:3 and 16:9 Pan & Scan, PAL and NTSC standards, MPEG2 issues, negative cut lists for contractual reasons. I think it is inevitable, especially in the marketplace that you folks are serving every day, that these people are going to ask about these things. The question "gee, what are we going to do about this?" is what we really need to start asking now. By and large, where the money is coming from that is likely to drive these new forms of television almost always begins with commercials—in this case, high-definition commercials. So I think the new formats to be expected are completely digital, with HD acquisition, which then gets digitized, and then the digital bits get repurposed continually into different forms.

**CF:** What will happen to videotape?

**MP:** I think you'll see 601 interlace at least until the year 2007 when the U.S. government said it will officially shut it down— but that is to be re-evaluated in 2004. The multicasting of many channels that Tom mentioned, where 601 is going to be around for a long time, is because broadcasters can say "I can do four or five channels of 601." And once you multiply that factor by four you are talking about much more programming and much more repurposing. Different versions—maybe one version is channel 38.2, which is the PG-rated version. Just like DVDs do today, I think you'll start to see a lot of similarity between the ratings that exist on DVD that will exist on these channels. Those are all versions you have to manage in editorial and that is something that nonlinear is great at.

**CF:** How will masters be archived?

**MP:** Your ultimate archive will still be available for some time, and that is the original film negative. For broadcast, you will create a production master on 1080 24p tape. The ultimate goal is a high-resolution, $1920 \times 1080$ 24p frame-to-frame relationship to the original film now existing within a tape format. The 24p decks have the ability to output via the SDI 601 that introduces 2:3 pulldown for the down-convert. So you can get a 601 output for editorial and the 601 deliveries from this HD deck. This is a 16:9 anamorphic 601 just like you would do today with a digital beta like in a 16:9 anamorphic mode. So a high-resolution, HD videotape format at 24 fps is the surest thing to bet on for archiving.

**CF:** What are some of the implications of graphics on a frame-based system?

**TO:** People are spending time a lot of time undoing the 2:3 pulldown in order to work on just the real film frames. So, ultimately, it is going to be a lot less work if you have just frames to manipulate: You have fewer of them, they don't have to be de-interlaced and then re-interlaced, you can transmit them to different graphic artists via the network faster—everything becomes much more efficient. The biggest thing has to do with titles and graphics in a multiformat world. Here, we are used to just having to create titles for a 601 4:3 aspect ratio. The work is going to multiply, simply because you will have to repurpose a title to provide for the 601 4:3 and 16:9 releases, the

PAL 4:3 and 16:9 releases, the HD releases, and so forth. So it will either be the user or the computer that facilitates this and makes it easier.

**CF:** What is 720p and 480p?

**MP:** This defines the $x$ and $y$ pixel values of the image. For example, 720 defines the number of pixels horizontally, multiplied by the amount of lines vertically. 'p' or 'I' define the scan format of the image as being either progressive or interlace. Can one actually see the difference in quality? That is hard to say, depending on viewing situations and monitoring devices. Many tests have indicated that a 720p/24 version of a program looks as good as the same program broadcast as 1080i.

Where do we stand as far as a broadcast standard? We look at 24p as being a mastering format at this time. Broadcasters for the most part are struggling with what HD standard they will actually broadcast. The 24p format offers the producer or content creator a single master that can be converted to all other standards maintaining a high quality product. For the most part, this is a down-convert to any of the other HD standards as well as to SDTV.

The important asset to maintain is the metadata, since resolution is the easiest element with which to deal. During the postproduction process, maintain all the metadata, or the creative decisions that were done on a particular frame or even on the pixel. Then these decisions can be recreated at any resolution, very much like via a batch process. What is left for you, the editor, or the production company is to do the work once. Make those decisions once and then apply them to all the other delivery mechanisms as a down-conversion or batch process. No one can point back to you, the producer, if your show is delivered as a 1080p/24 master, since everything can be delivered from this format to any other format.

When you are delivering anything below a 1080i master to the broadcaster, you are in essence giving them the right to up-convert the program for broadcast. If you are delivering as 720p, it will, for the most part, hold up quite well. That cannot be said in all instances for 480p or 480i material.

Delivering 1080p/24 is called a top-down approach, but what is sometimes forgotten or not considered is not only the versions as far as a delivery format, but versions of the actual content. This may be done for demographic reasons. Language and other reasons also impact the number of versions a show or spot will encounter. Most of these masters today are required as 601 uncompressed, as doing all these versions in a HDTV online quite can be cost-prohibitive, since many of these versions will not air in HDTV for many years to come. A lot of the work that Tom and I are doing right now is identifying the workflow and processes for all these content versions at 601 and those that are needed at HDTV, whatever that flavor is or will become.

The metadata is important since a producer can work today at 24p, but in a 601 level. Gain all the benefits that 24p offers, but not the cost associated with the new equipment, since this can all be done with existing NTSC and PAL equipment. By maintaining the metadata at a true 24-frame level, there is no conversion back and forth between PAL and NTSC, and all this can be recreated exactly at any resolution, since the same unique frame can always be identified. The resolution is not a factor until it needs to become a factor. When it does, apply the creative decisions preserved as metadata to the higher-resolution frames, then deliver again. This is referred to as a bottom-up approach, which makes much more economic sense when there are many content versions to create and when 601 is still a delivery requirement. A lot of this will play out over the next twelve ot eighteen months. 601 delivery requirements will not go away the day broadcasters go to HD. There will still be 601 delivery requirement and multicasting is also an issue that makes 601 attractive.

**TO:** Will 24 frame be the only format? Unfortunately, no. There will still be 24, 25, 30, and even 60 fps. The good news is that HD monitors are able to decode all these different formats, depending on the source signal being received. The delivery requirements for the next several years will still include PAL and NTSC SDTV, so we will still need to deal with the different formats well into the future.

**CF:** So how is this accomplished using today's equipment and 24p?

**MP:** The only acquisition format for 24p today is film, until Q1/Q2 2000, when HD 24 will be available. The film is transferred to either NTSC or PAL using all known standard processes. In NTSC there is a 2:3 pulldown inserted and PAL has a 4.1% speed increase. The resulting tapes then contain within their video signal the original film frames. The original 24 progressive frames are created during the digitizing process in either the Avid Film Composer or Avid Symphony Universal. Appropriate fields are either combined or dropped to recreate the original frames. These progressive frames are then stored on disk.

All editing is then done on full-film frames with a 1:1 relationship to the film. Timecodes can be tracked at all frame rates [24, 25, 30 DF, and NDF] as well as the original key code from the negative. All effects work and transitions are done at the 24-frame rate. Preserving this true 24-frame rate allows the system at any time to output five different speeds with a variety of frame rates and standards: 23.976 fps NTSC, 24 fps NTSC, 29.97 fps NTSC, 24 fps PAL, and 25 fps PAL.

All of the outputs are interlaced signals. If a user needs progressive frames, the frames on disk can be exported in a variety of formats for repurposing downstream.

The question that arises is as to the quality of the transcoding, from NTSC to PAL or from PAL to NTSC. For example, if the sequence originated as NTSC, the 24p frames were derived from this NTSC signal and stored as $720 \times 486$ 24-frame progressive for every second of material. When creating PAL, the progressive frames are played back 4.1% faster (now playing at 25 fps) with a slight resize to $720 \times 576$. The quality is actually much higher than standalone boxes that do the same thing, since they are exerting extra effort to facilitate an interlace-to-interlace conversion. When deriving PAL or NTSC from a progressive frame, there are no such motion artifacts, especially when dealing with pulldown within a NTSC signal to PAL. One must really think of this process as a retransfer of the finished film to either PAL or NTSC.

**TO:** Combine this with the aspect ratio management and you start to see how easily one can create the multiple versions needed for delivery: PAL, NTSC, as well as 16:9 and 4:3 versions within each standard. You can see now, how working at 24p at 601 uncompressed levels starts preparing the material for HDTV delivery when it is required. It is now a matter of applying the metadata to the new resolution.

**CF:** How does 24p convert to PAL?

**MP:** As mentioned earlier, when a sequence exists as 24-frame progressive, it behaves very much like a film that has had all the effects created and negative cut, and then retransferred back to tape. And like the telecine process, the timeline or sequence plays back 4.1% faster, creating a 1:1 relationship with the PAL video standard of 25 fps. Of course the sequence is now running faster, and its running length will be 4.1% shorter as an obvious consequence of the speed-up. The interlacing also happens during the output where each frame is represented as two fields in PAL. In NTSC, each frame is interlaced out but with a 2:3 pattern just like a film-to-tape transfer. This continuous 2:3 cadence is not only important in giving a perceived higher picture quality but is also useful for MPEG encoding downstream when an inverse telecine is applied.

**CF:** How much drive space does 24p use?

**MP:** When compared to NTSC data rates for uncompressed material, 24p versions of the same material compared to 60 fields will always take up 20% less space on the hard drive. So where a 60-field version would take up a rough average of 56 seconds per gig, the same in 24p would allow you to get 77 seconds per gig. When you start looking at half-hour and hour shows and the storage needs, it starts adding up.

**CF:** How much do editors need to know?

**TO:** I think it's important that editors know how to get to where their clients need to go. Editing is my profession, and while it would be great to think that all I have to do is figure out how to tell the best story with the material that I have, I also have to realize that, depending on what it is that I am editing, there are different people that need different things from me. On the films that I edit, it is often the case that I will have to export some frames and e-mail them to a design house working on a poster, or export the frames to someone working on a graphics workstation in order to previsualize a certain special effect. So, I think it's very important for editors to know how all this works on a conceptual level—the big picture approach. It will help you communicate better to everyone else in the production and postproduction process.

**CF:** Will today's equipment become obsolete?

**TO:** This is always a difficult thing to answer. Because the answer, really, is that when a piece of equipment was purchased, it was purchased with a particular task in mind—to perform a particular thing, to accomplish a particular form of editing or program delivery. Most of the time, a piece of equipment doesn't become obsolete simply because a new feature is added to a later model. Most of the time when a piece of equipment becomes obsolete it is because the nature of the program, or the job that is being done, has changed—it has been transformed in some way such that the piece of equipment can no longer do the things that the new job requires, or using the older piece of equipment simply takes much more time and then becomes very inefficient to use from a practical and business stance. So if you want to use a tape-to-tape 601 linear room to do 601 program delivery, you can still do that. But will it still be the most efficient way of doing that given some of the things we talked about earlier? That is a question really for the facility owner to reckon with.

**CF:** Could you give us some advice for film dailies specifications and FLEx files?

**MP:** For the most part nothing has changed to the process that is already in place. Facilities that transfer film-to-tape and provide transfer file databases already do everything that is required for a 24p process. It is more a matter of being conscious of the process, rather than passive. The minimum amount of information needed for a seamless 24p process, capture, edit, and output is:

1. Timecode
2. Key code
3. Pulldown

Everything else is gravy as far as the process is concerned. It seems that the most difficult part is actually making sure that the transfer facility provides this file. In most cases, the transfer file has to specifically be asked for in order to receive it. The only advice we would offer is to make sure that this is always asked for. Too much information is better than not enough information. If there is no plan to work at 24p—to ever go back to the negative, and so forth—there is nothing lost. It's just some extra information that lives alongside the media. But if there ever is a need to go back to the negative, retransfer selects, etc., then key code becomes a vital part of this process. By carrying the key code throughout the post process, the act of eye-matching is eliminated from the conform process. No need to spend time during the retransfer matching the key code to the offline timecode. No need in the conform room, making sure that the multilayers line up on the correct field or frame. All of this adds up to frame accuracy, a consistent look, and reduced costs in the postproduction process.

**Audience member:** It seems that it is imperative that proper transfer files are delivered as part of the process. We as editors have to insist that it is a necessary ingredient in what we do. It also the responsibility of AICE to educate the production companies to insist on getting this information, since it is usually they and not the editors that will negotiate this part of the process. We editors do not control which lab or facility will be used for any given job we do. It seems that we as an organization need to educate the production companies on this and do so very quickly.

**TO:** I think that as part of the education process, it would behoove the production companies to understand how important it is for them to have access to these FLEx files and how it will amount to savings. The time saved from not eye-matching, the time saved during the color-correction transfer are all real savings not to mention the fact that by using key code the final digital nonlinear conform will match exactly the offline edit.

**MP:** This is a great example of applying the metadata to another resolution. The offline edit is done at one resolution, a pull list is generated from the system, and only the takes used are retransferred. The online now consists of just redigitizing the new elements from the newly created FLEx files. The sequence will automatically relink to the new sources based on that common key code. This is instantaneous. Once you see how this works in just the 601 workflow, imagine the cost savings when applied to film, to HDTV transfer, or even film scanned at 2K resolution. The savings can be tremendous as well as the workflow accelerated.

**CF:** I would like to thank Michael and Tom for their participation. For further information, you can also check out their Web site at www.24p.com.

**MP:** Thank you very much.

**TO:** Thanks, Chris. A great pleasure for us both.

# Glossary

**ADR**  Additional dialogue replacement, accomplished by playing back the scene in question in a loop while the actor matches the timing and delivery of the lines in sync to the on-screen visual.

**AES/EBU**  American Engineering Society/European Broadcasting Union.

**AIFF**  Audio Interchange File Format.

**answer print**  The first version of the film that contains optical effects and the complete and mixed optical soundtrack.

**arena programming**  Instances where, typically sporting events, such as boxing matches, are beamed into a civic auditorium via satellite.

**art direction**  Often referred to as "the look of the film"—extends to the photographic tone, the costumes, the sets, the set dressing, props, and so forth.

**ASCII**  American Standards Code for Information Interchange.

**aspect ratio**  The aspect ratio of an image is measured by the amount of units across (horizontally) in relation to the amount of units down (vertically). Thus, an aspect ratio of (1.33:1) signifies that for every four units across, there are three units down.

**asymmetric compression**  Asymmetric compression techniques require a greater amount of processing power, and almost always during the compression stage. Once the material has been compressed, it can be decompressed with far fewer processing requirements.

**ATM**  Asynchronous Transfer Mode (ATM) is not in and of itself a network, but, rather a packaging scheme for data.

**AVI**  Audio/Video Interleaved. Similar to QuickTime, AVI is the corresponding extension to Intel-based CPUs.

**bandwidth**  Refers to the number of bits per second of material. The CPU is tasked with processing a number of bits per second when digitizing; that number becomes a limiting factor. The computer can process only a certain number of frames and a certain amount of information for each frame every second.

**bins**  Based on the concept of film bins, which are canvas containers used to hang film strips, bins have become associated with nonlinear editing systems as the location for storing footage.

**blow-up**  The ability to enlarge a section of a picture.

**blue screening**  Technique by which selective colors (usually blue or green) are removed in order to composite layers of film.

**budgeting**  Both above-the-line and below-the-line categories. Above-the-line costs are usually the producer, director, some A-list actors, some directors of photography, and some editors.

**camera operator**  Person responsible to the director and the DP in terms of composition, focus, and camera movement. Any item relating to what the camera actually sees and is captured on the film frame is the responsibility of the camera operator.

**casting**  The process of deciding which actors will be used to portray the film's characters.

**cast list**  This list contains all characters in alphabetical order.

**CCD**  Charged-coupled device.

**CD-I**  Compact Disc Interactive.

**CD-ROM**  Compact Disc, Read-Only Memory.

**chroma subsampling**  A technique used to reduce the file size of an image by reducing the amount of color information.

**circle of confusion**  Refers to the circumference of a point of light on the exposed film that is within acceptable focus.

**circled takes**  The takes that the director feels can be utilized during the editing stage.

**color timer**  Person who sets the density, contrast, and color from scene to scene for a film.

**compression**   To reduce in volume and to force into less space.

**costume designer**   Person responsible for researching and designing the costumes and related accessories such as hats, gloves, and jewelry.

**dailies screening**   A viewing of the results of each day's shot film. Notes are taken concerning performances, quality of both picture and sound, and which takes are preferred for editing.

**DAT**   Digital Audio Tape.

**data transfer rate**   The amount of information that a computer storage drive can write and read in a certain amount of time. Also called Read/Write Speed or Transfer Speed.

**DAW**   Digital Audio Workstation. DAWs use optical discs or magnetic disks to offer random access, nonlinear editing of audio.

**DFW**   Digital Film Workstation.

**dial-up**   Dial-up phone service is exactly that: an ordinary telephone in a home or office. A modem is used to transmit and to receive digital data. The channel that the data can travel through is small, at 56 Kbits/sec (Kilobits; Kbps).

**digital backlot**   Through digital technology, footage that is many years old that is reconstituted and digitally composited.

**digitize**   To convert continuous analog information to digital form for computer processing. Also digitizing and digitization.

**director of photography (DP)**   Interprets the written page and the director's vision into moving images. The choice of film negative type, lighting equipment, and camera lenses all fall to the domain of the director of photography.

**DLP**   Digital Light Processing systems are based on breakthroughs made by the Texas Instruments Corporation and its Digital Micromirror Device (DMD) chip.

**DNLE**   Digital, nonlinear editing.

**DOF**   Depth-of-field.

**Dolby stereo digital**   An optical soundtrack that is comprised of blocks of data that are located between the sprocket holes on one edge of 35mm Dolby Stereo SR-D prints.

**down-conversion**   The method of extrapolating a smaller image size from a larger image size.

**DS-0**   DS-0 is the basic unit used to measure fiber optic capacity. At 64 kbps, one DS-0 channel is required to send a single voice call.

**DS-1**   DS-1, also known as digital service-one, has a capacity of 1.5 Mbps.

**DS-2**   DS-2 has a capacity of approximately 6 Mbps.

**DS-3**   DS-3 has a capacity of approximately 45 Mbps. At 45 Mbps/sec, a DS-3 line can be used to transmit compressed video.

**digital theater systems (DTS)**   A dual system where the digital audio is recorded and played back from CD-ROM discs.

**DTV**   Digital television refers to signals that are transmitted as digital ones and zeroes and are then decoded into pictures and sounds that are visible and audible.

**dual finish cognizant**   The desire to leave the editing process with lists that can be used to create a finished videotape master and a cut film negative for both videotape and film release.

**dual system**   By utilizing two different systems, one for recording picture and one for recording sound, film shooting is often called a dual-system approach.

**DVI**   Digital Video Interactive. A compression method consisting of a programmable chipset and software. DVI supports both still images and motion video and can be both asymmetric and symmetric in nature. A current implementation can decode and encode in DVI as well as JPEG.

**DX codes**   The manufacturer markings available on a film that will automatically set the exposure index in the camera to match the film rating.

**edgenumbers**   Identifying codes spaced at constant intervals on film negative.

**Ethernet**   Ethernet is a form of local area network. It consists of a cable (coaxial), which can extend to approximately 1.25 miles and can offer up to 1000 nodes (computers and peripheral devices). Ethernet operates on a principle known as Carrier Sense Multiple Access (CSMA). Whereas other LANs require computers to "wait their turn" before sending information, CSMA allows a computer to send information and, during a period when the cable is not in use, another computer can begin sending its information. Ethernet is rated at a bandwidth capability of 10 Mbits/sec, which is what the system is capable of delivering. However, because multiple computers can be waiting to transmit, the more practical throughput (the amount of data which can regularly be processed in seconds) in actuality is about 1 Mbit/sec (about 100 KBytes/sec).

**FDDI**   FDDI (Fiber Digital Data Interconnect) is a transmission method that uses fiber optics to transmit and receive signals. Fiber optics transmit energy by directing light instead of electrical signals. Electrical signals are encoded into light waves, transmitted, and received and decoded back into electrical signals. FDDI is often offered in two configurations, bandwidths of 100 Mbits/sec and 200 Mbits/sec. However, in much the same fashion that there are trafficking issues in networks using Ethernet, there are similar throughput constraints for FDDI networks. Because of this, a 100 Mbit/sec FDDI network will most likely deliver about 2 MB/sec.

**final cut**   Stage that signifies that no further picture editing will be done.

**flash convertor**   Used to convert analog signals to digital signals. Through the flash convertor it is possible to convert frame(s) of video into data that can then be interpreted by computers.

**flops**   Done to reverse the line of action so that left and right are switched.

**foley artist**   Person who watches a scene and recreates many of the sound effects that the scene requires such as a series of footsteps walking to a door, the jangling of keys, and the opening of a door.

**fractals**   A compression technology that utilizes fractal patterns to represent every possible pattern that can exist. By dividing a picture into small pieces, these smaller sections can be searched and analyzed fairly quickly. On a smaller level, instead of trying to find the pattern for the entire picture, the search is for smaller patterns of pixels.

**freeze frame**   An optical effect which is created by repeating a single film frame while the new negative is exposed for as many frames as are necessary to arrive at the required duration for the freeze.

**FTFT**   Film to tape to film to tape refers to the ability to generate a color-corrected EDL from a one-lite EDL.

**gaffer**   Person responsible to the DP in all areas of lighting including maintenance, selection of electrical equipment, and placement of and setting the levels for each light.

**GPS**   Global Positioning Satellite.

**Hazeltine**   A machine that analyzes the film negative and sets the initial timing lights. By aligning the positive print alongside and in-sync with the negative, the notes based on the A positive are then matched to the negative during the Hazeltine process.

**ISDN**   (Integrated Services Digital Network) A transmission method that is designed to combine various sorts of information, from telephone transmissions to fax to images and sounds, into one digital network. ISDN requires that a communications link be placed at the transmitting and receiving areas. At 64 Kbits/sec, the bandwidth is not that much greater than dial-up service. However multiple channels of ISDN can be combined, up to 24 channels, depending on how many are needed.

**in-camera timecode**   Timecode data exposed onto the film negative between the perforations. The timecode rate is established by the running speed of the camera.

**ink numbers**   The process of coding (also known as inking) numbers on the mag track which match the film's edgenumbers.

**interlaced scanning**   Video signals consist of two fields of alternatingly scanned lines which are then interlaced together to create a viewable frame.

**internet broadcasting**   Refers to the use of the Internet to deliver and view programming which otherwise and previously would have been available on terrestrial or satellite-based broadcasting services.

**JPEG**   Joint Photographic Experts Group is a form of hardware-assisted compression. JPEG is based on still images, also called continuous tone images. JPEG employs discrete cosine transforms that are lossy algorithms. When a file is compressed using a JPEG-based processor, information about the original signal will be discarded and lost.

**key grip**   Person responsible to the DP to either facilitate or actually create the movement of a camera either via dolly, boom, jib, or crane.

**keycode**   Refers to all edgenumber formats that can be read by a barcode reader.

**KeyKode™**   The official name of the Eastman Kodak Corporation's offering of machine-readable edgenumbers.

**Kodak Picture Exchange**  This service functions as a database of digital images from stock footage houses as well as still images from various state film commissions.

**letterboxing**  Film transfers that preserve the aspect ratio of the film as originally shot.

**linear editing**  The principle of assembling the program from beginning to end. If changes are required, everything downstream of the change must be rerecorded. The physical nature of the medium enforces a method by which the material placed on that medium must be ordered.

**location scout**  Person who goes on location and brings back pictures based on the description set forth by the director and production designer. May work closely with film bureaus in each state.

**lossless compression**  The act of compressing information without irretrievably losing any of the data that represents that information. In order to be lossless, a great deal of analyzing must be done.

**lossy compression**  The act of compressing information that results in an inability to retrieve some portion of the data in the original message.

**makeup artist**  Person responsible for researching and designing the makeup for principal actors and extras. Works closely with the production designer in the important coordination of makeup with costume.

**macros**  Used by computer applications to "record" a certain repeated function.

**mired**  An abbreviation for micro reciprocal degrees. A system that is used to handle the conversions when adjusting from one color temperature to another.

**MOS**  Film that has been shot without sound being recorded.

**motion control**  The means by which camera operation, camera dolly, and object movements are repeatable through the use of computer guided programming.

**MPEG**  (Moving Picture Experts Group) A form of hardware-assisted compression. Whereas JPEG is based on still images, MPEG is based on motion. It is a lossy compression method.

**multiple versions**  The nonlinear editing system's capability of providing for multiple versions of a sequence without requiring additional copies of footage or degrading the signal by losing generations.

**negative cutter**  Person who is responsible for recreating the cuts on the original camera negative, yielding an exact duplicate of what the editor created on workprint.

**nonlinear editing**  The concept that the physical nature of the medium and the technical process of manipulating that medium do not enforce or dictate a model by which the material must be physically ordered. Changes can be made regardless of whether they are at the beginning, middle, or end of the sequence being edited.

**NTSC**  National Television System Committee. Motion video is normally played back at 30 frames per second, actually 30 fps non-drop frame and 29.97 fps drop-frame. The scan rate is 525 lines at 60 Hz.

**OMF**  (Open Media Framework) A format for file compatibility to fully describe all relationships between source material and effects.

**optical printer**  An optical printer is used to take one or more film elements, align them together and rephotograph the elements onto a new piece of film.

**PAL**  Phase Alternate Line. Motion video is normally played back at 25 frames per second. The scan rate is 625 lines at 50 Hz. PAL affords superior quality to NTSC by reversing the phase of its reference color burst on alternate lines.

**photo-CD**  A disc which can store pictures as well as sounds; these pictures can be viewed on a television screen or can be accessed via a computer.

**pixel**  A single point of an image's make-up.

**pixel matrices**  The number of pixels which are contained both vertically and horizontally over the span of the viewing screen.

**playlist**  A list of items to be played back in a certain order. Underlying principle behind virtual recording. A playlist determines what shots will be played and in what order.

**previsualization**  Technique used to create and judge concepts in a form that is not for final viewer consumption as part of the film proper.

**production designer**  Person responsible for the overall look of the film to achieve the mood and feel of a story.

**production illustrator**  The production illustrator provides sketches and storyboards for different film-making departments.

**production sound mixer**  Person responsible for recording all production sound, either synchronous (sync) or wild.

**progressive scanning**  The method by which an entire frame is displayed at the same time and in totality, unlike interlaced scanning.

**property master**  Person responsible for any props that are used by the actors.

**quantization**  The loss yeilded by process of sampling.

**QuickTime™**  A set of operating extensions to the Macintosh computer platform that allows Macintosh computers to display time-dependent media such as video, audio, and animation and to combine these media with time-independent media such as text and graphics.

**random access**  The ability to seek a section of material without having to proceed sequentially through the material to reach that location.

**repositions**  Moving a picture north, south, east, and west on predefined fields.

**rerecording mixer**  Person whose responsibilities include the mixing of dialogue, music, and sound effects.

**resolution**  The number of pixels that run across (horizontally) the screen and the number of rows of pixels, which run down (vertically) the screen. Additionally, the amount of bits-per-pixel can be used to calculate the overall resolution of an image.

**reverse action**  Created by printing the last frame first and working backwards until the first frame of action is reached.

**RISC**  Reduced instruction set computing.

**rough cut**  The first complete viewing of the entire film.

**script breakdown**  Method used to divide a script into eighths of a page. Filmmaking days can be described in the number of pages shot per day. For example, on Shooting Day 14, a total of 5 $\frac{3}{8}$ pages were completed.

**script supervisor/continuity**  Person who assists the director or assistant director by ensuring that dialogue is adhered to, or if changed, is noted accordingly. Also keeps the script notes and creates a lined script.

**Sony Dynamic Digital Sound (SDDS)**  The SDDS system provides eight discrete audio channels on film where the matrix of digital information is on the left side of the film print, adjacent to the picture, while on the right side the stereo optical track is present.

**SDTI**  Serial digital transport interface

**SECAM**  Sequential couleur à memoire. Like PAL, SECAM has a normal playback of 25 fps with a similar scan rate. It is primarily used in Eastern Europe and France.

**set decorator**  Person responsible for the visual look of the film through the use of furniture, carpeting, drapery, and the different artifacts that a character is most likely to have.

**set designer**  Person responsible for overseeing and executing the plans for the set and responsible for drafting detailed blueprints from drawings and verbal descriptions provided by the production designer.

**scoring mixer**  Person responsible for recording all the music that will be used in the film.

**sides**  The number of dialog parts for each actor.

**skip frames**  Used when motion needs to be accelerated by skipping frames during the printing. This will create a sped up effect when the new element is played back at sound speed.

**SMPTE**  Society of Motion Picture and Television Engineers.

**sound designer**  Person who uses recording techniques and multiple layers of sound to create specific effects.

**sound sweetening**  The process of taking sounds and changing them in some way.

**Steenbeck**  A film editing machine.

**storyboards**  A series of drawings that depict the visual breakdown of an entire scene as the director has planned for it to be shot.

**stretching frames**  Creates the appearance of an action being slowed down and is accomplished by repeating a frame for a specific amount of time.

**subsampling**  A technique for reducing the overall amount of data that will represent the digitized signal. When more samples are thrown away than meets the sampling theorem, subsampling is being done. When the sampling theorem is violated, many types of aliasing can be noted.

**symmetrical compression** Techniques that require an equal amount of processing power to compress and decompress an image. This is important because, in applications designed for editing, the compression of a frame must occur in real time. Decompressing that same frame must also occur in real time.

**synchronous optical network** SONET. An optical fiber delivery method which operates at higher rates than DS3 or T3 technology. STS signals can be combined to provide greater bandwidth. The optical channels (OCs) come in the following versions: OC-1, a 51 Mbit/sec channel; OC-3, a 155 Mbps channel; OC-12, a 622 Mbits/sec channel; OC-48, multiple 45 Mbps optical channels for a total of 2.4 gigabits.

**synthespians** Synthetically created actors.

**T1 and T3** T1 and T3 are best referred to as common carriers of signal that require dedicated systems installed at either end of two sites that will be in communication with each other. Often misinterpreted as meaning Terrestrial, T1 and T3 links are not solely terrestrial in nature; they can involve communicating using satellites as well as over land. T1 links have a bandwidth of approximately 1.5 Mbit/sec (about 150 KBytes/sec), which is about one-half greater than a network using Ethernet, but equal to 24 channels of ISDN. T3 links, on the other hand, have a very significant bandwidth of 45 Mbits/sec (about 4.5 MB/sec). Although T3 service is expensive to install and utilize, transferring data over these links is an extremely efficient method when large files are routinely sent and received.

**telecine** A device that is used to transfer film images from a film roll to either videotape or to digital disk.

**time-shifting** The ability to delay the live nature of a broadcasted program by recording the signal for later use or viewing.

**timing lites** Determine the amount of light and color that a film will be exposed to in the process of creating the release print.

**titles and effects supervisor** Person responsible for producing the main titles and end credits for a film.

**TOD** Time-of-day timecode, which runs on a 24-hour basis.

**up-conversion** The method of extrapolating a larger image size from a smaller image size.

**video tap** The output of a film camera that is converted to a video signal. Allows the image to be recorded and reviewed on videotape.

**visual effects producer** Supervises the plan for realizing the visual effects that the film requires.

**VITC** Vertical Interval Timecode.

**wavelets** A compression technology. A picture is first scaled and a set of wavelet functions (transforms) are run that seek to encode error. In this way, the information in the original picture is compared to the differences in the scaled version. Once the picture has been scaled and analyzed this transformation achieves information based in "wavelet space." Wavelet space is error. The goal is to store one of four portions of the picture and then to quantize the other three portions of the picture.

**white flag** A single line of 100% white across the entire width of the picture.

**wild sound** Sound that does not have a synchronous picture or recordings of sound effects that are available on the location and may be hard to obtain or create at a later time.

**workprint** The developed and printed film used for editing purposes.

# Bibliography

Alcatel & Pacific Bell. *The Cinema of the Future.* Richardson, TX: 1994.

ASC Press. *American Society of Cinematographers Camera Manual.* Hollywood, CA: ASC Press, 1993.

Balmuth, Bernard, A.C.E. *Introduction to Film Editing.* Boston: Focal Press, 1989.

Brower, Alexandra, and Wright, Thomas Lee. *Working in Hollywood.* New York: Avon Books, 1990.

Cinema Products. *Vidiflex Viewing System.* CA: 1990.

Cinesite. *Boundaries Not Included.* Cinesite, A Kodak™ Company, 1993.

Digital Theater Systems. *DTS-6 Installation and Operation Manual.* 1994.

Dolby. *Questions and Answers about Dolby Stereo Digital.* San Francisco: 1993.

Eastman Kodak Corporation. *Kodak Picture Exchange Backgrounder.* Rochester, NY: 1994.

Eastman Kodak Corporation. *In Camera.* Rochester, NY: Spring, 1994.

EDNet. *Entertainment Digital Network.* San Francisco, CA: 1993.

EDNet. Kobayashi, Tom, and Scott, Tom. *Fiber Optics Make It Easier.* San Rafael, CA: Dec. 1992.

Katz, Steven. *Film Directing Shot by Shot: Visualizing from Concept to Screen.* Boston: Focal Press, 1991.

Kennell, Glenn. *Digital Film Scanning and Recording: The Technology and Practice.* Rochester, NY: 1993.

Miller, Pat P. *Script Supervising and Film Continuity, Third Edition.* Boston: Focal Press, 1999.

Ohanian, Thomas A. *Digital Nonlinear Editing, Second Edition.* Boston: Focal Press, 1998.

Screenplay Systems. *Scriptor, Scheduling, and Budgeting User Guides.* Los Angeles, CA: 1994.

Singleton, Ralph S. *Film Scheduling.* Los Angeles, CA: Lone Eagle Publishing, Co., 1991.

Sony. *Post-Production Audio Mixing in the SDDS Format.* 1994.

Sony. *Sony Dynamic Digital Sound™.* InterBEE '93 Press Kit, 1993.

Wavefront Technologies, Inc. Columbia Pictures Profile Press Kit, 1994.

# Index